100
PARKS
5000
IDEAS

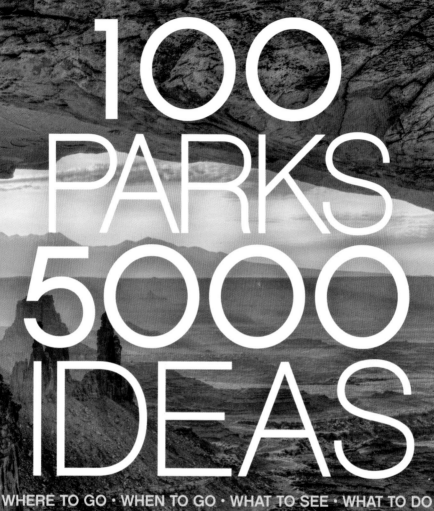

100 PARKS 5000 IDEAS

WHERE TO GO · WHEN TO GO · WHAT TO SEE · WHAT TO DO

JOE YOGERST

NATIONAL GEOGRAPHIC

WASHINGTON, D.C.

Contents

Opposite: Spring has sprung at the base of snowcapped Mount Rainier, where wildflowers bloom.
Previous: The sun rises in between Mesa Arch in Canyonlands National Park.

WARNING

RESTRICTED
WILDLIFE AREA

FOR NEXT 5 MILES PHOTOGRAPHY
AND OBSERVATION OF WILDLIFE
PERMITTED FROM ROAD ONLY

NO HIKING OFF ROAD

INTRODUCTION

I cannot imagine my life without parks. They were close friends from a very early age, especially those in the American West, where I was born and raised. And they remain among my most beloved companions. I'm drawn by their stunning landscapes, the sense of adventure, the chance to see wild things where they most belong—in the wild. But parks are also a place to clear the mind, contemplate the future, commune with your inner self without the distractions of everyday life.

While those sentiments may sound rather New Age, consider the fact that John Muir expressed a similar thought in 1912: "Everybody needs beauty as well as bread, places to play in and pray in, where nature may heal and give strength to body and soul alike." A fitting adage for any and all parks.

I was barely out of the cradle when my parents whisked me off to Yosemite National Park (p. 222) for my first camping experience and, as I still vividly recall, the first time I encountered a bear in the wild. Growing up in San Diego, I visited Balboa Park (p. 258) almost weekly, not just the celebrated zoo but the various museums (where I saw my first mummy), the sprawling lawns (where I played football and Frisbee with my friends), and the eucalyptus-filled canyons for the day camps I relished each summer.

Summers also featured family road trips that revolved around national parks—Crater Lake (p. 276), Carlsbad Caverns (p. 212), Zion (p. 194), Bryce Canyon (p. 194), the Grand Canyon (p. 190), and Yellowstone (p. 158), to name just a few. I devoured everything I could read about those parks: maps, brochures, and books that remain in my library all these years later. And I still have a box filled with the photos that I took in those parks, a collection that shows my photographic evolution from an old-fashioned Brownie box camera to my first single-lens reflex and Kodachrome.

When I look back at those formative years and the open spaces that were such a part of my life, I realize how parks helped shape the person I am today; they helped spark a lifelong passion for wildlife, learning, outdoor recreation, and conservation that eventually became my career.

I'm not the only one. By any definition, the parks of the United States and Canada have had a profound effect on billions of people. In 2017 alone, the U.S. National Park Service recorded more than 330 million visitors, and Parks Canada drew an additional 25 million. Add all of the people who visit city parks, state and provincial parks, wildlife refuges, and national forests, and the numbers are staggering—easily the number one tourist attraction in North America and possibly the world.

It always amazes me that the idea of setting aside open space for *public* use is a rather modern concept. I suppose that's because there was so much wilderness left and a widespread notion that nature was somehow infinite. By the late 19th century, people began to realize that such was not the case and that action was needed to protect a nation's natural assets.

Although the first national parks were declared in the 1870s and 1880s, the notion of creating a nationwide system of wild places didn't come along until the early 20th century—Parks Canada in 1911 and the U.S. National Park Service in 1916. Many of the city, state, and provincial park systems followed a similar time line. It's that shared legacy that forms the heart of this book: parks of all shapes, sizes, and functions.

By no means is *100 Parks, 5,000 Ideas* a list of the best parks in the United States and Canada. Rather, it's a window into the wide variety of green spaces scattered across this part of the world and the multitude of things that you can do in those parks and similar outdoor areas. And it certainly isn't an in-depth guide to any of these parks; I leave that to the local experts. But in the same way that childhood books sparked my own fascination with parks, I hope my words inspire your next visit.

—Joe Yogerst

A brown bear uses a roadside sign as a scratching post in Sable Pass, Denali National Park.

San Juan Island National Historical Park

North Cascades National Park

Olympic National Park

Mount St. Helens National Volcanic Monument

Mount Rainier National Park

WASHINGTON

Glacier National Park

Flathead Lake State Park

Columbia River Gorge National Scenic Area

MONTANA

NORTH DAKOTA

Theodore Roosevelt National Park

Oregon Dunes National Recreation Area

OREGON

IDAHO

Crater Lake National Park

Yellowstone National Park

Grand Teton National Park

SOUTH DAKOTA

Black Hills National Forest

Redwood National and State Parks

Sawtooth National Forest

WYOMING

Lassen Volcanic National Park

Missouri National Recreational River

CALIFORNIA

Point Reyes National Seashore

Lake Tahoe Basin Management Unit

Dinosaur National Monument

NEBRASKA

Golden Gate National Recreation Area

Golden Gate Park

Yosemite National Park

NEVADA

UTAH

Rocky Mountain National Park

Canyonlands National Park

COLORADO

Sequoia–Kings Canyon National Park

Bryce Canyon National Park

Glen Canyon National Recreation Area

KANSAS

Zion National Park

Death Valley National Park

Valley of Fire State Park

Four Corners parks

Red Rock Canyon National Conservation Area

Grand Canyon National Park

OKLAHOMA

Channel Islands National Park

Griffith Park

Valles Caldera National Preserve

Palo Duro Canyon State Park

Anza-Borrego Desert State Park

Joshua Tree National Park

ARIZONA

Wichita Mountains Wildlife Refuge

Balboa Park

NEW MEXICO

Carlsbad Caverns National Park

Guadalupe Mountains National Park

TEXAS

ALASKA

Denali National Park and Preserve

Wrangell–St. Elias National Park and Preserve

Big Bend National Park

Aransas National Wildlife Refuge

Lake Clark National Park and Preserve

Nāpali Coast parks

HAWAI'I

Padre Island National Seashore

Katmai National Park and Preserve

Kenai Fjords National Park

Haleakalā National Park

National Park of American Samoa

AMERICAN SAMOA

Hawai'i Volcanoes National Park

Parts of the United States

Voyageurs National Park

Isle Royale National Park

Boundary Waters Canoe Area Wilderness

Pictured Rocks National Lakeshore

Hiawatha National Forest

MINNESOTA

St. Croix National Scenic Riverway

WISCONSIN

Mississippi National River and Recreation Area

MICHIGAN

Mackinac Island State Park

MAINE

Acadia National Park

VT.

White Mountain National Forest

N.H.

Boston Common

Adirondack Park

NEW YORK

MASS.

Niagara Falls State Park

Blackstone River Valley National Heritage Corridor

CONN. R.I.

Cape Cod National Seashore

IOWA

Grant Park, Lincoln Park, and Jackson Park

Pennsylvania Wilds Conservation Landscape

Cuyahoga Valley National Park

PENNSYLVANIA

Gettysburg National Military Park

Central Park

Gateway National Recreation Area

NEW JERSEY

Pinelands National Reserve

OHIO

ILLINOIS

INDIANA

Chesapeake and Ohio Canal National Historical Park

MD.

DEL.

National Mall

D.C.

Assateague Island National Seashore

MISSOURI

Forest Park

WEST VIRGINIA

Shenandoah National Park

VIRGINIA

KENTUCKY

Colonial National Historical Park

Ha Ha Tonka State Park

Mammoth Cave National Park

Cape Hatteras National Seashore

Great Smoky Mountains National Park

NORTH CAROLINA

TENNESSEE

ARKANSAS

Chattahoochee-Oconee National Forests

SOUTH CAROLINA

Ouachita National Forest

Natchez Trace Parkway

	City Park
	National Forest
	National Historical Park
	National Historic Site
	National Marine Sanctuary
	National Military Park
	National Monument
	National Park
	National Preserve
	National Recreation Area
	National Scenic Area
	National Scenic River
	National Seashore/Lakeshore
	National Volcanic Monument
	National Wildlife Refuge
	State Park
	Other

MISSISSIPPI

ALABAMA

GEORGIA

LOUISIANA

Cumberland Island National Seashore

Jean Lafitte National Historical Park and Preserve

FLORIDA

PUERTO RICO

San Juan National Historic Site

El Yunque National Forest

Virgin Islands National Park

Vieques National Wildlife Refuge

Everglades National Park

National Key Deer Refuge

Dry Tortugas National Park

Biscayne National Park

John Pennekamp Coral Reef State Park

Bahia Honda State Park

Florida Keys National Marine Sanctuary

YUKON

Kluane National
Park and Reserve

NORTHWEST TERRITORIES

NUNAVUT

Wood Buffalo
National Park

Wapusk
National Park

BRITISH
COLUMBIA

ALBERTA

SASKATCHEWAN

MANITOBA

Jasper
National Park

Banff
National Park

Pacific Rim
National Park
Reserve

Stanley Park

Dinosaur
Provincial Park

Waterton Lakes
National Park

Parks of Canada

City Park
National Marine Park
National Park
National Park Reserve
Provincial Park

NEWFOUNDLAND AND LABRADOR

Gros Morne
National Park

QUÉBEC

PRINCE
EDWARD
ISLAND

Cape Breton
Highlands
National Park

Saguenay-St. Lawrence
Marine Park

NEW
BRUNSWICK

Prince Edward Island
National Park

NOVA SCOTIA

ONTARIO

Mont-Tremblant
National Park

Mount Royal Park

Algonquin
Provincial Park

Thousand Islands
National Park

New England & New York

Rocky Gorge, White Mountain National Forest, New Hampshire

Acadia National Park
Maine

One of the nation's most beloved parks, Acadia protects a patch of coastal Maine where the north woods tumble down to meet the wild Atlantic. The first national park east of the Mississippi River sprawls across half of Mount Desert Island and all of several smaller landfalls. For generations, it's been the place where New Englanders escape into nature and learn to cherish the wild side of Down East.

THE BIG PICTURE

Established: 1916

Size: 49,052 acres (198.5 sq km)

Annual Visitors: 3.5 million

Visitor Centers: Hulls Cove, Thompson Island

Entrance Fee: $25 per vehicle, $12 per person

nps.gov/acad/

Named after the French settlers who were expelled from Atlantic Canada by the British, Acadia is the nation's easternmost national park and one of the first places in the United States to see the sunrise each day. Most of the park is located on Mount Desert Island, with small portions on smaller islands and the mainland.

After starting life as a colonial fishing village, **Bar Harbor** gradually evolved into a Victorian-era getaway for the affluent, artists, and "rusticators" trying to get back to nature. Today the island town is the park's main tourist hub, a port of call for **whale-watching** and **sailing tours**, **lobster shacks**, and lodging.

At low tide it's possible to walk the **Bar Island Land Bridge** to a tiny portion of the national park on **Bar Island**. During the summer, a passenger ferry runs between Bar Harbor and **Winter Harbor** and the park's **Schoodic Peninsula**. Located near the **Village Green** in Bar Harbor, the Smithsonian-affiliated **Abbe Museum** is dedicated to the Wabanaki Alliance of Native America tribes that once lived along the Maine coast. Bar Harbor's other great collection is the **Dorr Museum of Natural History** at the College of the Atlantic with its displays of Maine wildlife and touch pools of live sea creatures.

Many of the park's major features are within easy reach of Bar Harbor, including **Hulls Cove Visitor Center**, the start of Acadia's scenic **Park Loop Road**, a sinuous 27-mile (43.5 km) route that includes a steep drive to the top of **Cadillac Mountain**. One can also hike from town (via several trails) to the 1,530-foot (466 m) summit for a view that

A starfish sits in a tide pool at Ship Harbor in Acadia National Park.

The surf surges through the rocks at Thunder Hole during daybreak.

takes in much of the park and nearby islands. Located just south of town, the park's **Sieur de Monts** area features the **Wild Gardens of Acadia**, the park's **Nature Center**, and an older branch of the **Abbe Museum**.

After looping around Cadillac Mountain, the one-way Loop Road reaches the coast at **Sand Beach.** Protected by the Great Head peninsula, this is probably the best place in the park to take a dip in the ocean. The 4.7-mile (7.5 km) stretch between Sand Beach and **Hunters Head** is Acadia at its best: a rugged, rock-strewn shore carved by wind and water over millions of years. The rush of water through **Thunder Hole**—and the roar it makes—epitomizes the forces that shaped the Acadia coast.

Loop Road curls inland to **Jordan Pond** and **Eagle Lake**, navigable by kayak, canoe, and low-horsepower motorboat. The lake area is laced with hiking trails and crushed-stone **carriage roads**, which were funded by John D. Rockefeller, Jr., between 1914 and 1940. Most of the park's carriage roads are open to foot, bike, and horse traffic.

Much less visited than the heart of the park, the area west of **Somes Sound** features trails along the shore

Above: A hiker takes in the sunrise atop Cadillac Mountain. Opposite: The Bass Harbor Head Lighthouse

of **Long Pond** (1 mile/1.6 km) and up **Bernard Mountain** (3.2 miles/ 5 km). Down along the coast are **Ship Harbor Nature Trail** (1.3-mile/ 2 km return) and the cliff-top **Bass Harbor Head Lighthouse**.

Reaching the park's **Isle au Haut** unit requires passage on two ferries, from mainland Stonington to Town Landing (year-round) and then onward to **Duck Harbor** (summer only), where trails lead to secluded coves and dramatic sea cliffs. During summer, ranger-led boat tours journey to far-off **Baker Island** with its pioneer homes and graveyard, 1855 lighthouse, and cluster of huge natural granite slabs dubbed the **"dance floor."**

For another blast from the past, hop across the bridge to **Trenton village** and the **Great Maine Lumberjack Show**, an homage to the timber industry that once dominated much of the state. The show includes log rolling, chainsaw carving, pole climbing, and other woodsy sports. Just up the road, **Scenic Flights of Acadia** offers aerial views of the national park, with tours that vary from 15 minutes to a couple of hours. Trenton is also home to many **"lobster pound" restaurants** and the national park's seasonal **Thompson Island Information Center** (May to October). ■

CHOW DOWN

• **Jordon Pond House:** An Acadia eating institution since the early 1900s, the house serves soups, sandwiches, salads, and popovers on a sprawling lawn beside Jordan Pond. *acadiajordanpondhouse.com*

• **Otter Creek Market:** A tasty place to breakfast or lunch between Sand Beach and Hunters Head, this old general store dispenses groceries and lobster meals. *ottercreekinn maine.com*

• **Beal's Lobster Pier:** Catering to both drive-up and boat-up customers, Beal's at Southwest Harbor serves lobsters a dozen ways, including burgers, rolls, salads, and stew. *bealslobster.com*

• **Mache Bistro:** Fine dining in Bar Harbor with a rotating menu that includes dishes like herb-crusted salmon with Provence brown-butter vinaigrette or grilled quail with spiced honey and fig jam. *machebistro.com*

White Mountains

New Hampshire

The Old Man in the Mountain (a stone face profile on Cannon Mountain) might have disappeared, but the White Mountains—granite highlands that tower over the rest of New England—remain as solid as ever. Protected within the confines of three state parks, six federal wilderness areas, and the largest national forest in the Northeast, the mountains provide a year-round playground that includes a hundred miles of the Appalachian Trail and a half dozen winter sports areas.

THE BIG PICTURE

Established: 1918

Size: 750,852 acres (3,039 sq km)

Annual Visitors: 5 million

Visitor Centers: Gateway (North Woodstock), Lincoln Woods, Flume Gorge (Franconia Notch), Summit (Mount Washington), North Conway Village

Entrance Fee: $5

fs.usda.gov/main/white mountain/

Visitors were flocking to the White Mountains, one of the cradles of tourism in North America, as early as the 1820s to experience the region's heady blend of high peaks, scenic lakes, and lush northern forest. By the end of the 19th century, there were more than 20 "grand" hotels dotting the area—sprawling Victorian compounds where wealthy families from Boston and New York decamped for the entire summer. Snow sports took off after 1933 when **Wildcat Mountain** became the region's first established ski area.

Much of the early hoopla focused on **Mount Washington**, at 6,288.2 feet (1,916.6 m) the highest peak in New England and the most prominent mountain east of the Mississippi. First summited in 1642, the bald-topped peak continues to fascinate both serious hikers and casual visitors who take one of the two "easy" ways to the top.

Opened in 1861 as a carriage route, the vertiginous **Mount Washington Auto Road** climbs 7.6 miles (12.2 km) to the summit. Visitors can make the drive on their own or opt for a guided van tour. The company that manages the toll road also provides a hiker shuttle and snow coach tours during the winter. On the western side of the peak, the **Mount Washington Cog Railway** runs vintage carriages pulled by steam or biodiesel locomotives to the top from April to November. The three-hour round-trip includes plenty of time to take in the view, undertake a short hike, or explore various summit attractions.

Surrounded by the national forest, **Mount Washington State Park** covers 60 acres (.24 sq km) of the summit, a small but action-packed

Autumn colors take over the White Mountains of New Hampshire.

A hiker crosses a wooden walkway along the Zealand Falls Trail to an Appalachian Mountain Club hut in the White Mountains.

tract that includes the modern **Sherman Adams Summit Building** with its café, shop, and hiker's information desk; the **Mount Washington Observatory,** and its new **Extreme Mount Washington** museum; and **Tip Top House Historic Site**.

Trails radiate from the top of Mount Washington across the **Presidential Range**, a crescent-shaped chain of other lofty peaks, most of them named after U.S. presidents. The network includes a tough 160-mile (257.5 km) section of the **Appalachian Trail**, as well as the strenuous, 23-mile (37 km) **Presidential Traverse** across 10 peaks.

Franconia Notch is the region's other great natural attraction, a glacier-gouged mini-Yosemite with granite walls towering nearly 2,000 feet (609.6 m). The **Pemigewasset River** and scenic **Franconia Notch Parkway** (Interstate 93) flow through the bottom of the narrow valley. **Old Man of the Mountain**—a rock formation that resembled a human face—hovered 1,200 feet (365.76 m) above the valley until 2003 when it suddenly collapsed. Just off the parkway, the **Old Man of the Mountain Memorial** features seven steel profiles that help visitors imagine the site before the Old Man fell.

Stretching the entire length of the valley, **Franconia Notch State Park** offers numerous hiking trails, a campground, the **Cannon Mountain Aerial Tramway**, and the **New England Ski Museum**. Visitors can swim in the park's **Echo Lake** or trek an elevated wooden walkway up the **Flume**, a granite gorge with waterfalls and covered bridges. The 10-mile (16.1 km) **Franconia Notch Bike Path** also runs the full length of the pass.

At the bottom end of the notch, the **Loon Mountain** winter sports resort and spa, the **Mountain Club on Loon**, looms above the western end of the **Kancamagus Scenic Byway**. Considered one of America's premier routes for fall foliage, "The Kanc" meanders 34.5 miles (55.5 km) between Lincoln and Conway along the southern edge of the White Mountains. In addition to the region's largest assemblage of hotels and restaurants, **North Conway Village** hosts the **Mount Washington Observatory Weather Discovery Center**, the shop-until-you-drop **Settlers Green Outlet Village**, and a terrific viewpoint,

LAY YOUR HEAD

Hotels

• **Omni Mount Washington Resort:** Historic grand hotel near the base of Mount Washington; restaurants, bars, shops, pool, spa, golf course, zip line, snow sports, guided tours; from $259. *omnihotels.com*

• **Squam Lake Inn:** Cozy B&B near "Golden Pond" in the White Mountain foothills; from $179. *squamlakeinn.com*

• **Mount Coolidge Motel:** Cool retro digs and cabins on the Pemigewasset River in Franconia Notch; heated pool, riverside barbecues, and picnic tables; from $65. *mtcoolidgemotel.com*

• **Bartlett Inn:** Pet-friendly B&B near Crawford Notch and Attitash ski area; art gallery, outdoor pool, lawn games, discount lift tickets; from $105. *bartlettinn.com*

Camping

• **National forest:** 21 developed campgrounds; Barnes Field and Hancock open year-round; from $18.

• **State parks:** Franconia Notch, Crawford Notch; from $25.

the **Cathedral Ledge**, in Echo Lake State Park.

The other great pass through the White Mountains is **Crawford Notch**, which starts about 20 miles (32.2 km) north of Conway. While not nearly as spectacular as Franconia, Crawford appeals to those who prefer their nature with far fewer people. **Crawford Notch State Park** boasts a number of hiking routes,

from the easy **Saco River Trail** along the valley bottom to more challenging treks like the 4-mile (6.4 km) route to 140-foot (42.7 m) **Arethusa Falls** and **Frankenstein Cliff**.

First constructed in the 1930s by the Works Progress Administration (WPA), **Attitash Mountain Resort** winter sports area lies near the foot of the valley. In addition to Highway 302, the **Conway Scenic**

Railroad makes its way through Crawford Notch on a five-hour round-trip journey between North Conway and Bretton Woods on tracks laid in the 1870s. The kid- and canine-friendly "Notch Train," which operates between June and November, includes a glass-ceiling dome car and first class with a three-course lunch.

Bretton Woods, one of the

The Mount Washington Cog Railway, constructed in 1869, is the oldest in the country.

region's recreational hubs, lies in a broad valley shadowed by the Presidential Range. The colossal red-roofed building crowning a rise in the middle of the valley is the **Omni Mount Washington Resort**, opened in 1902 and the last of the grand hotels that once dominated the White Mountains. A national historic landmark, the hotel offers public tours that highlight its Tiffany glass, Italian stucco, Prohibition-era speakeasy, and the **Gold Room** where the 1944 Bretton Woods Conference established the gold standard and the International Monetary Fund.

The valley also harbors an **18-hole golf course**, the **Bretton Woods Ski Area** (62 ski/snowboard trails and 10 lifts), a forest canopy **zip line**, and the Mount Washington Cog Railway base station.

The foothills along the southern edge of the White Mountains are speckled with lakes, farms, and bucolic villages like **Holderness**, on a wooded isthmus between the twin **Squam Lakes**. The movie *On Golden Pond* was filmed on location here in 1981, and the lakes also provide a nesting place for loons, bald eagles, and many other birds. Get an up-close look at the wild things that roam the White Mountains—black bears, mountain lions, river otters, coyotes, raptors—at the excellent **Squam Lakes Natural Science Center**. The center also offers 90-minute guided boat tours of the nearby lakes. **Rattlesnake Mountain** affords incredible views of the lake region.

The **Museum of the White Mountains** in Plymouth showcases the region's history, culture, and nature through artwork and artifacts. In nearby Rumney, **Polar Caves** is a cluster of nine caverns that visitors navigate via wooden walkways and staircases. The private park also

The snow-covered view at the 6,288-foot (1,916.6 m) summit of Mount Washington

features outdoor rock climbing, rappelling, and a guided via ferrata adventure across a huge granite rock face. A self-guided nature trail winds through **Quincy Bog Natural Area**, which protects a typical White Mountains wetlands.

Around 5 percent of White Mountain National Forest lies across the border in western Maine. **Brickett Place**, an 1830 farmhouse in Stow, doubles as a historic site

and jumping-off point for hikers bound for the area's **Caribou-Speckled Wilderness**. Visitors can dig for amethyst, feldspar, topaz, garnet, and other precious stones at the **Deer Hill and Lord Hill Mineral Collecting Areas** (free permit required). During winter, **New England Dogsledding** offers guided trips in the national forest's **Evans Notch/Wild River** area. ■

DID YOU KNOW

• The summit of Mount Washington endured the second highest wind speed ever recorded on the Earth's surface on April 12, 1934: 231 miles an hour (371.76 km/hour).

• Constructed in 1819, Crawford Path, between Crawford Notch and the top of Mount Washington, is the nation's oldest maintained footpath.

• So many landscape painters flocked to the region during the 19th century that an entire artist

movement, the White Mountain School, was born.

• A historical marker on Route 3 near Lincoln, New Hampshire, in the White Mountains, indicates the spot where New Hampshire couple Betty and Barney Hill were allegedly abducted by aliens in 1961.

• More than 150 hikers and climbers have perished on Mount Washington since the first recorded death in 1849—most from weather-related hypothermia.

Cape Cod National Sea Shore
Massachusetts

THE BIG PICTURE

Established: 1961

Size: 43,607 acres (176.47 sq km)

Annual Visitors: 4.1 million

Visitor Centers: Salt Pond; Province Lands

Entrance Fee: $20 per vehicle, $3 per person at beaches (Memorial Day to Sept. 30)

nps.gov/caco/

Much more than just a pretty beach, Cape Cod National Seashore safeguards a range of natural habitats from salt marshes and heathlands to stands of pine and oak forest, and freshwater features like kettle ponds and sphagnum bogs. Its human heritage is just as rich and diverse, with a history that spans Pilgrims and presidents, radio pioneers and an artist colony hidden among the cape's many rolling sand dunes.

"Local boy does good" could easily have been the headline when Cape Cod National Seashore became a reality in 1961. Local son John F. Kennedy, who spent many summers on the Cape, created the park with a stroke of a pen in the Oval Office.

The designation came just in the nick of time to save the area from a massive subdivision development that would have devastated many of the Cape's ecosystems and closed off much of the area to public use. Shaped like a muscle-flexing arm, the Cape flaunts a mixed bag of farms, fields, villages, and conservation areas.

The national seashore covers the peninsula's entire east coast as well as the head of the peninsula around Provincetown.

For many, first contact with the park comes at the **Salt Pond Visitor Center** in Eastham, which rotates four 12-minute films about the Cape's natural and human history. Outside are the Braille-enabled **Buttonbush Nature Trail** (0.3 mile/ .48 km) and the **Nauset Marsh Trail**, which loops 1.3 miles (2.1 km) along the edge of wildlife-rich Salt Pond and Nauset Marsh.

Henry David Thoreau called the 40-mile (64.4 km) stretch of continuous sand along the Cape "the Great Outer Beach." Over the years, various sections have taken on their own appellations—Coast Guard, Marconi, Head of the Meadow, Race Point, and so on—each with a distinct personality and story to tell.

Starting from the visitor center parking lot in Eastham, the 1.6-mile (2.6 km) **Nauset Bike Trail** (open to walkers too) meanders through

A least tern keeps its egg warm in her nest.

From soft sands to prime fishing, Race Point Beach in Cape Cod has lots to offer.

thick woods to a glacial erratic called **Doane Rock** before reaching the ocean at **Coast Guard Beach**. It was here, on November 9, 1620, that the Pilgrims on the *Mayflower* first stepped ashore in the New World before anchoring near what is now Provincetown. In addition to being a great place to swim in summer, the beach affords access to sandy **Nauset Spit,** where nature writer Henry Beston lived while writing *The Outermost House* (1928). For those who want to get out on the water, **Goose Hummock** in Orleans runs four-hour guided kayak tours of Nauset Salt Marsh during the summer.

From Coast Guard Beach it's an easy stroll along the sand or drive along Ocean View Drive to **Nauset Light Beach**, another excellent place to wade into the surf. As well as the beach's namesake red-and-white beacon, the older **Three Sister Lighthouses** (dating from the 1830s) can be found in the pine forest behind

the shore. Next up the shore is **Marconi Beach**, where radio pioneer Guglielmo Marconi dispatched America's first transatlantic wireless message in 1903. The old radio station is long gone, but its elevated site offers splendid views across the coast. Nearby, the **Atlantic White Cedar Swamp Trail** (1.2 miles/ 1.9 km) leads through a variety of Cape ecosystems.

The national seashore briefly sprawls across the whole peninsula, nearly encircling the village of **Wellfleet**, settled in 1763 and now renowned for its many art galleries. Facing onto Cape Cod Bay, this portion of the park includes family-friendly **Duck Harbor Beach**, the classic Cape Cod–style **Atwood-Higgins House** (built in 1730), and the rambling **Great Island Trail**, a serious 8.8-mile (14.2 km) trek via sections that are sometimes submerged at high tide. Wellfleet is the northern terminus of the **Cape Cod**

Rail Trail, a 22-mile (35.4 km) paved biking and hiking route along an old railroad right-of-way that runs all the way to Dennis on the south coast via Eastham, Orleans, and Nickerson State Park. Old-fashioned **Wellfleet Drive-In Theater** offers alfresco movies during the summer.

Settled by English colonists in 1700, **Truro** is the next town north along the Cape. Built in 1848, **Truro Town Hall** is a gem of 19th-century Cape architecture, while the modern **Truro Vineyards** offers wines made from locally grown Chardonnay, Cabernet Franc, and Merlot grapes. East of town, the park's **Pamet Area Trails** amble through old cranberry bogs in the Pamet River Valley and the twin summits of **Bearberry Hill**.

A little farther up the coast is the national seashore's eclectic Highland area. Truro Historical Society maintains the **Highland House**

LAY YOUR HEAD

Hotels

• **Inn at the Oaks:** B&B tucked in a classic 1870 Cape Cod Victorian manse near Salt Pond; from $75. *innattheoaks.com*

• **Crowne Point Inn:** Spread across six historic structures, the inn is two blocks off the water in Provincetown; pool, spa, ghost; from $109. *crownepointe.com*

• **Even'tide Resort Motel & Cottages:** This modest Wellfleet resort is like a time trip back to the 1950s; indoor pool, sundeck, freshwater ponds; from $89. *eventidemotel.com*

• **Chatham Bars Inn:** Grand old beach hotel on Aunt Lydia's Cove in Chatham; restaurant, bar, private beach, swimming pool, tennis, wildlife cruises, sailing, fishing; from $295. *chathambarsinn.com*

• **HI Truro Hostel:** Summer-only youth hostel near the Pamet Area Trails; from $45. *hiusa.org*

Camping

• **Dune's Edge** (Provincetown), **North of Highlands** and **Horton's** (North Truro), **Paine's** and **Maurice's** (Wellfleet), **Nickerson State Park** (Orleans); from $22.

Museum, dedicated to the life and times of the Cape's bygone Native American inhabitants and European settlers. Visitors can climb 69 steps to the lantern room atop **Highland Light Station** (erected in 1857) or play a round of nine at **Highland Links** (established in 1892). After inheriting the decommissioned North Truro Air Force Station in 1994, the Park Service created the **Highland Center**. Among its various scientific and artist tenants is the **Payomet Performing Arts Center**, a seaside venue for plays, concerts, and circus camps.

Just before Highway 6 crosses that motel-spangled sandbar into Provincetown, the slightly elevated area on the right is called **Pilgrim Heights**. A short loop trail (0.7 mile/ 1.13 km) leads to a spring where it's believed the Pilgrims sipped their first freshwater in the Americas. Another trail leads to **Small's Swamp**, where Native Americans and early colonists once lived. From Pilgrim Spring, a paved biking/hiking trail follows the Old King's Road along the edge of a salt marsh to the **Head of the Meadow Beach** (it can also be reached by motor vehicle via a turnoff from Highway 6).

Crowning the head of the peninsula, **Provincetown** is the springboard for exploring the national seashore's northern extreme. Although the Pilgrims briefly anchored here in 1620—and penned the Mayflower Compact aboard their ship—the town wasn't founded until 1727. Celebrated for its progressive ways and alternative lifestyles, Provincetown hosts the annual **Fantasia Fair** and **Women's Week**, as well as the popular **Provincetown Film Festival**. Lined with shops, bars, art galleries, B&Bs, and eateries of all persuasion, helter-skelter **Commercial Street** runs the length of the waterfront.

Provincetown Museum and its 252-foot (76.8 m) **Pilgrim Monument** celebrate the 1620 landing and the town's long, colorful history. And the view from the top of the Italian Renaissance–style tower is outstanding. The well-respected **Provincetown Art Association and Museum** displays works by various artists who have rendered the Outer

Fishing boats docked at the Cape Cod Provincetown Port

A parkgoer paddles his canoe through the beautiful twilight waters of Gull Pond in Wellfleet, Massachusetts.

Cape in paintings, sculptures, and other mediums. Be sure to explore the **Winthrop Street Cemetery**, where some of the graves predate the town's founding.

The town is also home base for many of the outfitters offering guided tours and adventure sports in and around the national seashore. **Art's Dune Tours** take 4x4 passengers deep into the sand barrens on the outskirts of town, trips that combine coastal ecology and the **dune shacks** where Eugene O'Neill and the poet Harry Kemp, among others, once lived and created. **Moment Sailing Adventures** offers summertime day trips and two-day overnight journeys around Cape Cod Bay. **Provincetown Aquasports** rents kayaks and paddleboards and leads tours of **Herring Cove Tidal Lake** and **Provincetown Harbor**.

Province Lands Visitor Center is the gateway to the national seashore's northern exposures, including the 1-mile (1.6 km) **Beech Forest Trail** (some of the park's best fall foliage can be found here) and the **Old Harbor Life-Saving Station Museum**, which conducts buoy rescue demonstrations in the summer. The **Province Lands Bike Trail** loops 7 miles (11.3 km) through the area, connecting **Herring Point Beach** on Cape Cod Bay with **Race Point Beach** on the open Atlantic. ■

CHOW DOWN

• **Captain Linnell House:** Oysters, escargot, and classic chowder are just a few of the delights at this elegant Orleans eatery inside the 1840 house of sea captain Ebeneezer Linnell. *linnell.com*

• **Provincetown Portuguese Bakery**: Malasada to die for, plus soups, sandwiches, meat pies, fish cakes, and dozens of different bakery items.

• **The Beachcomber:** Oceanfront eatery on Cahoon Hollow Beach in Wellfleet featuring a raw bar, lobster rolls, fish tacos, crab cakes, and other maritime favorites. *thebeachcomber.com*

• **Mac's Shack:** Creative coastal cuisine from around the world is the forte of this 1857 clapboard house restaurant on Wellfleet Harbor. *macsseafood.com/restaurants/macs-shack/*

• **The Knack:** This trendy roadside stand near the big roundabout in Orleans serves gourmet burgers, seafood rolls, and sandwiches. *theknackcapecod.com*

The sunset paints the sky in pinks and purples over
Race Point Light in Provincetown, Massachusetts.

① Central Park, New York
Frederick Law Olmsted set the tone in the mid-19th century when he transformed more than 800 acres (3.24 sq km) of Manhattan's vestigial countryside into a landscaped wonderland called Central Park. In its wake came other handcrafted urban green spaces like Chicago's Grant Park, Golden Gate Park in San Francisco, and Balboa Park in San Diego.

② National Mall, Washington, D.C.
The cherry trees that bloom around Washington's Tidal Basin each spring were originally a gift from the Japanese government planted along the waterfront of West Potomac Park between 1912 and 1920. Among other places to witness the pink extravaganza are Vancouver's Stanley Park and the Missouri Botanical Garden, near Forest Park in St. Louis.

③ Great Smoky Mountains, Tennessee and North Carolina
Hiking or driving from the lowest to the highest elevations of Great Smoky Mountains National Park offers the botanical equivalent of traveling from Georgia to Maine up the Atlantic seaboard. Five types of forest—pine-and-oak, northern hardwood, spruce-fir, cove hardwood, and hemlock—blanket the park's peaks and vales.

④ Florida Keys and Everglades, Florida
Along the shorelines of the Florida Keys parks and the Everglades are mangroves, thick tidal vegetation that protects the coast against storms and provides a nursery for infant fish and other sea creatures.

⑤ Theodore Roosevelt National Park, North Dakota
The wild grasslands that once covered much of North America are preserved in places like Theodore Roosevelt National Park in North Dakota. If you can't make it to North Dakota, other parks that preserve virgin prairie include Missouri National Recreational River in Nebraska and Dinosaur Provincial Park in Alberta.

THE TOP

10

BOTANICAL ADVENTURES

Parks where the flora often overshadows the fauna.

⑥ Anza-Borrego Desert, California
Deserts often foster a biodiversity greater than that of forested areas. Anza-Borrego Desert State Park is renowned for its riot of spring wildflowers and wide variety of cacti and other succulents that thrive in the California park's arid environment.

Central Park, as viewed from a nearby skyscraper, adds green space to Manhattan.

⑦ Redwood and Sequoia, California
Discover the difference between coastal redwoods (the world's tallest trees) and giant sequoias (the world's largest trees) in California. The former congregate along the coast in Redwood National Park and its allied state parks; the latter are found at Sequoia National Park and other spots along the Sierra foothills.

⑧ Mount St. Helens, Washington
One of the results of the 1980 eruption of Mount St. Helens was thousands of toppled-over trees, an eerie gray horizontal forest that resembled a jumble of giant toothpicks when seen from above. Since then, the forest has recovered with surprising vigor, new trees sprouting among their fallen comrades at the national volcanic monument.

⑨ El Yunque, Puerto Rico, and Olympic, Washington
Rain forest comes in two varieties: the steamy tropical version found in Hawaiian state and national parks, as well as El Yunque National Forest in Puerto Rico, and the moss-covered temperate "jungle" of Washington's Olympic National Park.

⑩ Denali, Alaska
Although some consider it a cold-weather desert, tundra is surprisingly diverse and photogenic, especially in the fall when the foliage renders an explosion of color every bit as dazzling as the deciduous forest in Alaska's Denali National Park.

Boston Common
Massachusetts

THE BIG PICTURE

Established: 1634

Size: 50 acres (0.2 sq km)

Annual Visitors: 2.98 million

Visitor Center: Weekdays 8:30 a.m. to 5 p.m.; weekends 9 a.m. to 5 p.m.

Entrance Fee: None

boston.gov/parks/boston-common

The oldest public park in the United States, Boston Common started life in 1634 as a collective cow pasture for the city's Puritan community. Now the rambling green space provides a quick and easy escape from urban life, a mixed bag of lawns, trees, and water features that's equally cherished by local residents, workers, and visitors to the largest city in New England.

It's not a far stretch to claim that Boston Common has played a larger role in the history of America than any other green space in the entire nation.

In addition to grazing their cows, the Puritans used the Common as a place to hang Quakers and other undesirables. The Massachusetts militia utilized it as a training ground for revolution until the British occupied Boston and the redcoats began an eight-year encampment on the Common. During the Civil War era, the park provided a venue for abolitionist rallies and troops. A century later, civil rights and anti–Vietnam War demonstrators marched across the manicured lawns.

From George Washington and John Adams to Charles Lindbergh, Martin Luther King, Jr., and Judy Garland, many famous people have appeared before the masses on Boston Common. Two of the largest crowds ever were in attendance for a 1979 open-air Mass by Pope John Paul II (400,000 people) and the 2017 Women's March (175,000 people).

The evolution from pasture to city park was slow and somewhat random. The last public execution took place in 1817. Cows weren't banned until the 1830s, the same decade in which the Common was enclosed by an iron fence and many of the pedestrian walkways were added. Many statues and memorials were erected during a flurry of monument building in the early 20th century.

Boston Common Visitor Information Center—which also serves as the official start of the Freedom Trail through downtown Boston—overlooks **Parkman Plaza** on the park's east side (Tremont Street). In addition to maps, books, and souvenirs, the visitor center is the starting point for the **Walk Into History** and **African-American Patriots** walking

The Boston Common, covered in more than 37,000 American flags honoring those who died in the Revolutionary War

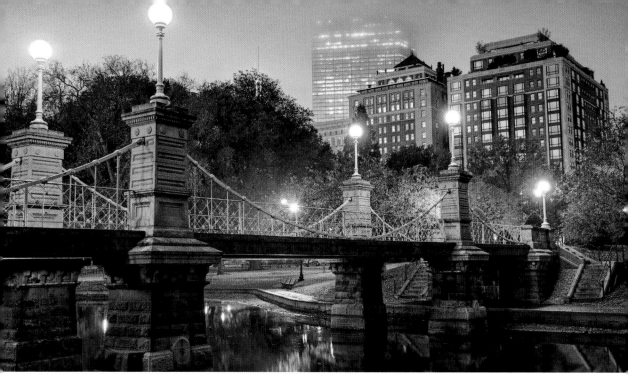

A view of the city from the Public Garden on a foggy fall morning

tours. The first leg of the 2.5-mile (4 km) **Freedom Trail** cuts diagonally across the Common to the golden-domed **Massachusetts State House**, built in the 1790s on Beacon Hill. As it exits the park, the trail passes the **Shaw Memorial**, a bronze monument that honors Colonel Robert Gould Shaw and the first African-American volunteer unit that fought in the Civil War.

Frog Pond, the lone survivor of the three lakes that once graced the Common, is the focal point for many of the park's annual and seasonal activities. With **ice-skating** in winter and playing in the **spray pool** during the summer, the pond is a magnet for kids. Nearby are the **Frog Pond Café** snack bar, a **carousel**, and free **yoga** sessions.

Musicians, thespians, protesters, and politicians take the stage at the Greek Revival–style **Parkman Bandstand**, the venue for a wide variety of rallies, protests, and performing arts. The Common also boasts its own graveyard—the **Central Burying Ground**. Opened in 1756, the cemetery is the last resting place of painter Gilbert Stuart, composer William Billings, and both British and American troops killed in action during the Revolution.

Often considered part of the Common, the **Boston Public Garden** on the west side of Charles Street is actually a separate park. Founded in 1837 as the nation's first public botanical collection, the Garden contains a wide variety of trees, shrubs, and flowers. The famous **swan boats** on the garden lake have been around since 1877. ◾

EVENT HORIZON

• **Ancient Fishweir Project:** Members of the Wampanoag and other Massachusetts tribes collaborate with Boston school kids to stage a May through June festival that combines public art and education with Native American rituals and performances. *fishweir.org*

• **First Night:** Boston rings in the new year with the People's Parade to Boston Common, followed by a skating spectacular on Frog Pond and early evening fireworks display over the park. *firstnightboston.org*

• **Shakespeare on the Common:** A tradition since 1996, the Commonwealth Shakespeare Company presents the Bard alfresco under summer night skies. *commshakes.org*

• **Boston Freedom Rally:** Legalization of marijuana is the focus of this September gathering that includes live music, food stalls, and plenty of paraphernalia. *masscann.org/rally/*

Blackstone River Valley National Heritage Corridor

Rhode Island & Massachusetts

THE BIG PICTURE

Established: 1986

Size: 400,000 acres (1,619 sq km)

Annual Visitors: 500,000

Visitor Centers: Pawtucket, Woonsocket, Uxbridge, Worcester

Entrance Fee: None

nps.gov/blac/
blackstoneheritagecorridor.org

Dedicated to the legacy of the 19th-century industrial revolution in New England, the Blackstone River Valley represents a new kind of national park, one dedicated to the works of people rather than nature, as well as one that comprises hundreds of separate properties and structures rather than a contiguous area. Another unique characteristic of the corridor is the fact that it's a joint effort of federal, state, and local authorities; the private sector; and nonprofits.

Spread along both banks of the Blackstone River between Providence, Rhode Island, and Worcester, Massachusetts, the National Heritage Corridor embraces 25 cities and towns that sparked the industrial revolution in the United States and helped transform the nation into a global economic powerhouse.

The tale of the region's evolution from farm to factory is told in the historic factories, mills, warehouses, transportation links, schools, churches, and other institutions that make up the 46-mile-long (74 km) stretch. Whether you start your exploration of the corridor from the south or north, it's a fascinating journey into America's past, a story that has seldom received the attention it deserves.

For those who prefer a chronological passage, the place to start is Pawtucket, Rhode Island, and the **Blackstone River Valley Visitor Center** on the grounds of the **Slater Mill**. Founded in 1793, Slater was the nation's first successful textile spinning factory. Today you can tour the old mill buildings, catch weaving and spinning demonstrations, or watch a short informative film, "Hidden in the Blackstone Valley."

State Highway 122 leads north to Lincoln, Rhode Island, and **Blackstone River State Park**, where a towpath leads along a barge canal built in the 1820s. Regional transportation is the focus of the **Captain Wilbur Kelly House Museum**. The park itself is an ideal place to slip a canoe, kayak, or paddleboard into the river or access the middle section of the **Blackstone River Bikeway**.

Across the river, the colossal red-brick **Ashton Mill** and its neat rows of worker homes (historically restored into modern housing) offer the corridor's best example of a 19th-century factory town. In nearby Cumberland, the **Blackstone River Theatre** showcases the valley's dance, music, and folk-art traditions.

Farther upriver, **Woonsocket** offers more than 30 structures on the National Register of Historic Places, including mills, schools, homes, and places of worship dating from the city's 19th-century textile boom days. The **Museum of Work and Culture** focuses on a wave of French Canadians who worked in Rhode Island's textile mills. Woonsocket is home port for the **Blackstone Valley Explorer**, a 40-passenger riverboat that offers history and nature tours.

Across the border in Massachusetts, a self-guided walking tour in the town of **Uxbridge** runs a broad gamut from 18th-century churches

Taking in the sunny weather, a woman kayaks on the Blackstone River.

and farmhouses to 19th-century mills and commercial buildings. On the outskirts of town, **Blackstone River and Canal Heritage State Park** highlights the vital role of canals in the industrial revolution. Among the park's many outdoor activities are hiking, biking, horseback riding, canoeing, fishing, and cross-country skiing.

Now the second largest city in New England (after Boston), **Worcester** retains many of its industrial revolution landmarks, including worker-funded **Mechanics Hall** (built in 1855) and the colossal **Worcester Corset Factory** (1895), as well as the wonderfully restored **Salisbury Mansion** (1772). Paintings by Winslow Homer, Thomas

Cole, John Singer Sargent, and other 19th-century American masters are on display at the excellent **Worcester Art Museum**. For nature lovers, the Audubon Society's **Broad Meadow Brook Wildlife Sanctuary** offers a variety of trails through 400 acres (1.62 sq km) of marsh, meadow, and woodland on the edge of Worcester. ■

LAY YOUR HEAD

Hotels

• **Hotel Providence:** Opened in 1882 and called the Blackstone Hotel for many years, this restored classic lies in the Downtown Providence Historic District; restaurant, bar, fitness studio; from $143. *hotelprovidence.com*

• **Pillsbury House:** Period antiques and regional artwork flavor this cozy B&B in an 1875 Victorian manse in Woonsocket; from $125. *pillsburyhouse.com*

• **Putnam House:** Set on two bucolic acres of the Blackstone Valley, the main house of this B&B was built in

1737; from $95. *putnamhousebandb .com*

• **Samuel Slater:** Docked in Central Falls, Rhode Island, this authentic 40-foot (12.2 m) canal boat with full kitchen and bathroom can sleep four; book via Airbnb; from $149. *rivertourblackstone.com/site/slater/*

Adirondack Park

New York

Adirondack—the largest park of any kind in the lower 48 states—was created in 1892 to safeguard the timber and water resources of upstate New York. While it still performs those functions, it's also the state's recreational treasure, a wonderland of woods and water that shelters 3,000 lakes, 30,000 miles (48,280.3 km) of rivers and streams, and more than a hundred rustic towns and villages.

Protected by the state constitution as a "forever wild" preserve, Adirondack Park sprawls from Lake Champlain and Lake George to the St. Lawrence Valley. With half of the land in private hands and the other managed by public agencies, the park is a patchwork quilt of farms and orchards, summer camps and winter resorts, wilderness areas and wild forests.

Within the famous "blue line" that delineates the Adirondack, native flora and fauna flourish. Moose and mountain lion, black bear and beaver, muskrat and mink

THE BIG PICTURE

Established: 1892

Size: 6.1 million acres (24,584.8 sq km)

Annual Visitors: 10 million

Visitor Centers: Newcomb, Lake Placid, Paul Smiths

Entrance Fee: None

visitadirondacks.com
apa.ny.gov

are among the many animals that call the region home. A mix of temperate and boreal forest means the park is also blessed with an equally impressive array of plant life—more than 1,200 native species.

With a rich human history and assortment of water sports, **Lake George** is gateway to the park's eastern sector. Snap panoramic photos of the lake region from the top of **Prospect Mountain.** Or get out on the water aboard the *Mohican,* first launched in 1908 and one of several vintage steamboats that offers guided lake cruises. Perched near the lake's southern end, **Fort William Henry** is the faithful re-creation of a British bastion that saw action in the French and Indian War and was featured in *The Last of the Mohicans.* At the opposite end of the lake, **Fort Ticonderoga** played a pivotal role in the American Revolution and is now home to one of North America's largest collections of 18th-century weapons and uniforms.

Heading west, **Pharaoh Lakes Wilderness** offers 70 miles (112.7 km) of hiking trails, as well as winter snowshoeing and cross-country skiing. The whitewater paddling is top-notch in the **Hudson Gorge Wilderness,** which safeguards a 12-mile (19.3 km) stretch of the upper Hudson River. True to its

Historic buildings and a cannon at Fort Ticonderoga

The calm waters of Seventh Lake in the Fulton Chain of Lakes region create the perfect sunset reflection.

name, the **High Peaks Wilderness** includes 5,343-foot (1,628.5 m) **Mount Marcy**—the highest point in New York—and 40 other mounts that reach over 4,000 feet (1,219.2 m). You can also hike to **Lake Tear of the Clouds**, where the Hudson starts its journey to New York City.

Learn more about the region's human and natural history at the **Adirondack Interpretive Center** in Newcomb. Just up the road in Tupper Lake, the **Wild Center** offers live animal encounters, interactive nature exhibits, guided hikes, and canoe trips, plus the elevated quarter-mile (0.4 km) **Wild Walk** trail through the treetops. Located in a classic 1870s resort hotel, the **Adirondack Experience** at Blue Mountain Lake spins the region's human story through exhibits, artifacts, workshops, demonstrations, and a research library.

Lake Placid is the region's winter sports hub. Host of the 1932 and 1980 Winter Olympics, the town offers everything from skiing, snowboarding, and ice-skating to ski jumping and bobsledding at the same places where gold medals were won. The **Lake Placid Winter Olympic Museum** in Herb Brooks Arena details many of the town's athletic exploits including the legendary "Miracle on Ice" hockey game of 1980. The Olympic venues can be toured throughout the year,

MEET THE NEIGHBORS

• **Saratoga National Historical Park:** Considered one of the turning points of world history, the 1777 battle that took place on this site turned the tide of the Revolutionary War in favor of the Americans and made Benedict Arnold a (temporary) hero.

• **Thousand Islands State Parks:** From Burnham Point near Lake Ontario to Cedar Island in Chippewa Bay, this eye-catching archipelago is protected within the confines of 11 New York state parks.

• **Green Mountain National Forest:** Autumn foliage and archaeological sites, wildlife, and eight wilderness areas spangle this Vermont version of the Adirondacks ecosystems.

• **Fort Stanwix National Monument:** Located on the strategic south flank of the Adirondacks, the fort played a pivotal role in the struggle between the British, French, and the Six Nations Confederacy to control upstate New York.

Above: Snow-covered trees cover the High Peaks of the Adirondacks. Opposite: A rushing stream in Adirondack Park

including the **Olympic Speed Skating Oval** where American phenom Eric Heiden won his five gold medals and the massive towers of the **Olympic Ski Jumping Complex** on the south side of town.

Mere mortals can experience the adrenaline rush of speeding down the Olympic course with a professional driver at the **Lake Placid Bobsled Experience**. The **Mt. Van Hoevenberg Olympic Complex** also offers biathlon and cross-country skiing adventures. And anyone can ski or snowboard the Olympic runs at **Whiteface Mountain**, which offers 11 lifts and 87 total trails.

Nearby **Saranac Lake** is the architectural gem of the Adirondacks, celebrated for its Victorian-era **tuberculosis "cure cottages"** and the extravagant Craftsman-style **Great Camps** where wealthy families once summered. The town also boasts the hand-carved **Adirondack Carousel** and the **Saranac Laboratory Museum**, where groundbreaking research on TB was carried out between 1894 and 1964. Nearly 200 structures in the village are on the National Register of Historic Places. ■

LAY YOUR HEAD

• **The Point:** On Upper Saranac Lake, this Rockefeller take on the 19th-century Adirondacks "great camp" is now the epitome of a rustic chic resort; restaurant, bar, billiards, boating, hiking, ice-skating; from $1,700 all inclusive. *thepointsaranac.com*

• **Mirror Lake Inn:** Within walking distance of the Winter Olympic Museum in Lake Placid, the inn features indoor and outdoor pools, private beach, and full-service spa; restaurants and bar; boating, fishing, and winter snow activities; from $169. *mirrorlakeinn.com*

• **Adirondack Loj:** Built in 1927 and run by the Adirondack Mountain Club (ADK), this rustic lodge offers private rooms and bunk houses; restaurant, library, game room, boat rental, swimming, and High Peaks Information Center for hikers; private doubles from $169. *adk.org*

From the sunset reflection on Heart Lake to the changing leaves, fall arrives in the Adirondacks.

Niagara Falls State Park

New York

THE BIG PICTURE

Established: 1885

Size: 400 acres (1.62 sq km)

Annual Visitors: 9.5 million

Visitor Center: Niagara Falls, New York

Entrance Fee: None

niagarafallsstatepark.com

From honeymooners and tightrope walkers to movie stars and landscape painters, people have long been drawn to Niagara Falls. A wet, wild, and thunderous divide between the United States and Canada, the massive cascade is both a scenic wonder and cultural phenomenon that reflects the ongoing human quest to triumph over nature—a clash that Niagara has won more often than not.

Formed around 12,000 years ago during the last ice age, Niagara Falls is no more than a hiccup in the epic movement of freshwater from the Great Lakes to the Atlantic Ocean. But what a hiccup it is—the most powerful waterfall in North America and one of the most painted, penned, and photographed landmarks on Earth.

Niagara's three separate cascades (American, Bridal Veil, and Horseshoe) are arrayed across a 3,400-foot (1,036.3 m) rock wall. An average of more than 750,000 gallons (2.8 million L) of water tumbles over the falls every second—enough to fill more than 4,000 Olympic-size pools every hour. Below the falls, the short but historic Niagara River runs 36 miles (57.9 km) to Lake Ontario, dividing New York State from Ontario

province. Scattered along the way are four other state parks—**Whirlpool, Devil's Hole**, **Joseph Davis**, and **Fort Niagara**—with their own unique take on the Niagara Corridor.

The first European to describe the falls was Father Louis Hennepin, a French priest traveling with the La Salle expedition of 1678. But tourism didn't take off until the early 19th century, when honeymooners began to arrive en masse. By the 1870s, an alliance of artists, landscape architects, and conservationists lobbied to put Niagara under state control in order to stem rampant commercialization, a campaign that culminated in 1885 when the American side of the falls became the nation's first state park.

The state park is split into mainland and island sections; the latter offers better waterfall viewing, and the former boasts more attractions. Located at the foot of Old Falls Street, the state park **Visitor Center** offers information, interactive exhibits, souvenirs, and the **Niagara Adventure Theater**, which screens a 30-minute film on the natural and human history of the falls.

Just steps away is the **Niagara Falls Observation Tower**, which provides an outstanding view of the American falls and a partial glimpse of Horseshoe. Directly below the tower is the dock for *Maid of the*

The stately grounds of Old Fort Niagara in New York State

The view of gushing and powerful Niagara Falls from the U.S. perspective

Mist, a tour boat service that's been taking visitors into the spray of Horseshoe Falls since 1848 (blue rain ponchos are included with your ticket to board). Walking paths lead to other viewpoints and attractions like the **Niagara Gorge Discovery Center** interactive museum, the **Schoellkopf Power Station** ruins, and **Aquarium of Niagara**.

Inside the Discovery Center, the **Niagara Gorge Trailhead Center** gives information on eight trails along the Niagara River leading downstream from Goat Island to the **Artpark**. Some of the trails (like the 1.3-mile/2.1 km **Whirlpool Rapids Trail**) require boulder hopping, while others (like the 3.2-mile/5.15 km **Robert Moses Trail**) are paved, flat, and easy to navigate.

Goat Island, which separates Horseshoe from American and Bridal Veil, can be reached on foot over a pedestrian bridge or vehicle on the First Street Bridge. In addition to vertigo-inducing views like **Terrapin Point**, the island is home to **Cave of the Winds**, an eclectic attraction that combines a tribute to inventor **Nikola Tesla** (who figured out how to harness the power of Niagara to create alternating current) and wooden stairs that plunge 175 feet (53.34 m) into Niagara Gorge for a close-up view of Bridal Veil Falls. ■

DID YOU KNOW

• The origin of "Niagara" is Native American; it may derive from a word meaning "the strait."

• In 1901—after experimenting with a cat that survived the plunge—63-year-old Michigan schoolteacher Annie Edson Taylor became the first person to go over the falls in a wooden barrel. She survived.

• The Niagara River Corridor was the world's first internationally recognized Audubon Important Bird Area.

• More than 600 plant species have been recorded on Goat Island, including 140 of the 170 trees native to western New York. Although the falls had been a popular honeymoon destination since the early 1800s, Marilyn Monroe inspired a whole new generation of newlyweds when she starred in the 1953 film *Niagara*.

Gateway National Recreation Area

New York & New Jersey

Even the nation's largest metropolitan area has its quiet, back-to-nature spaces—beaches, bays, marshes, and parklands in this eclectic park along New York's City's Atlantic coast. History, wildlife, and outdoor recreation are the big attractions at this great escape from the Big Apple, scattered across Long Island, Staten Island, and a small slice of the Jersey Shore.

THE BIG PICTURE

Established: 1972

Size: 26,607 acres

Annual Visitors: 8.6 million

Visitor Centers: Floyd Bennett Field, Great Kills, Sandy Hook

Entrance Fee: None

nps.gov/gate/

This national recreation area (NRA) takes its name from the fact that tens of millions of migrants entered the nation via New York Harbor. And while only a small part of the park carried out immigration functions, its shoreline was often the first land these arrivals spotted after their long Atlantic passage.

Gateway is divided into three distinctive sections. By far the largest, Jamaica Bay Unit protects an archipelago of unspoiled islands and recreation areas along the Brooklyn and Queens waterfronts. Staten Island Unit safeguards parklands and two tiny islands along the east coast of New York's least-populated borough. Sandy Hook Unit embraces an entire peninsula at the northern extreme of the Jersey Shore.

Brooklyn's **Floyd Bennett Field** was the world's most celebrated airfield during the 1930s, when Amelia Earhart, Howard Hughes, and Wiley Post, among others, used the field as a staging post for numerous world-record flights. In addition to a **Visitor Contact Station** (the visitor center), the old airport now features the **Hanger Row Historic District**, the **North Forty Natural Area** (hiking in summer, cross-country skiing in winter), an **archery range, model aircraft flying area**, myriad **bike paths,** a sports complex with **indoor ice-skating** and **rock climbing**, and a year-round public **campground**.

Jamaica Bay shelters 16 large islands and numerous smaller landfalls, all of them within the NRA. **Broad Channel Island** can be accessed by road or subway, but reaching the others requires some sort of watercraft. **Kayaking** is the best bet for birding, fishing, and sightseeing, with numerous spots around the bay to slip a boat into the water, including Canarsie Pier, the Mill Basin, and the old seaplane ramp at Floyd Bennett. **Wheel Fun Rentals** in Marine Park rents kayaks and paddleboards for use on the bay.

Out on the Rockaway Peninsula, **Fort Tilden** blends secluded shorelines, coastal dunes, rare maritime forest, historic gun and missile batteries, and **Rockaway Theatre Company** stage productions. Nearby **Jacob Riis Park** offers a magnificent art deco bathhouse and pitch and putt golf course.

A pudgy tree swallow at Jamaica Bay Wildlife Refuge

Standing strong, the Sandy Hook Light is among the oldest lighthouses remaining in the United States.

The park's **Staten Island** section includes several large waterfront parcels. Centered around a bay of the same name, **Great Kills** harbors several marinas, a long sandy strand, and a natural area laced by hiking and biking trails. Literally in the shadow of the Verrazano-Narrows Bridge, **Fort Wadsworth** boasts the longest continuous military history for a U.S. fortress. Rangers elucidate the site's Dutch, British, and American history on guided tours.

Technically a barrier spit, the slender **Sandy Hook Peninsula** extends 6 miles (9.7 km) into the Atlantic and was largely under U.S. Army control from the 1850s to 1974. **Fort Hancock** retains many of its historic structures, used now for research, education, and the **Sandy Hook Visitor Center**. Towering above the old base is **Sandy Hook Lighthouse**, commissioned in 1764 and still active.

Reached by ferry from Manhattan or road through northern New Jersey, Sandy Hook lives up to its name with seven beaches on both its bay and ocean sides. **Biking**, **hiking**, **boating**, and **birding** are among the favorite pastimes. During the warm summer months, rangers lead guided **canoe cruises** on Sandy Hook Bay. ■

LAY YOUR HEAD

Hotels

• **Inn Your Element:** Modern B&B on Rockaway Peninsula makes a great base for exploring Jamaica Bay, Fort Tilden, and Jacob Riis Park; from $115. *innyourelement.com*

• **Harbor House:** Manhattan skyline and Statue of Liberty views highlight this cozy B&B on the Staten Island waterfront within walking distance to Fort Wadsworth; from $79. *nyharborhouse.com*

• **SeaScape Manor:** Pet-friendly B&B with ocean views in the town of Sandy Hook; from $145. *seascapemanorbb.com*

Camping

• Gateway NRA offers camping at three sites: Floyd Bennett Field in Brooklyn (tents and RVs), Fort Wadsworth on Staten Island (tents), and Sandy Hook in New Jersey (tents). Fees start at $30 per night or $210 per week.

Central Park
New York

As much a part of the city's image as the Statue of Liberty and Times Square, it's hard to imagine the Big Apple without leafy Central Park. Sculpted in the 1850s and a template for hundreds of urban parks around the world, the huge green space stretches 51 blocks right through the middle of helter-skelter Manhattan.

THE BIG PICTURE

Established: 1858

Size: 843 acres (3.4 sq km)

Visitors: 42 million

Visitor Centers: The Dairy, Belvedere Castle, Dana Discovery Center, Chess & Checkers House, Columbus Circle Kiosk

Entrance Fee: None

centralparknyc.org
nycgovparks.org/parks/central-park/

By the early 1800s, New York's elite felt their city needed a large recreational parkland similar to those already established in London and Paris. The most obvious site was an area of villages and farms mostly inhabited by recent Irish immigrants and free African Americans. Wielding eminent domain, the city fathers evicted the residents and announced a design competition for the proposed park.

Prominent American landscape architect Frederick Law Olmsted and British American architect Calvert Vaux won. But in a stinging rebuke to the elites who envisioned the park as a highbrow playground, Olmsted announced their creation would be "a democratic development of the highest significance," intended for all New Yorkers and not just the privileged. And that's exactly what it became: an egalitarian space where people of every persuasion could relax, run around, smell the roses, and savor fresh air.

Olmsted and Vaux would be pleased to know that their original design remains largely intact. The Mall and the Bethesda Fountain, the Reservoir and Harlem Lake, the Ball Ground and the North Meadow are all original features. The early menagerie evolved into the Central Park Zoo, and their vision of an art museum on Fifth Avenue soon became the Metropolitan Museum of Art.

Visitors have numerous ways to enter the park, but none as spectacular as **Grand Army Plaza** at the corner of Fifth Avenue and 59th Street. A gold equestrian statue of **General Sherman** by celebrated American sculptor Augustus Saint-Gaudens looms over the square, as do some of New York's most prestigious hotels. With its gargoyles and Gothic spire, the **Sherry-Netherland** is a masterpiece of 1920s urban architecture; recently discovered after decades beneath white paint, the lobby's precious neo-Renaissance ceiling has been meticulously restored.

Walkways lead to the outdoor **Wollman Rink** (ice-skating in winter, roller skating the rest of the year) and the family-friendly **Central Park Zoo**. Managed by the Wildlife Conservation Society (WCS), the collection is small but incredibly diverse, including lemurs and snow leopards, grizzly bears and sea lions, penguins and boa constrictors, most of them housed in modern habitats. The menagerie also includes the **Tisch Children's Zoo**

Changing autumn leaves make an archway above visitors to Central Park.

An aerial view of Central Park captures the 843-acre (3.4 sq km) green space, smack in the middle of Manhattan.

and the sensory overload **4-D Theater**. Beyond the zoo, the **Dairy** building originally dispensed fresh milk to urban families but is now a visitor center with a gift shop for Central Park information, maps, and souvenirs.

Lined by statues of celebrated writers and shaded by one of the last remaining stands of American elm trees, the **Mall** leads north to the **Bethesda Terrace and Fountain**, among the earliest structures built in the park and a popular spot for selfies. They overlook the **Lake**, one of the park's primary water features. In addition to a popular restaurant and bar, **Loeb Boathouse** offers rowboats and guided rides on a Venetian gondola. The lake's north shore is edged by a heavily wooded area with rock outcrops called the **Ramble**, Olmsted's ode to raw nature. The **Conservatory Water** draws model boating enthusiasts, their miniature yachts flitting between statues of **Hans Christian Andersen** and **Alice in Wonderland.**

Central Park's midsection is dominated by four large and very different landmarks—a lake, a field, and two world-class museums.

Perched on either side of midpark are the **Metropolitan Museum of Art** (the Met) and the **American Museum of Natural History** (AMNH). One of the world's foremost collections, the Met's two million works span nearly every part of the globe and all historical eras. The **sculpture garden** on the roof offers excellent views of Central Park, as do the floor-to-ceiling windows of the gallery that houses the ancient Egyptian **Temple of Dendur**. The AMNH is one of the world's largest museums of any kind. Dedicated to nature, science, and human culture, the collection embraces more than 33 million specimens and artifacts.

EVENT HORIZON

• **GMA Summer Concert Series:** Between May and September, *Good Morning America* hosts weekly performances by the biggest acts in popular music on Rumsey Playfield.

• **Central Park Conservancy Film Festival:** A full week of free open-air movies in the park at the end of August where patrons are encouraged to bring blankets, drinks, and picnic dinners. *central parknyc.org*

• **Rolex Central Park Horse Show:** Grand Prix show jumping takes over the Wollman Rink in September. *cphs.coth.com/*

• **Macy's Thanksgiving Day Parade:** The iconic event always starts at 77th Street and Central Park West. The night before, watch the giant balloons being inflated behind the American Museum of Natural History. *macys.com/social/parade/*

• **Columbus Circle Holiday Market:** Yuletide foods, crafts, clothing, and decorations are offered by more than a hundred vendors at this outdoor bazaar held from Thanksgiving weekend to Christmas Eve.

The museum's **Hayden Planetarium** offers exhibits and shows about earth and space science under the direction of noted astrophysicist Neil deGrasse Tyson.

Renamed in honor of Jacqueline Kennedy Onassis in 1994, the **JKO Reservoir** once supplied fresh drinking water to New York City. Today it's renowned for its mile-and-a-half (2.4 km) jogging track, equestrian trail, pink-blossomed cherry trees, and the two dozen species of water birds that frequent the park's largest lake.

The most prominent park feature not in the Olmsted-Vaux plan, the **Great Lawn**, serves as both a sports complex and concert venue where Simon and Garfunkel, Plácido Domingo, Elton John, and the New York Philharmonic have performed for crowds numbering as high as a half million people. The big open space started life as a reservoir and served as a Hooverville for the homeless during the Great Depression before its current form took shape in the 1950s. On the edge of the lawn, the open-air **Delacorte Theater** presents free Shakespeare in the Park during the summer. The adjacent **Shakespeare Garden** is planted with flowers, herbs, and trees mentioned in works by the Bard. Rounding out the area's trio of cultural offerings is the **Swedish Cottage Marionette Theatre** and its popular family puppet shows.

The park's north end reaches deep into Harlem and reflects that neighborhood's heritage with features like the **Duke Ellington Memorial** at Fifth Avenue and 110th Street— the first monument to an African-American artist in New York City (dedicated in 1997). Harlem's

A view of the San Remo luxury apartment building from the cast-iron Bow Bridge

renaissance in recent years has also revitalized the north end.

Dana Discovery Center on Harlem Meer offers a year-round slate of exhibits, education programs, and holiday events. One of the few parts of Central Park that doesn't adhere to Olmsted's rustic vision, the 6-acre (.02 sq km) **Conservatory Garden** includes manicured French, English, and Italian beds, plus a magnificent Gilded Age gateway that once fronted the Vanderbilt Mansion on Fifth Avenue.

Having served as a British encampment during the Revolutionary War and an American base in the War of 1812, the north end is also rich in military history. Remnants of those days remain, including the 1814 **Blockhouse** (the park's oldest surviving structure) and the site of **Fort Clinton**, a 1776 British bastion.

Central Park is surrounded by a number of other museums and historic structures. Anchored by the Met, the section of Fifth Avenue between 82nd and 110th streets is called the **Museum Mile**. The stretch includes the Frank Lloyd Wright–designed **Guggenheim Museum** (modern art) and the small but superb **Frick Collection** (Old Masters and furnishings), as well as the **Jewish Museum, Museum of New York City**, **El Museo del Barrio** (Latin American and Caribbean art), and **Cooper Hewitt**, **Smithsonian Design Museum** located in the 1903 Carnegie Mansion. At the top of the Museum Mile, the new **Africa Center** is slowly evolving from a policy and special events center into a museum of African arts and culture.

Among the iconic structures on Central Park West are the **Dakota Apartments**, erected in the 1880s on the corner of West 72nd Street and home to many celebrities, from

football star Joe Namath and dancer Rudolph Nureyev to actress Lauren Bacall, composer Leonard Bernstein, and John Lennon (who was murdered in front of the Dakota in 1980). The **Imagine memorial** honoring Lennon is across the street in the park's **Strawberry Fields** area. Just up the street is the **New-York Historical Society** museum and archives.

Central Park Conservancy offers guided tours of the park that revolve around topics like children's sculptures, beginning birding, fall foliage, art in the park, northern woods, and even a Hounds Hike dog walk if you want to see it all. ∎

CHOW DOWN

• **Loeb Boathouse:** A two-in-one eatery—the casual Express Cafe and the more formal Lakeside Restaurant—plus an outdoor bar. *thecentralpark boathouse.com*

• **Tavern on the Green:** A New York eating institution since 1934, the gourmet tavern serves lunch, dinner, and Sunday brunch. *tavernonthegreen .com*

• **Cantor Roof Garden Bar:** Cocktails and light snacks are the forte of this alfresco hangout on the roof of the Met. The museum offers six other bars and restaurants. *metmuseum .org/visit/dining*

• **Kerbs Boathouse Café:** Snack bar in a restored copper-roofed structure overlooking the Conservatory Water.

• **Harlem Meer Snack Bar:** Next to the Dana Discovery Center, this vegetarian outlet is the only place to grab a bite or drink in the north end. Try the falafels. *maozusa.com*

The Mid-Atlantic

Cherry blossom trees bloom along D.C.'s Tidal Basin.

Shenandoah National Park
Virginia

A throwback to the days when this was the western frontier of European civilization in North America, Shenandoah National Park offers a patchwork quilt of wilderness and pastoral landscapes underpinned with stories from 300 years of American history. Arrayed along the Blue Ridge Mountains of western Virginia, the park is just 75 miles (120.7 km) from Washington, D.C., yet light-years distant from the nation's capital in ambience and attitude.

"Build it and they will come" may derive from the celebrated baseball movie *Field of Dreams*, but the dictum could just as easily apply to the creation of Shenandoah National Park. Inspired by Yellowstone and other parks in the West, a national reserve in the Blue Ridge Mountains was first proposed in 1901. When the campaign stalled, Virginians took it upon themselves to make the park a reality. Using eminent domain, the commonwealth bought out around 5,000 small landholders and donated the parcels to the federal government.

A sleeping white-tailed deer fawn

THE BIG PICTURE

Established: 1935

Size: 199,173 acres (806 sq km)

Annual Visitors: 1.4 million

Visitor Centers: Dickey Ridge, Byrd/Big Meadows, Loft Mountain

Entrance Fee: $25 per vehicle, $10 per person

nps.gov/shen

The park was finally established the day after Christmas 1935.

Stretching more than 100 miles (161 km) along the Blue Ridge, the park unfolds as a long, thin island of green between the Shenandoah Valley in the west and the Piedmont region on the east. Within that extenuated form there's a lot to behold: wooden hollows and breezy summits, waterfalls and mountain streams, more than 500 miles (804.67 km) of hiking trails, and nearly 80,000 acres (323.75 sq km) of designated wilderness.

Constructed in the 1930s by the Civilian Conservation Corps (CCC), **Skyline Drive** snakes its way across the park, 105 miles (168.98 km) of scenic overlooks, trailheads, picnic areas, and campgrounds between Front Royal in the north and Rockfish Gap in the south. The other way to traverse the length of Shenandoah is hiking the hundred or so miles (161 km) of the **Appalachian Trail** that run across the park.

In addition to Front Royal and Rockfish Gap, the park is accessible from Luray and Sperryville by way of the **Thornton Gap Entrance Station**, as well as from Elkton and Stanardsville via **Swift Run Gap Entrance Station**.

The sweeping skies and hills of Shenandoah National Park

NORTH DISTRICT

Although it's the closest part of the park to major metropolitan areas, the North District offers some of the more secluded terrain, a quiet part of Shenandoah that many people zip through on their way to the park's more celebrated attractions farther south. And that's quite all right for those who prefer their parks with fewer folks along the trails.

Dickey Ridge Visitor Center near Front Royal presents a great introduction to the park with exhibits on Shenandoah's human and natural history and plenty in the way of information and maps. From the visitor center parking lot, you can pick up two short walking routes—the **Fox Hollow Loop** and **Snead Farm Road**—that meander through the remains of bygone farms, including an old barn and grave sites.

Overall Run Falls—at 93 feet (28.35 m), the tallest cascade in the park—is reached via trails from **Hogback Overlook** or **Matthews Arm**. It can be tough going: The main route (a 5.1-mile/8.2 km round-trip) features an elevation change of 1,291 feet (393.5 m). Much easier is the 1.7-mile (2.74 km) **Traces Trail**, which loops through the woods around the Matthews Arm Campground. The Appalachian Trail leaps across Skyline Drive near **Beahms Gap**, a great opportunity for those who want to hike a short portion of the trail but not the entire 2,200 miles (3,540.6 km) from Maine to Georgia.

LAY YOUR HEAD

Hotels

• **Lewis Mountain Cabins:** Restored with modern comforts, these cabins were at the forefront of the segregation struggle in the 1940s; open March to November; from $133. *goshenandoah.com/lodging/lewis-mountain-cabins*

• **Skyland:** The historic 1890s resort transformed into a modern wilderness lodge; restaurant, bar, gift shop, horseback rides; from $105. *goshenandoah.com/lodging/skyland*

• **Hotel Laurance:** A 12-room boutique hotel tucked into an 1830 mercantile town in Luray near Thornton Gap Entrance Station; from $129. *hotellaurance.com*

Camping

• Drive-in campgrounds at Matthews Arm, Big Meadows, Loft Mountain, and Lewis Mountain open seasonally, early spring through late fall; $15-$20 per night.

CENTRAL DISTRICT

Shenandoah's middle section is the park's highest and most popular area, with more vehicles in the turnouts and more hikers along the trails, especially during the busy summer months when the wooded highlands offer refuge from Virginia's notorious heat and humidity.

It's also where Shenandoah tourism was born in the 1800s, long before the park became a reality. **Skyland** was originally envisioned as a mountaintop real estate development, but when that was slow to get off the ground, flamboyant owner George Freeman Pollock transformed the lofty plot into a summer vacation oasis. Many of the old buildings remain, including recently restored **Massanutten Lodge** (built in 1911), several of its rooms decorated with early 20th-century furnishings and others dedicated to Addie Nairn Pollock and the women who frequented Skyland in the early days.

Skyland offers a convenient parking place and jumping-off spot for a number of nearby trails, including the easy, 1.3-mile (2.1 km) **Limberlost Trail** through a forest that Addie Nairn saved from logging by purchasing the old-growth hemlock trees for $10 each. The hemlocks long ago succumbed to insects and were replaced by the magnificent laurels that shade the path today.

Among other routes in the area are the short but steep ascent to **Stony Man** peak (1.6 miles/2.6 km), the **Whiteoak Canyon Trail** (2-7.3 miles/ 3.2-11.75 km) to a series of six waterfalls, and the **Skyland Stable Trail** for horseback riders. Hikers can also reach **Old Rag Mountain** from Skyland. The shorter and more popular routes to the celebrated peak—from Berry Hollow and Route 600—are found along the eastern edge of the park.

Hawksbill Summit—the park's highest point at 4,051 feet (1,234.75 m)—is reached from trails that start at two parking spots along Skyline Drive about halfway between Skyland and Big Meadows. Despite the elevation gain, the trails are not as difficult as one might expect.

Learn more about park history at the **Byrd Visitor Center**, which lies about halfway along Skyline Drive (milepost 51) in the **Big Meadows** area. The park's largest open space is a great place to spot wildlife in the early morning or late afternoon, especially the black bear and whitetail deer that feast on the meadow berries and other vegetation. A 1.4-mile (2.25 km) trail drops down to

One of the most popular hikes in Shenandoah leads to the Dark Hollow Falls.

70-foot (21.3 m) **Dark Hollow Falls**. Big Meadows also boasts a lodge, campground, and amphitheater for ranger talks and other programs.

Rapidan Camp is downhill from Big Meadows. Built in 1929, the rural retreat served as a wilderness White House during the presidency of Herbert Hoover. **Brown House**, the presidential cabin, has been historically refurnished. The **Prime Minister's Cabin** offers exhibits on Hoover's life and times. **Mill Prong Trail** is the easiest way to hike to Rapidan (4.1 miles/6.6 km round-trip). From spring to fall, the Park Service offers 2.5-hour **guided van tours** from Byrd Visitor Center.

Six miles (9.6 km) south of Big Meadows, **Lewis Mountain Campground** was the scene of an ongoing segregation struggle that pitted the National Park Service against local business and political interests. Developed by a private concession, it opened in 1939 as the park's only picnic ground and campsite for "Colored People" and remained that way until 1950 when Shenandoah was fully integrated in line with Park Service policy.

SOUTH DISTRICT

Seclusion returns in the park's bottom end, like its northern counterpart much less crowded than the popular middle zone. Visitor services cluster at **Loft Mountain** with

A native Shenandoah salamander (*Plethodon shenandoah*)

its campground, camp store, and amphitheater for interpretive programs. The nearby **Frazier Discovery Trail** (1.2-mile/1.9 km loop) offers a short scramble to an awesome viewpoint over the park. Another short hike is the 1-mile (1.6 km) **Blackrock Summit Trail**, which climbs through a boulder- and rock-strewn talus slope on its way to another lofty vista.

Farther south, **Riprap–Wildcat Ridge Trail** offers a strenuous 9.8-mile (15.77 km) hike across rugged terrain that includes rock formations, stream crossings, waterfalls,

and swimming holes, as well as a portion of the Appalachian Trail.

The park finally peters out at **Rockfish Gap**, a large gap in the Blue Ridge Mountains between the Shenandoah Valley and eastern Virginia. Following trails blazed by Native Americans, European settlers were passing through the gap as early as the 1740s. A roadside tavern in the pass provided a meeting place in 1818 where Thomas Jefferson, James Madison, James Monroe, and other interested parties developed a plan for creating the University of Virginia. ■

CHOW DOWN

• **Thornton River Grille:** Modern American cuisine made with farm-to-table products from the Piedmont region is showcased on the menu at this popular Sperryville restaurant. *thorntonrivergrille.com*

• **Lafayette Inn:** Crab cakes, braised lamb, and pork are just a few of the specialties at this Stanardsville eatery also known for its happy hour and Sunday brunch. *thelafayette.com*

• **Spelunker's:** Frozen custard and freshly made burgers are the main attractions at this vintage drive-in along South Street in Front Royal. *spelunkerscustard.com*

Standing above the clouds, white wisps surround the hills of Shenandoah.

Assateague Island
Virginia & Maryland

Stretching 37 miles (59.5 km) along the coasts of Maryland and Virginia, wild and wondrous Assateague Island offers a vision of what the entire mid-Atlantic shore must have been like before humans arrived. Beaches and bays, marshes and maritime forests, wild horses and sandy motoring draw both nature buffs and those who view the great outdoors as a place to test their mettle.

THE BIG PICTURE

Established: Wildlife refuge (1943); state park (1956); national seashore (1965)

Size: Wildlife refuges (14,000 acres/56.65 sq km); state park (855 acres/3.46 sq km); national seashore (41,320 acres/ 167.21 sq km)

Annual Visitors: 2.3 million

Visitor Centers: Assateague Island, Bateman Center, Toms Cove

Entrance Fees: State park ($3-$6 per vehicle); national seashore ($20 per vehicle)

nps.gov/asis; fws.gov/refuge/ Chincoteague; dnr.maryland.gov

Split between Maryland and Virginia, this long barrier isle is shared by Assateague Island National Seashore, Chincoteague National Wildlife Refuge, and Assateague State Park. Remoteness and the ever changing topography, shaped by wind and waves, kept the island from being settled until the mid-1800s. Settlers are responsible for the feral horses that have come to symbolize Assateague, although local legend says they may have escaped from the Spanish galleon that wrecked along the coast in 1750.

There are only two ways to reach the island: from Ocean City or Berlin, Maryland, in the north or the island town of Chincoteague on the Virginia shore. Those arriving from the north normally stop at the **Assateague Island Visitor Center** before crossing Sinepuxent Bay to **Assateague State Park**. In addition to 2 miles (3.2 km) of sandy beach, the state park offers kayaking, canoeing, and oceanfront camping.

The **Nature Center** offers interpretive programs and aquariums with some of the creatures that dwell in local waters and beaches. **Rackliffe House,** a restored 18th-century coastal plantation house, is now home to the **Coastal Maryland Heritage Center.**

Bayberry Drive continues south into **Assateague Island National Seashore**, where the shoreline suddenly gets much wilder. **North Beach** and **South Beach** feature similar recreational activities as the state park. Beyond the end of the road is the **Over Sand Vehicle (OSV) Zone,** a long stretch of beach to the Virginia state line open to 4x4 drivers with special permits and safety equipment. Horseback riding, hiking, and paddling are also allowed on the OSV Zone.

First settled in 1650, **Chincoteague**

A fence traverses the sand dunes at Assateague Island National Seashore.

A wild mare, one of many free horses that live on the island, stops for a drink along the marsh at sunrise.

village is gateway to the Virginia half of Assateague. Every July, local "saltwater cowboys" organize a round-up of feral horses and host a **Pony Swim** across Assateague Channel at slack tide. The **Museum of Chincoteague Island** boasts historic artifacts and model ships, and **Chincoteague Pony Center** tenders pony rides and exhibits on the 1961 movie *Misty of Chincoteague*. **Assateague Tours** offers canoe and kayak rentals, as well as two-hour guided tours.

Maddox Boulevard leaps the channel to **Chincoteague National Wildlife Refuge**, which preserves most of the Virginia end of Assateague Island. In addition to hiking and boating, the wildlife refuge allows fishing, crabbing, and clamming, as well as big game and waterfowl hunting.

Bateman Visitor Center offers exhibits, a bookshop, and information on refuge events and activities. Nearby are the red-and-white-striped **Assateague Lighthouse** (1867), the

Wildlife Loop Trail (3.25 miles/ 5.23 km) across a marshy area, and the **Woodland Trail** (1.5 miles/ 2.4 km) through a pine forest. Chincoteague's **wild beach** stretches 10 miles (16.1 km) to the Maryland border.

Although technically part of the wildlife refuge, the southern tip of

Assateague Island is managed by the National Park Service. **Toms Cove Visitor Center** is the jumping-off point for the nearby recreational beach, as well as an **OSV Zone** along Toms Cove Hook where off-road vehicles and horseback riding are allowed between September 1 and March 14. ∎

MEET THE NEIGHBORS

• **Virginia Coast Reserve:** The longest expanse of coastal wilderness on the East Coast, the VCR includes 14 barrier and marsh islands managed by the Nature Conservancy.

• **Wallops Flight Facility:** Located on the Virginia mainland opposite Chincoteague Island, NASA welcomes visitors to a rocket launch site that supports scientific and exploratory missions into outer space.

• **Janes Island State Park:** This Maryland preserve includes hiking trails, campsites, cabins, a marina, and 30 miles of water trails through a 2,900-acre (11.736 sq km) salt marsh along the eastern edge of the Chesapeake Bay.

• **Fenwick Island State Park:** This barrier island in southern Delaware includes a stretch of beach ideal for swimming, surfing, and sunbathing, as well as access to Little Assawoman Bay.

Gettysburg National Military Park
Pennsylvania

THE BIG PICTURE

Established: 1895

Size: 5,989 acres (24.24 sq km)

Annual Visitors: 1 million

Visitor Center: Gettysburg National Military Park Museum

Entrance Fee: Military park (free); museum ($15 per person)

nps.gov/gett

The battle that decided the fate of a nation unfolded among the woods, rocks, and golden fields of Gettysburg in July 1863. The bloody three-day clash blunted a Confederate invasion of the North and turned the tide of the entire Civil War. The hallowed battleground is an enduring reminder that a house divided against itself cannot stand.

Robert E. Lee never meant to make a stand in southern Pennsylvania in summer 1863. He wanted to drive his Army of Northern Virginia much deeper into Union territory and force Abraham Lincoln into pleading for peace, a move that would have split the United States into two independent nations.

But when Yankee forces blocked his advance near Gettysburg, Lee had no choice but to engage the enemy on unfavorable ground—Union forces in the rocky heights, Confederates attacking across open fields. Played out July 1-3, 1863, the Battle of Gettysburg included nearly 200,000 troops and the largest casualty count of any other Civil War encounter.

Nobody should visit the national military park without first stopping at the **Gettysburg Museum and Visitor Center** on Old Baltimore Pike. One of the finest of its kind in the entire National Park System, the highly interactive collection includes firearms, uniforms, documents, photos, and many other relics of the battle and its aftermath. The complex also offers the restored **Gettysburg Cyclorama** depicting Pickett's Charge, shows a film called "**A New Birth of Freedom**," a resource room with a computer bank for learning more about the conflict, and tours with licensed battlefield guides.

Visitors can tour the grounds on their own or follow a self-guided, 24-mile (38.6 km) **Auto Tour** that starts outside the visitor center. The driving tour includes 16 stops at major landmarks and monuments. It's also possible to hike or bike the park. **Confederate Trails** and its sister company, the **Victorian Carriage Company**, offer guided horseback rides and horse-drawn carriage tours of the battlefield.

A commemorative statue of a Civil War Union soldier

A Civil War cannon rests, as if ready for combat at any moment, on the battlefields of Gettysburg.

Like the auto tour, many first-time visitors opt to explore the battlefield in chronological order. Trying to hold back the Confederate tide until reinforcements arrived, Union troops took a stand on **McPherson Ridge** and **Oak Hill** during the first day of the battle, but were pushed back into Gettysburg town and the heavily wooded heights on the far side.

Using **Seminary Ridge** as their staging ground, the Confederates launched major assaults on the second day of battle against Union forces dug in on **Cemetery Ridge**. At the same time, they tried to outflank the Yankee lines with attacks on **Culp's Hill** in the north and **Little Round Top** in the south. The clash for Little Round Top ended with a legendary downhill bayonet charge by Col. Joshua Chamberlain and the 20th Maine Volunteer Infantry Regiment—one of the most famous actions of the entire Civil War.

Day three commenced with the largest artillery bombardment of the war, a barrage reportedly so loud it could be heard in Philadelphia and Baltimore. Starting from the present-day **Virginia Memorial**, Maj. Gen. George Pickett led 12,500 Confederate troops across the void. The

Confederate troops got as far as the **Angel**, the **Copse of Trees,** and the **High Water Mark** on Cemetery Ridge before the attack was repulsed—and for all intents and purposes, the Confederate cause lost, although the war would continue for another two years. ■

DID YOU KNOW

• Abraham Lincoln wrote the final draft of his Gettysburg Address in the David Wills House in downtown Gettysburg, a property that's been part of the national military park since 2009.

• Lincoln delivered his most celebrated speech at the Soldiers' National Cemetery, on the outskirts of Gettysburg, on November 19, 1863, at the dedication ceremony for the graveyard.

• The Shriver Museum, located in the 19th-century home of a Civil War soldier in Gettysburg town, explores the roles that civilians played in the epic battle.

• Eisenhower National Historic Site on the edge of the battlefield showcases the farm where the 34th president hosted world leaders during his presidency and then retired to. Tickets and shuttle buses are available at the Gettysburg Battlefield visitor center.

Colonial National Historical Park
Virginia

THE BIG PICTURE

Established: 1930

Size: 9,349 acres (38.2 sq km)

Annual Visitors: 3.3 million

Visitor Centers: Jamestown, Yorktown, Williamsburg

Entrance Fee: $14 per person

nps.gov/colo

One of the more distinct units of the U.S. National Park System, Colonial National Historical Park offers a journey through early American history that includes the English colonial settlement at Jamestown and the Yorktown battlefield where the Revolutionary War came to a dramatic end. The 23-mile (37 km) Colonial Parkway connects these historic sites with Williamsburg as it meanders through Virginia's lush tidewater countryside.

Scattered along the James and York Rivers and the mouth of the Chesapeake Bay, Colonial National Historical Park sprawls across more than 260 years of U.S. history. The Declaration of Independence may have been penned in Philadelphia, but this is where America as a nation was born—the place where the first English settlers came ashore and where George Washington's Continental Army finally overcame the redcoats.

Separating fact from fiction is the goal at **Jamestown**, where the real-life stories of Capt. John Smith, John Rolfe, and Pocahontas are often clouded by modern myth and movies. The first permanent English settlement in the New World was actually founded by Captain Christopher Newport in 1606. After sputtering at first—including starvation, cannibalism, and brief abandonment—the settlement eventually survived and thrived.

A joint venture between the National Park Service and Preservation Virginia, **Historic Jamestowne** includes the ruins of **Fort James** and other 17th-century structures, as well as the **Voorhees Archaearium** archaeological museum, where thousands of Jamestown artifacts are displayed. Living history programs, archaeological walking tours, and other interpretive programs illuminate the area's rich history, while the **Glasshouse** continues the heritage of America's first industrial factory. Motorists, cyclists, and hikers can explore **Jamestown Island** on a **Loop Drive** shaped like a figure eight. On the mainland opposite the island, the state-run **Jamestown Settlement** re-creates the 16th-century colony through living history programs and reproduction buildings.

Created between 1930 and 1957 by the National Park Service to link the region's historic sites, **Colonial Parkway** starts its ramble across the peninsula at Jamestown. Ten miles

The waterside view of Ringfield Plantation along the Colonial Parkway

Historic brick twin arch bridges from the Colonial Parkway in Williamsburg

(16.1 km) up the pike is **Williamsburg**, founded in 1632 and Virginia's capital through most of the 18th century. Although technically not part of the park, the town preserves many distinguished colonial buildings and is renowned for its living history programs. Among Williamsburg's many attractions are the **Abby Aldrich Rockefeller Folk Art Museum**, the **DeWitt Wallace Decorative Arts Museum**, and the **College of William and Mary**.

Colonial Parkway continues another 13 miles (20.92 km) across the peninsula to **Yorktown**, where Washington and his French allies defeated Lord Cornwallis in October 1781 in the last major battle of the American Revolution. **Yorktown Battlefield Visitor Center** offers historical exhibits (including Washington's campaign tents); an orientation film, "**The Siege of Yorktown**"; and a shop with books, audio tours, and reproduction items.

The 98-foot-high (29.87 m) **Yorktown Victory Monument**, crowned by a figure of "Liberty," rises near the visitor center. Ranger-led guided tours take you down **Main Street** in Yorktown village and along the **1781 siege line** that determined the fate of two nations. Two motor routes totaling 16 miles (25.75 km)—the **Battlefield Tour** and the **Allied Encampment Tour**—ramble through a landscape still defined by redoubts, trenches, and other earthwork defenses constructed for the siege and battle.

Yorktown village harbors many historic structures, including the Georgian-style **Nelson House** and **Moore House**, where the surrender negotiations took place on October 17, 1781. **Yorktown Victory Center** is a state-operated living history museum that revolves around civilian and military life during the Revolution. ■

EVENT HORIZON

• **Pedal the Parkway:** Motor vehicles are banned from the Colonial Parkway on the first Saturday in May as cyclists flood the historic route.

• **Jamestown Landing Day:** The 1607 founding of the first permanent English settlement is marked with special programs on the second Saturday in May.

• **At Christmas Be Mery:** Historic Jamestown celebrates the season with a night of caroling, dancing, the firing of Christmas guns, and a seasonal bonfire.

• **Yorktown Summer:** Artillery demonstrations, a young soldiers program, and colonial-era musical performances take over the battlefield from June to August.

• **Before the Siege:** Life under the British invaders is the focus of this Yorktown living history event over Labor Day weekend.

Chesapeake & Ohio Canal

Virginia, Maryland, District of Columbia & West Virginia

Nearly 200 miles (321.87 km) of the Potomac River between Washington, D.C., and Cumberland, Maryland, fall within the confines of the Chesapeake & Ohio Canal National Historical Park. Along the way are numerous other riverside heritage areas and parklands that offer history, culture, and outdoor recreation, most notably Harpers Ferry with its various links to the Civil War.

The "Grand Old Ditch" was the brainchild of George Washington, who after the Revolutionary War founded a company to improve navigation along the Potomac River between the Chesapeake Bay and the Allegheny Mountains.

But the full-blown scheme didn't come about until 1828 when construction began on the Chesapeake & Ohio Canal (commonly called the C & O Canal) alongside the Potomac. Over the next 32 years, the waterway expanded to 184.5 miles

THE BIG PICTURE

Established: 1938

Size: 19,586 acres (79.26 sq km)

Annual Visitors: 4.8 million

Visitor Centers: Cumberland, Hancock, Williamsport, Ferry Hill, Brunswick, Great Falls, Georgetown

Entrance Fee: None

nps.gov/choh

(296.92 km) of canals, aqueducts, culverts, and one very long tunnel. The canal's major purpose was transporting coal downstream from the Allegheny region. But the waterway also became a means for forest and farm products—as well as whiskey, salt, and even blocks of ice—to make their way to the nation's capital and beyond.

The C & O Canal operated until 1924, when damage from a major flood proved too great for the government to repair. The national historical park was established just a few years later (1938) to highlight the role of the C & O in America's development and history, and provide recreational outlets within easy reach of major East Coast cities.

The park provides a major **hiking and biking** route between Washington, D.C., and the foothills of the Appalachian Mountains. Special hiker/biker campsites are located roughly every 5 to 7 miles (8-11.3 km) along the towpath. But there's plenty of scope to explore the park by road, water, and horse. The **mobile tour app** of sights along the entire canal is available for download on smartphones.

Cumberland Visitor Center in the Maryland panhandle marks the canal's upstream terminus with

Colorful buildings line the perimeter of the C & O Canal.

Under a purple sunset, waters rush through Great Falls, which separates the Maryland and Virginia sides of the park.

exhibits on C & O history, as well as a 19th-century feeder dam and guard lock. Across the river is a **log cabin** that young George Washington used as a command post during the French and Indian War, and nearby is the **Allegheny Museum**, which preserves the region's history and culture in a lovely neoclassical building.

About 30 miles (48.28 km) downstream from Cumberland, the **Paw Paw Tunnel** is the canal's major engineering feat. The 3,118-foot-long (950.37 m) brick passageway is part of a **Tunnel Hill Trail** that also affords awesome views over the Potomac valley. **Hancock Visitor Center** is located in the historic Bowles House, built in 1785 on a plot of land that originally belonged to Lord Baltimore.

Between Hancock and Williamsburg, **Four Locks** preserves the remains of a classic towpath community including a mule barn, one-room schoolhouse, and **Lockhouse 49**, where visitors can stay overnight. More history awaits in **Williamsport**, where a self-guided walking tour takes in canal works around the Cushwa Basin, including an aqueduct attacked by Confederate troops in 1863.

A footbridge carrying the **Appalachian Trail** leaps across the Potomac at Harpers Ferry. Perched above the canal, the Civil War gun batteries of **Maryland Heights** are linked by hiking trails. Erected in 1831 as a canal-side hotel, **Great Falls Tavern Visitor Center** offers tours in an 1870 mule-drawn packet boat and access to the nearby **Billy Goat Trail**, a 4.7-mile (7.56 km) hike that includes a 40-foot (12.19 m) cliff face and views of the nearby southern terminus of the C & O, **Georgetown Visitor Center** in Washington, D.C., lies beside two recently restored locks. ■

Harpers Ferry in the fall, as viewed from Maryland Heights

❶ Metropolitan Museum of Art, New York

A Central Park landmark since it opened in 1870, the beloved Met safeguards more than two million works of art ranging from an ancient Egyptian temple through the Great Masters and 20th-century masterpieces. The medieval Cloisters in Manhattan's Fort Tryon Park is also part of the Met collection.

❷ Immigration Museum, New York

The main immigrant intake building is now a three-story museum that details the "peopling of America" from the 1550s through modern times, including the 12 million immigrants who passed through Ellis Island. Part of Statue of Liberty National Monument, the museum offers ranger-guided tours and a genealogical collection where visitors can trace their roots.

❸ Gettysburg Museum of the Civil War, Pennsylvania

The nation's best battlefield museum covers the entire war from Fort Sumter through Appomattox, with emphasis on the bloody clash that unfolded around Gettysburg in summer 1863 and Lincoln's famous address. The collection also includes the Gettysburg Cyclorama, an epic football-field-long oil painting of the battle by Paul Philippoteaux.

❹ Smithsonian Institution, Washington, D.C.

The world's largest museum and research complex, with 19 museums, most of them located on or beside the Mall in the nation's capital. Sometimes referred to as the "Nation's Attic," it includes the Air and Space Museum, American History Museum, National Portrait Gallery, American Indian Museum, and National Museum of African American History and Culture.

❺ Art Institute of Chicago, Illinois

Rising amid the greenery of Grant Park, the institute introduced the city to world-class art when it opened in 1879. The permanent collection is especially known for its Impressionist and modern works.

THE TOP

10

MUSEUMS

North America's parks feature a treasure trove of art and artifacts.

❻ Museum of Westward Expansion, Missouri

Located beneath the Gateway Arch on the St. Louis riverfront, the recently revamped museum examines America's Manifest Destiny and how it affected all of those involved in the nation's relentless expansion after the Louisiana Purchase. Exhibits are now lit by natural light filtered through a transparent ceiling that also affords views of the arch above.

The lifelike Fénykövi elephant stands in the rotunda of the Smithsonian Museum of Natural History.

❼ California Academy of Sciences, California

Charles Darwin was one of the original consultants on this cutting-edge science and nature academy, founded in 1853. The Golden Gate Park museum encompasses the Steinhart Aquarium, Morrison Planetarium, a living rain forest beneath a 90-foot (27.43 m) glass dome, and a remarkable, environmentally friendly green roof.

❽ Autry Museum of the American Western, California

Founded by celebrated "Singing Cowboy" Gene Autry, this expansive museum in Los Angeles's Griffith Park ranges from Native Americans and 19th-century cowboy culture to Western music and movies. Among its many excellent collections are firearms, fashion, cowboy art, and movie memorabilia. The Autry also hosts film screenings, culinary events, live music, and lectures.

❾ Mingei International Museum, California

Located along the Prado museum row in San Diego's Balboa Park, the offbeat Mingei features historical and contemporary folk art, crafts, and designs from all epochs and every corner of the world. Exhibitions focus on everyday objects that double as artworks. The collection contains more than 26,000 pieces from 141 countries.

❿ Royal Tyrrell Museum, Alberta

Many of the primordial bones uncovered in nearby Dinosaur Provincial Park are on display at this landmark on the Alberta prairie. Among the 40 mounted skeletons are a complete *Tyrannosaurus rex*, triceratops, and woolly mammoth. Visitors can also cast fossils and test their bone-hunting skills at a simulated fossil dig.

National Mall

Washington, D.C.

The large green space that became the National Mall was part of the original design for the nation's capital. But the park is more than just a pretty face. It's also a depository of American culture, a place of solemn remembrance, and a spot where history was made by those like Martin Luther King, Jr., Gen. Douglas MacArthur, and every U.S. president since Thomas Jefferson.

THE BIG PICTURE

Established: public open space (1790s); national park (1965)

Size: 6,547 acres (26.49 sq km)

Annual Visitors: 24 million

Visitor Centers: White House, U.S. Capitol, Smithsonian Institution

Entrance Fee: None

nps.gov/choh/index.htm
nps.gov/nama/

Even before there was a District of Columbia, the National Mall was taking shape in the minds of those planning the capital of the new American nation. In his ambitious plan of 1791, French-American military architect Pierre Charles L'Enfant sketched a "grand avenue" between the Capitol Building and Potomac River. The grand avenue was never realized, but a large open space was set aside for later development.

British troops marched across the Mall in 1814 on their way to burning the White House and Capitol during the War of 1812. The Snow Riot of 1835, America's first large-scale race protest, was waged around the edge of the Mall. And until abolition in 1862, the park was sometimes used for slave auctions and as holding pens for African-American chattel. The area didn't become an official park until the 1850s, when landscape architect

Andrew Jackson Downing created a blueprint that was gradually rolled out over the next 50 years, laying the foundation for the Mall as we know it today.

WEST END

Fifteenth Street divides the National Mall into contrasting halves. The east end is dominated by the U.S. Capitol Building and the Smithsonian Institute museums. The western half is largely set aside for memorials honoring great Americans and those who gave their lives for country or cause.

Modeled after the obelisks of ancient Egypt that honored the pharaohs, the **Washington Monument** took 40 years (1848-1888) to construct. It soars 555 feet (169.16 m) above the Mall and is still D.C.'s tallest structure. With a view that spans northern Virginia to Maryland, the summit can be reached via a recently renovated elevator. The monument provides a dramatic backdrop for the **National Sylvan Theater**, an outdoor venue for concerts, plays, dance, religious services, and other events.

Just north of the monument lies a large oval green space, the **Ellipse**, used over the centuries as a billeting

The National World War II Memorial in Washington, D.C.

One of the most iconic views in D.C.: the Washington Monument seen from the Lincoln Memorial across the Reflecting Pool

ground for troops, a pasture for military livestock, a field for some of the country's first professional baseball games, and, more recently, home to the **National Christmas Tree**. Flanking the Ellipse are the **Art Museum of the Americas**, which specializes in the works of Latin America and Caribbean artists, and **Freedom Plaza**, laid out like a miniature version of L'Enfant's original plan for Washington, D.C.

That very familiar-looking building beyond the Ellipse is **1600 Pennsylvania Avenue**. The White House was originally constructed in 1792 and then rebuilt after the British torched it during the War of 1812. Daily tours of the presidential home must be reserved months ahead through a congressional office or embassy. However, the **White House Visitor Center**, with exhibits on historic occasions and presidential families, requires no reservations.

The **Reflecting Pool** is surrounded by poignant tributes to

American troops who fell on foreign fields of battle: the **World War II Memorial**, the **Vietnam Veterans Memorial** with its long black granite walls, the **Vietnam Women's Memorial**, and the **Korean War**

Veterans Memorial. Tucked away to one side is leafy **Constitution Gardens** and an island shrine that honors the **56 signers of the Declaration of Independence**.

South of Independence Avenue,

MEET THE NEIGHBORS

- **Rock Creek Park:** The national capital's other iconic green space is also managed by the National Park Service.

- **Smithsonian's National Zoo:** Home to around 300 species—many of them rare and endangered creatures—housed in modern exhibits like Elephant Trails, Cheetah Conservation Station, and Asia Trail (where the pandas live). *nationalzoo.si.edu*

- **Nature Center:** Local plants and animals are the focus of this natural history museum which also hosts the only planetarium in the U.S. national park system, as well

as the Rock Creek Visitor Center and ranger-led nature programs. *nps.gov/rocr/planyourvisit/nature center.htm*

- **Rock Creek Horse Center:** Equestrian complex with guided trail rides (on 13 miles/20.9 km of bridle paths) and horseback riding lessons. *rockcreekhorsecenter.com*

- **Rock Creek Ramble:** One of Teddy Roosevelt's stomping grounds during his years in Washington, this forested area is explored via a 3.1-mile (5 km) loop trail. *nps.gov/rocr/index.htm*

a waterfront path lined with cherry blossom trees loops around the tranquil **Tidal Basin** to memorials for three other great Americans: **Thomas Jefferson**, **Franklin Delano Roosevelt**, and **Martin Luther King, Jr.** It's a most fitting spot to remember the civil rights leader, within earshot of the place where Dr. King delivered his legendary "I Have a Dream" speech in 1963 on the steps of the **Lincoln Memorial**. The 19-foot-high (5.8 m) figure of a seated Honest Abe—sculpted by Daniel Chester French from 175 tons (177.8 metric tons) of white Georgia marble—is arguably America's most recognizable statue.

EAST END

Founded in 1846 as a means to increase human knowledge and diffuse it around the world, the **Smithsonian Institution** is one of the world's premier scientific, historical, and cultural bodies. The "Nation's Attic" was originally lodged inside the **Smithsonian Institution Building** (known as The Castle), but over the years it has grown into 19 separate museums, the vast majority of them huddled around the eastern end of the Mall. The distinctive red sandstone Castle harbors the **Smithsonian Information Center**. Out front is the **Smithsonian Carousel**, a vintage 1947 merry-go-round with 60 wooden horses.

The **National Air and Space Museum** is the most popular of the Smithsonian's collections, a spectacular tribute to the human quest to rise above and beyond planet Earth. Among its famous flying machines are the Wright Brothers' *Flyer,* Charles Lindbergh's *Spirit of St. Louis,* and the Apollo 11 command module that brought the three astronauts safely home after the first moon landing.

The erudite ensemble around the Castle also includes the **National Museum of the American Indian**, four magnificent art galleries—the **Freer**, the **Sackler**, the **Hirshhorn**, and the **African Art Museum**—and the aromatic **National Garden**.

Farther west are the **Forest Service Information Office** (for those who want to learn more about visiting national forests) and the **U.S. Holocaust Memorial Museum**.

The National Air and Space Museum holds the largest collection of air- and spacecraft in the world.

Across the grassy space where people gather to watch presidential inaugurations are three more indispensable collections. The **National Museum of Natural History** has evolved from static displays like the Hope Diamond to a virtual motion triceratops skeleton and exhibits on climate change and human impact on the world.

Rather than a stuffy assembly of artifacts, the **National Museum of American History** delights with pop culture favorites like Judy Garland's ruby slippers from *The Wizard of Oz* and Julia Child's kitchen. The newest member of the Smithsonian family is the **African American History and Culture Museum**, a striking building dedicated in 2016 by President Obama.

The only museum along this stretch that isn't in the Smithsonian stable is the **National Gallery of Art**, a massive accumulation of global creativity housed in two buildings and an outdoor sculpture garden. The collection spans 500 years of artistic genius and includes the only da Vinci ("Ginevra de' Benci") in the Western Hemisphere. Directly behind the gallery is the **Newseum**, a high-tech museum dedicated to print and electronic journalism. Across Pennsylvania Avenue is the **National**

A statue at the new National Museum of African American History and Culture honors 1968 Summer Olympics athletes.

Archives, where original copies of the Declaration of Independence, Louisiana Purchase Treaty, and Emancipation Proclamation are on public display.

Although museums dominate the eastern end of the Mall, they are overshadowed by the imposing **Capitol Building** with its trademark dome and stately facade. Like the White House, the original capitol was burned by the British during the War of 1812 barely more than a decade after it was finished. It wasn't

until after the Civil War that the present structure was finally completed. Tours of the interior should be booked well in advance.

Capitol Hill is also home to the **U.S. Supreme Court** and **Library of Congress**, the world's largest storehouse of books, maps, photos, films, and posters. Another Capitol Hill resident is the **Belmont-Paul Women's Equality National Monument**, a tribute to the woman suffrage and equal rights movements inside two historic houses. ∎

EVENT HORIZON

• **National Cherry Blossom Festival:** The Tidal Basin turns pink during this spring fest with roots in a gift of 3,020 cherry trees from Japan in 1912; late March or early April. *nationalcherry blossomfestival.org*

• **Earth Day:** This is celebrated in April by a mass gathering on the Mall. Over the years, the event has varied from concerts and environmental activities to rallies and teach-ins. *earthday.org*

• **Rolling Thunder:** Nearly a half million bikers gather around the Mall over the Memorial Day Weekend as motorcycle-riding vets honor prisoners of war, those missing in action, and others who have served in the military. *rollingthunderrun.com*

• **Fourth of July:** National birthday events around the Mall include military band concerts, fireworks over the Washington Monument, and a

dramatic reading of the Declaration of Independence held at the National Archives.

• **Smithsonian Folklife Festival:** A summer tradition since 1967, this two-week cavalcade of American music, dance, crafts, and cooking in late June and early July has a different theme each year. *festival.si.edu*

Cherry blossom branches frame the Jefferson Memorial.

Pinelands National Reserve

New Jersey

THE BIG PICTURE

Established: 1978

Size: 1.16 million acres (4,694.35 sq km)

Annual Visitors: 1 million

Visitor Centers: Southampton Township, Batsto

Entrance Fee: Bass River State Forest ($5-$20 per vehicle); national reserve and other state forests (none)

nps.gov/pine

New Jersey's reputation as the Garden State endures in this thick knot of woods about halfway between Atlantic City and Trenton. From the notorious Jersey Devil (a legendary mythological beast) to Mafia intrigue, the forest is also immersed in local folklore and legend. Poor soil kept settlers away, but today, those who love the outdoors flock to the Pinelands for hiking, biking, hunting, boating, and winter sports.

Created in 1978 to safeguard the Pine Barrens from housing subdivisions and other development, the Pinelands National Preserve includes a dozen New Jersey state forests or wildlife management areas, and several national wildlife refuges.

The nonprofit **Pinelands Preservation Alliance** maintains a visitor center and museum in Southampton Township, just off Highway 206 on the northern fringe of the Pinelands. The complex includes three historic structures plus a bookstore, **native** **plant garden**, and **nature trail** through a grassland habitat. Farther up Route 206, **Pinelands Adventures** in Shamong offers canoe and kayak rentals, guided hikes and paddles, as well as history, culture, and nature tours of the Pine Barrens.

Wharton State Forest is the largest single tract within the preserve, as well as the largest state park in New Jersey. Crisscrossed by numerous streams and rivers, the park offers plenty of scope for fishing and boating. But terra firma is its strongest card, with routes like the **Penn Branch** mountain biking trail (19.2 miles/30.9 km), **Burnt Mill** equestrian trail (12 miles/19.3 km), and a massive slice of the 53-mile (85.3 km) **Batona Trail**, a hiking path that snakes across the Pinelands. Bygone **Batsto Village**, a hub for iron smelting and glassmaking during the 18th and 19th centuries, is also found in the state forest.

Whitesbog Historic Village in Brendan T. Byrne State Forest was founded in the 1870s as a company town for producing commercial cranberries and blueberries. Today this tribute to the Pinelands' past includes a working **General Store** with various berry delicacies, an antique engine

A baby opossum hangs by its tail in Pine Barrens.

A lake on the Westecunk Creek in the Pine Barrens reflects the glowing sky.

museum, art gallery, and old barrel factory, as well as live music performances, living history programs, and the annual **Whitesbog Blueberry Festival** in June.

Penn State Forest shelters two of the Pinelands' geographical landmarks. **Oswego Lake** provides one of the state's top spots for canoeing and kayaking, as well as fishing and swimming. But the park's most unusual attraction is the **Pygmy Pine Plains**, where the trees grow no more than four feet (1.2 m) tall. **Double Trouble State Park** offers another blend of Pine Barrens nature and history, a one-time cranberry company town surrounded by the pristine Cedar Creek watershed.

Many of the tidal wetlands and shallow bays between Toms River and Atlantic City are protected within the confines of the **Edwin B. Forsythe National Wildlife Refuge**. Located on the Atlantic Flyway, deer, fox, raptors, songbirds, and migratory birds are the main attraction. But deer, otter, muskrat, mink, and other creatures can often be spotted from trails that wind through the refuge. Also along the coast, the **Jacques Cousteau National Estuarine Research Reserve** in Tuckerton welcomes visitors for hiking, birding, and ecological exhibits. **Great Egg Harbor National Scenic and Recreational River** cuts across the southern Pinelands. **Palace Outfitter's** in Mays Landing rents canoes and kayaks to explore the 129-mile (207.6 km) river system.

Pinelands Scenic Byway is a meandering 130-mile (209.2 km) route through the heart of the barrens between Tuckerton near the Atlantic coast and Port Elizabeth on the **Maurice River**. Thirty-five miles (56.3 km) of the Maurice and its tributaries are another national scenic and recreational river that flows into **Delaware Bay**. Near the river's mouth, the **Bayshore Center at Bivale** is home base for the **Delaware Bay Museum and Folklife Center** and a restored oyster dredging schooner, named the *A. J. Meerwald* (New Jersey's official state tall ship). ∎

Pennsylvania Wilds

Pennsylvania

Sprawling across a huge expanse of the Allegheny Mountains, the Pennsylvania Wilds Conservation Landscape is a compilation of smaller parks and a megapark in its own right that protects one of the largest tracts of wilderness between the Great Lakes and the eastern seaboard.

THE BIG PICTURE

Established: 2003

Size: 2.1 million acres (8,498.4 sq km)

Annual Visitors: 12 million

Visitor Centers: Elk Country (Benezette), Kinzua Bridge State Park, Brookville

Entrance Fee: None

pawilds.com; visitanf.com

The Wilds encompasses 2.1 million acres (8,498.4 sq km) of pristine forest and mountains in north-central Pennsylvania, an area that includes Allegheny National Forest, eight state forests, 50 state wildlife areas, and 29 state parks.

By the turn of the 20th century, the area was heavily logged and environmentally degraded. Through more than 100 years of conservation, the hardwood forest bounced back and the wildlife returned, in particular the elk population, now the largest in the U.S. Northeast. A loose confederation of civic, private, and nonprofit entities banded together in the early 21st century to create the Pennsylvania Wilds.

Elk Country Visitor Center in Benezette gives park visitors the lowdown on the region's natural and human history, as well as three nature trails where elk are often seen. The visitor center lies along **Elk Scenic Drive,** a 127-mile (204.39 km) motor route with two dozen posted stops, including **Gilbert Farm Elk Viewing Area, Sinnemahoning State Park, Cranberry Swamp Natural Area,** and **Karthaus Canoe Launch** on the Susquehanna River.

Often called the "Grand Canyon of Pennsylvania," **Pine Creek Gorge** is a 45-mile-long (72.4 km) rift in the Allegheny Plateau that's nearly 1,500 feet (457.2 m) at its deepest point. **Leonard Harrison State Park** on the east rim and **Colton Point State Park** on the west rim are among the best places to gaze into the belly of this geological beast. You can also hike the gorge using various routes, including the 65-mile (104.61 km) **Pine Creek Rail Trail** along an old railroad right-of-way between Wellsboro and the Jersey Shore. Nearby **Cherry Springs State Park** is renowned for its stargazing, a certified international dark sky preserve where as many as 10,000 stars can be seen on any given night.

Highway 6, another scenic route, rambles across the top of the Wilds. The **Pennsylvania**

A grazing bull elk pauses in the Elk State Forest.

The Clarion River is surrounded by lush greenery and tree-covered hills.

Lumber Museum in Galeton highlights the region's timber industry and forest recovery. **Kinzua Bridge State Park** preserves the remains of a Victorian-era railroad viaduct (once hailed as the "Eighth Wonder of the World") recently converted into a 600-foot-long (182.88 m) **Sky Walk** with glass floors that render views of the forest.

Allegheny Reservoir backs up 24 miles (38.6 km) behind the dam, all the way into upstate New York. Among the lake's many activities are boating, fishing, swimming, waterfront camping, and hiking in the surrounding national forest lands. In nearby Bradford, the **Zippo/Case Museum** revolves around the iconic metal lighter brand, manufactured locally since 1932.

The western Wilds is anchored by **Allegheny National Forest** and its 600 miles (965.6 km) of all-season trails for hiking, biking, cross-country skiing, and other winter activities. Among its many paths is an 87-mile

(140 km) segment of the **North Country National Scenic Trail**, while **Longhouse National Scenic Byway** provides 29 miles (46.67 km) of scenic motoring around Allegheny Reservoir. The national forest also offers 76 miles (122.31 km) of all-terrain vehicle trails and the **Trails at Jakes Rocks** mountain biking loop.

Running along the southern edge of the national forest, the designated Wild and Scenic **Clarion River** provides another glimpse of primordial Pennsylvania. **Cook Forest State Park** is home to the **Ancients**—a grove of old-growth white pines and hemlocks that towers cathedral fashion above the forest floor. **Clear Creek State Forest** safeguards laurel fields where Pennsylvania's state flower blooms each summer. ∎

EVENT HORIZON

• **Laurel Festival:** Pennsylvania's state flower grabs the limelight during this week-long June fest in Wellsboro that includes food, drink, music, and the big Laurel Festival Parade. *wellsboropa.com*

• **Woodsman Show:** Logrolling, tree felling, ax throwing, and chainsaw carving count among the many events at this August festival in Galeton. *woodsmenshow.com*

• **PA Great Outdoors Elk Expo:** This August event at Elk Country Visitor Center features kids' activities, wagon rides, educational exhibits, and the annual elk hunting license draw. *elkexpo.com*

• **Autumn Leaf Festival:** This nine-day event in September celebrates the arrival of fall in Clarion County with the Tournament of Leaves Parade and other events. *clarionpa.com*

Cape Hatteras National Seashore

North Carolina

Created by a string of long, lanky barrier islands floating off the North Carolina mainland, Cape Hatteras forms a huge blip in the Atlantic coast about halfway between Florida and New York. Over the years, its geographical prominence has attracted everyone from early English settlers and the Wright brothers to millions of modern outdoor adventure seekers.

Established as the nation's first national seashore in 1953, Cape Hatteras stretches more than 70 miles (112.65 km) along the Outer Banks of North Carolina and is co-managed by the Wright Brothers National Memorial on Bodie Island and Fort Raleigh National Historic Site on Roanoke Island.

Pea Island National Wildlife Refuge squeezes between two sections of the national seashore, while yet another unit of the National Park Service, **Cape Lookout National**

THE BIG PICTURE

Established: 1953

Size: 30,351 acres (122.83 sq km)

Annual Visitors: 2.4 million

Visitor Centers: Bodie Island, Hatteras Island, Ocracoke Island

Entrance Fee: None

nps.gov/caha; nps.gov/choh/index.htm

Seashore, is located directly to the south. These various bits and pieces make for one of the longest conservation and recreation areas along the entire eastern seaboard.

In addition to Sir Walter Raleigh and Wilbur and Orville Wright, many others have left their mark on the cape, including notorious 18th-century pirate Blackbeard, military aviation innovator Billy Mitchell, and groundbreaking weather reporter Lucy Stowe.

Cape Hatteras also boasts a rich natural history, from millions of migrating shorebirds, sea turtles, and marine mammals to a constantly evolving landscape sculpted by wind and water, evidenced by the new island that formed off Cape Point in April 2017.

HATTERAS ISLAND

One of America's longest islands, Hatteras stretches nearly 50 miles (80.47 km) from stem to stern, a sandy barrier between Pamlico Sound and the open Atlantic. In addition to the lion's share of the national seashore, the island shelters seven tiny settlements totaling around 4,000 year-round residents. The island takes its name from the Hatteras Indians who inhabited its sandy shores when the English arrived in 1585.

An aerial view of the Cape Hatteras coastline captured on a stormy day

The Bodie Island Lighthouse sits in view of the Morning Marsh Boardwalk on North Carolina's Outer Banks.

There are two ways to reach the island: scenic **State Route 12**, which leaps a bridge over Oregon Inlet from Bodie Island in the north, or the year-round **free ferry** from Ocracoke Island in the south. **Hatteras Island Visitor Center** delivers the scoop on seashore recreation, from beach activities and boating to fishing, hiking, and waterfowl hunting. It's also the place to pick up off-road vehicle (OVR) permits to drive the 28 miles (45.1 km) of beach that are open to motorists either seasonally or year-round.

Just behind the visitor center are the **Museum of the Sea** in the old lighthouse keeper's quarters and the 210-foot-high (64 m) **Cape Hatteras Light**, built in 1870 and currently the world's second tallest brick lighthouse. Self-guided climbs of the structure ($8) are available April through October. **Cape Point** also harbors the island's only lifeguard-protected beach, a small World War II **British sailor cemetery**, and the small sandy island that arose from the Diamond Shoals in 2017. Another military relic is **Billy Mitchell Airfield**, where the aviator pioneered naval airpower in the 1920s.

The **Salvo** and **Haulover Day Use Areas** on Pamlico Sound are the best places to slip a canoe or kayak into the water, as well as hubs for kite-boarding and windsurfing. **Avon village** boasts a fishing pier on the island's ocean side as well as the historic **Little Kinnakeet U.S. Life Saving Service Station.** Farther north along Route 12 is the visitor center for **Pea Island National Wildlife Refuge**, which protects around 400 bird species and nesting sea turtles.

BODIE ISLAND

The northernmost link in the Outer Banks, Bodie is no longer an island but a 72-mile-long (115.87 km) peninsula that connects to the mainland at its northern end. Only the southern tip is part of the National Seashore. **Bodie Island Visitor Center** lodges inside another historic lighthouse keeper's residence between Roanoke Sound and **Coquina Beach**. The 156-foot (47.55 m) **Bodie Island Lighthouse** is open to visitors spring through fall, while the boardwalk path to a **wildlife observation deck** overlooking a freshwater pond is open year-round. The stretch of sand between Coquina and Oregon Inlet is open to **off-road vehicles** with a National Park Service permit.

Sixteen miles (25.75 km) north of the visitor center, **Wright Brothers National Memorial** marks the spot in Kitty Hawk where the Ohio siblings staged the first sustained, powered flight in a heavier-than-air machine on December 17, 1903. Exhibits at the **visitor center** spin their legendary tale. Visitors can walk the **flight line** where the world-shattering event took place, explore a reproduction of the **1903 Camp Buildings**, and scramble to the top of Big Kill Devil Hill with its **Wright Brothers Monument** and panoramic views.

From **Whalebone Junction**, a bridge leaps the sound to **Roanoke Island**, where Sir Walter Raleigh established a small settlement in 1585. Later that decade, Virginia Dare became the first English child born in North America. By 1590, all 120 colonists had vanished without a trace, and no one has ever determined their fate. **Fort Raleigh National Historic Site** preserves earthworks and archaeological artifacts from the ill-fated colony and tells the story in a long-running outdoor summer theater production, *The Lost Colony*. The historic site also features two nature trails and the **Elizabethan Gardens**, created by the Garden Club of North Carolina as a beautiful living memorial to the lost colonists.

OCRACOKE ISLAND

One of the quirkiest islands along the Atlantic seaboard, Ocracoke is probably more renowned for its history and folk culture than its mosaic of beaches, marshes, and coastal dunes. Sir Walter Raleigh ran aground on the island, while Edward Teach (aka Blackbeard the Pirate) used it as his favorite hideout until his death in 1718 at the hands of troops from the Virginia colony.

A memorial in Kill Devil Hills celebrates Orville and Wilbur Wright's successful flight.

Ocracoke is served by **three ferries**: from Hatteras Island to the north, Cedar Island to the south, and Swan Quarter on the North Carolina mainland. The national seashore embraces the island's entire Atlantic shore, including long stretches that are open to off-road vehicles. **Ocracoke Day Use Beach** is one of only three strands in the national seashore staffed with lifeguards during the summer. About halfway up the island, the **Pony Pen** safeguards a herd of wild "Banker" horses cared for by the National Park Service since the 1960s.

Ocracoke village, which hugs the shore of a snug harbor called Silver Lake, is the center of most island activities, including the **national park visitor center** with ranger-led programs during the summer.

Founded in the mid-18th century, the village is like a time capsule of the bygone Outer Banks— including a local English-language dialect, High Tider, still spoken by some residents. Outfitters based in the village offer a variety of **outdoor activities** around the island, including sports fishing, kayaking, kite boarding and surfing, and sailing as well as boat and golf cart rentals.

One of the nation's oldest coastal

An egret rests high above Hatteras Island.

beacons, **Ocracoke Lighthouse,** was erected in 1823 and is one of more than 200 structures included within the **Ocracoke Historic District** (which covers most of the village). The town also boasts three museums: the **Ocracoke Preservation Society's** history collection, the **Working Waterman's Exhibit**, and **Teach's Hole Blackbeard Exhibit**.

The **Ocracoke Festival** in June— three days of folk music, storytelling, arts and crafts, and coastal cuisine— is the high tide of a festival-filled year. Among the island's other top events are the **Firemen's Ball** over Memorial Day weekend, the **Classic**

Old-Time 4th of July Parade, the **Ocracoke Fig Festival** in August, **Blackbeard's Pirate Jamboree** in October, and the **Oyster Roast and Shrimp Broil** in December.

Although **Portsmouth Island** lies just off Ocracoke, it's part of Cape Lookout National Seashore. Founded in 1752, Portsmouth was once a thriving little seaport. The last residents left in 1971, but the Park Service has restored the post office, general store, school, lifesaving station, and several private homes. Rangers lead **walking tours** during the warmer months. Boat services is available from Ocracoke. ■

LAY YOUR HEAD

Hotels

• **Inn at Pamlico Sound:** Highly popular boutique hotel on the lagoon side of Hatteras Island; restaurant, swimming pool, movie theater, kayaks, paddleboards; from $91. *innonpamlicosound.com*

• **Ocracoke Harbor Inn:** Small family-run hotel on Silver Lake in the heart of Ocracoke village; balconies, cottages, boat dock, sport fishing; from $100. *ocracokeharborinn.com*

• **Sanderling Resort:** High-end, full-service beach resort on the ocean side of Bodie Island; restaurants, bars, indoor and outdoor pools, spa, fitness center, bike rentals, beach chairs; from $159. *sanderling-resort.com*

• **White Doe Inn:** Victorian-style B&B in Manteo village on Roanoke Island; restaurant, spa services, picnic and dinner baskets; from $195. *whitedoeinn.com*

Camping

• The national seashore offers beach-front campgrounds at Oregon Inlet, Cape Point, Frisco, and Ocracoke; $20-$28 per night.

The South

The historic Avenue of Oaks on St. Simons Island, Georgia

Great Smoky Mountains National Park

North Carolina & Tennessee

Sprawling across more than 800 square miles (2,072 sq km) of the southern Appalachians, Great Smoky Mountains is the nation's most visited national park, as well as the anchor for scores of other adventure and entertainment activities in Tennessee and North Carolina. While hiking, camping, and horseback riding count among its cornerstone activities, the park also elucidates the lives of the Cherokee Indians and European settlers who once called the Smokies home.

THE BIG PICTURE

Established: 1934

Size: 522,419 acres (2,114.15 sq km)

Annual Visitors: 11.3 million

Visitor Centers: Oconaluftee, Sugarlands, Cades Cove, Clingmans Dome, Gatlinburg

Entrance Fee: None

nps.gov/grsm

This was the park that almost didn't happen. By the time Congress got around to declaring Smoky Mountains National Park in the 1934 around 80 percent of its forest cover was already decimated and much of the land was in private hands. Through funds provided by the state governments of Tennessee and North Carolina, as well as donations from wealthy conservationists, the Park Service bought out the logging operations and more than 1,200 small landowners and began the arduous task of restoring the mountains to their former glory.

The Smokies take their name from the haze that often fills the mountain valleys in the early morning, caused by thick vegetation that emits large amounts of moisture and organic compounds that form a natural mist that's especially thick on calm, sunny, humid days. The Cherokee people called it *shaconage* ("blue like smoke"), a description that seemed apt to the Europeans who began settling the region in the 1790s and adopted a translation of the Native American name as their own.

While some of the highest peaks in the eastern United States are certainly one of the park's major attractions, what really makes the Smoky Mountains special is the incredible variety of flora and fauna. It's often been said that moving from the lowest to highest elevations within the park is the biological equivalent of traveling from Georgia to Maine—such is the diversity of life-forms. Overall, the park safeguards more than 1,500 species of flowering plants and 240 types of birds, around 50 kinds of fish, and more than 100

Dew covers the flowers of a fringed phacelia.

Early fall colors begin to emerge against the morning mist in Great Smoky Mountains National Park.

different native trees. In addition, there are five distinct types of forest within the park: pine-and-oak, northern hardwood, spruce-fir, cove hardwood, and hemlock.

While the vast majority of visitors never stray far from Highway 441 through the heart of the park, the best hiking, camping, and wildlife viewing—and pure communing with nature—unfold in the quiet corners of the Smoky Mountains far away from the paved roads and the touristy towns that flank the park on both sides.

NORTH CAROLINA

Located just outside Cherokee, the **Oconaluftee Visitor Center** is the starting point for most visitors entering the park from North Carolina. In addition to a sizable bookstore and information desk, the center offers exhibits on Smoky

Mountains history, in particular the Cherokee Indians and the early European settlers and their ancestors. Behind the visitor center, the **Mountain Farm Museum** gives

insight into the lives of the people who once farmed the region, with hands-on exhibits and historic buildings brought from elsewhere in the park. Just up the road, the

LAY YOUR HEAD

Hotels

• **LeConte Lodge:** Perched at 6,400 feet (1,950.72 m) on the eponymous peak, this rustic accommodation is the highest guest lodge in the eastern United States and the only noncamping accommodation inside the park; it can be reached only by hiking; from $148 per night, including dinner and breakfast. *lecontelodge.com*

• **Grove Park Inn:** On the National Register of Historic Places, this Asheville institution opened in 1913 as the first big resort hotel in the Smoky Mountains region;

restaurants, bars, spa, golf, tennis, history tours; from $169. *omni hotels.com*

• **The Lodge at Buckberry Creek:** Rustic design and fabulous views help this mountaintop B&B near Gatlinburg channel the national park lodges of old; kitchenettes, fireplaces; from $150. *buckberry lodge.com*

Camping

• Ten developed campgrounds and five drive-in horse camps inside the park; $17.50–$29 per night.

Mingus Mill is a relic of the days when corn was the region's main crop and water-driven mills the mechanism for grinding it into flour and cornmeal.

Beyond the mill, **Highway 441** starts its forest-flanked climb into the heart of the mountains. The former site of the **Smokemont** lumber village renders the first opportunity for camping, hiking, and horseback riding through outfits like **Smokemont Riding Stables**. Trails in the Smokemont area lead to the historic **Carver Cemetery** and the **Oconaluftee Baptist Church** (built in 1896).

The road continues its ascent to **Newfound Gap** on the Tennessee–North Carolina border (elevation 5,046 feet/1,538 m), where a viewpoint looks out over much of the Smokies. A stone monument marks the spot where FDR dedicated the

park in 1940. There's also a chance to hike a short portion of the **Appalachian Trail**, which leaps across the highway between the parking lot and monument. A side road leads to **Clingmans Dome**, at 6,643 feet (2,024.79 m) the highest point in the park, third highest peak in the eastern United States, and the highest place along the entire length of the Appalachian Trail. From the observation tower, it's sometimes possible to see to a distance of 100 miles (160.9 km). Although closed to motorized traffic in winter, **Clingmans Dome Road** is open for cross-country skiing, snowshoeing, or even walking through the ridgeline's high-altitude spruce-fir forest.

The North Carolina side features several off-the-beaten-track diversions where the quiet side of the Smokies is there for the taking. Once **Cataloochee** was one of the

region's largest settlements, a legendary apple-growing valley. Among the many 19th-century buildings that remain are two churches, the school, and several private homes. The lush valley also supports a herd of **wild elk**. Another journey into the past is the drive along **Heintooga Ridge Road** and the one-way continuation along gravel **Balsam Mountain Road** that leads into a remote section of the park that few people ever explore and is closed in winter.

TENNESSEE

Gatlinburg and adjacent **Pigeon Forge** are the gateway to the park's Tennessee sector, longtime holiday towns that offer a huge selection of accommodation, dining, and roadside attractions. Visitors can pick up information or find out what's happening inside Great Smoky Mountains at the **National Park**

The 3-mile (4.8 km) round-trip hike to Grotto Falls is well worth the effort, especially for an escape from summer heat.

Information Center in Gatlinburg or **Sugarlands Visitor Center** on Highway 441 just inside the park.

The Sugarlands' main attraction is a popular loop that includes **Cherokee Orchard Road** and the **Roaring Fork Motor Nature Trail**, a route that offers a microcosm of the park in terms of both natural attractions and what visitors can do. The path leads through old-growth forest to the **Noah "Bud" Ogle Nature Trail** (0.7 mile/1.13 km) onto a historic farmstead and the **Rainbow Falls Trail** (5.4-mile/8.7 km round-trip) to a lovely cascade. The Roaring Fork portion is closed in winter.

Little River Road runs east from Sugarlands to the **Elkmont historic area** and a large valley called **Cades Cove** that was another densely populated area prior to National Park status. Motorists or bikers can pick up a self-guide tour book at the orientation shelter near the drive entrance and follow the **11-mile (17.7 km) loop road** to historic structures like the grist mill, three old churches, and bygone homes like Tipton Place. **Cades Cove Trading Company** rents bikes.

Although most visitors treat Cades Cove as a dead end, intrepid drivers can follow two other routes out of the valley (although both are closed in winter). **Rich Mountain Road** is a one-way, 8-mile (12.9 km) route over oak-studded terrain to **Townsend** and eventually back around to Pigeon Forge. **Parson Branch Road** heads in the other direction, a solitary one-way drive to Highway 129 at the park's western extreme. From there, motorists can continue to **Fontana Lake**, which delineates much of the park's southern boundary. At 480 feet (146.3 m), **Fontana Dam** is the tallest concrete dam east of the Rockies. The

Visitors take in the stunning park scenery from Clingmans Dome viewing point.

Tennessee Valley Authority maintains a visitor center beside the dam (open May to October), while **Fontana Marina** offers kayak, paddleboard, and pontoon boat rentals, as well as guided hikes and boat tours.

Another quiet side of the park is the **Greenbrier Cove**, about a 20-minute drive from Gatlinburg via Highway 321. **Porter's Creek** through the valley is well known for trout fishing. And the cove is the jumping-off point for several noteworthy hikes including the **Brushy Mountain Trail** (9.1 miles/14.65 km) to **Mount LeConte**. ∎

MEET THE NEIGHBORS

• **Blue Ridge Parkway:** The nation's longest linear park stretches 469 miles (754.78 km) between Great Smoky and Shenandoah national parks. The southern end is just 0.2 mile (.32 km) from Oconaluftee Visitor Center.

• **Biltmore Estate:** Beyond its famous manse, the 8,000-acre (32.4 sq km) private park features hiking, biking, horseback riding, river float trips, paddleboarding, clay shooting, fly-fishing, Segway tours, carriage rides, and Land Rover off-road driving courses.

• **Pisgah National Forest:** More than a half million acres (2,023.4 sq km) of the Appalachians in North Carolina fall within a national forest that boasts about 1,600 miles (2,574.95 km) of hiking paths and 245 miles (394.29 km) of mountain biking trails.

• **Trail of Tears National Historic Trail:** Commemorates the Cherokee Indians who were forced from the Southeast and marched overland to Oklahoma in the 1830s. Several of the "round-up routes" start near the Smokies.

• **Manhattan Project National Historical Park:** The Oak Ridge, Tennessee, unit of this multistate park includes the X-10 graphite reactor used to develop the first atom bombs.

A summer sunset over Great Smoky Mountains National Park

Ouachita National Forest
Arkansas & Oklahoma

THE BIG PICTURE

Established: 1907

Size: 1.78 million acres (7,203.4 sq km)

Annual Visitors: 1.2 million

Visitor Centers: Jessieville, Mount Ida, Mena, Waldron, Hochatown

Entrance Fee: Day use fees in some areas

fs.usda.gov/ouachita

The oldest national forest in the South, Ouachita offers a patchwork quilt of mountains and valleys in Arkansas and adjacent Oklahoma. As America expanded westward, the rugged region was largely ignored by pioneers seeking easier lands to settle, leaving islands of wilderness that remain largely untouched to this day, places that seem as remote today as when the national forest was first declared in the early 20th century.

Native Americans roamed the Ouachita region for thousands of years prior to the arrival of the first Europeans—a Spanish expedition led by Hernando de Soto that explored the area in 1541 until a clash with Tula Indians sent them retreating back to the lowlands.

Although no one knows for sure where the battle took place, a monument at **Caddo Gap** commemorates the fateful encounter.

Nearby **Lake Ouachita**, which backs up behind **Blakely Mountain Dam**, is one of the South's largest reservoirs and the best place for water recreation in the national forest. The self-proclaimed Striped Bass Capital of the World is renowned for fishing, as well as boating, camping, and scuba diving in its crystal-clear waters. The lake's unique **Geo-Float Trail** is a 16-mile (25.75 km) boating route with a dozen points of geological interest, including **Zebra Rock**, one of the world's largest quartz-crystal "Arkansas diamond" seams. Shared by hikers, runners, and mountain bikers, the **Lake Ouachita Vista Trail** runs more than 40 miles (64.37 km) along the lake's southern shore.

Mount Ida is one of the largest towns inside the national forest. Founded in the 1840s during a short-lived silver boom, the backwoods outpost offers a good selection of lodging, restaurants, and rock hound shops, as well as two **crystal mines** that are open to the public.

Two of the park's best outdoor adventures are located in the southwest. The **Eagle Rock Loop** is a rugged 27-mile (43.45 km) trail that normally takes several days to trek; it rises over nine mountains and requires nine stream crossings. The nearby **Cossatot River** is one of the more gnarly whitewater runs between the Rockies and the Appalachians,

A green anole lizard sits on a bolete mushroom.

Orange and auburn take over the forests of the Ouachita Mountains come autumn.

including a stretch of rapids that drop 40 feet (12.19 m) in an eighth of a mile (0.2 km).

Although smaller than the Arkansas units, the Oklahoma portions of the national forest are packed with scenic wonders and outdoor activities. **Red Slough Wildlife Management Area** offers 5,814 acres (23.5 sq km) of wetlands and bottomland hardwoods near the Red River; alligators and more than 300 bird species have been recorded in the reserve. **Kerr Arboretum and Botanical Area** near Big Cedar offers three nature trails through a wide variety of indigenous trees, shrubs, and flowers.

Towering above far eastern Oklahoma, the lofty **Winding Stair Mountain National Recreation Area** offers numerous campsites, forest trails, and impressive vistas. The area's premier hiking, biking, and equestrian route is **Horsethief Springs Trail**, an 11-mile (17.7 km) loop from **Cedar Lake**.

Two long-distance routes meander through the national forest. **Ouachita National Recreational Trail** spans a refreshingly remote 192 miles (309 km) between **Talimena State Park** in Oklahoma and Perryville, Arkansas. The path varies between 600 and 2,600 feet (182.9-792.5 m) above sea level as it wanders up,

down, and around the region's rugged topography. Much of the route is multiuse (hikes and cycling). For those who prefer stepping on a gas pedal rather than a dirt trail, **Talimena National Scenic Byway** is a 54-mile (86.9 km) route through the Ouachita region including portions of old-growth forest. ■

MEET THE NEIGHBORS

• **Hot Springs National Park:** Hiking trails, hot springs, and historic "Bathhouse Row" are all part of the oldest federally protected park (1832) in the foothills of the Ouachita Mountains.

• **Fort Smith National Historic Site:** The 19th-century brick bastion served as a gateway to the West, terminus of the Trail of Tears, jail for notorious outlaws, and courthouse for "Hanging Judge" Isaac Parker.

• **Showman's Rest:** This shady cemetery in Hugo, Oklahoma, is the last resting place for numerous circus and carnival performers, including animal trainers, trapeze artists, and clowns, who once wintered here.

• **Crater of Diamonds State Park:** Anyone can dig for gemstones—and take them home—at the world's only public diamond mine, located near Murfreesboro, Arkansas. Around 30,000 diamonds have been unearthed by visitors since the 1970s.

Chattahoochee-Oconee National Forests

Georgia

THE BIG PICTURE

Established: 1936

Size: 866,468 acres (3,506.5 sq km)

Annual Visitors: 2.9 million

Visitor Centers: Brasstown Bald, Anna Ruby Falls, Tallulah Gorge, Black Rock Mountain

Entrance Fee: $3-$5 per person at national forest day use sites

fs.usda.gov/main/conf/

Much of the northern Georgia is swathed in this sprawling national forest, which includes the headwaters of numerous rivers flowing from the bottom end of the Appalachian range. Just a short drive from the Atlanta metropolitan area, the region also includes several popular state parks and one especially famous Wild and Scenic River.

If you start humming a famous banjo tune while driving through the Chattahoochee region, it's probably from the movie *Deliverance*, filmed on location in the national forest in the 1970s. The movie exposed what a lot of local people already knew—that many of the rivers, valleys, and forests of north Georgia are incredibly remote, with possibilities around every bend.

The fictional "Cahulawassee River" of *Deliverance* is really the **Chattooga River**, which demarcates the eastern end of the national forest as well as the border between Georgia and South Carolina. The first Wild and Scenic River east of the Mississippi, the Chattooga is the only such stream in the eastern United States where outfitters can operate commercial **whitewater rafting trips**. **Nantahala Outdoor Center** is one of several companies that run the river's gnarly Class II-IV rapids.

Whitewater trips end downstream at **Lake Tugalo**, where excellent **bass fishing** goes hand-in-hand with **recreational boating** (both motorized and muscle propelled). Nearby **Tallulah Gorge** is sometimes called the "Grand Canyon of the South," a gaping hole in the earth's surface carved by the fast-flowing Tallulah River. Trails lead along the north and south rims to a suspension footbridge and viewpoints of the **six waterfalls** in the bottom of the gorge. It's also possible to descend 1,000 feet (304.8 m) to the gorge floor, but the state park issues just 100 permits each day on a first-come, first-serve basis.

All told, the national forest maintains more than 450 miles (724.2 km) of hiking, biking, and horseback riding trails. By far the most celebrated of these is the southern start (or end) of the **Appalachian Trail**. Starting from **Springer Mountain**, America's most celebrated wilderness path leads more than 76 miles (122.31 km)

Amicalola Falls State Park in Chattahoochee National Forest

In a series of cascades, Minnehaha Falls descends about 100 feet (30.5 m) over a steeped rock formation.

across the national forest before crossing into North Carolina. Less ambitious hikers can follow a short trail (0.8 mile/1.28 km) to **Anna Ruby Falls**, a twin cascade that tumbles more than 200 feet (60.96 m) down a rock face.

Georgia's highest point, 4,784-foot (1,458.16 m) **Brasstown Bald**, is reached via a 1.2-mile (1.93 km) paved trail from the parking lot. The **visitor center** at the summit features an observation tower and a surprisingly good museum that features a tiny locomotive once used to haul timber down the mountain, as well as a cave-like geology exhibit, and an animatronics version of Arthur Woody (the "father" of Chattahoochee National Forest).

From Brasstown Bald, visitors can hike the **Arkaquah Trail** (5.5 miles/ 8.85 km) to the park's **Track Rock Gap Petroglyph** site, where the region's ancient Native American inhabitants carved images in the soft soapstone. A Cherokee village sat nearby until 1838, when the residents were forcibly relocated to Oklahoma via the infamous Trail of Tears.

Located in the Piedmont country east of Atlanta, **Oconee National Forest** features two recreational lakes (boating, fishing, swimming, camping), as well as the old frontier settlement of **Scull Shoals** and **Dyar Pasture Recreation Area**, a 60-acre (.24 sq km) freshwater wetlands and bird sanctuary. ■

LAY YOUR HEAD

Hotels

• **Beechwood Inn:** An excellent wine cellar, farm-to-table restaurant, and gourmet cooking classes make this Clayton inn the most elegant place to stay in the Chattahoochee region; from $199. *beechwoodinn.ws*

• **Glen Ella Springs Inn:** Surrounded by forest, this bucolic B&B is just a 10-minute drive from Tallulah Gorge; restaurant, swimming pool, outdoor fire pit; from $165. *glenella.com*

• **Unicoi Adventure Lodge:** State park digs with zip line, water sports, archery and air gun range, mountain biking, fly-fishing, and global positioning system scavenger hunts; from $89.

Camping

• **National forests:** Campgrounds at 30 sites in the two national forests; $4-$16 per night.

• **State parks:** Camping available at Tallulah Gorge, Black Rock Mountain, Moccasin Creek, Vogel, and Unicoi; $15-$55 per night.

Natchez Trace Parkway

Mississippi, Alabama & Tennessee

THE BIG PICTURE

Established: 1938

Size: 52,302 acres (211.66 sq km)

Annual Visitors: 6.3 million

Visitor Centers: Tupelo, Mount Locust, Jackson

Entrance Fee: None

nps.gov/natr

Stretching 444 miles (714.5 km) between Nashville, Tennessee, and Natchez, Mississippi, the trace is one of America's oldest overland routes, a path originally blazed by Native Americans and later used by settlers, soldiers, slaves, and bandits as the American frontier expanded into the Mississippi Valley. A scenic and recreation route created in the 1930s, the modern parkway roughly follows the path of the old trace through forest, fields, and historic towns.

Researchers estimate the Natchez Trace first took shape around 10,000 years ago, when the region's early indigenous peoples carved out a trade route between the Cumberland and Mississippi Rivers. Following the Louisiana Purchase (1803), Thomas Jefferson expedited development of the trace to bolster American rule over the Lower Mississippi Valley.

From Andrew Jackson and Meriwether Lewis to Great Awakening preachers and Civil War soldiers, few other routes have played a greater role in American history. Most travelers today drive the trace, but the route is also ideal for cycling, and parts of it welcome hikers and horseback riders.

You can start at either end of the trace or anywhere between. But the city of **Natchez** on the banks of the Mississippi seems as logical a place as any. Leaving the antebellum mansions behind, the parkway starts off Liberty Avenue on the eastern edge of town.

It seems appropriate that the first landmark along the way is **Emerald Mound**, one of the earliest human structures along the trace. A ceremonial center used by Native Americans between the 13th and 18th centuries, the grass-covered rise is the nation's second largest pre-Columbian mound. Just up the road is **Mount Locust**, the route's only remaining "stand," or roadside inn (founded 1780), as well as a visitor center for those headed north along the parkway.

Visitors can walk a portion of the original route at mile marker 41.5, a much trafficked section called the **Sunken Trace** that dips below surface level. This section of the trace—in particular, **Port Gibson** and **Raymond**—was drawn into Grant's Vicksburg Campaign during the Civil War. The main action unfolded in the riverside town of **Vicksburg**, just 20 miles (32.19 km) west of the trace.

A section of the Old Natchez Trail known as "sunken trail" because of erosion

The John Gordon House, built for the ferry operator in the 1800s, is one of the few remaining buildings on the Old Natchez Trace.

After skirting around **Jackson**, Mississippi, the trace hugs the shore of **Barnett Reservoir** and **Cypress Swamp** (with its wooden boardwalk trail) as it rolls into northern Mississippi. A long section of the trace north of mile marker 200 is steeped in Native American heritage, including the 2,000-year-old **Bynum Burial Mounds** and the abandoned Choctaw village at **Pigeon Roost**.

Located about midway along the trace, **Tupelo**, Mississippi, is renowned as the birthplace of Elvis Presley. But the city also boasts the official **Natchez Trace Parkway Visitor Center**, with a book store, orientation film, and exhibits on the route's natural and cultural history.

The trace slices across the northwest corner of Alabama, leaping the **Tennessee River** on a modern bridge across the same stretch of water once plied by the Colbert Ferry. Perched along the north bank, **Rock Spring Nature Trail** provides easy access to the lush riverside environment. Not far downstream is **Shiloh National Military Park**, where another great Civil War battle took place.

A replica roadside inn just after crossing into Tennessee marks the site where **Meriwether Lewis** passed away, possibly by his own hand. A little farther up the road are trails through the woods to the **Fall Hollow** cascades, **Jackson Falls**, and another short hiking section of the original trace. The trace finally peters out on the south side of **Nashville**, not far from historic **Franklin**. ■

LAY YOUR HEAD

Hotels

• **Stone House Musical B&B:** Tucked into a Greek Revival–style mansion in the Natchez Historic District, this inn features live classical music, as well as an antique map gallery and antebellum billiards room; from $135. *josephstonehouse.com*

• **Moon Lake Farm:** This rustic B&B sits on a 75-acre (0.3 sq km) spread on the outskirts of Tupelo; horseback riding, fishing, farm animals; from $129. *moonlakefarm.com*

• **The Alluvian:** Boutique hotel in downtown Kosciusko, the Mississippi town that gave the world Oprah Winfrey; spa, cooking school, gourmet Italian restaurant; from $215. *thealluvian.com*

• **Magnolia House:** Located near the northern end of the trace in Tennessee, this cozy B&B occupies a 1905 Craftsman-style home within walking distance of Franklin historic district; from $175. *bbonline.com/tn/magnolia*

Jean Lafitte National Historical Park & Preserve
Louisiana

Much like the gumbo of Louisiana's bayou country, Jean Lafitte is a delicious stew that includes many of the ingredients that make the region such a tasty place to visit. The park's five units range from Cajun culture and American military history to alligators and bird life, as well as a visitor center in the heart of New Orleans's French Quarter.

Named for the French pirate who aided Andrew Jackson at the Battle of New Orleans, Jean Lafitte celebrates the unique culture, the quirky history, and the natural attributes of the Mississippi Delta region in southern Louisiana.

Located on Decatur Street in the Vieux Carré, the park's **French Quarter Visitor Center** renders a broad overview of New Orleans history and the state's eclectic human and natural heritage through exhibits, films, and a shop that sells local

THE BIG PICTURE

Established: 1978

Size: 22,421 acres (90.73 sq km)

Annual Visitors: 456,000

Visitor Centers: French Quarter, Chalmette, Barataria, Lafayette, Eunice, Thibodaux

Entrance Fee: None

nps.gov/jela

books and music. Five days each week, there's a ranger talk on local history and culture.

Downriver from New Orleans—and reached by driving or cruising aboard the ***Creole Queen* paddle wheeler**—is **Chalmette Battlefield**. It was here, on January 8, 1815, that the fabled Battle of New Orleans took place, Andrew Jackson and his ragtag band of American defenders arrayed against a superior force of British Army regulars. Located next to the obelisk monument, the **battlefield visitor center** illuminates the War of 1812 and its last clash. This riverfront site also includes the historic **Malus-Beauregard House** (built in the 1830s) and **Chalmette National Cemetery**, where Americans who fell in more than a half dozen wars are buried.

Located on the southern outskirts of New Orleans, **Barataria Preserve** protects 23,000 acres (93.1 sq km) of Louisiana wetlands, one of the best places in the metropolitan area for bird-watching and close encounters of the alligator kind. The visitor center features hands-on exhibits and films. But the real action is outdoors, trekking the **Plantation Loop** (3.2 miles/5.45 km), raised boardwalk **Palmetto Trail** (0.9 mile/1.45 km), and other routes into the bayou.

A dragonfly perches in the Jean Lafitte National Historical Park.

An old plantation that survived the Battle of New Orleans (1815) sits in fine condition in Chalmette, St. Bernard Parish.

The other three units of Jean Lafitte are deep in **Acadiana**—the region settled by French exiled from Canada in the 1700s, as well as the birthplace of Cajun culture. **Wetlands Acadian Cultural Center** in Thibodaux illuminates Cajun culture through museum exhibits on regional cooking, clothing, and folk art, as well as films, Cajun music jams, and plays performed in a 200-seat theater. The center also offers guided boat tours of **Bayou Lafourche**, ranger-led walking tours of historic **Thibodaux**, and *Cercle* **Francophone** sessions where visitors can hear Acadiana French speakers interacting.

The **Acadian Cultural Center** in Lafayette, the unofficial capital of Acadiana, presents a similar slate of exhibits, art shows, and live performances on Cajun themes, including regular dulcimer jams and a 35-minute film, *The Cajun Way: Echoes of Acadia.* During spring and fall,

rangers lead boat tours of nearby **Bayou Vermilion** from a dock at **Vermillion Heritage and Folklife Park**, which preserves historic Cajun and Creole structures brought from around Louisiana.

Prairie Acadian Cultural Center in Eunice, to the west, revolves around the Prairie Cajuns, a subset of regional culture. The center is especially attuned to local music,

from swamp pop to zydeco. Every Saturday, the center throws a party, called **"The Cajun Way,"** that features local music, dance, and cooking demonstrations. Later in the day, the action moves next door to the historic **Liberty Theater**, where the *Rendez-vous des Cajuns* show is an evening celebrating live music often billed as a Cajun version of the Grand Ole Opry. ◼

CHOW DOWN

• **Ruby's:** Just a block away from the cultural center, this Cajun eatery in downtown Eunice features crawfish étouffée, jambalaya, stewed catfish, and other regional specialties.

• **Fremin's:** Nouvelle Cajun and Creole dishes—like smoked duck and andouille gumbo, crawfish tortellini carbonara, and calamari creolaise—is the forte of this edgy

restaurant tucked into a historic townhouse near the Thibodaux waterfront. *fremins.net*

• **La Cuisine de Maman:** Maybe mother made dishes like the brisket po'boy and seafood gumbo, but did she really drink the crawfish-topped Cajun Bloody Marys they serve at this Lafayette eatery? *bayouvermiliondistrict.org*

Everglades National Park

Florida

Sprawling between Lake Okeechobee and the Gulf of Mexico, the Everglades is one of the world's largest tropical wetlands. About 20 percent of the region is protected within the confines of Everglades National Park, the third largest national park in the lower 48 states. While the park's main purpose is preserving a wilderness like none other in North America, the Everglades also provides plenty of scope for outdoor adventure.

Although technically a wetland, perhaps it's best to think of the Everglades as the nation's slowest, widest river—a constant stream of freshwater roughly 60 miles (96.56 km) wide, moving at a speed of around 2.5 miles (4 km) per day as it makes its way south to Florida Bay.

The Seminole people called the region Okeechobee ("river of grass").

And while a large part of the Everglades is covered in razor-sharp sawgrass, the region also encompasses mangrove swamps, tropical hardwood hammocks (island forests), pine and cypress forests, freshwater prairie, and various marine and estuarine habitats.

Although the entire coast is open to exploration via watercraft, land-

THE BIG PICTURE

Established: 1934

Size: 1.5 million acres (6,070.3 sq km)

Annual Visitors: 1 million

Visitor Centers: Ernest F. Coe, Flamingo, Shark Valley, Gulf Coast

Entrance Fee: $25 vehicles, $8 per person

nps.gov/ever

bound visitors have three options for entering the park: **Flamingo** in the southwest, **Shark Valley** in the northeast, and **Gulf Coast** in the northwest.

The **Ernest F. Coe Visitor Center** is the place to start for those making the 38-mile (61.15 km) drive to **Florida Bay**. Some of the park's best hikes are just beyond the visitor center, including the short, easy **Gumbo Limbo Trail** (0.4 mile/.64 km) and **Anhinga Trail** (0.8 mile/1.28 km), which wind through a wildlife-rich hammock called Royal Palm, and the 6.1-mile (9.8 km) **Long Pine Key Trail** through the park's largest remaining stand of native pines.

Main Park Road continues through a variety of ecosystems—the freshwater prairie, stunted cypress forest, mangrove and coastal marsh—to Flamingo on the shore of Florida Bay. Badly damaged by Hurricane Irma in 2017, the area has slowly recovered with the reopening of the **Flamingo Visitor Center**, beachfront campground, and boat and bike rentals. In addition to paddling along the shore of Florida Bay, the area boasts a number of inland routes, including the **Nine Mile Pond Loop** (14.48 km) and the **Bear Lake Canoe Trail**.

Flamingo is the southern terminus

Great blue herons, the largest heron in North America, exchange nesting materials.

Lily pads and water grasses cover large portions of the waterways in the Everglades.

of the Everglades' ultimate kayak/canoe experience—the **Wilderness Waterway**—a 99-mile (159.32 km) meander through mangroves and marshes with raised platform "chickee hut" campsites along the way. An entire week is recommended for those who want to make the complete journey between Flamingo and Everglades City.

Reached via the historic **Tamiami Trail** highway across the Everglades, **Shark Valley Visitor Center** is the gateway to a much different park experience—a chance to explore the freshwater grasslands and hammocks of the Shark River Slough. You won't come across any sharks, but this might be the best place in the entire park to view crocodiles, turtles, and bird life at close range. The 15-mile (24.14 km) **Shark Valley Tram Road** expedites hiking, biking, and a narrated tram tour to a 65-foot (19.81 m) **Observation Tower** with views across the wet

wilds. Seasonally, rangers lead full moon and meteor shower bike rides to the tower.

Thirty-six miles (57.9 km) from Naples, the **Gulf Coast Visitor Center** and the town of **Everglades City** anchor the park's northwest corner. Daily boat tours are available to the remote **Ten Thousand**

Islands archipelago along the Gulf of Mexico. Gulf Coast is also a jumping-off spot for the Wilderness Waterway, as well as shorter paddle routes like the **Turner River Canoe Trail**. Everglades City is home to several **airboat tours** that explore parts of the Everglades outside the national park. ■

MEET THE NEIGHBORS

- **Big Cypress Reserve:** Another 729,000 acres (2,950.16 sq km) of the South Florida wilderness are protected by this federal preserve on the north side of Everglades National Park, including the primary range of the endangered Florida panther.

- **Ten Thousand Islands National Wildlife Refuge:** Just west of the Gulf Coast, the coastal reserve features boating, hiking, camping, fishing, and wildlife viewing.

- **Fruit and Spice Park:** Founded in 1944, this historic botanical garden along the eastern edge of the Everglades in Homestead cultivates more than 500 varieties of fruit, nut, and spice trees from around the world.

- **Everglades Alligator Farm:** Located in Homestead near the national park's Flamingo entrance, this vintage Florida attraction features airboat rides as well as snakes, lizards, turtles, and more than 2,000 gators.

A red mangrove grows in Florida Bay.

Florida Keys
Florida

The world's third longest barrier reef (after those in Australia and Belize), the Florida Keys stretch 190 miles (305.77 km) along the southern fringe of Florida. Anchoring either end of the 800-island chain are marine-focused national parks—Biscayne and Dry Tortugas—and along the way are numerous other nature reserves and recreation areas, including several state parks and the Florida Keys National Marine Sanctuary.

THE BIG PICTURE

Established: Biscayne (1980); Dry Tortugas (1992)

Size: Biscayne (173,000 acres/ 700.1 sq km); Dry Tortugas (64,701 acres/261.8 sq km)

Annual Visitors: Biscayne (446,000); Dry Tortugas (54,000)

Visitor Centers: Dante Fascell/ Biscayne, Eco-Discovery Center/ Key West

Entrance Fees: Biscayne (none); Dry Tortugas ($10)

nps.gov/bisc
nps.gov/drto

Formed around 130,000 years ago when the sea level was 20 to 30 feet (6.1-9.14 m) higher than its present level, the Florida Keys are one of the nation's natural wonders. Dividing the open Atlantic from the Gulf of Mexico, the islands present an amazing array of terrestrial and marine nature, as well as myriad ways to enjoy the water.

BISCAYNE

Despite the fact that it's perched at the southern end of the Miami-Dade metropolitan area, Biscayne Bay remains refreshingly unspoiled, a medley of mangroves, sandy islands, shallow bays, and coral reefs within sight of the skyscrapers of downtown Miami.

Boating is by far the best way to explore the park, although it does boast a razor-thin mainland (comprising mostly shore-hugging mangrove swamps), several campgrounds, and one lengthy hiking trail.

Overlooking the bay at the end of Southwest 328th Street in Homestead, the **Dante Fascell Visitor Center** at Convoy Point is the hub for many park activities, including ranger-led interpretive talks and a **Park After Dark** program that runs a broad gamut from story slams and sea shanty sing-alongs to evening cruises and paddles.

The visitor center shop is the place to sign up for water activities operated by the **Biscayne National Park Institute**, including **snorkel trips** to the outer reef, **boat trips** to Boca Chita, **guided paddling excursions** through the mangroves, **all-day sailing adventures**, and transfers to the campsite on Elliott Key. The shop also rents canoes, kayaks, and paddleboards.

On the other side of Biscayne Bay is the top end of the Florida Keys, a string of sandy barrier islands that have helped protect the coast against hurricanes and tidal surges for thousands of years. **Elliot Key** is by far the largest, home to a secluded campground where rangers give fireside chats in the evening, as well as a **hiking**

Anglers search for bonefish in the clear waters of Biscayne.

Colorful coral and reef fish are among many of the sights on offer under the waters of Biscayne National Park.

trail that runs the entire length of the island.

Just off the north end of Elliott, **Boca Chita Key** boasts the park's other campground, as well as an ornamental lighthouse, built in the 1930s. Down at the southern end of the chain are the **Adams Key** day use area and **Jones Lagoon**, renowned for its resident upside-down jellyfish and named after 19th-century African-American settlers Israel and Moiselle Jones and their sons, King Arthur and Sir Lancelot.

Beyond the islands are the coral gardens, with fixed mooring buoys at popular dive or snorkel spots like **Elkhorn Reef, Anniversary Reef**, and **The Drop**. The area is littered with the remains of ships that came afoul of the coral heads. The park's **Marine Heritage Trail** links wrecks like the 19th-century steamer *Arra-*toon *Apcar* (1878), the Havana-bound steamer *Alicia* (1905), and the iron-hulled cargo ship *Lugano* (1913).

DRY TORTUGAS

One of the most remote places in the lower 48 states is the Dry Tortugas float in the Gulf of Mexico around 70 miles (112.65 km) west of Key West. In addition to marking the western end of the Florida Keys, the archipelago is blessed with an array of both natural and human history.

The **Florida Keys Eco-Discovery Center** in Key West—

DID YOU KNOW

• Ponce de León "discovered" the Florida Keys during a 1513 expedition and named the islands Los Martires ("the martyrs").

• From the 1948 movie *Key Largo* to Jimmy Buffett songs and Ernest Hemingway's prose, the Keys have inspired many works of art.

• Looe Key Reef in the Florida Keys National Marine Sanctuary hosts the world's only underwater music festival, a July event that attracts harp-playing "mermaids" and other costumed musicians.

• The place where treasure hunter Mel Fisher found the Spanish galleon *Atocha* is also in the national marine sanctuary. The spot is marked not by an "X" but by a sunken barge that Fisher used as his salvage base.

A glass-bottom boat allows visitors a peek underwater at Coral Reef State Park.

DeHavilland Turbo Otter. Those who fly in also have plenty of time to tour the fort and snorkel.

Garden Key is dominated by **Fort Jefferson**, a massive citadel that once guarded the passage between the Florida Strait and the Gulf of Mexico. Construction began in 1846 on the fort that would eventually grow into the largest brick masonry structure in the Western Hemisphere. During the Civil War it served as a prison for unruly or mutinous Union soldiers. Following the war, four of the Lincoln assassination conspirators (including Dr. Samuel Mudd) were imprisoned at Fort Jefferson. A **self-guided tour** route takes visitors around the fort's major features. During peak seasons, rangers conduct living history and stargazing programs, as well as historical and ecological walks.

Beyond the fort, Garden Key features a **beachfront campground**, several good **snorkeling spots**, and great **bird-watching**. A 1-mile (0.6 km) trail leads from Garden Key across a sandy isthmus to **Bush Key** (open September to January when the resident birds are not nesting).

Those with their own boat can also visit **Loggerhead Key** with its towering lighthouse, **Little Africa** coral gardens, and the wreck of the windjammer *Avanti*.

OTHER FLORIDA KEYS PARKS

Extending all the way across the chain from Biscayne Bay to the Dry Tortugas, the **Florida Keys National Marine Sanctuary** is one of the nation's largest and most important underwater reserves. The Eco-Discovery Center also serves as a visitor center for this vast underwater park. Basically any water in

a cooperative venture between the Park Service and other state and federal agencies—has all the information you need for visiting the Dry Tortugas. Unless you have your own boat, there are only two ways to reach the park: ferry and seaplane.

Yankee Freedom III, a high-speed catamaran, makes the trip daily, a voyage of just over two hours between the Key West waterfront and **Garden Key**. The craft also carries campers and their equipment, as well as canoes or kayaks. Day passengers have nearly five hours on the park's main island. **Key West Seaplane Adventures** makes the trip in about 40 minutes in a 10-passenger

LAY YOUR HEAD

Hotels

• **The Gardens:** An oasis of tranquility in the midst of helter-skelter Key West, this chic little boutique is just a block off busy, bar-swamped Duval Street; swimming pool, wine gallery, outdoor bar, bike rental, pet friendly; from $229. *gardenshotel.com*

• **Kona Kai:** On the leeward side of Key Largo, this old-time resort transports you back to a kinder, gentler time in the Keys; pool, art gallery, spa treatments, yoga, tennis courts, beach, kayaks, paddleboards, resident iguanas; from $219. *konakairesort.com*

• **Hampton Inn:** Located just off the Florida Turnpike in Homestead, this five-story hotel is just 15 minutes from the Biscayne National Park visitor center; swimming pool, free Wi-Fi and breakfast, resident duck family; from $143. *hamptoninn3.hilton.com*

Camping

• **Biscayne:** Primitive campsites on Elliot Key and Boca Chita Key; $25 per night.

• **Dry Tortugas:** Beachside campground on Garden Key beside Fort Jefferson; $15 per night.

---

the keys below the mean high-tide mark is part of the sanctuary.

Covering 2,900 square nautical miles (9,946.72 sq km), roughly the same size as Everglades National Park, the sanctuary is best explored by boat. Outfitters in Key West and Key Largo offer guided trips including **Key West Eco Tours**, which tenders guided kayak, paddleboard, and catamaran tours of the mangroves and inshore waters.

Living up to its name, **John Pennekamp Coral Reef State Park** in Key Largo is blessed with stunning underwater scenery, pristine reefs like the **Grecian Rocks, Molasses Reef,** and **Christ of the Deep** with its 9-foot-tall (2.74 m) submerged Jesus. The nation's first underwater park is named after the crusading editor of the *Miami Herald* newspaper, one of those who helped preserve the reef in the 1950s. The park concessionaire offers scuba, snorkeling, and glass-bottom boat tours, as well as canoe, kayak, paddleboard, and powerboat rentals. On shore, the visitor center boasts a pretty good little **aquarium** with creatures that frequent the reef.

The U.S. Fish and Wildlife Service maintains four federal wildlife refuges on the Keys, including the **National Key Deer Refuge** on Big Pine Key and neighboring No Name Key. After nearly going extinct in the 1950s, the deer have rebounded to around 800 individuals but are still highly endangered. The best time to see them is early morning, normally just off the roadways. The refuge offers several short hiking trails and a submerged quarry, **Blue Hole**, which attracts a variety of wildlife.

Bahia Honda State Park on the island of the same name boasts one of the Keys' best beaches, as well as the remains of an immense bridge built for Henry Flagler's **Florida East Coast Railway**. The park also facilitates scuba, snorkeling, paddle sports, fishing, and bird-watching, as well as seafront camping. ■

An aerial view of Fort Jefferson in Dry Tortugas National Park.

① Yellowstone National Park, Wyoming

America's version of the Serengeti Plains features an array of large mammals, from apex predators like the grizzly bear and wolf to herbivorous herds of bison, elk, and pronghorn antelope. The Lamar Valley is renowned for some of the park's best wildlife viewing, especially in winter when many of the animals take shelter in the snowy vale.

② Saguenay–St. Lawrence National Park, Quebec

The rich underwater feeding grounds at the confluence of the Saguenay and St. Lawrence Rivers in Quebec attract a broad range of marine mammals, including 10 types of whale, as well as seals, sharks, porpoises, and more than 300 bird species. Kayak trips and scenic boat cruises along the Saguenay Fjord are the ideal way to view them.

③ Florida Keys, Florida

The world's third longest barrier reef is a giant living thing all on its own. Biscayne and Dry Tortugas national parks, and Pennekamp Coral Reef State Park offer pristine coral gardens where snorkelers and scuba divers can mingle with tropical fish, sea turtles, and other denizens of the deep. The Keys also boast great bird watching.

④ Everglades National Park, Florida

Florida's "river of grass" is renowned for its alligators, but the vast park is home to many other creatures: West Indian manatees, a subspecies of the mountain lion called the Florida panther, four different species of sea turtle, and the very rare American crocodile. Feathered friends also thrive in the wetlands, with more than 360 species on the park's bird list.

⑤ Aransas National Wildlife Refuge, Texas

More than 400 different bird species have been recorded in this feather-friendly Texas Gulf Coast refuge. Among the other creatures that dwell in its four distinct ecosystems are sea turtles, manatees, alligators, peccaries, coyotes, and bobcats.

THE TOP

10

WILDLIFE ENCOUNTERS

These parks offer close encounters of the wild animal kind.

⑥ Wichita Mountains National Wildlife Reserve, Oklahoma

One of the places that saved the American bison from extinction, this Oklahoma reserve's mix of shortgrass prairie and red-rock canyons shelters a vast array of animals viewed from roads and trails. They range in size from huge buffalo, Rocky Mountain elk, and feral longhorn cattle to the black-tailed prairie dogs that inhabit several "towns" in the park.

An alligator surfaces in the blue swamp of the Everglades.

⑦ Wapusk National Park, Manitoba

Set along the shores of the Hudson Bay in northern Manitoba, Wapusk is considered the best place on the planet to observe and photograph polar bears in the wild. Peak viewing times are the fall migration back into the sea ice and midwinter when mother bears emerge from their dens with cubs. Thousands of beluga whales congregate offshore in the summer.

⑧ Channel Islands National Park, California

Astride the migration route of humpbacks, orcas, and gray whales and home at any one time to 30,000 seals and sea lions, the Southern California archipelago is renowned for marine mammals. There are also copious birdlife and rare land creatures like the island fox, island spotted skunk, and island deer mouse.

⑨ Wrangell-St. Elias National Park and Preserve, Alaska

Alaska's giant national park harbors a vast array of typical northern latitude creatures. Brown bears, caribou, Dall sheep, mountain goats, and moose are the "big five" terrestrial animals, while humpback whales, orcas, sea lions, harbor seals, and porpoises inhabit Icy Bay and other parklands along the Gulf of Alaska.

⑩ Katmai National Park and Preserve, Alaska

One of the great spectacles of North American wildlife takes place at Katmai each summer: dozens of brown bears (aka grizzlies) fishing for spawning salmon in the Brooks River. The huge Alaska park is also home to scores of inland and coastal bird species and 42 different mammals including the gray wolf, sea otter, and humpback whale.

Mammoth Cave National Park
Kentucky

The world's largest known cave system hides beneath the woods of central Kentucky, more than 400 miles (643.73 km) of underground passages that have already been discovered and untold other caverns that await exploration by future spelunkers. Aboveground, the national park's pristine wilderness—a mix of woodland and rivers—can be explored via hiking, biking, paddling, and horseback.

THE BIG PICTURE

Established: 1941

Size: 586,000 acres (2,371.5 sq km)

Annual Visitors: 587,000

Visitor Center: Mammoth Cave

Entrance Fee: None

nps.gov/maca

Mummified remains found inside Mammoth Cave show that Native Americans and their ancient ancestors used the subterranean wonder as a sacred site for around 6,000 years. But it wasn't until the 1790s that the aperture became known to the greater world, when a pioneer bear hunter accidentally stumbled on the cave.

In the early 19th century, Mammoth was mined for its saltpeter (used in gunpowder production) before evolving into a full-fledged tourist attraction in the 1830s. Many of the chamber's rooms and landmarks were named during that period, which also featured underground music concerts and religious services. The cavern also featured in the heated Kentucky Cave Wars of the early 20th century as competing cave owners battled to attract paying customers. The disputes were eventually settled when the cave system came under the National Park Service in 1941.

Located about 10 miles from Cave City, Kentucky, the **Historic Entrance** to Mammoth Cave is surrounded by a tourist village that includes a hotel, cottages, campground, camp store, and cemetery, as well as the national park **visitor center**. Five other entrances are strung out along **Cave City Road**.

Nobody can enter Mammoth Cave without joining a guided tour. At the very basic level, this includes short introductory visits like the self-guided **Mammoth Cave Discovery** ($5) and ranger-led **Mammoth Passage** ($7). A dozen other tours focus on specific sections or adventures in the underground world, including the **Frozen Niagara** formation ($13), the throwback **Violet City Lantern** experience ($18), the physically demanding **Grand Avenue** tour ($26), and the subterranean waterways of the **River Styx** ($15).

The spectacular Frozen Niagara section of Mammoth Cave

Cavers stand in the New Discovery Bore Hole of Mammoth Cave, first discovered in 1939.

Wannabe spelunkers can learn the ins and outs of exploring beneath the surface with the national parks **Introduction to Caving** program ($26) or venture into lesser-known parts of the Mammoth system on a **Wild Cave** adventure ($55) that mandates crawling, sliding, and free climbing plus a good amount of dirt, mud, water, and maybe even bat guano.

Advanced reservations are recommended for all cave tours, in particular the specialty ones. Youth and senior rates are available on most of these adventures.

Aboveground, the park offers plenty of scope for outdoor recreation in a Kentucky wilderness spangled with more than 1,200 species of flowering plants and 84 kinds of trees, including hickory, oak, cedar, and pine. The slow-flowing **Green River** snakes 25 miles (40.23 km) across the park from east to west and is suitable for canoeing, kayaking, fishing, and swimming. **Mammoth Cave Canoe**

and Kayak is one of several outfitters that offer guided paddle trips down the river.

Bikers have a choice of four routes within the park, including the rambling **Mammoth Cave Bike and Hike Trail**, a 9-mile (14.48 km) gravel path between Park City and the cave entrance that follows the route of a train service that once

brought visitors to the park. Mammoth also boasts dozens of **hiking trails**, including a number of short jaunts around the visitor center and "frontcountry" along the park's southern fringe. The backcountry features 65 miles (104.6 km) of trail doable by foot or horse, with primitive campsites for those engaged in multiday treks. ∎

MEET THE NEIGHBORS

• **Daniel Boone National Forest:** This green sash across eastern Kentucky embraces more than 600 miles (965.6 km) of hiking, biking, and horse trails, as well as a vast underground world of its own.

• **Land Between the Lakes National Recreation Area:** Wedged between the Kentucky and Cumberland Rivers, this U.S. Forest Service park runs a broad gamut from paddle trails and powerboating to a bison range and a planetarium.

• **Abraham Lincoln Birthplace National Historical Park:** Honest Abe came into the world in a log cabin on this site in 1809.

• **Kentucky Horse Park:** This working thoroughbred spread in Lexington, in bluegrass country, features the Horseracing Hall of Champions, International Museum of the Horse, Rein of Nobility, Show Jumping Hall of Fame, and Breeds Barn Show with horses from around the globe.

Wild Texas Coast

Texas

Stretching along a third of the U.S. Gulf Coast, the Texas shore is a patchwork of lagoons, bays, peninsulas, and barrier islands. Although much of the coast is developed—including cities like Houston, Galveston, and Corpus Christi—sizable portions remain wild and untamed, a vision of what the entire shoreline must have been like in pre-Columbian times. Two of the most significant wilderness areas are protected by Aransas National Wildlife Refuge and Padre Island National Seashore.

ARANSAS NATIONAL WILDLIFE REFUGE

Located on the Blackjack Peninsula and offshore Matagorda Island, Aransas traces its roots to the 1930s when FDR, recognizing its importance as a breeding ground for migratory birds, created the reserve by executive order.

The park's iconic species is the whooping crane, nearly driven to extinction during the first half of the 20th century but now on the road to recovery thanks in large part to

THE BIG PICTURE

Established: Padre Island (1962); Aransas (1937)

Size: Padre Island (130,434 acres/527.8 sq km); Aransas (114,657 acres/464 sq km)

Annual Visitors: Padre Island (650,000); Aransas (80,000)

Visitor Centers: Malaquite; Aransas

Entrance Fees: Padre Island ($10 per vehicle, $5 per person); Aransas ($3 per person)

nps.gov/pais
fws.gov/refuge/Aransas

Aransas. Besides more than 400 bird species, the refuge is also home to alligators, manatees, sea turtles, bobcats, coyotes, white-tailed deer, peccaries, and scores of other species that inhabit its coastal dunes, wetlands, oak woodlands, and sandy prairies.

Severely damaged by Hurricane Harvey in 2018, **Aransas Visitor Center** at the park's northeast entrance has been replaced by a contact station where visitors can collect maps and birding checklists, or check out binoculars and field guides to the animals that dwell in the refuge. The old visitor center parking lot is the place to leave your vehicle and strike off on the **Heron Flats Trail** (1.4 miles/2.25 km) along a coastal lagoon, one of the best places in the park for bird and alligator spotting.

The main park road continues south along the shore of **San Antonio Bay** past a **fishing pier** (it doubles as a lookout for dolphins and rays) and an **oak sanctuary** that attracts a variety of animals. Anchoring the bottom end of the road are a 40-foot (12.19 m)

Bird-watchers look to the skies for whooping cranes along the Intracoastal Waterway.

Purple seaside morning glories line the entrance to the beach and ocean on Padre Island.

Observation Tower that offers the best chance in the park to spot whooping cranes and the popular **Big Tree Trail** (0.7 mile/1.12 km) through some of the largest oaks. The big birds are most common during the cooler period between mid-October and mid-March. The refuge's inland portions are best explored via a one-way **Auto Tour Loop** that starts at the tower.

Offshore is the reserve's **Matagorda Island Unit**, a 38-mile-long (61.2 km) barrier island comprising salt marshes, tidal flats, sandy beaches, and thick brush. Activities include hiking, biking, fishing, camping, and visiting an **1852 lighthouse** at the island's north end. Among the creatures that frequent the island are white-tailed deer,

alligators, and a wide variety of birds including whooping cranes (especially around **Panther Point**). As no private motor vehicles are allowed in the unit, private boat is the only way to access Matagorda.

PADRE ISLAND NATIONAL SEASHORE

The world's single longest barrier isle, Padre stretches 113 miles (181.85 km) from north to south, the Gulf of Mexico on one

---

DID YOU KNOW

• Aransas NWR is a key stop on a Great Texas Coastal Birding Trail that runs all the way along the state's Gulf shore from Port Arthur to Brownsville.

• Padre Island was one of eight remote places on the short list for the first atomic bomb test in 1945; the Trinity Site in New Mexico was the "winner."

• Thanks to Aransas, the nation's whooping crane population has rebounded form just 15 individual birds that wintered at the refuge in 1941 to more than 600 today.

• Padre Island is named for Father José Nicolás Ballí, a Spanish priest who inherited the island from his grandfather and later founded the first European settlement on Padre.

EVENT HORIZON

- **Padre Island Kite Day:** Kites of all shapes and sizes take to the air above Malaquite Beach in February.

- **Barefoot Mardi Gras:** The community of Padre Island just outside the park is the setting for a wild and crazy carnival celebration held before Ash Wednesday.

- **Sea Turtle Festival:** The public can watch or even take part in this July release of baby Kemp's ridley sea turtles at Padre Island's Malaquite Beach.

- **National Wildlife Refuge Week:** Tours, talks, and walks are all part of the fun at Aransas during this annual October event.

- **Christmas Bird Count:** Volunteers comb Aransas NWR in December and January to tally local birds during this popular annual nationwide program.

- **Texas SandFest:** Master sculptors from around the world put their sand-sculpting skills to the test at this annual April competition in Port Aransas.

side and supersalty Laguna Madre on the other. Although it's just a half hour from downtown Corpus Christi, nearly all of the island's north side remains refreshingly undeveloped.

Like other national seashores, the park wears two very different hats: human recreation and environmental conservation. Padre Island supports a wide range of outdoor pursuits, from **beach driving, bicycle riding**, and **water sports** to **birding, fishing**, and an organized **sea turtle release**. At the same time, it strives to protect the fragile coastal ecosystems within its boundaries.

The majority of visitor services (and the only paved roads) cluster near the north end, where the **Malaquite Visitor Center** offers information, exhibits, and a picnic area. Nearby are the park's main campground, the short **Grasslands Nature Trail** through the dunes, and the **Bird Island Basin** boating and windsurfing area.

Visitors with high clearance and four-wheel drive can continue along the **wild beach** south of Malaquite—60 miles (96.56 km) of sand stretching down to **Mansfield Channel**. But there are no facilities of any kind along the way, and drivers should always be on the lookout for shifting tides and soft spots where they can get stuck. Four-wheel-drive vehicles with high clearance are highly recommended. Driving off the beach is forbidden. Primitive camping is allowed along the entire length of the wild beach. ■

Above: Bivalve shells Opposite: Months-old whooping crane siblings in Aransas

Cumberland Island National Seashore
Georgia

THE BIG PICTURE

Established: 1972

Size: 36,415 acres (147.4 sq km)

Annual Visitors: 51,000

Visitor Center: St. Marys

Entrance Fee: $7 per person; $28 round-trip/person ferry

nps.gov/cuis

Georgia's coast is protected by scores of offshore landfalls known collectively as the Sea Islands. Cumberland Island anchors the southern end of the archipelago with one of the nation's premier national seashores, a park that blends incredible coastal nature, a wide range of "unplugged" beach and water activities, and eccentric history.

The largest of Georgia's barrier islands, Cumberland offers a montage of maritime forest, marshes, coastal dunes, and a pristine 16-mile-long (25.75 km) beach that feral horses share with sea turtles and prehistoric-looking horseshoe crabs. Behind the shore, the bygone plantation fields have faded back into a moss-strewn wilderness where alligators and bobcats find a home.

The only way to reach the 56-square-mile (145.04 sq km) island is by private boat, the public ferry from St. Marys on the Georgia mainland, or the Greyfield Inn ferry from Amelia Island in northern Florida. The **Cumberland Island National Seashore Visitor Center** overlooks the riverfront in St. Marys. In addition to exhibits, a bookstore, and information desk, the center is the place to check ferry reservations, make reservations for the **Lands and Legacies van tour**, or check what ranger-led activities are happening on the day of your visit.

Cumberland Island National Seashore Museum is on Osborne Street, two blocks up from the waterfront. The collection spans several thousand years of island history, from the indigenous Timucuan culture through the British colonial and early American plantation/slavery periods, and the arrival of the Carnegies. Opposite the visitor center, **St. Marys Submarine Museum** honors the legacy of the underwater warriors at the U.S. Navy submarine base at nearby Kings Bay.

The **Cumberland Island Ferry** transports camping equipment to the National Seashore but not canoes, kayaks, or pets. Reaching the island's leeward (western) shore, passengers disembark at docks beside the **Sea Camp Ranger Station** or the **Ice House**, which presents a time line of island history, as well as exhibits on the Carnegie family legacy. Just steps away are the ruins of the ghostly **Dungeness mansion**, erected in 1884 by Thomas Carnegie as a family seaside retreat and later destroyed in a 1959 fire.

There are several ways to explore the island, including hiking, biking and the van tour (which takes five to

The ruins of Cumberland Island Mansion

Reddish brown wild horses graze leisurely along the white-sand beaches of Cumberland Island National Seashore.

six hours). **Sea Camp Ranger Station** offers bike rentals.

Many visitors head straight for the island's long, wild **Atlantic strand**. The ocean looks enticing, but there are no lifeguards and rip currents are frequent. Better to walk the shore, a long beachcombing adventure that may include encounters with the wild horses that graze the seagrass behind the sand. **Sea Camp Beach** and **Stafford Bridge** campgrounds are nearly hidden in the woods behind the shore.

Main Road leads north from Sea Camp past the historic **Greyfield Inn** hotel to **Plum Orchard**, a meticulously restored 1898 Carnegie family mansion decked out in stunning furnishings, artwork, and ambience of the island's Edwardian era. Rangers lead 45-minute tours of the mansion.

Perched near the island's north end is the **Settlement,** founded by former slaves in the 1890s. Now a ghost town, the village retains many of its historic structures, including the **First African Baptist Church** where John F. Kennedy, Jr., and Carolyn Bessette were married in 1996.

The island's many hiking trails ramble over the dunes, through the palmetto-studded woodlands, and beside marshes and freshwater ponds flush with wildlife. Among the noteworthy routes are the **Southend Loop** (1.7 miles/2.74 km), the **Roller Coaster Trail** (3 miles/4.8 km), and the long **Parallel Trail** (6.1 miles/9.8 km) down the middle of the island. ▪

LAY YOUR HEAD

Hotels

• **Greyfield Inn:** Carnegie family manse transformed into a romantic inn on Cumberland Island; rates include full board and private ferry transfer from Fernandina Beach, Florida; from $525. *greyfieldinn.com*

• **Riverview Hotel:** Perched on the St. Marys waterfront near the Cumberland Island ferry pier, this historic property has been owned and operated by the Brandon family since the 1920s; restaurant, bar; from $79. *riverviewhotelstmarys.com*

• **Elizabeth Pointe Lodge:** Upscale inn on Amelia Island; 50-minute drive to St. Marys; restaurant, pool, beach; from $249. *elizabethpointelodge.com*

Camping

• Developed campgrounds at Sea Camp and Stafford Beach, ferry access permits required; $12-$22 per night.

• Three wilderness campgrounds at Hickory Hill, Yankee Paradise, and Brickhill Bluff, no restrooms or showers on site; $9 per night.

The sun rises above Cumberland Island.

Wichita Mountains Wildlife Refuge
Oklahoma

THE BIG PICTURE

Established: 1901

Size: 59,020 acres (238.8 sq km)

Annual Visitors: 1.7 million

Visitor Center: Open daily 9 a.m. to 5 p.m.; closed Thanksgiving, Christmas Day, and New Year's Day

Entrance Fee: None

fws.gov/refuge/Wichita_Mountains

With a herd of 650 bison and nearly 400 other species, the Wichita Mountains of south-central Oklahoma are considered one of the nation's best places to view and photograph North American animals in their natural habitat. The refuge's landscapes are also compelling, a mosaic of sheer rock canyons, mixed grass prairie, and lakeside wetlands, as well as oak and cedar forest.

The oldest of the 556 refuges managed by the U.S. Fish and Wildlife Services, Wichita Mountains was established in 1901—six years before Oklahoma became a state. The refuge preserves a pristine slice of the Great Plains, rolling grasslands fringing the only highlands for miles in every direction. Wichita Mountains played a key role in saving the **American bison** from almost certain extinction. The herd traces its roots to 15 animals transferred in 1907 from the New York Zoological Park. The great Comanche chief Quanah Parker was among the enthusiastic crowd that greeted the bison as they arrived by train in the nearby town of Cache and were then shuttled to the reserve in wagons.

The bison are free to roam anywhere they want in the refuge, but are often seen grazing the big meadow on the south side of **Quanah Parker Lake** and the grasslands along Highway 49 through the middle of the park.

Most visitors access the park from the east side via Highway 49, which skirts the south side of 2,464-foot (751 m) **Mount Scott**, the park's second highest peak. A motor road and footpath climb to the summit and its bird's-eye view of the refuge, nearby **Lake Lawtonka**, and the historic town of **Medicine Park**. The 1.5-mile (2.4 km) **Mount Scott Nature Trail** leads from the picnic area at the base of the mountain to **Lake Elmer Thomas Recreation Area**.

Farther along Highway 40, a side road shoots off to a wildlife viewing

A colorful lizard sunbathes in the Wichita Mountains.

Atop the Wichita Mountains, a breathtaking landscape of rock, tree, and water awaits.

tower overlooking **Lake Jed Johnson** and **Holy City of the Wichitas**, a cultural curiosity. Built by the Works Progress Administration during the Great Depression, the "city" comprises 22 stone structures (including a Last Supper banquet hall and Pontius Pilate's throne room) and an outdoor amphitheater, where the nation's longest running passion play takes place each year during the Easter season.

With its natural history exhibits and air-conditioning, the **Visitor Center** offers refuge to those seeking information, maps, or perhaps just a respite from the Oklahoma summer heat. There's also a short film, as well as animal checklists. Among the park's other noteworthy species are elk, deer, prairie dogs, beavers, coyotes, bobcats, and feral Texas longhorn cattle.

From the visitor center, Highway 49 continues westward to side roads and trails that lead into the heart of the Wichita Mountains. About 2 miles (3.2 km) past **Dolores Campground**—the only place where the general public can stay overnight in the refuge—is a turnoff to **Lost Lake,** the woodsy **Boulder Picnic Area**, the aptly named **Narrows** rock climbing area, and the **Dog Run Hollow Trail System** (which includes a 5.7-mile/9.17 km loop to **French Lake**).

Back on the highway, pause at the busy little **prairie dog town** before taking a left turn onto **Indianhoma Road**, which shoots past the refuge headquarters and another popular rock climbing wall. A short side road leads to one of the park's most scenic spots—a rocky overlook for gorgeous **Treasure Lake**. This is also the start of the rugged 2.4-mile (3.86 km) **Charon Gardens Trail**, which leads through a boulder-strewn wilderness area in the heart of the Wichita range. ◼

The Midwest

Lake Kabetogama in the Ash River area of Voyageurs National Park, Minnesota

Isle Royale National Park
Michigan

Floating near the top of Lake Superior, Isle Royale affords a glimpse of what much of the Great Lakes region must have been like in prehistoric times. Although Native American tribes no longer inhabit the national park's thick woods or rocky shores, those ancient hunters, fishermen, and copper miners would still feel right at home on an island the Ojibway called Minong ("good place") because of its natural abundance.

Closer to Canada than to the United States, Isle Royale is one of the more secluded spots in the lower 48 states. The island's boreal forest harbors a wide range of wild things including moose, beaver, otter, and a few remnant gray wolves. While the island is renowned for backpacking and kayak camping, there's also plenty of scope for day hikes, shorter paddles, lake fishing, and wreck diving.

Isle Royale National Park is closed to the public during the winter because of harsh weather and a tempestuous Lake Superior. Between mid-April and the end of October, there are only three ways to reach

THE BIG PICTURE

Established: 1940

Size: 571,790 acres (2,313.9 sq km)

Annual Visitors: 28,000

Visitor Centers: Rock Harbor, Windigo, Houghton

Entrance Fee: $7 per person per day

nps.gov/isro

the island: ferry, seaplane, or private boat.

Passenger-only ferries—no private vehicles are allowed in the park—run from Houghton and Copper Harbor (Michigan) and Grand Portage (Minnesota). The voyage from Houghton to Rock Harbor takes around six hours, from Copper Harbor to Rock Harbor around three hours, and from Grand Portage to Windigo around one and a half hours.

Day boaters don't need a special permit but are required to pay the same entrance fee as everyone else. Boaters staying overnight at campgrounds, docks, or anchorages need to obtain a backcountry permit from the Park Service.

The quickest way to reach the park is flying. **Isle Royale Seaplanes** offers 35-minute flights from Houghton to both Rock Harbor and Windigo.

Perched on an 11-mile (17.7 km) inlet of the same name, **Rock Harbor** is the main port of call and staging point for hiking and paddling trips. In addition to the ferry pier, campground, and store, the waterfront hamlet is home to the **Rock Harbor Visitor Center** with interpretive programs and exhibits on Isle Royale's natural and human history. On the other side of Snug Harbor, **Rock**

A red fox ventures out from the forest of Isle Royale National Park.

The coastal areas of Isle Royale, like Rock Harbor (above), were once submerged beneath prehistoric lake waters.

Harbor Lodge offers canoe, kayak, and motorboat rentals, as well as cruises aboard the **MV *Sandy***.

Hikers can set off on a number of trails in the Rock Harbor area, including the shoreline loop **Scoville Point** (4.2 miles/6.76 km), the walk to **Suzy's Cave** (3.8-mile/6.1 km round-trip), and the longer trek to the top of **Mount Franklin** (10-mile/16.1 km round-trip) with its views across the water to Ontario. Named after Ben Franklin, the summit is one of the landmarks along the 42.5-mile (68.4 km) **Greenstone Ridge Trail**, which runs the entire length of the island to Windigo. Paddlers can make their way from Rock Harbor to the historic **Edisen Fishery**, **Rock Harbor Lighthouse** (built in 1855), little **Raspberry Island,** and the trailhead for short hikes to **Hidden Lake** and **Lookout Louise**.

The island's only other outpost of civilization, **Windigo**, offers docking facilities, campgrounds, cabins, and a visitor center on **Washington Harbor** near the western end of Isle Royale. Several of the area's hikes are ideal for day-trippers including the **Windigo Nature Trail** (1.2 miles/1.9 km) and the 1.8-mile (2.89 km) hike up to **Grace Creek Overlook**. Better still is the 9.4-mile (15.13 km) **Huginnin Cove Loop**, which traverses cedar swamps, beaver ponds, rocky cliffs, and an old copper mining area on its way to the north shore and back. ∎

DID YOU KNOW

• Moose and wolves didn't colonize Isle Royale National Park until the early 20th century; before that, caribou and lynx were the island's most abundant mammals.

• Only the introduction of off-island packs will save Isle Royale's wolves from almost certain extinction because of the limited gene pool.

• Archaeological digs suggest that Native Americans had been mining copper on Isle Royale as early as 1500 B.C.

• Benjamin Franklin allegedly badgered the British into ceding Isle Royale to the Americans after the Revolutionary War because he secretly knew about the island's copper deposits.

• Isle Royale was nearly deforested during the 19th century by miners searching for copper veins, so the island's so-called old-growth forest is little more than a century old.

• The Isle Royal Greenstone found along the island's rocky shores is Michigan's official state gemstone.

Pictured Rocks NLS & Hiawatha NF
Michigan

Secluded by three of the Great Lakes, Michigan's Upper Peninsula has always felt off the beaten track, a vast expanse of woods and water inhabited by a vast array of wild things. Once defined by copper mining, the "U.P." has morphed into a outdoor adventure wonderland centered around scenic gems like Pictured Rocks National Lakeshore and Hiawatha National Forest.

PICTURED ROCKS NLS

Created by ancient oceans and carved by the ice ages, Pictured Rocks National Lakeshore offers a 40-mile (64.37 km) stretch of sandstone cliffs, sandy beaches, and sand dunes set against a backdrop of ponds, streams, and waterfalls.

The name derives from the minerals that stain the coastal cliffs, the orange tones of the Jacobsville Formation, the grayish white of the Munising Formation, and the brownish hues of the Au Train Formation, mixed with blue-green copper and white limonite.

THE BIG PICTURE

Established: Pictured Rocks (1966); Hiawatha (1931)

Size: Pictured Rocks (73,236 acres/296.4 sq km); Hiawatha (894,836 acres/3,621.3 sq km)

Annual Visitors: Pictured Rocks (781,000); Hiawatha (1.5 million)

Visitor Centers: Pictured Rocks (Munising Falls, Grand Sable); Hiawatha (Munising, Rapid River)

Entrance Fees: None

nps.gov/piro
fs.usda.gov/hiawatha

Munising Falls Interpretive Center anchors the park's western end, just steps away from its namesake cascade and a short drive from **Sand Point** on Lake Superior. Hike 5 miles (8.05 km) along the coastal cliffs or drive the forest to **Miners Castle,** the best place to view the park's geological kaleidoscope.

The park's secluded middle sector can be accessed only by foot or unpaved roads. But it's worth the effort, especially the **Chapel Basin**, where a small lake, waterfall, and stone formations betray the area's glacial lineage. **Beaver Basin Wilderness Area** is rife with indigenous wildlife: black bears, bald eagles, beavers, otters, deer, and even the occasional timber wolf.

True to its name, **Twelve Mile Beach** (19.3 km) provides the park's longest stretch for beachcombing. Looming above the beach's east end, **Au Sable Light Station** has been protecting the coast since 1874. The shore gradually rises to the 300-foot-high (91.44 m) **Grand Sable Banks** and its rolling sand dunes.

Backpackers can walk the **Lakeshore–North Country Trail**— part of a 4,600-mile (7,402.9 km)

Come fall, maple leaves cover the forest floor in vibrant yellows and oranges.

A kayak is one of the best means of exploring the intricate arches and formations of Pictured Rocks National Lakeshore.

hiking route between North Dakota and Vermont—along the park's entire shoreline. **Pictured Rocks Kayaking** is one of several Munising-based outfitters that offers guided paddle trips along the park's multi-colored shore.

HIAWATHA NF

Named after the legendary Mohawk chief, Hiawatha National Forest spans the Upper Peninsula on either side of Pictured Rocks. In addition to extensive woodlands and lakes, the forest includes scenic shorelines along three Great Lakes: Superior, Huron, and Michigan.

Hiawatha also embraces offshore treasures like **Grand Island National Recreation Area**. Accessible by ferry from Munising, the island has hiking and biking trails, beachside campsites, historic sites, and its own chromatic cliffs. **Grand Island Ferry Service** offers passage from Munising; bus tours of the island; and bike, kayak, and paddleboard rentals.

Six historic lighthouses are scattered along Hiawatha's shore, including the picture-perfect **Point Iroquois Light Station** (commissioned in 1870) near Sault Ste. Marie. Starting from Point Iroquois, **Whitefish Bay Scenic Byway** leads west along the coast of Lake Superior to wilderness beaches and dramatic viewpoints.

In addition to the three Great Lakes, the national forest offers permit **fishing** on more than 75 smaller lakes and ponds, as well as **canoeing** and **kayaking** along six Wild and Scenic Rivers.

With as much as 200 inches (5.58 m) of snow every year, Hiawatha provides plenty of scope for **winter activities** as varied as ice fishing, ice-skating, dogsledding, and snowshoeing. Snowmobilers and cross-country skiers can explore around 3,000 miles (4,828 km) of snowy roads and trails. ■

MEET THE NEIGHBORS

• **Apostle Islands National Lakeshore:** Wisconsin's northern shoreline features 21 islands and 12 miles (19.31 km) of mainland on Lake Superior.

• **Porcupine Mountains Wilderness State Park:** Hiking, biking, boating, and snow sports are the main activities in Michigan's biggest state park, one of the largest wilderness areas in the Midwest.

• **Seney National Wildlife Refuge:** This migratory bird bastion also boasts hiking and biking trails, mushroom and berry picking, paddle sports, and winter activities.

• **Sault Historic Sites:** Spread across downtown Sault Ste. Marie, this urban history park includes the Museum Ship *Valley Camp* (a 1917 cargo vessel), Water Street Historic Block, and the 210-foot (64 m) Tower of History.

Miners Beach Falls is tucked away in the east end of Lake Superior.

Mackinac Island State Park
Michigan

Long a linchpin for control of the Upper Great Lakes region, Mackinac Island more than made up for its diminutive size with a strategic location second to none. Three nations (France, Great Britain, and the United States) competed for control of the pivotal island in three different wars. Just three years after the founding of Yellowstone, Mackinac became the nation's second national park, although its federal status was short-lived.

Named after a local Native American term for "turtle," Mackinac Island lies in a narrow strait between Michigan's Lower and Upper Peninsulas. French Jesuits established a mission there in 1670, but lost the island to the British during the French and Indian War.

THE BIG PICTURE

Established: 1875 (national park); 1895 (state park)

Size: 1,770 acres (7 sq km)

Annual Visitors: 1 million

Visitor Center: Mackinac Island City

Entrance Fee: $13 per person

mackinacparks.com
mackinacisland.org

The Americans took possession after the American Revolution, but the British snatched it back during the War of 1812.

Mackinac later served as a fur trading post, fishing port, and Victorian-era vacation destination. Its brief stint as a national park coincided with the final years (1875-95) of the U.S. military occupation, when the federal government transferred Fort Mackinac to the state of Michigan. The entire island was named a national historic landmark in 1960.

The island is reached by ferry from **Mackinaw City** on the Lower Peninsula and **St. Ignace** on the Upper Peninsula, historical places in their own right. The ferry rides include views of the **Mackinac Bridge**, one of the world's longest suspension spans. Passengers disembark at **Mackinac Island City.** Don't be shocked by the lack of cars: Walking, cycling, and horses are the only way to get around the motor-vehicle-free island.

Just steps from the ferry pier, **Mackinac Island State Park Visitor Center** is the place to pick up maps and information before striking off to the waterfront or up the hill to **Fort Mackinac.** Built in 1780 by

Fort Mackinac, outfitted with vintage artillery pieces, watches over the state park.

A horse-drawn carriage makes its way through fog and the tree-lined roads of Mackinac Island.

the British as a bulwark against American expansion into the Upper Great Lakes, the stout limestone bastion commands a 150-foot (45.72 m) bluff. Many of the original buildings remain, including the **Officers' Stone Quarters** (built in 1780) and the **Post Hospital** (1828). Guides clad in period uniforms give tours and demonstrations, including cannon firing.

The island's **Historic Downtown** sprawls beneath the bluffs. Horse-drawn carriages add a touch of nostalgia, although the roads are now paved.

Among the scores of historic structures is **Biddle House**, constructed around 1780 and furnished as a family home might have been then, including an open-hearth kitchen where cooking demonstrations are carried out.

Built in 1902 as a private home, the **Governor's House** is now the official summer residence of Michigan's chief executive. Visitors can visit the manse on guided tours. Dedicated to regional art and

EVENT HORIZON

- **Lilac Festival:** Purple reigns supreme over the island during this 10-day June celebration that includes a grand parade, dog and pony show, concerts and culinary events, as well as special land and water tours.

- **W. T. Rabe Stone Skipping Contest:** This annual Fourth of July competition brings together amateur and professional stone skippers from around the world to test their skill on the surface of the Mackinac Strait.

- **Chicago Yacht Club Race to Mackinac:** The world's oldest annual freshwater distance race (founded in 1898) spans 333 miles (535.9 km) of Lake Michigan in mid-July, followed by a porch party at the Grand Hotel. *cycracetomackinac.com*

- **Fudge Festival:** Fudge-infused cocktails, fudge-making demonstrations, sugar-sack races, and Miss Michigan Sugar are all part of the fun at this August celebration of the island's sticky heritage.

culture, the **Mackinac Art Museum** occupies the old Indian Dormitory, built in 1838.

Explore the rest of Mackinac on 70 miles (112.65 km) of vehicle-free roads and trails, including **Michigan Highway 185**, which circumnavigates the island along the shoreline. In addition to an old cedar forest and rock formations sacred to the local Native Americans, the backcountry also boasts the **Wawashkamo Golf Club**, a nine-hole course opened in 1898.

Great Turtle Kayak Trips offers guided kayak tours, paddleboard yoga sessions, and overnight camping paddles to nearby **Bois Blanc Island**. Individual horseback riding and guided trail rides are available at **Cindy's Riding Stable**. Several companies on the island, including

Mackinac Wheels, rent bikes to help you get around.

On the mainland side of Mackinac Strait, **Colonial Michilimackinac State Park** revolves around an historic fort and trading post where costumed interpreters, demonstrations, exhibits, videos, and archaeological digs spin tales of life on the 18th-century Northwest frontier. ∎

LAY YOUR HEAD

• **Grand Hotel:** With its massive white facade, this historic 1887 hotel is truly grand; restaurants, bars, spa, shops, golf, tennis, lawn games, pool, bikes, horseback riding; from $329. *grandhotel.com*

• **Mission Point:** This dog- and kid-friendly resort sprawls across 18 acres of island waterfront; restaurants, bars, spa, cinema, golf, bikes, kayaks, pool, lawn games; from $119. *missionpoint.com*

• **Main Street Inn:** Located on Main Street in the village, this three-story Victorian throwback offers homemade fudge with nightly turndown service; from $105. *mainstreetinnandsuites.com*

• **The Inn at Stonecliffe:** 1904 mansion transformed into a boutique hotel on a secluded spot along the island's western shore; restaurant, bar, pool, bikes, horseback riding; from $154. *theinnatstonecliffe.com*

Above: A historic main street of Mackinac Island Opposite: Saint Ann's Catholic Church sits in the center of Mackinac Island Harbor.

Ha Ha Tonka State Park

Missouri

THE BIG PICTURE

Established: 1978

Size: 3,709 acres (15 sq km)

Annual Visitors: 534,000

Visitor Center: April through October. Open 10 a.m.-5 p.m. daily; November through March not regularly staffed.

Entrance Fee: None

mostateparks.com/park/ ha-ha-tonka-state-park

Wildlife and water, geology and history come together at this central Missouri state park that borders Lake of the Ozarks. Ha Ha Tonka was born as the private estate of Kansas City tycoon Robert Snyder, who built a European-style castle overlooking a deep gorge with a bountiful spring—the "smiling waters" that give both the big house and park their Native American name.

Although the park is renowned for its karst (limestone) topography, the main attraction is **Ha Ha Tonka Castle**, now a ruin. Work on Snyder's dream house began in 1905, but he was killed in an auto accident the following year and never lived to see its completion. Gutted by fire in 1942, all that remains of the castle are the eerie stone walls—the sort of thing Frankenstein tales are born from. Still, the **stone terrace** out back offers panoramic views of the 250-foot-deep (76.2 m) gorge and the twisting Niangua Arm of Lake of the Ozarks.

Just downhill from the Ha Ha Tonka castle, the **Dell Rim Trail** (0.3 mile/.48 km) leads across a wooden boardwalk to the partially restored ruins of the **Water Tower** and an overlook of the 150-foot-deep (45.72 m) **Whispering Dell Sinkhole**, where a cool, moist microclimate nourishes rare plants.

Another trail leads down into an even larger limestone sinkhole, named the **Colosseum** because of its arena-size proportions. A **natural bridge**, which you can walk over or under, leaps the sinkhole. The bridge once served as the dramatic entrée to Snyder's castle. Vehicles are banned from traversing the natural rock structure. Nearby **River Cave**—host to several bat species and the blind grotto salamander—can be explored on ranger-guided tours.

Away from the karst formations, the park is largely wilderness, a vast expanse of old-growth oak woodland protected within the confines of the **Ha Ha Tonka Oak Woodland Natural Area**. Visitors can get a flavor of this backcountry by following the 1-mile (1.6 km) **Acorn Trail** or the 7-mile (11.26 km) **Turkey Pen Hollow Trail**. Home to

The majestic arches and ruins of Ha Ha Tonka castle

The lake at the Schell Osage Conservation Area in the Ozarks reflects a glowing sunset.

more than 500 native plant species, the area also harbors dolomite glades filled with wildflowers, as well as natural habitats for many bird and reptile species.

The best way to access the lower portions of the park is via the 1.5-mile (2.4 km) **Spring Trail**, which drops down 316 wooden steps (200 vertical feet/60.96 m) to the gorge floor and aquamarine **Ha Ha Tonka Spring**. Emerging from a limestone wall, the spring flushes 58 million gallons (219.6 million L) of crystal-clear water each day into the **Trout Glen Pool**. The small lake is a great place to scope out local wildlife: otters, muskrats, turtles, frogs, and dozens of bird species. The trail continues along the southern edge of the pond to the ruins of a pioneer-era **gristmill** including the spillway and old

grinding stone. A small bridge leads over to an **unnamed island** where trails lead to a cave and dolomite boulders.

Beyond the gristmill lies **Lake of the Ozarks,** the massive reservoir created after the Osage River was dammed in 1929. One of the great water recreation hubs of the Midwest, the lake facilities encompass fishing, swimming, wakeboarding, waterskiing, and boating, as well as houseboat vacations. Boat docks on both side of the cove cater to waterborne visitors to the state park. The south dock is also used for casting fishing lines or launching canoes and kayaks. Despite its fishy moniker, angling is actually banned in Trout Glen Pool.

There is no overnight camping in Ha Ha Tonka State Park. But there are numerous lakeshore resorts along

the Niangua Arm (off Highway 5) as well as the **Cottage by the Castle B&B** just west of the park. ■

MEET THE NEIGHBORS

• **Lake of the Ozarks State Park:** Missouri's largest state reserve offers 85 miles (136.79 km) of beautiful shoreline on the eponymous lake (including two swimming beaches) and Ozark Caverns.

• **Mark Twain National Forest:** Adventure opportunities abound in this multiunit federal reserve that includes much of the 350-mile (563.27 km) Ozark Trail system.

• **Ozark National Scenic Riverways:** This paddling paradise protects the wild and scenic Current and Jacks Fork Rivers.

Boundary Waters & Voyageurs
Minnesota

Extending for 200 miles (321.87 km) along the U.S.-Canada border in northern Minnesota, Voyageurs National Park and the adjacent Boundary Waters Canoe Area Wilderness (BWCAW) offer the largest expanse of wilderness in the entire Midwest. Boat is the main way to explore these parks, a mosaic of woods and water that seems little changed from the days when French fur traders, called *voyageurs,* crisscrossed the region in birch-bark canoes.

BOUNDARY WATERS

Part of Superior National Forest, the BWCAW features more than 1,200 miles (1,931.2 km) of boating routes through a vast warren of rivers, streams, and lakes. Those on foot can explore the area via 15 hiking trails. Saved from mining and timber extraction by early 20th-century conservationists, the canoe area provides

THE BIG PICTURE

Established: Boundary Waters (1978); Voyageurs (1975)

Size: Boundary Waters (1 million acres/4,046.9 sq km); Voyageurs (218,200 acres/883 sq km)

Annual Visitors: Boundary Waters (195,000); Voyageurs (237,000)

Visitor Centers: Boundary Waters (Grand Marais, Ely, Crane Lake); Voyageurs (Rainy Lake, Kabetogama Lake, Ash River)

Entrance Fees: Voyageurs (none); Boundary Waters ($16 per person)

nps.gov/voya; fs.usda.gov/superior

a glimpse of what the landscape and daily life were like in bygone days.

The 57-mile (91.7 km) **Gunflint Trail** between **Grand Marais** and **Lake Saganaga** is the eastern gateway to the Boundary Waters, providing access to two dozen official entry points where paddlers can begin. Near the end of the road, **Chik-Wauk Museum and Nature Center** offers insight into the region's human and natural history.

The historic iron mining town in **Ely** is the jumping-off point for the middle and western sectors, as well as home to the **International Wolf Center**, the **North American Bear Center**, and the **Dorothy Molter Museum**, dedicated to a woman who lived alone in the Boundary Waters for 56 years.

Hikers take to the 65-mile (104.6 km) **Border Route Trail** between Swamp River and Mac-Farland Lake, a circuitous route over ridgelines and along watercourses, including **Pigeon River**, which divides Minnesota from Ontario. Farther west, the **Kekekabic Snowbank Loop** expedites 73 miles (117.48 km) of wilderness walking.

Mushrooms grow from a birch stump in Voyageurs National Park.

A man paddles his canoe through Rainy Lake, which runs along 929 miles (1,495 km) of shoreline in Voyageurs National Park.

VOYAGEURS

Named for the 18th-century French trappers who blazed the watery trails through this region, Voyageurs is farther west along the U.S.-Canada frontier. The national park is much more welcoming to motorists than the canoe area. But only just. Forty percent of the park is water, and all of its 200 campsites can be reached only by boat or foot.

Rainy Lake Village anchors the park's west end with waterfront lodges, cabins, stores, boat ramps, and a visitor center. It's also the springboard for boating on **Lake Rainy** and hiking the **Black Bay** or **Anderson Bay** area. During summer, visitors can hop the *Voyageur* for a scenic lake tour or a ranger-led canoe trip. **Rainy Lake Houseboats** rents motorized craft for fishing or exploring the park.

Kabetogama Lake Visitor Center on the south shore offers similar boat and canoe tours, as well as living history walks, campfire talks, stargazing programs, and a weekly boat shuttle to **Locator Lake Trailhead** on the remote **Kabetogama Peninsula**. Although it's strenuous, the peninsula's **Cruiser Lake Trail** (9.5 miles/ 15.28 km) is considered the park's best route for encounters with wolves or moose.

Farther east along Kabetogama Lake, **Ash River Visitor Center** offers ranger-led wildlife viewing in canoes. Hikes in the area range from the easy **Blind Ash Bay Loop** (2.5 miles/4 km) to the multiday **Kab-Ash Trail** (28 miles/48 km).

Rather than hibernate through the winter months, Voyageur relishes the arrival of snow. Hiking paths morph into **cross-country and snowshoe trails**, and the frozen lakes transform into venues for **ice fishing** and **snowmobiling.** Motorists can take a spin (sometimes literally) on the **Rainy Lake Ice Road** (7 miles/11.26 km) around the north side of the peninsula and the **Kab-Ash Ice Road** (9.3 miles/14.97 km) across frozen Kabetogama Lake. ◼

DID YOU KNOW

• Connected by a string of narrow passages, the Namakan Chain of Lakes allows paddlers to move between Boundary Waters and Voyageurs without having to portage or otherwise leave the water.

• A U.S. Customs post at Crane Lake and Canadian Customs post at Sand Point expedite boaters who want to flit back and forth between the two nations (bring your passport).

• The watery wilderness on the Canadian side of the border from Boundary Waters is protected within the confines of Ontario's Quetico Provincial Park.

• Downstream from Boundary Waters, the Pigeon River flows past the Grand Portage—an 8.5-mile (13.68 km) footpath around rapids and waterfalls blazed by 18th-century French trappers. Grand Portage National Monument honors both the voyageurs and the regions' Native American cultures.

❶ Saguenay-St. Lawrence Rivers, Quebec

The confluence of these two great Quebec rivers creates ideal environmental conditions for a wide variety of aquatic life, including a great gathering of whales, seals, and other marine mammals. The best ways to see the critters are by guided boat trips on the St. Lawrence and camping kayak trips down the fjord-like Saguenay.

❷ Thousand Island Paddling Trail, Ontario

Make like the French *voyageurs* of old on this 50-mile (80.47 km) kayak/canoe trail down the St. Lawrence River between Kingston and Brockville, Ontario. Energetic oarsmen can make the voyage in a single day, but it's better to go slow, camping at nine secluded overnight stops in Thousand Islands National Park.

❸ *Maid of the Mist,* New York

Sure it's an overhyped, touristy thing. But the guided boat ride that glides along the bottom of Niagara Falls is also historic, established in 1848 when the mighty cascade was first coming into its own as a global attraction. Cruises are offered daily from late April to early November.

❹ Chattooga River, Georgia and South Carolina

The raging whitewater boundary between Georgia and South Carolina, the Chattooga was the first designated wild and scenic river east of the Mississippi, as well as the waterway where much of the movie *Deliverance* was filmed. Rapids range up to Class IV on a rafting run. *Southern Living* magazine called whitewater rafting "the Number 1 thing every Southerner ought to do."

❺ Namekagon–St. Croix Rivers, Wisconsin and Minnesota

Starting in northern Wisconsin, the Namekagon and St. Croix Rivers offer a slow-motion float trip down to the St. Croix's confluence with the mighty Mississippi on the outskirts of the Minneapolis–St. Paul metropolitan area. Stretching around 200 miles (321.87 km), the national scenic riverway offers numerous places to camp overnight.

THE TOP

10

RIVER TRIPS

By cruise ship or kayak, river journeys offer a novel way to explore many parks

❻ Big Bend, Texas

Everything is huge in Texas including the Rio Grande, which marks the southern boundary of the Big Bend parks and the U.S.-Mexico border. It takes three weeks to raft the entire 231 miles (371.76 km) of the Big Bend River through Santa Elena Canyon and the Great Unknown. And you will encounter plenty of Class III and IV rapids along the way.

A hiker navigates the watery trek through the Narrows in Zion.

❼ Grand Canyon, Arizona

In 1869, John Wesley Powell was the first explorer to make a whitewater trip on the Colorado River through the bottom of the Grand Canyon. Float trips range from three days for a quick dip to 18 days to make the complete 188-mile (302.56 km) journey between Lee's Ferry and Whitmore Wash.

❽ The Narrows, Utah

Proving that you don't need boats to navigate a river, this epic day hike in Zion National Park entails walking *in* the Virgin River as it threads a slot canyon called the Narrows. The trek can be undertaken as a 7.2-mile (11.59 km) return from Zion Canyon or a 16-mile (25.75 km) one-way walk from Chamberlain's Ranch. It's best to hike the Narrows in late spring and summer when water levels are low and temperatures high. Do not hike if there's rain in the forecast—flash floods can occur.

❾ Columbia River, Oregon

A 120-passenger paddle wheeler, *Queen of the West,* plies the Columbia River in Oregon and Washington between April and November on a week-long voyage that includes the spectacular Columbia River Gorge and a side trip to Mount St. Helens National Volcanic Monument.

❿ Tatshenshini-Alsek Rivers, Alaska

Grizzly bears, icebergs, and an ever present feeling that you have reached the end of the earth highlight a float trip down the remote Tatshenshini and Alsek Rivers between the Yukon and the Gulf of Alaska. The full journey takes at least a week and a half.

Mississippi & St. Croix National Rivers
Minnesota & Wisconsin

THE BIG PICTURE

Established: Mississippi NRRA (1988); St. Croix NSR (1968)

Size: Mississippi NRRA (53,775 acres/217.7 sq km); St. Croix NSR (92,738 acres/375.3 sq km)

Annual Visitors: Mississippi NRRA (436,000); St. Croix NSR (772,000)

Visitor Centers: Mississippi NRRA (Science Museum of Minnesota, St. Anthony Falls); St. Croix NSR (St. Croix Falls, Trego)

Entrance Fees: none

nps.gov/miss; nps.gov/sacn

The Minneapolis–St. Paul metropolitan area is blessed with two mighty waterways: the Mississippi River running right through the middle of the urban area and the St. Croix River along the city's eastern edge and its border with Wisconsin. Together the rivers offer more than 300 miles (482.8 km) of nature, history, and outdoor fun.

MISSISSIPPI NATIONAL RIVER AND RECREATION AREA

A 72-mile (115.87 km) stretch of the Mississippi through the middle of the Twin Cities has been transformed from a hardworking industrial river into an outdoor recreational paradise over the past 30 years.

Boating and fishing are the most obvious activities, but the meandering park is also a great place to hike or bike, learn about the past, snowshoe or cross-country ski, or watch the amazing array of birds that dwell along the Mississippi.

Perched on the St. Paul waterfront, the **Science Museum of Minnesota** features an excellent Mississippi River Gallery as well as the main **MNRRA Visitor Center** where visitors can sign up for the popular **Fish with a Ranger** and **Bike with a Ranger** programs. Across the river, **Padelford Riverboats** offers Mississippi tours on authentic replica stern-wheelers.

In Minneapolis, **St. Anthony Falls Visitor Center** overlooks the largest waterfall on the entire 2,320-mile (3,733.68 km) length of the Mississippi. The nearby riverside neighborhoods like the **Mill District, North Loop,** and **Northeast Riverfront** are flush with historic buildings filled with shops, restaurants, nightclubs, and cultural institutions like the **Mill City Museum** and **St. Anthony Main Theatre**.

Minneapolis traces its roots to the 1820s with **Fort Snelling,** which presents living history programs and preserves the slave quarters where Dred Scott and his wife lived prior to the landmark 1857 Supreme Court case that reinforced slavery in the

Among many park treasures, bald eagles perch along the rivers.

Sandstone and forested cliffs along the Dalles border the St. Croix River in Minnesota.

United States. Riverside trails lead to 53-foot-high (16.16 m) **Minnehaha Falls**, which features in Longfellow's "Song of Hiawatha."

ST. CROIX NATIONAL SCENIC RIVERWAY

Born of Wisconsin's north woods, the St. Croix River was named as one of the nation's original eight Wild and Scenic Rivers in 1968. The park includes a lengthy tributary, the **Namekagon.** Together the two rivers provide more than 250 miles (402.3 km) of fishing, paddling, swimming, waterfront camping, and other outdoor adventures.

The **fishing** is nothing short of epic. A combination of clean water and varied aquatic habitats lures anglers with the prospect of catching small-mouth bass, trout, muskellunge (known as muskies), pike, and other game fish. **Hayward** and **Fly Dog** are among the outfitters that offer guided trips.

One of the more popular paddling routes is an easy 6-mile (9.6 km) float down the **Dalles**, a spectacular gorge on the St. Croix between **Interstate State Park** and **Osceola Landing**.

Those who want to get far away from the summer crowds can paddle a 20-mile (32.18 km) stretch of the Namekagon between **Trego Dam** and **McDowell Landing** through a largely road-less area considered one of the best in the park for wildlife viewing.

Hikers can tackle a portion of the 1,200-mile (1,931.2 km) **Ice Age National Scenic Trail** that loops around **St. Croix Falls** on the Wisconsin side or the 12-mile (19.3 km) **St. Croix Trail** along the Minnesota bank. **Governor Knowles State Forest** and **St. Croix State Park** offer hiking, biking, and horseback routes that morph into winter snowmobile and cross-country ski trails.

There's history too. Founded in the 1830s, riverside **Stillwater** was the "Birthplace of Minnesota." The **Warden's House Museum** spins tales from those days. And many of the other historic buildings are now home to cafés, wine bars, antique shops, and art studios. ■

LAY YOUR HEAD

Hotels

• **Nicollet Island Inn:** Built in 1893 as a door factory, the three-story brick structure in Minneapolis is now a romantic boutique hotel; restaurant, spa services; from $179. *nicolletislandinn.com*

• **Hewing Hotel:** Located several blocks from the Minneapolis riverfront, this upscale urban hotel was once a farm machinery warehouse; restaurant, rooftop pool, fitness center; from $251. *hewinghotel.com*

• **Ann Bean Mansion:** Six blocks off the St. Croix River in Stillwater, the opulent home of a 19th-century lumber baron is now a cozy bed-and-breakfast; from $169. *annbeanmansion.com*

Camping

• St. Croix National Scenic Riverway features more than 70 primitive campsites, plus more in the riverside state parks and state forests.

The confluence of the St. Croix and Mississippi Rivers

Missouri National Recreational River

Nebraska & South Dakota

Follow in the wake of intrepid explorers Lewis and Clark, Custer's ill-fated Seventh Cavalry, the fearless Chief Standing Bear, and legendary steamboat captain Grant Marsh along a stretch of America's longest, largely untamed river. Visitors can explore the famed waterway by canoe or kayak, hiking or biking trails, or along scenic highways that meander along both sides of the Big Muddy.

A ribbon of wild water between Fort Randall, South Dakota, and Ponca, Nebraska, the Missouri National Recreational River (MNRR) covers approximately 100 miles (160.9 km) of the Missouri River, plus short stretches of the Niobrara River and Verdigre Creek, both located in north-central Nebraska.

A piping plover soars above the national recreation area.

THE BIG PICTURE

Established: 1978

Size: 69,000 acres (279.2 sq km)

Annual Visitors: 119,000

Visitor Centers: Ponca State Park, Lewis and Clark, Niobrara State Park, Fort Randall Dam

Entrance Fee: None to the MNRR; $4-$6 per vehicle for state parks and recreation areas

nps.gov/mnrr

The park is divided into two sections on either side of Lake Lewis and Clark: **59-Mile District** (94.9 km) in the east and **39-Mile District** (62.7 km) in the west—the only two sections of the Missouri between Montana and its confluence with the Mississippi that have never been dammed or channelized. Several state parks, recreation areas, and wildlife refuges are also found within its boundaries.

From easy half-day float trips to week-long camping expeditions, paddlers have a huge amount of choice when it comes to tackling the **MNRR Water Trail** that runs through the park. Along the way are a dozen campgrounds and 29 canoe/kayak access points, as well as small towns like Niobrara, Springfield, and Yankton.

Before heading downstream, boaters and motorists can learn more about the watery wilds they are about to traverse at the **Fort Randall Dam Visitor Center**, which hosts exhibits on the region's cultural and natural history, early explorers, and paleontology. Below the massive dam are the ruins of **Fort Randall**, a military outpost from 1856 to 1892. Only the base chapel remains standing (barely),

Completed in 1957 by the U.S. Army Corps of Engineers, the Gavins Point Dam is the most downstream dam on the river.

while the old cemetery speaks volumes of those who once lived and died on the American frontier.

Downstream along the south bank is **Karl E. Mundt National Wildlife Refuge**, one of the nation's most important bald eagle habitats, especially during the winter when as many as 300 of the majestic birds come to roost. The north shore is bounded by the **Yankton Sioux Indian Reservation** almost all the way down to **Niobrara**, where Lewis and Clark camped near the junction of the Missouri and Niobrara Rivers.

Niobrara State Park offers waterfront trails and campsites, as well as regional human and natural history exhibits at the **Cramer Interpretive Center**. Named after a great Ponca tribal leader, **Chief Standing Bear Memorial Bridge** is the only road crossing between Fort Randall and Gavins Point. Beyond the bridge, the Missouri flows into **Lake Lewis**

and Clark, a popular boating and fishing venue with marinas, campgrounds, and hiking trails.

Gavins Point Dam offers several waterfront sights, including the **National Fish Hatchery and Aquarium**, where visitors can view many of the marine creatures that inhabit the river, and the U.S. Army Corps of Engineers' **Lewis and Clark Visitor Center**. Perched on the north bank, **Yankton** was the first capital of the Dakota Territory (1861). A replica of the original **Territorial Capitol** building graces the waterfront.

Downstream from Yankton, the Missouri flows past **Bow Creek Recreation Area** (a mix of wetlands, forest, and prairie), lofty **Mulberry Bend Overlook,** and the various hiking and biking trails of **Ponca State Park**, where the riverside woods include a 370-year-old oak tree. ∎

MEET THE NEIGHBORS

• **Lewis and Clark National Historic Trail:** Scenic motor routes flank the Missouri National Recreational River on the north and south. *nps.gov/lecl*

• **Outlaw Trail Scenic Byway:** Route 12 along the south side links Fort Randall, Niobrara, and Ponca with turnoffs to Old Baldy Overlook, the Ponca Tribal Museum, Mulberry Bend, and other landmarks.

• **Native American Scenic Byway** and **Oyate Trail:** A combination that runs parallel to the north shore between Fort Randall and North Sioux City, with possible stops at the Dakota Territorial Museum in Yankton, National Music Museum in Vermillion, and Spirit Mound Historic Prairie along the way.

Cuyahoga Valley National Park
Ohio

Ohio's Cuyahoga River made headlines in the 1960s as one of the nation's most tainted waterways, so polluted that it actually caught fire on occasion. Since then, the Cuyahoga has become a poster child for waterway restoration, a renaissance most evident along the 22 miles (35.4 km) of river between Akron and Cleveland that flow through Cuyahoga Valley National Park.

A mosaic of forest and farmland, the Cuyahoga Valley lies amid what was once the heartland of American industry. Divided by the Ohio & Erie Canal and a coal-carrying railroad—and home to a major industrial dump—the area certainly played its part in the industrial revolution, but not without side effects. It took nearly a

THE BIG PICTURE

Established: 2000

Size: 32,572 acres (132.5 sq km)

Annual Visitors: 2.2 million

Visitor Centers: Boston Store, Canal Exploration Center, Hunt House

Entrance Fee: None

nps.gov/cuva

quarter century (1987-2011) to clean up the toxic mess left behind by various industries. Ironically, both the canal and train are now among the park's major attractions, converted from industrial uses into ways to explore the area via land, rail, and water.

Constructed in the 1820s and 1830s beside the river, the **Ohio & Erie Canal** shuttled freight between the Akron area and the lakeshore for nearly 30 years, until the advent of the railroad made it redundant. Only short portions of the canal remain inside the park—behind **Wilson's Feedmill**, north of the lofty **Route 82 Bridge**, and beside the **Canal Exploration Center** with its interactive maps and games that explore the role of canals in developing the American frontier. However, most of the old **Towpath Trail** is still intact, an 85-mile (136.8 km) recreational trail meant for hiking and biking that runs 20 miles (32.2 km) through the heart of the park.

The tracks that once carried coal trains have found new life as **Cuyahoga Valley Scenic Railroad** (CVSR), a 51-mile (82 km) route between Akron Northside Station and Rockside Station with seven stops inside the national park. In addition to its regular sightseeing

A steam locomotive makes its way through Cuyahoga Valley National Park.

The 65-foot (19.8 m) Brandywine Falls is one of the park's most popular attractions, with a boardwalk viewing area.

service, the train hosts Thomas the Tank Engine family rides, beer- and wine-tasting rides, and a holiday season Polar Express.

Several water bodies in the park—including **Kendall Lake** and **Horseshoe Pond**—are ideal for **canoeing** or **kayaking**. However, the Park Service recommends that only experienced paddlers attempt passage down the rock-strewn Cuyahoga River. **Fishing** is allowed along the entire length of the river inside the park, with the possibility of angling any of the 65 species that have returned to the river since its impressive cleanup.

Besides the towpath, the park boasts numerous other hiking routes, including a lengthy portion of the cross-state **Buckeye Trail**.

LAY YOUR HEAD

Hotels

• **Inn at Brandywine Falls:** Built in 1848, this bucolic B&B overlooks the falls. The Greek Revival house is furnished with Ohio art and antiques; from $149. *innatbrandywinefalls.com*

• **Stanford House:** Historic 1843 farmhouse near Boston Store that offers individual room rentals from May to October; shared bathrooms, full kitchen; from $50. *conservancy forcvnp.org*

• **Silver Fern B&B:** An 1875 home in historic Peninsula village within walking distance of the canal towpath and train station; from $115. *silverfern bnb.com*

Camping

• **Stanford House:** Five primitive campsites available Memorial Day to October 31; $25 per night. *conservancy forcvnp.org*

• **Heritage Farms:** Private camping on the outskirts of Peninsula; from $25 per night. *heritagefarms.com*

Above: A covered bridge along Everett Road Opposite: Ledges Trail (2.2 miles/3.5 km) leads to one of the park's best overlooks.

Other popular walks are the 2.2-mile (3.5 km) loop to **Ledges Overlook** with its views across the valley and the 1.5-mile (2.4 km) loop to **Brandywine Falls**. The park's major equestrian route is the 19-mile (30.58 km) **Valley Trail South** between **Brecksville Reservation** and the 19th-century **Everett Covered Bridge**, the last of its kind in the region.

For those who like to combine hiking and sleuthing, the national park hosts **geocaching** adventures and is part of a **Canalway Questing** network that includes 40 adventures in and around the valley. With more than 250 bird species counted in the park—including numerous wetlands birds and raptors—Cuyahoga is great for **bird-watching** too. It's one of more than 80 stops on the **Lake Erie Birding Trail** that stretches across northern Ohio and 28 islands

of Lake Erie. The park also boasts four **golf courses**.

Cuyahoga stays active throughout winter. Short but sweet, the pistes at the park's **Boston Mills** and **Brandywine** ski resorts offer challenges for

both beginner and veteran skiers and snowboarders; or enjoy the **Polar Blast** snow tubing and snowshoeing along the Towpath Trail, the area around Kendall Lake, and **Oak Hill** on the river's west bank. ∎

DID YOU KNOW

• The Cuyahoga River takes its name from the Native American term *ka-ih-ogh-ha* (crooked), an apt description of the uniquely contorted stream.

• Spanning Furnace Run, the bright-red Everett Covered Bridge is one of the last of 2,000 covered spans that once graced Ohio.

• Cuyahoga Valley Scenic Railroad hosts annual wine- and beer-tasting events called The Grape Escape and Ales on Rails.

• The park's artsy side includes big-name concerts at Blossom Music Center and plays at the outdoor Porthouse Theatre.

• Cuyahoga Valley also administers the David Berger National Memorial in Beachwood, which honors the Cleveland-born weightlifter who was taken hostage and killed during the Munich massacre while competing for Israel at the 1972 Summer Olympics.

Forest Park
Missouri

The "Heart of St. Louis" is what locals call the huge green space on the western side of downtown. And Forest Park beats in many different ways. Among its splendors are art, architecture, animals, world-class museums, and numerous ways to get your cardio workout. Living up to its name, the park also boasts more than 45,000 trees under which to nap, read, or picnic.

THE BIG PICTURE

Established: 1876

Size: 1,300 acres (5.26 sq km)

Annual Visitors: 13 million

Visitor Center: Dennis and Judith Jones Visitor and Education Center

Entrance Fee: None

forestparkforever.org

Of all the various things the 1904 Louisiana Purchase Exposition bestowed on the world, the most endearing (if you don't count the ice cream cone) is Forest Park in St. Louis. The park was actually founded more than a quarter century earlier, But it was the world's fair that endowed Forest with many of its permanent features and much of its cachet as a world-class urban park.

The excellent **St. Louis Zoo** sprouted from a walk-through flight cage that brought exotic birds to the fair. Today the menagerie safeguards more than 16,000 animals spread across six major habitats, including creatures like the echidna, sifaka, and gerenuk that are rarely seen in zoos. Behind-the-scenes animal care and "geek" tours provide a glimpse of everyday zookeeper life, while a carousel, miniature railroad, and interactive children's zoo appeal to younger visitors.

On the park's north side, the **St. Louis Art Museum** occupies the Palace of Fine Art, a neoclassical structure inspired by the ancient Baths of Caracalla in Rome. The museum covers a wide range of historical epochs and every corner of the globe. Among its highlights are the South Pacific and Mesoamerican collections, European Impressionists, and 20th-century German art.

The park's **Museum of Missouri History** (built with world's fair profits) features a permanent exhibit, Looking Back at Looking Forward, about the 1904 expo and the Summer Olympic Games that took place in Forest Park that same year. Newest of the park's trio of great museums is the **St. Louis Science Center** boasting animatronic dinosaurs, amazing science demonstrations, and a hyperboloid-shaped planetarium.

Given its Olympic heritage, Forest Park is also well endowed with sports facilities including two **golf courses**, three **tennis centers**, an **archery range**, winter **ice-skating rink**, and numerous **ball fields**. Paddleboats and stand-up paddleboards can be rented along the shore of **Post-Dispatch Lake**, surrounded by recently restored natural grasslands and wetlands that provide a habitat for birds

A statue of King Louis IX of France, namesake of St. Louis

The white marble Nathan Frank Memorial Bandstand, dedicated in 1925, sits in the center of Pagoda Lake.

and other creatures. A stream connects the lake with other water features like **Lake Eisenhower** and the **Grand Basin**, another relic of the 1904 world's fair.

A **dual recreational path** for walking, biking, and jogging circumnavigates the entire park. However, the best hikes for nature lovers are in the 60-acre (.24 sq km) **Kennedy Forest**, the 24-acre (.097 sq km) **Deer Lake Savanna**, and the wetlands **Prairie Complex**, where minks, martens, turtles, and a wide array of birds can be spotted.

A wondrous art deco greenhouse, the **Jewel Box**, looks just as astonishingly modern today as when it opened in 1936. The adjacent amphitheater, the **Muny**, stages nine weeks of musical theater during the summer under the adept direction of the Municipal Theatre of St. Louis.

The park's other alfresco performance space is **Art Hill**, a venue for outdoor concerts and films (and picnics with a view).

Based at the **Dennis and Judith Jones Visitor and Education Center** beside the history museum, **Forest Park Forever conservancy** offers free public nature classes, bird-watching programs, and **Heart of the Park walking tours** on a variety of topics. ■

MEET THE NEIGHBORS

• **Gateway Arch National Park:** The 630-foot (192 m) Gateway Arch anchors a riverside park that also includes the Old Courthouse and the Museum of Western Expansion.

• **Ulysses S. Grant National Historic Site:** Before his time as general and president, Grant and his family farmed this bucolic property 10 miles (16 km) from downtown St. Louis. Five historic buildings illuminate his life and times.

• **Missouri Botanical Garden:** Little more than 1 mile (1.6 km) south of Forest Park, the 79-acre (.32 sq km) floral oasis, founded in 1859, is the nation's oldest botanical garden in continuous operation.

• **Columbia Bottom Conservation Area:** Set at the confluence of the Mississippi and Missouri Rivers, this state park features hiking and biking trails through forested areas, around wetland ponds, and along the two great rivers.

Chicago's Lakeside Parks
Illinois

The wetlands that once bordered Lake Michigan may have been replaced by skyscrapers, but Chicago still boasts a green facade, a string of waterfront parks that rambles for more than 20 miles (32.18 km) down the coast of the Windy City. Named after American presidents, the three main parks offer various ways and means to pass the time, from fine art and exotic animals to outdoor concerts and an array of winter sports.

GRANT PARK

In the 1830s, Chicago's founding fathers had the foresight to set aside a large tract of lakeside land as a "public space forever to remain vacant of buildings." Debris from the Great Chicago Fire of 1872 was used as landfill to expand the park into Lake Michigan. Another huge change came on the cusp of the 21st century, when the park's north end was reimagined into a radically modern green space.

Buckingham Fountain lies at the very heart of the park. Unveiled in 1927, the colossal fountain (one of the world's largest) spouts water and colored lights on evenings between May and October. The gurgling waters are flanked by formal gardens with outdoor cafés and paths leading to the **Petrillo Music Shell**, the epicenter for big events like the annual **Lollapalooza** music fest.

The massive structure rising just west of the band shell is the **Art Institute of Chicago**. One of the world's premier art museums, it holds all-time classics like Grant Wood's "American Gothic" and the Post-Impressionist masterpiece "A Sunday on La Grande Jatte—1884" by Georges Seurat.

Grant Park's other epic collections are located on a sprawling **Museum Campus** that protrudes into Lake Michigan. A giant of research and scientific discovery for more than a century, the massive **Field Museum** is renowned for its dinosaurs, ancient Egyptian artifacts, and priceless gem collection. More than 32,000 creatures inhabit the cutting-edge **Shedd Aquarium**, which features Amazon and Caribbean habitats, as well as beluga whales, dolphins, sharks, and penguins. **Adler Planetarium** crowns the nearby waterfront, celebrated for both its outer space shows and drop-dead gorgeous views of the Chicago skyline.

The permanent art installation "Agora" by Magdalena Abakanowicz

Sailors guide their boat along Lake Michigan, with the downtown Chicago skyline and beachfront in full view.

Soldier Field—called Grant Park Stadium when it opened in 1924—anchors the park's southern end. Home of the Chicago Bears football team, the stadium is also the city's largest concert venue and stages a number of headline acts every summer.

Chicago ushered in the 21st century by morphing a mishmash of railroad tracks, parking lots, and scruffy open space into the well-manicured **Millennium Park**, a place where art and architecture complement the lush vegetation. Anish Kapoor's stainless steel "**Cloud Gate**," which resembles a giant floating silver bean, is *the* place to snap selfies in Chicago. The elegant **Jay Pritzker Pavilion** (designed by Frank Gehry) hosts the Grant Park Music Festival, the Grant Park Symphony Orchestra, and other performing arts events. The granite-and-glass **Crown Fountain** presents a modern-

istic foil to the Buckingham, while the schizophrenic **Lurie Garden** displays two entirely different takes on urban horticulture—shade-loving and full-sun plants.

Like a giant silver anaconda, **BP Pedestrian Bridge** snakes its way across Columbus Drive to the park's

latest innovation: **Maggie Daley Park**. This cutting-edge urban playground features rock-climbing walls, tennis courts, a children's **Play Garden** with six different environments, and a sinuous, quarter-mile (0.4 km) **Skating Ribbon** that converts to ice in winter.

LAY YOUR HEAD

Hotels

• **Chicago Athletic Association:** Recently restored to its 1890s grandeur, this chic hotel in Grant Park features Chicago music and sports history; restaurants, bars, fitness facilities, pet friendly, free loaner bikes; from $169; *chicago athletichotel.com*

• **Hotel Lincoln:** Across from Jackson Park, this historic boutique

hotel lies within easy walking distance of the zoo, museums, and beaches; restaurant, bar, rooftop yoga, free loaner bikes, pet friendly; from $109. *jdvhotels.com*

• **W ChicagoLakeshore:** Hip highrise hangout near Navy Pier, Ohio Street Beach, and the Lakeshore Trail; restaurant, bar, spa, gym, pet friendly; from $159. *wchicago-lake shore.com*

Buckingham Fountain illuminated against downtown Chicago

Japanese Island was originally a feature of the 1893 Columbian Exposition.

LINCOLN PARK

Stretching 18 miles (28.9 km) down the Chicago shoreline, **Lakefront Trail** connects Grant Park with the city's other great waterfront green spaces. The multiuse path facilitates walking, jogging, skating, and biking. **Divvy Bike** rental stations are located at a number of spots along the trail.

Heading north from Grant Park, the trail curls around a mesmerizing forest of skyscrapers to **Navy Pier**. Opened in 1916, the 3,300-foot-long (1,005.8 m) quay once served as a Great Lakes training facility for the U.S. Navy. Now it's more like a theme park that includes carnival rides, indoor ice-skating, lake cruises, and lakeside green spaces like **Milton Lee Olive Park**. Among its other permanent tenants are the **Chicago Children's Museum** and **Chicago Shakespeare Company**.

Two miles (3.2 km) farther north along the shoreline trail is **Lincoln Park**, which started life as a cluster of cemeteries. Most of the graves were relocated and the waterfront land was converted into a public park in the 1860s and named after the recently assassinated president. Its biggest draw is the free **Lincoln Park Zoo**, one of the oldest in the Western Hemisphere and home to more than 1,100 animals. Many of the zoo's older exhibits have been replaced in recent years by much more spacious

Other landmarks and cultural institutions are on **Michigan Avenue**, along the park's western edge. Lodged inside a gorgeous Beaux Arts building, the **Chicago Cultural Center** presents a year-round slate of free exhibitions and performances. Opened in 1890, the **Chicago Athletic Association** was a cradle of college football as well as a hotbed of American jazz and blues with Duke Ellington and Muddy Waters, among many others. Down the street, the **Chicago Symphony Center** offers a much different sort of music. Get more kicks at the corner of Adams and Michigan, where a sign marks the official start of **Historic Route 66.**

EVENT HORIZON

- **Craft Brews at the Zoo:** Wild beasts and wicked beers in Lincoln Park; mid-June. *lpzoo.org/craft-brews*

- **Taste of Chicago:** The world's largest food festival consumes Grant Park in early July.

- **Lollapalooza:** The huge alternative music fest has been permanently based in Grant Park since 2005; early August. *lollapalooza.com*

- **Chicago Air and Water Show:** Blue Angels and other aerial acrobatics soar over North Street Beach in mid-August.

- **Chicago Jazz Festival:** Four days of free performances in Millennial Park punctuate the end of the Windy City summer. *jazzinchicago.org/jazzfest*

modern habitats like the indoor/outdoor **Regenstein African Journey**.

The park's wildlife theme continues at the **Peggy Notebaert Nature Museum**, a family-friendly collection that features a living butterfly house with more than 40 species of the fluttery creatures, an indoor Wilderness Walk through three habitats once found along Chicago's lakeshore (prairie, savanna, and dune), and several outdoor nature trails along **North Pond**. The nearby **Lincoln Park Conservatory** is the municipal botanical garden, and the **Chicago History Museum** spins tales of the Windy City.

A huge advantage that Lincoln has over Grant Park is water access. The longest stretch of sand in the city of Chicago, **North Avenue Beach** simmers during the summer with beach volleyball, sandcastle construction, and swimming in Lake Michigan. **Chicago Sailboat Charters** at Belmont Harbor offers sailboat and motorboat rentals between late spring and early fall.

JACKSON PARK

South from Grant Park, the Lakeshore Trail meanders 6 miles (9.6 km) along the waterfront to sprawling **Jackson Park**. Landscape architects Frederick Law Olmsted and Calvert Vaux—already renowned for designing New York's Central Park—proposed a water-centric park with lagoons, bridges, and bathing areas. It took more than 20 years for their plan to become a reality as the template for the **World's Columbian Exposition of 1893.**

Many of the water features created for the world's fair linger, including the two **lagoons** with their waterfront trails and a restored habitat, **Bobolink Meadow**, that comes as close to anything else in Chicago

• **Park Grill:** Modern American cuisine and international favorites beneath the Cloud Gate in Millennium Park. *parkgrillchicago.com*

• **Buck's Four Star Grill:** Casual burgers, beer, and other bites near Buckingham Fountain. *bucks fourstargrill.com*

• **Kim and Carlo's Chicago Style Hot Dogs:** One of the last traditional hot dog carts is permanently parked between the Field Museum and Shedd Aquarium.

• **Castaways Bar and Grill:** Salads and sandwiches on the top deck of a ship moored at North Street Beach. *castawayschicago.com*

• **North Pond:** Gourmet farm-to-table fare in a classic Arts and Crafts structure in Lincoln Park. *northpondrestaurant.com*

to showing what the lakeshore must have been like before European settlement. The **Garden of the Phoenix** on Wooded Island is another holdover from 1893, a lovely Japanese garden with a koi pond, meditation pavilions, and the recently added "Skylanding" sculpture by Yoko Ono.

The only building remaining from the 1893 fair is the Palace of Fine Arts, home now to the **Museum of Science and Industry** overlooking the Columbia Basin. Another structure will soon rise on the other side of the basin, the **Barack Obama Presidential Center**. Scheduled to open in 2021, the three-building complex will house the 44th president's official library and museum.

The 18-hole **Jackson Park Golf Course** (opened in 1900) had the first municipal links in the Midwest. The park also offers several places to dip your toes into chilly Lake Michigan, including **63rd Street Beach** with its historic bathing pavilion. ▪

Auburn leaves line the lawns and sidewalks of Grant Park.

The Rocky Mountains

Dream Lake reflects the sunrise and peaks of Rocky Mountain National Park.

Yellowstone & Grand Teton National Parks
Wyoming

The mountains aren't as high as those in Colorado, and the rivers are not as wide as those in Montana and Idaho, but the highlands of western Wyoming may be the most spectacular part of the entire Rockies. Yellowstone and Grand Teton, neighboring national parks, typify the reasons why people decided to preserve, rather than pave, Mother Nature's enduring treasures.

THE BIG PICTURE

Established: Yellowstone (1872); Grand Teton (1929)

Size: Yellowstone (2.2 million acres/8,903 sq km); Grand Teton (310,000 acres/1,254.5 sq km)

Annual Visitors: Yellowstone (4.1 million); Grand Teton (3.3 million)

Visitor Centers: Yellowstone (Mammoth, Canyon, Fishing Bridge, Grant Village, Old Faithful); Grand Teton (Colter Bay, Jenny Lake, Craig Thomas, Rockefeller Preserve)

Entrance Fees: $30 per vehicle, $15 per person

nps.gov/yell; nps.gov/grte

Rarely do two parks complement each other so well. Yellowstone has the wildlife, the massive canyon, the simmering volcanic underbelly. Grand Teton boasts spectacular snowcapped peaks, their profile reflected in fjord-like lakes and a slowly flowing river. No matter what the season, the parks present an amazing array of sights, smells, sounds, and outdoor activities relished by more than seven million combined visitors each year.

YELLOWSTONE

If ever a park had a flair for the dramatic it's Yellowstone—geysers, grizzlies, and its very own grand canyon, as well as trendy towns and backcountry trails that rarely see human bootprints. After all these years, the world's very first national park is still one of its most imposing, a blend of land and water, forest and field, wildlife and geothermal features that often seem to be living things.

It seems remarkable in hindsight that someone recognized the uniqueness of Yellowstone—and suggested that steps be taken at once to preserve such an incredible landscape—at the very time that America was realizing its Manifest Destiny by "conquering" much of the West.

A golden spike had finished the first transcontinental railroad just three years earlier, and the Little Big Horn was still four years in the future when Ulysses S. Grant created Yellowstone National Park with the flourish of his pen in March 1872. The president was acting at the request of geologist Ferdinand V. Hayden, who had surveyed the region the previous summer. The genius of his expedition was

"Blondie," a blond grizzly bear, grazes in a field of wildflowers in Grand Teton.

Arresting views of the Teton range and curving river valley can be seen from the Snake River Overlook.

including a photographer and landscape painter who rendered images of the Yellowstone country to show those in Washington exactly what needed saving.

When we look at those early photos and paintings today, it's as if nothing has changed in the century and a half since Yellowstone was established. And that's the enduring appeal of the park: a large, unspoiled canvas of the American West. In the words of Hayden, "remarkable curiosities which have required all the cunning skill of nature thousands of years to prepare."

Tucked up on the northwest corner of Wyoming with parts spilling over into Montana and Idaho, the massive park offers five different approaches that feed into the **Grand Loop Road**, a figure-eight highway

in the middle of the park. Rather than a single focus, Yellowstone has five main hubs—Old Faithful, Grant Village, Lake Village, Canyon Village, and Mammoth Hot Springs—each of them linked to a unique geological or geographical phenomenon.

The most impressive entry is from **Gardiner**, Montana, in the northwest, a road that ducks beneath the famous **Roosevelt Arch** and meanders along the Gardiner River to **Mammoth Hot Springs** and the park headquarters. **Albright Visitor Center** is located in the historic bachelor officers' quarters of old **Fort Yellowstone**, where the U.S. Cavalry kept watch over the park before the National Park Service was born. That sulfur smell that permeates the air is from the hot springs, a cluster of limestone **travertine terraces** that cascade down a hillside like a steaming waterfall.

From Mammoth, the Great Loop Road shoots due east to the **Tower-Roosevelt** area and the broad **Lamar Valley**, the best place in Yellowstone to get a glimpse of the wolves that were reintroduced to Yellowstone in 1995. Bison and elk also frequent the valley with its lush grasslands. Veering in a southward direction, the road runs past 132-foot (40.23 m) **Tower Fall** and the start of the **Mount Washburn Trail** (6.2-mile/9.9 km round-trip) to the summit of a 10,243-foot (3,122 m) peak with a **fire lookout tower** that provides a spectacular view over just about all of Yellowstone.

As the name implies, **Canyon Village** lies on the edge of the park's biggest "ditch"—the gaping **Grand Canyon of the Yellowstone**—an immense multicolored trench that stretches 24 miles (38.6 km) and rises as much as 1,200 feet (365.7 m)

Above: A white wolf surveys Yellowstone. Opposite: Old Faithful Geyser erupts.

above the **Yellowstone River**. Trails lead to outstanding viewpoints like Artist's Point on the south rim and Lookout Point on the north rim, two of the best places to snap selfies with 308-foot (93.8 m) **Lower Yellowstone Falls** as a backdrop. **Canyon Visitor Education Center** in the village revolves around the park's geology and the supervolcano that underlies Yellowstone.

Continuing the clockwise journey around the Grand Loop, the road climbs up the river valley to **Yellowstone Lake**. The largest high-altitude lake in North America, the sky-blue pool offers the park's best opportunities for boating, fishing, and waterfront camping. Given the lake's chilly water, even during the height of summer, swimming is discouraged and often dangerous. **Bridge Bay Marina** offers rental boats, guided fishing charters, and scenic lake cruises, as well as shuttle services to remote campsites along the 141-mile (226.9 m) lakeshore.

Perched on the lake's **West Thumb**, busy little **Grant Village** lies at the junction of the Loop Road and the highway running up

from the South Entrance and Grand Teton. In addition to another visitor center, the village hosts several

DID YOU KNOW

- Ranger-led activities, including guided snowshoe walks, continue through the colder months at Mammoth, Old Faithful, and West Yellowstone.

- Cross-country ski trails are located at six places within Yellowstone and three spots in Grand Teton.

- Jackson Hole Mountain Resort on the south side of Grand Teton offers downhill skiing and snowboarding.

- Guided snowmobile and snowcoach tours are allowed on Yellowstone roadways during the winter "snowover" months when they are closed to motorized traffic.

- Yellowstone Forever offers unique cold season programs like Wolves in Winter and a winter landscape photography field seminar.

stores, a gas station, a boat ramp, and an amphitheater with summer ranger programs.

Turning to the west, the Grand Loop cuts across the **Continental Divide** (and into the Pacific drainage) at two different points before cruising downhill into **Old Faithful Village** and the park's largest cluster of visitor services. Opened in 1904, **Old Faithful Inn** is a masterpiece of national park rustic architecture, in particular the lobby with its massive yet cozy stone fireplace and soaring timber ceiling.

The main event is just outside: **Old Faithful Geyser**, which erupts around 17 times per day to an average height of 130 feet (39.6 m). Visitors can learn more about the geothermal forces at the **Old Faithful Visitor Education Center** and then hike the **Upper Geyser Basin**

along the **Firehole River**, home to around 60 percent of the world's geysers. Curving around to the west, the road continues to other geothermal wonders like the **Midway Geyser Basin** and its **Grand Prismatic Spring** and the **Lower Geyser Basin** with its **Fountain Paint Pot.**

Madison features an information station and bookstore at the junction where the highway from **West Yellowstone** in Idaho joins up with the main park road. The Grand Loop continues to the **Norris Geyser Basin**, where geological wonders like **Artist Paintpots, Roaring Mountain,** and **Steamboat Geyser** are complemented by the indoor exhibits of the **Museum of the National Park Ranger** and **Norris Geyser Basin Museum** with its distinctive 1920s "parkitecture." Visitors can also explore the eerie

Norris-Canyon Blowdown with its ghost trees or fly-fish for trout in the swift-flowing **Gibson River**.

GRAND TETON

Without much warning, the Grand Tetons rise 7,000 feet (2,133 m) almost straight up from the Jackson Hole Valley—serrated granite peaks so perfectly proportioned they seem born from the mind's eye of a landscape artist rather than Mother Nature. Named by French-speaking trappers who ventured through the region in the early 19th century, they are the youngest mountains in the Rockies and certainly the most handsome, their gorgeous facades mirrored in six lakes and sinuous Snake River along their eastern edge.

The Hayden Expedition of the early 1870s that brought Yellowstone

Technicolor teal and yellows make up the Morning Glory Pool at Yellowstone.

into the limelight also illuminated the Grand Teton through innovative photography and landscape paintings. But with settlement already underway in Jackson Hole, it would take more than a half century—and the substantial wealth of the Rockefeller family—to exert enough pressure on government officials and purchase enough private lands for the national park to become a reality.

U.S. Highway 89 runs the length of the park between the funky town of **Jackson Hole, Wyoming,** and Yellowstone's southernmost entrance. Along the way are numerous pull-outs with views of the peaks beyond the Snake River and Jackson Lake. **Craig Thomas Discovery and Visitor Center** near Moose Junction provides a great overview of the area's natural forces and human history with a high-definition movie about the park, various ranger-led activities, and the excellent **Vernon Collection** of local Native American artifacts.

This southeastern corner of the park boasts some of the best wildlife. Beaver, otters, and moose are a few of the creatures found around **Schwabacher's Landing** on the Snake River; bison, antelope, and elk are some of the animals that frequent the sagebrush-covered area on the north side of the **Gros Ventre River**. There are also historical relics, like the photogenic **Mormon Barns** and the log-cabin-style **Chapel of the Transfiguration** in the **Menors Ferry Historic District**.

A dozen outfitters offer scenic float trips down the **Snake River,** including **Barker-Ewing** and **Solitude**. Guided fishing trips are available through **Snake River Angler**.

On the western side of the river, **Teton Park Road** and the adjacent **biking/hiking path** meanders

The sun sets over the mountains at Antelope Flats in Grand Teton.

through the heart of the park to divine **Jenny Lake** and its visitor center. **Jenny Lake Shuttle** provides scenic cruises and water taxi service to the western shore for short hikes to **Hidden Falls** or **Inspiration Point** or challenging ascents of the park's highest peak: 13,770-foot (4,197.1 m) **Grand Teton**. Jenny Lake is also a springboard for day hikes to **Paintbrush Canyon** and secluded **Leigh Lake**.

Farther north, **Jackson Lake** offers paddle sports, sailing, waterskiing, and windsurfing. Boat rentals, scenic cruises, and guided fishing trips are available at **Colter Bay Marina**. Landlubbers can trek the **Hermitage Point Trail** (9 miles/ 14.5 km) from the marina to a secluded stretch of lakeshore.

Grand Teton's mountainous western half is roadless and best explored on foot along more than 230 miles (370.2 km) of trails with varying degrees of difficulty. A stroll through the lake district along the **Lupine Meadows Trail** and **Taggart Lake Trail** (7 miles/11.26 km one way) is relatively flat and easy and affords amazing views. Put some oomph into the hike with steep-ascent side trips to **Amphitheater Lake** or **Garnet Canyon**.

Snatch a glimpse of the back (western) side of the Teton Range on two of the park's most challenging hikes: the trail up **Granite Canyon** to **Marion Lake** (18.5-mile/29.7 km return) and up **Death Canyon** to the **Static Peak Divide** (16.3-mile/ 26.2 km return). ■

Glacier & Waterton Lakes National Parks
Montana & Alberta, Canada

THE BIG PICTURE

Established: Glacier (1910); Waterton Lakes (1895)

Size: Glacier (1,013,322 acres/4,100.7 sq km); Waterton Lakes (247.10 acres/505 sq km)

Annual Visitors: Glacier (3.3 million); Waterton Lakes (536,000)

Visitor Centers: Glacier (Apgar, St. Mary, Logan Pass); Waterton Lakes (Waterton Village)

Entrance Fees: Glacier ($30 per vehicle, $15 per person); Waterton Lakes (C$7.80 per person)

nps.gov/glac; pc.gc.ca/pn-np/ab/waterton

"Crown of the Continent" is an apt nickname for this pair of parks, which feature some of the most impressive mountain scenery in North America. Joined together since 1932 as the world's first international peace park, Glacier National Park in Montana and Watertown Lakes National Park in Alberta offer a contiguous high-country wonderland of rock, ice, water, and wood.

GLACIER

This beloved park in northwestern Montana takes its name from its many glaciers *and* the glacial forces that shaped its rugged topography over two million years. While the park is still home to more than a dozen glaciers, even more impressive are the massive U-shaped valleys and hulking granite peaks carved by long-ago ice flows.

Nobody leaves the park without driving at least a section of **Going-to-the-Sun Road**. Constructed during the Great Depression by Civilian Conservation Corps workers, the 50-mile (80.5 km) route could easily double as a roller-coaster ride up and over the Continental Divide. Whether you start from Lake McDonald in the west or Lake St. Mary in the east, your hands will surely be sweaty by the time you finish.

Among the many landmarks along Going-to-the-Sun are **Avalanche Creek** with its ancient hemlock-cedar forest, a wicked switchback called the **Loop**, a roadside **Weeping Wall**, and the overlook for big **Jackson Glacier**. The Continental Divide splits the road at the 6,646-foot-high (2,025.7 m) **Logan Pass**, where a visitor center and bookstore provide shelter from the chilly highland weather. Moun-

A juvenile cougar, known as a territorial hunting species, looks out from the brush.

A short but challenging Glacier Park day hike ends with views of Hidden Lake and of mountains in the distance.

tain goats, bighorn sheep, and marmots inhabit the rocky slopes around Logan Pass, which is also a hub for several great hikes, including the family-friendly **Animal Super Heroes Trail** and the 1.5-mile (2.4 km) nature trail to **Hidden Lake**. The other great place to hike along the road is the western end of Lake St. Mary, where trails lead to **three splendid waterfalls**.

Apgar Village anchors the western end of road with its lakeside hotels, restaurants, shops, and visitor center. During summer, scenic cruises are offered along **Lake McDonald**; kayaks, canoes, rowboats, and paddleboats are also available for rent. **Camas Road** heads north from the village to lakeshore access at **Rocky Point** and a bridge over the **North Fork Flathead River**

that provides a great perch for snapping scenic shots of the front range. A rough gravel road continues into the park's rarely visited **North Fork Area** and supersecluded camping spots beside **Kintla Lake** and **Bowman Lake**.

Highway 2 loops around the south end of Glacier, flitting in and out between the park and two national forests (Flathead and Lewis

CHOW DOWN

• **Eddie's Café:** Buffalo meatloaf and huckleberry cobbler are a few of the locally flavored dishes at this lakeside favorite in Apgar Village—only open May–October.

• **Mountain Bar:** Microbrews and burgers top the menu at this hangout at St. Mary Lodge (June–September).

• **Royal Stewart Dining Room:** Braised bison stew and pineapple red curry count among the house specials at this elegant eatery in Waterton's Prince of Wales Hotel, open from May–September.

• **Tupelo Grille:** Soulful Cajun and other Southern dishes are served in

cozy surroundings on the main drag in Whitefish.

• **The Huckleberry Patch:** Fresh-from-the-oven pies and other treats, including jam, honey, and fudge, are on the menu in Hungry Horse village near West Glacier.

and Clark). About halfway along is **Goat Lick Overlook**, where you can gaze across the valley at a lofty railroad trellis and possibly spot Rocky Mountain goats clinging to the cliffs.

Glacier's east side is bounded by the **Blackfeet Nation** and reservation towns like **East Glacier** that cater to park visitors. Just outside East Glacier is a spectacular but lesser-known part of the park: **Two Medicine**, where the Blackfeet once undertook sacred rites of passage. Trails meander around three lakes and along a creek to **Running Eagle**

Falls, which gushes through a giant stone orifice.

St. Mary lies at the eastern end of Going-to-the-Sun Road. In addition to a lodge, cabins, and several eateries, the hamlet offers another national park visitor center. Just beyond the park entrance, a large grassy area, **Two Dog Flats**, is a great place to look for bear or elk. Ninety-minute boat tours of **St. Mary Lake** depart from a floating dock at **Rising Sun Campground**.

Another elongated valley, **Many Glaciers**, tenders some of the park's most popular hikes, including a

5.5-mile (8.8 km) trail to the base of **Grinnell Glacier**, a strenuous climb up to **Swiftcurrent Pass** (6.6 miles/10.6 km), and a relatively easy jaunt to **Ptarmigan Falls** (2.5 miles/4 km). Scenic boat tours of **Swiftcurrent Lake** and **Lake Josephine** include a quarter-mile (0.4 km) hike between the two water bodies. Kayaks, canoes, and rowboats are available for rent.

Two private companies run motorized tours inside the park. The legendary **Red Bus Tours** operates in vintage, oak-framed vehicles from the 1930s, and the Blackfeet-owned and -operated **Sun Tours** interprets the park from an authentic Native American perspective.

Visitors should always be aware that Glacier is bear country—bruins of both the black and grizzly variety. Bear spray is essential, even on short walks. As one Glacier ranger explains, "A grizzly doesn't care if you're walking 10 yards or 10 miles."

The national park is mostly shuttered in winter. But nearby **Whitefish**, Montana, is a hub of cold weather sports with a ski and snowboard resort ranked in the U.S. top 10 by *Ski Magazine*. Among other winter activities in and around Whitefish are horse-drawn sleigh rides, snowmobiling, Nordic skiing, dogsledding, fat biking on snowy trails, and ice climbing. **Glacier Adventure Guides** in Whitefish offers guided snowshoeing, cross-country skiing, and winter camping inside the national park.

WATERTON LAKES

The Oregon Treaty of 1846 set the boundary between Great Britain and the United States along the 49th parallel—right through the middle of the Rockies and cleaving Waterton Lakes and Glacier. Yet it's

At 6,094 feet (1,857.5 m), Iceberg Lake sits in the shadows of a 3,000-foot (914.4 m) pinnacle wall.

almost impossible to think of the parks as separate entities. One may fly the Maple Leaf and the other the Old Glory, but to the hikers, climbers, and grizzly bears that roam between the two, they are mirror images of one another. Waterton Lakes is much smaller than its American cousin—about an eighth the size of Glacier. But the mountains are just as majestic, the lakes perhaps even more enticing, and the wildlife just as rich.

The massive Kenow Fire of 2017 devastated nearly half the park, leaving areas that will take decades to recover. But the blaze spared most of **Waterton Village** in the heart of the park, including the iconic **Prince of Wales Hotel**. A national historic site, the hotel was constructed in the mid-1920s by the Great Northern Railway, an offbeat design that blends Edwardian English and alpine touches. The **Parks Canada Visitor Centre** on the outskirts of the village gives information on park activities and interpretive programs.

Deepest in the Canadian Rockies, **Waterton Lake** stretches out from the village, its upper and lower halves separated by a narrow strait, the **Bosporus**. Private powerboats are banned, but muscle-powered watercraft—kayaks, canoes, paddleboards, and rowboats—are most welcome. Swimming and scuba diving are other possibilities.

The **MV International** plies the upper lake on two-hour transborder scenic cruises that pause for a half hour at **Goat Haunt**. The vessel also drops hikers at **Cryptic Landing**, the trailhead for hikes to **Hell Roaring Falls** and several other cascades, as well as **Cryptic Lake** on the U.S.-Canada border. It's about a 10-mile (16 km) round-trip, with considerable elevation gain, to the

The Prince of Wales Hotel overlooks epic scenery in Waterton Lakes National Park.

lake and back. Passports are required for crossing the border.

Cameron Lake, which also straddles the international border, lies at the southern end of the gorgeous **Akamina Parkway** (10 miles/16 km). Another route through the park's west side is the **Red Rock Parkway** (9 miles/14.48 km),

named for the colorful canyon where it dead-ends. For a complete change in scenery, explore the prairie and wetlands that dominate the park's northwestern sector. More than 250 bird species have been spotted at **Maskinonge Lake**, and there's also a **Bison Paddock** with a small herd of buffalo. ■

LAY YOUR HEAD

Hotels

• **Lake McDonald Lodge:** Swiss-chalet-style lodging on the lakeshore; restaurants, bar, general store, lake cruises, horseback riding; from $113. *glaciernationalpark lodges.com/lodging/lake-mcdonald -lodge*

• **St. Mary Lodge:** Rustic cabins and motel-style rooms at the eastern end of Going-to-the-Sun; restaurants, bar, general store, gas station; from $119. *glacierparkinc .com/lodging/st-mary-lodge-resort*

• **Garden Wall Inn:** B&B tucked inside a restored Victorian manse in downtown Whitefish; gourmet

breakfast, afternoon hors d'oeuvres, evening drinks; from $115. *gardenwallinn.com*

• **Prince of Wales Hotel:** Historic Canadian national park lodge with stunning views of lakes and mountains; restaurant, lounge, gift shop, afternoon tea; from C$249. *glacier parkinc.com/lodging/prince-of -wales-hotel*

Camping

• **Glacier:** 13 developed campgrounds with fees ranging from $10-$23 per night.

• **Waterton Lakes:** 3 campgrounds with fees from $C15.70 per night.

Avalanche Creek, Glacier National Park, Montana

Rocky Mountain National Park

Colorado

There's much ado about altitude at this remarkable park in the Colorado Rockies. In addition to having the highest average elevation of any other U.S. national park, Rocky Mountain boasts 70 peaks rising to more than 12,000 feet (3,657.6 m). In the shadow of these mighty summits are valleys carved by wild rivers, placid alpine lakes, and an amazing array of flora and fauna.

The old frontier town of **Estes Park** has long been the gateway to Rocky Mountain National Park. **Art galleries** and **artisanal alcohol** (breweries, distilleries, and wineries) are the twin pillars of the downtown scene. Opened in 1909, the **Stanley Hotel** (Stephen King's inspiration for *The Shining*) offers guided history tours and evening ghost tours to guests and the general public.

A pair of elk in Rocky Mountain National Park

THE BIG PICTURE

Established: 1915

Size: 265,461 acres (1,074.28 sq km)

Annual Visitors: 4.4 million

Visitor Centers: Beavers Meadows and Kawuneeche (year-round); Fall River and Alpine (seasonal)

Entrance Fee: $20 per vehicle, $10 per person

nps.gov/romo

There's also plenty of outdoor action. The bright red cars of the **Estes Park Aerial Tramway** sail to the summit of **Prospect Mountain**, where the view often extends 100 miles (160.9 km) along the snow-capped Front Range. Strewn with sculptures and shady sitting spots, **Estes Park Riverwalk** meanders along the banks of two rivers that cut through town. The nonprofit **Rocky Mountain Conservancy** partners with the national park on a wide range of guided tours, seminars, and family activities like geocaching, fly-fishing, and art in the park.

From Estes, two routes lead into the national park. Highway 36 shoots to **Beaver Meadows Visitor Center**, with its information desk, natural history exhibits, and backcountry permit office; Highway 38 makes its way to **Fall River Visitor Center** and a similar set of services. The two roads converge at **Deer Ridge Junction**, the start of the celebrated **Trail Ridge Road**, an extraordinary 48-mile (77.2 km) drive that leads up and over the Continental Divide. Owing to snow cover, the route is open only between Memorial Day and mid-October. Places to pause along the drive range from the **Highest Point** (12,183 feet/ 3,713.4 m)

Boulder Field, on Longs Peak trail, sits 12,750 feet (3,886.2 m) above sea level and offers picturesque hiking and camping.

and the lofty **Alpine Visitor Center** to the half-mile (0.8 km) **Tundra Communities** hike and several sections of the strenuous **Ute Trail** across the rocky highlands.

Trail Ridge Road eventually dips into the **Kawuneeche Valley**. Few visitors make their way this far, lending the region an end-of-the-earth feel. It is here that the **Colorado River** starts its 1,450-mile (2,333.5 km) journey to the Gulf of California as streams tumbling down from the **Never Summer Mountains**. The **Colorado River Trail** (3.1 miles/4.9 km) heads upstream past cliffs that often shelter herds of bighorn sheep. Farther south, **Holzwarth Historic Site** spins tales of a German immigrant family that homesteaded the valley in the 1860s.

The park's other legendary auto route, **Old Fall River Road** is an 11-mile (17.7 km), one-way climb from **Horseshoe Park** to **Chapin Pass** and the **Alpine Visitor Center**. Be forewarned: It's mostly gravel and features numerous switchbacks. Along the way are the slot canyon that funnels the 25-foot (7.6 m) **Chasm Falls** and views of

DID YOU KNOW

- A one-night stay at the supposedly haunted Stanley Hotel in 1974 inspired a young down-and-out writer named Stephen King to pen *The Shining*. The eerie novel became his first best seller.

- In 1976, Rocky Mountain National Park was named one of the first UNESCO World Biosphere Reserves—areas that reflect a balanced relationship between humans and nature.

- Named after the daughter of a mining company executive, Lulu City in the Kawuneeche Valley enjoyed a brief boom as a silver town in the 1880s.

- Its geology shaped by glacial dynamics over hundreds of thousands of years, the park still harbors more than two dozen glaciers tucked into the cirques of the Mummy Range and along the Continental Divide through the heart of the park.

Above: The Cache la Poudre River Opposite: An ancient bristlecone pine tree overlooks the Rocky Mountain forest.

13,000-foot (3,962.4 m) peaks within the **Mummy Range**.

Known for broad meadows and alpine lakes, Rocky Mountain's southeast sector is accessed via **Bear Lake Road**. The park's largest open space, **Moraine Park,** is a favorite grazing place for elk and mule deer; an easy 5.5-mile (8.85 km) trail loops around the entire meadow. Farther up the road are trailheads for **Hollowell Park, Sprague Lake, Storm Pass, Glacier Gorge,** and the shoreline path around handsome **Bear Lake**—hikes that vary from easy to strenuous depending on their length and elevation gain. Several of these trailheads are also jumping-off spots for ascents of 14,259-foot (4,346.1 m) **Longs Peak**, the park's highest mountain.

The park's **Hidden Valley** ski area (open 1955 to 1991) is perma-nently closed. But families still flock to the old slopes for **sledding and tubing**. And anyone willing to hike up the slopes can **ski or snow-board** back down (but must yield to sledders). ■

MEET THE NEIGHBORS

• **Arapaho & Roosevelt National Forests:** Surrounding the national park, these Forest Service reserves are a hiking/climbing paradise including 10 wilderness areas, hun-dreds of trail miles, and some of the highest peaks in all the Rockies.

• **Golden Gate Canyon State Park:** Iconic Rocky Mountain scenery and a gold rush legacy color this popu-lar state reserve just west of Denver.

• **Eldorado Canyon State Park:** Rather than gold metal, this deep indentation in the Rockies takes its name from the way the sun glis-tens off its 800-foot-high (243.8 m) red-rock walls. The rugged park boasts more than 500 rock climbing routes.

• **Lory State Park:** Twenty-five miles (40.2 km) of hiking trails are the main attraction of a park that marks the transition between prairie and mountains near Fort Collins.

• **Arapaho National Wildlife Refuge:** Set along the secluded Illinois River in north-central Colo-rado, the reserve features a 6-mile (9.7 km) auto tour through habitat that nurtures moose, elk, beaver, otters, coyotes, pronghorn, and more than 200 bird species.

Sawtooth National Forest

Idaho

Teddy Roosevelt played a hand in the creation of many western parks, including Sawtooth National Forest, which he declared with the stroke of a White House pen in 1905. Named for the jagged mountain range that rises above central Idaho, the reserve shelters more than just trees. Sagebrush prairie, alpine tundra, lakes, and rivers are also part of the Sawtooth experience.

Some of the nation's wildest places are found within the confines of this enormous national forest, which nearly became a national park in the 1960s. Opposition by extractive industries (like mining and logging) stonewalled the legislation. Nonetheless, the federal government extended environmental protection to vast tracts of the national forest by creating a national recreation area and large wilderness area.

Life in the national forest largely revolves around the big **Sawtooth Valley**, all of which falls within the boundaries of the national recreation area. Carved by the head-waters of the **Salmon River**, the

THE BIG PICTURE

Established: 1905

Size: 2.1 million acres (8,498.4 sq km)

Annual Visitors: 1.5 million

Visitor Centers: Redfish (near Stanley), Sawtooth National Recreation Area (near Ketchum)

Entrance Fee: $5 per vehicle daily trailhead parking pass

fs.usda.gov/main/sawtooth

lush vale shelters most of the park's human residents and tourist services. **Redfish Visitor Center** is the place to grab informative brochures and wilderness permits, as well as books, maps, posters, and other items at the Sawtooth Interpretive and Historical Association shop. Starting from the visitor center, **Fishhook Creek Nature Trail** (.25 mile/0.4 km) runs across boardwalks on wetlands favored by beavers. The eclectic **Stanley Museum**, tucked inside a log cabin, presents exhibits on the region's natural and human history.

The valley offers all sorts of outdoor recreation, from summer fly-fishing and horseback riding to winter snowmobiling and cross-country skiing. It's also the starting point for whitewater rafting with local companies like **Sawtooth Adventure** and **White Otter** that organize float trips on the tranquil **Upper Salmon**, as well as the gnarly **Middle Fork** and **River of No Return**. The valley's largest water body, **Redfish Lake,** is the place for boating, waterskiing, and swimming at **Orval Hanson Point Beach**. Or mellow out at the **free outdoor concerts** staged three times a week during the summer at Redfish Lake Lodge.

The sun peeks through a forest of golden aspens in Sawtooth, Idaho.

There's plenty of space for camping on the lakeshore below Castle and Merriam Peaks in the Sawtooth Range.

The fabled **Sawtooth Wilderness** —217,088 acres (878.5 sq km) of pristine forest, alpine tundra, and snowy peaks—lies along the western edge of the valley. In addition to an environment that hasn't been disturbed by human activity since the 1930s, the wilderness is said to have some of the nation's cleanest, clearest skies. Twenty-three trailheads provide access to more than 350 miles (563.27 km) of footpaths, including starting points from **Redfish Lake** that are ideal for day hikes rather than overnight trips. All motorized and wheeled transport is banned; the only way to explore the wilderness is hike, horse, snowshoe, or ski. With 50 peaks over 10,000 feet (3,048 m), the area is also a magnet for climbers.

Three new wilderness areas— **Hemingway-Boulders, Jerry Peak**, and **White Clouds**—were created in 2015 on the east side of the national forest. Their combined area, 275,696 acres (1,115.7 sq km), actually exceeds Sawtooth Wilderness.

Starting out from Stanley, **Sawtooth Scenic Byway** (Highway 75) runs south through the valley, over 8,701-foot (2,652.1 m) **Galena Summit** and down into the **Big Wood River Valley** before reaching **Ketchum** and **Sun Valley** on the south side of the national forest. In addition to copious winter sports, the twin mountain towns offer art galleries, interesting eateries, a lively performing arts center, and the **Ketchum/Sun Valley Heritage and Ski Museum**. The most famous sight is probably **Ernest Hemingway's grave** in the municipal cemetery. ◾

MEET THE NEIGHBORS

• **Craters of the Moon National Monument:** Black lava beds and dark skies draw visitors to this twisted landscape located in southeast Idaho.

• **Salmon-Challis National Forest:** The wild Middle Fork of the Salmon River and the Frank Church–River of No Return Wilderness are the main draws at Sawtooth's northern neighbor.

• **Morley Nelson Snake River Birds of Prey National Conservation Area:** Hundreds of eagles, owls, falcons, and hawks mate and raise their chicks at this national conservation area southwest of Sawtooth.

• **Minidoka National Historic Site:** More than 9,000 Japanese American citizens were forced to relocate to this remote, desolate camp during World War II.

A 10-mile (16.1 km) round-trip hike circumvents Sawtooth Lake.

Dinosaur National Monument

Colorado & Utah

Thousands of dinosaur bones have been uncovered in this real-life Jurassic Park, as well as evidence of early human inhabitants and relics of pioneer days when this remote region was home to trappers, outlaws, and a legendary woman rancher. While ancient bones might be the main attraction, the park also offers plenty of outdoor adventure in arid badlands and along two great wild rivers.

THE BIG PICTURE

Established: 1915

Size: 210,844 acres (853.26 sq km)

Annual Visitors: 315,000

Visitor Centers: Quarry and Canyon

Entrance Fee: $20 per vehicle, $10 per person

nps.gov/dino

Paleontologist Earl Douglass of the Carnegie Museum of Natural History discovered the park's famed fossil beds in 1909. Although many of his early finds were removed for study and display at the Pittsburgh museum, it was Douglass who suggested preserving the main quarry in situ beneath a permanent roof to create "one of the most astounding and instructive sights imaginable."

His dream was finally realized in 1957 when the **Quarry Exhibit Hall** was finished. The glass-and-steel structure encases a 150-foot-long (45.72 m) wall embedded with visible fossilized bones from giant creatures like the *Allosaurus, Camarasaurus, Stegosaurus, Diplodocus,* and *Apatosaurus* that roamed the region more than 56 million years ago.

Just down the hill, **Quarry Visitor Center** gives the scoop on the rest of the park. Catch a 12-minute film, browse the bookstore, or ask at the information desk about ranger-led programs and outdoor recreation opportunities in the park. Linking the visitor center and exhibit hall, **Fossil Discovery Trail** (1.2 miles/ 1.9 km) leads to three digs with exposed bones that Douglass worked in the early 20th century.

Cub Creek Road runs east from the visitor center along the north bank of the Green River. It's not a long drive, but there's plenty to see and do along the way including the ancient petroglyphs and pictographs of the **Swelter Shelter**, rendered by the prehistoric Fremont people who inhabited the area around 1,000 years ago. After dark, rangers offer stargazing programs at **Split Mountain Campground**.

A half dozen trails in the Cub Creek area illuminate different aspects of the Dinosaur experience. The **Sound of Silence Loop** (3.2 miles/

Rapids await whitewater rafters on the Yampa River.

The 250-mile (402.3 km) Yampa River cuts through Dinosaur National Monument, where it meets the Green River in the middle.

5 km) meanders through various rock layers and a rich desert environment; **River Trail** (2 miles/ 3.2 km) along the waterfront is best for bird-watching; **Hog Canyon Trail** (1.5-mile/2.4 km round-trip) runs beneath a shady canopy of trees into a classic box canyon of the type that outlaws once used as hideouts. At the end of the road is **Josie Bassett Morris Ranch** and the log cabin where the intrepid rancher (and perhaps her outlaw lovers) lived between 1914 and 1964.

Roughly 30 miles (48.3 km) east of the dinosaur quarry via Highway 40, **Canyon Visitor Center**, near the small town of Dinosaur, is the only gateway to the park's vast and rugged midlands. A 32-mile (51.5 km) scenic road, **Harpers Corner Drive**, leads parkgoers to lofty overlooks of the canyon country carved by the Green and Yampa Rivers. At the very end of the road, **Harpers Corner Trail** (3-mile/ 4.8 km round-trip) rambles through

pinyon-juniper forest to a vertigo-inducing overlook perched 2,500 feet (762 m) above the Green River. Those with off-road vehicles can follow primitive **Echo Park Road** (13 miles/20.9 km) down to the Yampa River shoreline or **Yampa Bench Road** (27 miles/43.45 km) all the way over to **Cactus Flat** in the park's eastern extreme.

The best way to explore the park's roadless wilderness is on a **whitewater rafting** trip. Commercial outfitters like **Adrift Adventures** and **Don Hatch River Expeditions** offer single-day float trips through **Split Mountain Canyon**, as well as multiday camping trips through the **Gates of Lodore** or along the **Yampa River** with Class III and IV rapids. ■

MEET THE NEIGHBORS

• **Fossil Buttes National Monument:** America's "aquarium in stone" preserves the fossils of ancient sea creatures at this rich dig in southwest Wyoming.

• **Seedskadee National Wildlife Refuge:** More than 300 species of bird, mammal, fish, and reptile inhabit this remote reserve along 36 miles (57.9 km) of the Green River in Wyoming.

• **Flaming Gorge National Recreation Area:** Just upstream from

Dinosaur National Monument, a 500-foot-high (152.4 m) dam creates a massive reservoir with 320 miles (514.9 km) of crimson-colored shoreline and myriad ways to enjoy the water.

• **Fort Bridger State Historic Site:** Several hundred years of overland movement are documented in this Wyoming outpost that sits astride the path of the Oregon, California, Mormon, Pony Express, and Cherokee Trails.

Flathead Lake State Park
Montana

The largest freshwater lake in the western United States is one of Montana's best kept secrets. Flathead Lake State Park is split into six separate sections—five around the 160-mile (257.5 km) shoreline and one on the lake's largest island. The mild climate created by all that water provides perfect conditions for growing the famous Flathead cherries, as well as grapes that stoke small wineries along the lakeshore.

THE BIG PICTURE

Established: 1941

Size: 2,620 acres (10.6 sq km)

Annual Visitors: 313,000

Visitor Center: None

Entrance Fees: Montana residents free; nonresidents $6 per vehicle, $4 per person

stateparks.mt.gov

Flathead Lake State Park is the largest relic of Lake Missoula, a huge inland sea that covered much of the Northwest during the last interglacial age. Home for centuries to Native American peoples, most of the lakeshore now falls within the **Flathead Indian Reservation** of the Confederated Salish and Kootenai tribes.

The largest of the six sections is the only one you can't reach by road, **Wild Horse Island**. The name derives from the Salish-Kootenai pasturing their horses there to keep them from being rustled by other tribes. The island's terrain varies from rocky shoreline and pine-filled valleys to Palouse prairie grasslands, habitats that shelter bighorn sheep, mule deer, bald eagles, and even a few remnant wild horses. The park is day use only; no overnight camping is allowed.

From Wild Horse Island, you can gaze across the water at the park's **Big Arm Unit** on the western shore. Ponderosa pines and juniper trees shade a waterfront campground with a pebble beach, boat ramp, and dock. The hip little park also offers overnight stays in Mongolian-style yurts with balcony views of the lake.

Yellow Bay Unit on the eastern shore is probably the prettiest stretch of Flathead, set around a tranquil bay protected by a wooded peninsula. Camping, boating, and swimming are the main activities, but Yellow Bay is also a great place for waterskiing and walk-in scuba diving. The large building at the top of the bay is the **Flathead Lake Biological Station**, which offers tours of labs that monitor the health of the Flathead watershed.

The other three sections of Flathead Lake State Park are the **West Shore Unit** near Rollins, the **Finley Point Unit** near Polson, and the **Wayfarers Unit** on the southern edge of Bigfork. All of these parks feature lakeside camping, boating, swimming, and fishing.

Busy little towns at either end of the lake—**Polson** on the south shore

Bighorn sheep are among the wildlife residents of Flathead Lake State Park.

A beautiful alpine lake, deep in the Swan Mountain Range, reflects its surroundings in the morning light.

and **Bigfork** in the northeast—host most of the visitor services, including outfitters for fishing, kayaking, powerboating, and other aquatic pursuits.

Polson's **KwaTaqNuk Resort and Casino** offers daily 90-minute scenic lake cruises as well as weekend dinner and brunch cruises on a large modern boat with indoor and outdoor seating. Down the shore, **Flathead Rafting Company** specializes in guided kayak trips on the lake, as well as kayak, paddleboard, and flatwater raft rentals for those who want a self-guided excursion.

Up in Bigfork, **Flathead Lake Sailing and Charters** stages scenic sunset and champagne cruises on vintage 1920s racing sloops and classic wooden motorboats. In addition to summer kayak, paddleboard, and mountain bike rental, **Base Camp Bigfork** extends the adventure into winter with cross-country skiing, snowshoeing, and dogsledding.

More than a dozen native and introduced fish species inhabit the lake, including trout, salmon, pike, perch, sturgeon, bass, and whitefish.

Outfitters like **Bagley Guide Service** in Bigfork offer half- and full-day fishing charters. A state/tribal fishing license is required for both boat and shore fishing. ■

LAY YOUR HEAD

Hotels

• **KwaTaqNuk Resort:** Waterfront rooms and lake cruises in downtown Polson; casino, café, marina; from $95. *kwataqnuk.com*

• **Bridge Street Cottages:** Cute modern cottages with full kitchens along the bank of the Swan River in downtown Bigfork; air-conditioning, Internet, daily housekeeping; from $125. *bridgestreetcottages.com*

• **Mountain Lake Lodge:** Fireplace suites make for cozy digs both summer and winter at this east shore lodge near Bigfork; restaurants, bar, swimming pool, gym, fire pit, putting green; from $149. *mountainlakelodge.com*

Camping

• Campgrounds at all five mainland units of Flathead Lake State Park; no camping on Wild Horse Island. Seasons vary, but all campgrounds are closed for three or four months in winter. Fees are $6-$24 per night (residents), $12-$34 per night (nonresidents).

• Yurts at Big Arm Unit are $54-$64 (residents), $66-$72 (nonresidents).

❶ Dalvay-by-the-Sea, Prince Edward Island

Set along the north shore of Prince Edward Island, this elegant Victorian manse was constructed in 1896 by Scottish American industrialist Alexander Macdonald as a family summer home and named after his birthplace in Scotland. In the late 1930s, Parks Canada transformed Dalvay into a resort hotel for the newly established Prince Edward Island National Park.

❷ Mount Washington Resort, New Hampshire

The last of two dozen grand hotels that once graced New Hampshire's White Mountains, Mount Washington Resort was opened in 1902 in the Bretton Woods valley. Railroad tycoon Joseph Stickney imported 250 Italian craftsmen to embellish his hotel with stained glass windows, elaborate molding, and intricate woodwork.

❸ Skyland Resort, Virginia

Eccentric developer George Freeman Pollock opened this Shenandoah mountain retreat in 1895, long before the area became a national park. Located astride the highest point of Skyline Drive, the rustic resort offers dreamy views, hiking and horseback riding trails, and accommodation in historic cabins.

❹ Greyfield Inn, Georgia

It may look antebellum, but the graceful Greyfield was actually built in 1900, one of several mansions created by the Carnegie family, who summered on Georgia's Cumberland Island during the late 19th and early 20th centuries. Family heirlooms decorate the public areas and guest rooms of a hotel still owned and operated by Carnegie descendants.

❺ Old Faithful Inn, Wyoming

Constructed mainly from lodgepole pine, the rustic geyser-field lodge is the world's largest log "cabin" and a Yellowstone landmark since 1904. Set beneath a huge gabled roof, the building's awe-inspiring atrium lobby rises seven stories above a massive stone fireplace. Many of the original furnishings remain in both the guest rooms and public areas like the very popular Bear Pit bar.

THE TOP

10

HISTORIC LODGES

With distinctive architecture and quirky history, lodges set the mood in many national parks.

❻ Banff Springs Hotel, Alberta

Opened in 1888 by the Canadian Pacific Railway as a way to attract more train-traveling tourists to the Rockies, the majestic lodge is set against a backdrop of snowcapped peaks and evergreen forest. The detailed Scottish baronial architecture gives it the feel of a fairy-tale castle rising in the wilderness.

The majestic Banff Springs Hotel overlooks Bow River in Banff National Park.

❼ El Tovar Hotel, Arizona

The Fred Harvey Company, which pioneered tourism in much of the Southwest, had the prescience to open a hotel overlooking the Grand Canyon in 1905, more than a decade before the geological wonder became a national park. Constructed primarily of wood and stone, the arts and crafts–influenced architecture was an early example of the National Park Service rustic style that imbued structures with a definite sense of place.

❽ The Inn at Death Valley, California

Formerly called the Furnace Creek Inn, this desert lodging attracted a glitzy Hollywood crowd when it opened in 1927. The romantic oasis setting near Furnace Creek village in Death Valley is complemented by California Mission architecture, towering palm trees, and a swimming pool fed by desert spring water.

❾ Majestic Yosemite Hotel, California

Longtime visitors to the Sierra Nevada park will always think of this noble hotel by its original name—the Ahwahnee Hotel. Opened in 1927, the lodge has hosted many famous people over the years, from President Kennedy and Queen Elizabeth to Judy Garland and Lucille Ball.

❿ Cavallo Point Lodge, California

With a panoramic view across the water to the Golden Gate Bridge, Alcatraz Island, and downtown San Francisco, the Marin Headlands hotel offers an elegant stay beside the bay in Golden Gate National Recreation Area. Constructed in the early 1900s, the Colonial Revival–style buildings once housed U.S. Army officers and their families.

Black Hills National Forest
South Dakota

Rising like a wooded island from a prairie sea, the Black Hills of South Dakota offer the highest (and some would say *only*) elevation between the Great Lakes and the Rocky Mountains. Sacred to the Lakota Sioux and renowned for its diverse outdoor recreation, the legendary hills are protected within the confines of a large national forest and smaller state and national parks.

The Lakota Sioux called their hallowed heights He Sápa ("black mountains"), a reference to the dark color of the forest mantle when viewed from the surrounding plains. The name endured through a very tumultuous history that included Custer's infamous Black Hills Expedition of 1874, the murder of Wild Bill Hickok, and the creation of two of the largest sculptures in the world.

THE BIG PICTURE

Established: 1897

Size: 1.25 million acres (5,058.57 sq km)

Annual Visitors: 3 million

Visitor Centers: Pactola, Norbeck, Mount Rushmore, Wind Cave, Jewel Cave

Entrance Fees: Black Hills National Forest (none); Custer State Park ($20); Wind Cave and Mount Rushmore ($10); Jewell Cave ($12)

fs.usda.gov/blackhills

Most of the highlands fall within Black Hills National Forest, a mixed bag of recreation, logging, grazing, and mining in a national forest that sprawls across 1.25 million acres (5,058.57 sq km) of native woodland and prairie. The Forest Service **Pactola Visitor Center**, located west of Rapid City, features exhibits, interpretive programs, a bookstore, and information on activities in the national forest. In addition to copious hiking and biking trails, the Black Hills offer plenty of scope for camping, horseback riding, rock climbing, boating, fishing, quad biking, cross-country and downhill skiing, and snowshoeing.

One of the best ways to discover the Black Hills is cruising the **Peter Norbeck National Scenic Byway**, a 68-mile (109.4 km) route that does a rough figure eight around the middle of the park. If cycling is your preferred mode of transport, consider a ride along the **Mickelson Bike Trail**, which follows 109 miles (175.4 km) of the old railroad path between Edgemont and Deadwood.

Deadwood was once the most notorious city in the West. Founded

Washington, Jefferson, Roosevelt, and Lincoln carved into Mount Rushmore

One of more than 15 lakes in the Black Hills, 19-acre (.07 sq km) Sylvan Lake sits in Custer State Park.

as a gold rush boom town in the 1870s, the entire city is now a national historic landmark district. Among the town's many attractions are the **Adams Museum** of local history, **Mount Moriah Cemetery** (where Calamity Jane and Wild Bill Hickok are buried), and the **Tatanka: Story of the Bison**, which offers a Northern Plains Indians interpretive center and large outdoor bison sculptures. High above Deadwood, the **Mount Roosevelt Friendship Towers** (built in 1919) offers awesome views of the town and Black Hills.

Higher still is **Black Elk (Harney) Peak.** At 7,242 feet (2,207.4 m), it is the highest mountain in the United States east of the Rockies. Although located in the national forest, the peak is accessed from two trailheads in the **Sylvan Lake** area of **Custer State Park.** Driving the 18-mile (28.9 km) **Wildlife Loop Road** is sure to produce close encounters with some of the park's 1,300 resident bison. Custer is also

home to the summer stock theater of the **Black Hills Playhouse**.

More wonders lurk beneath the surface. **Wind Cave National Park** revolves around one of the world's longest caverns with more than 130 miles (209.2 km) of passages. Ranger tours explore the cave network's unusual subterranean wonders like frostwork, popcorn, and boxwork formations. The showpiece of **Jewel Cave National Monument** is even longer—more than 180 miles (289.7 km) of underground passages.

Yet the most celebrated sights in the Black Hills were made by humans. Presidents Thomas Jefferson, Teddy Roosevelt, Abraham Lincoln, and George Washington are immortalized on the granite face of **Mount Rushmore National Memorial**, sculpted by Gutzon Borglum and his son between 1927 and 1941. On the other side of Black Elk Peak, the immense, unfinished **Crazy Horse Memorial** by Korczak Ziolkowski (started in 1948) commemorates the great Lakota warrior. ◾

MEET THE NEIGHBORS

• **Devil's Tower National Monument:** Rising 1,267 feet (386.18 m) above eastern Wyoming, this remarkable volcanic butte was the nation's first national monument, established by President Teddy Roosevelt in 1906.

• **Badlands National Park:** Bison and bighorn sheep, rich fossil beds, and wildly eroded rock formations

are the main attractions of this flatlands park east of the Black Hills.

• **Agate Fossil Beds National Monument:** The bones of strange Miocene creatures like the *Amphicyon* bear dog, giant pig-like *Daeodon*, and *Palaeocastor* land beaver are among the well-preserved fossils unearthed at this site in northwest Nebraska.

Theodore Roosevelt National Park
North Dakota

THE BIG PICTURE

Established: 1978

Size: 70,446 acres (285.1 sq km)

Annual Visitors: 708,000

Visitor Centers: Painted Canyon, South Unit (Medora), North Unit

Entrance Fee: $25 per vehicle, $12 per person

nps.gov/thro

Although nature is the most compelling reason to visit this North Dakota park, the underlying theme is spiritual and emotional renewal, for it was in the remote badlands of the Dakota Territory that America's 26th president reinvented himself—and, by extension, the destiny of a nation—while recovering from personal tragedy. Teddy Roosevelt's time out west also sparked his passion for exploring and conserving wild places.

Enamored with the Western lifestyle, which he found both rugged and romantic, 25-year-old Teddy Roosevelt first ventured to North Dakota in 1883 to hunt bison and learn the cowboy way. A year later, he was back, an extended trip to mourn the recent loss of both his mother and first wife. Roosevelt bought a ranch on the Little Missouri River about 35 miles (56.3 km) north of Medora and threw himself into the therapy of working with cattle and horses.

TR would no doubt be proud of the park that bears his name. The cattle and cowpokes are long gone, but the prairies, badlands, and wooded gullies along the Little Missouri River look pretty much as they did in his day. The park is divided into three units separated by Little Missouri National Grassland. It also straddles two time zones: The South Unit is on Mountain Time and the North Unit on Central Time.

After all these years, **Medora** is still the belle of the Badlands as well as the main gateway to the park. Founded in 1883, the town retains many of its historic frontier buildings, including the **Chateau de Mores**, a rustic hunting lodge built by the French aristocrat, rancher, and duelist Marquis de Morès. Every summer the Wild West–themed *Medora Musical* review takes the stage at the Burning Hills Amphitheater.

South Unit Visitor Center in Medora shows a short film, "Refuge of the American Spirit," about TR's legacy. Out back is Roosevelt's rustic **Maltese Cross Cabin**, where the not yet president lived in 1883.

Wild buffalo graze and roam through the park's tall grasses.

The hills of Theodore Roosevelt National Park push through the clouds during sunrise.

Beyond the visitor center is **Peaceful Valley Ranch**, where buffalo roam the riverside pastures beside prairie dog towns.

A **36-mile (57.9 km) Scenic Loop** takes motorists into the Badlands east of the river, with plenty of overlooks and trailheads en route to discover the area's prairie flora and fauna. You need a horse or a good pair of hiking boots to explore the west bank's wilderness area and its **petrified forest.**

Roosevelt's home on the range from 1884 to 1885, **Elkhorn Ranch**, lies along the west bank of the Little Missouri River, about halfway between the other units. Stones mark the foundation of the former ranch house and outbuildings, with information boards that tell the tale of Roosevelt's cowboy days, his spiritual revival at this site, and the area's natural history.

The **North Unit** feels equally isolated. A paved **14-Mile Scenic Drive** (22.5 km) hugs the north bank of the Little Missouri to landmarks like the **Cannonball concretions** and **Oxbow Overlook**. The area is also home to the park's herd of longhorn cattle, a living reminder of the lifestyle that lured Roosevelt to North Dakota in the first place.

Hikers and horseback riders can also explore the park via sections of the 144-mile (231.75 km) **Maah Daah Hey Trail**, which connects all three units with primitive campsites along the way. Outside the national park, the trail is also open to cycling—it's the nation's longest continuous single-track mountain biking route. ■

MEET THE NEIGHBORS

• **Fort Union Trading Post National Historic Site:** For nearly 40 years (1828-67), Native Americans, frontiersmen, explorers, soldiers, and settlers passed through this outpost on the Upper Missouri.

• **Knife River Indian Villages National Historic Site:** A museum and reconstructed lodges along the Missouri River pay tribute to the Native Americans who lived here for thousands of years.

• **Fort Abraham Lincoln State Park:** Across the Missouri River from Bismarck, this longtime U.S. Army outpost is where Custer and the Seventh Cavalry were stationed before their fateful trip to the Little Bighorn.

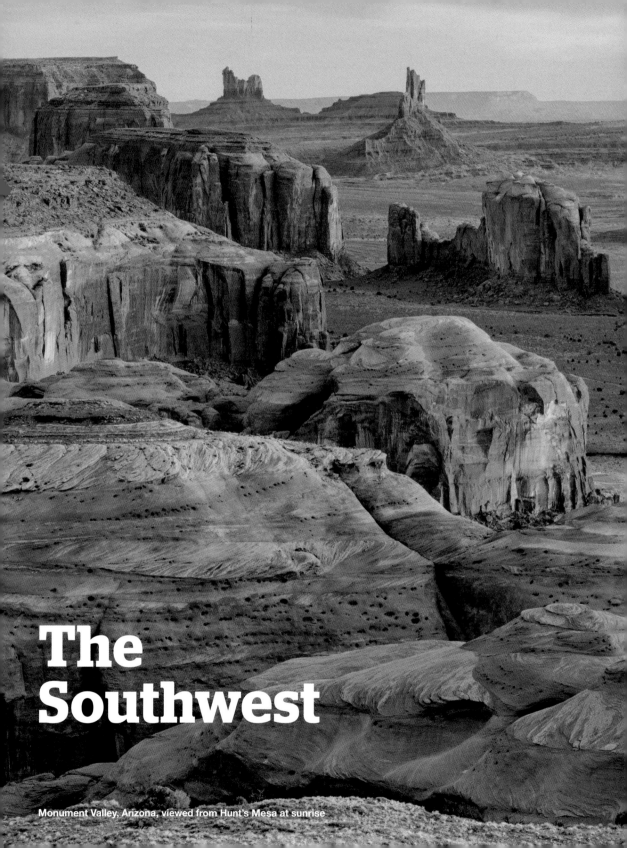

The
Southwest

Monument Valley, Arizona, viewed from Hunt's Mesa at sunrise

Grand Canyon National Park
Arizona

"Leave it as it is. You cannot improve on it. The ages have been at work on it, and man can only mar it," declared Teddy Roosevelt after a 1903 visit to the Grand Canyon. More than 100 years later, Arizona's "Big Ditch" continues to awe visitors—not so much from sheer size, although that's truly astounding, as from the park's blend of colors, shapes, weather, and wildlife.

Native Americans have lived in and around the Grand Canyon for at least 12,000 years, and Spanish explorers laid eyes on the rift in the 16th century. But it wasn't until 1869, when John Wesley Powell and his team became the first people to navigate the Colorado River through the canyon bottom, that it gained renown as a global landmark.

GRAND CANYON VILLAGE

With its exhibits on the park's natural and human history, **Grand Canyon Visitor Center** on the South Rim is an excellent starting point. You can leave your vehicle there and walk or take a shuttle bus to other landmarks along the South Rim. Right behind the visitor center are **Mather Point** and the 13-mile (20.9 km) **Rim Trail** to other

THE BIG PICTURE

Established: 1919

Size: 1.2 million acres (4,856.23 sq km)

Annual Visitors: 6.2 million

Visitor Centers: South Rim, North Rim

Entrance Fees: $30 per vehicle, $15 per person

nps.gov/grca

stunning viewpoints like **Yaki Point** to the east and **Yavapai Point** to the west, where a **geology museum** illuminates nearly two billion years of canyon history.

Beyond Yavapai Point (1.3 miles/ 2.1 km) is the **Village** and the eclectic architecture of its historic structures, which together comprise a national historic landmark district. Many of the buildings were designed by pioneering female architect Mary Colter, including the distinctive **Hopi House** (1905), a homage to the indigenous architecture of the Southwest that now houses the park's largest souvenir store and a Native American art gallery. **Verkamp's Visitor Center** (1906) harbors a bookstore, information desk, and exhibits on the canyon's pioneer history. Among other noteworthy structures are the **Kolb Studio** (1904) and **Lookout Studio** (1914), both vintage photo studios that now blend shopping and exhibit space.

The village **train station** (1910) is the terminus for the historic **Grand Canyon Railway**, a scenic passenger line that runs 64 miles (102.9 km) through the pine forest and meadows of the Coconino Plateau between the South Rim and Williams, Arizona. Passengers can ride the train as a day trip to the Grand Canyon or

One of the best ways to see the Grand Canyon: rowing the Colorado River

Breathtaking canyon and river views await hikers who walk the rocky stone trails.

combine it with overnights at South Rim lodging.

THE SOUTH RIM

During the slower winter months, you can drive all the way to Hermit's Rest. But during the busy peak season (March 1 to November 30), **Hermit Road** is closed to private vehicles west of the village. That leaves hiking and the shuttle bus as the two means to explore this awesome 7-mile (11.3 km) stretch of the South Rim. "Must see" stops along the way include the **Abyss** with its 3,000-foot (914.4 m) vertical drop-off and **Pima Point** where you can see a slice of the milk-chocolate-colored Colorado River far below. At the end of the road, **Hermits Rest** is a faux frontier cabin (host to a gift shop and snack bar) fashioned by Colter in 1914.

East of the main visitor center, **Desert View Drive** snakes 25 miles (40.2 km) along the South Rim to Desert View Watchtower near the canyon's easternmost extreme. The shuttle bus and Rim Trail run only as far as Yaki Point; beyond that, a private vehicle is necessary to access various viewpoints along the drive.

DID YOU KNOW

• Called Öngtupqa by the Hopi, the Grand Canyon is a sacred place of pilgrimage and prayer and considered a gateway to the afterlife by the region's indigenous people.

• The Grand Canyon's version of Area 51 traces its roots to 1909, when explorer G. E. Kinkaid claimed to have discovered an ancient Egyptian city—filled with mummies and hieroglyphics—inside a massive cavern.

• The coldest temperature ever recorded in the park was a mind-numbing −22°F/−30°C (on the North Rim in 1985).

• Grand Canyon National Park is in the midst of a two-decade program to reduce after-dark illumination in order to achieve International Dark Sky Park status.

• Using new dating techniques, scientists have revised the canyon's age from five to six million years to as old as 70 million years.

• The canyon harbors an estimated 1,000 caves; only 335 have been recorded and only one, Cave of the Domes on Horseshoe Mesa, is open to the public.

Most cars whiz past the **Shoshone Point** turnout because it doesn't overlook the canyon, but the relatively easy 2.2-mile (3.5 km) trail from the parking lot to the edge is one of the least crowded along the South Rim, and the view from the end is well worth the trek.

Grand Canyon aficionados debate which overlook along this stretch is best, from the aptly named **Grandview Point** to **Moran Point** with its view of Hance Rapids and **Lipan Point,** where you can gaze down on that big bend in the Colorado River. Tucked between the turnoffs is the small but interesting **Tusayan Museum** with exhibits on local Native American culture. Behind the museum, a short self-guided trail leads to the **Tusayan Ruin**, the remains of a 12th-century Puebloan village and one of 4,300 archaeological sites so far identified inside the national park.

Inspired by the Puebloan style, Colter fashioned the nearby **Desert View Watchtower** in 1932 as a perch for an even higher view down into the canyon. Eighty-five steps lead to an observation deck that sits more than 5,000 feet (1,524 m) above the canyon floor, past murals of ancient Native American life rendered by Hopi artist Fred Kabotie. A snack bar, store, and gas station round out Desert View's amenities.

THE NORTH RIM

From Desert View Tower, the drive to the Grand Canyon's North Rim is nearly 200 miles (321.87 km). But it's a journey into a whole different world. For starters, the North Rim averages a thousand feet (304.8 m) higher than its southern counterpart. That may not seem like an awful lot, but that extra elevation makes a huge difference in climate, vegetation, and even the animals you come across. The North Rim is slightly cooler in the summer and often inaccessible during winter because of snowstorms. Tourist facilities are open only from May 15 to October 15.

Once again, the **Visitor Center** is a great place to start, especially if you plan on hiking the rim trails or driving the spur roads. **Grand Canyon Lodge** (1937) balances on the very edge of the chasm, and its back patio offers perhaps the best place in the entire park to sit, stare, and contemplate the geological wonder that spreads out before you. For an even more vertiginous view, hike the short (0.5-mile/0.8 km) trail to **Bright Angel Point.**

Scattered around the village are trailheads to paths including the 4.7-mile (7.5 km) **Uncle Jim Loop**, the 9.6-mile (15.45 km) **Widforss Trail** to a very secluded overlook, and the 9.8-mile (15.7 km) **Ken Patrick Trail** all the way over to **Point Imperial,** the highest point on the North Rim, with views into the canyon's northeastern corner. You can also drive to Point Imperial via **Cape Royal Road**, which switchbacks up onto the **Walhalla Plateau** and other celebrated panoramas like **Vista Encantada** and **Angels Window**. Adventurous drivers can test their mettle on the rough, unpaved road that leads out to **Sublime Point**, 18 miles (28.9 km) west of the village. Four-wheel drive and high clearance are essential; a tow strap and saw (for cutting down fallen trees) are highly recommended.

THE CANYON

Given the absence of roads, there are only three ways to explore the Grand Canyon below the rims: hiking, mule trips, and river flat trips.

Around 40,000 people a year backpack into the canyon for overnight stays that can vary from one night to several weeks. Far more people are day hikers who venture a short distance down one of three main trails for a taste of what it's like to stare up at the imposing canyon walls.

Whether on a multiday trek or an hour-long hike, walkers should always check out trail and weather conditions before plunging down the path. The most timely and accurate information is available from the national park visitor centers or the

Backcountry Information Center on the South Rim.

Bright Angel Trail from the South Rim is the safest and best maintained route into the canyon and includes shade structures, emergency phones, toilets, and taps for refilling water bottles. With a trailhead just west of the South Rim Village, the Bright Angel dives quickly downward via a series of switchbacks to **Indian Garden** (4.8 miles/7.7 km) and a suspension bridge over the Colorado River to **Bright Angel Campground** (9.5 miles/15.3 km) and nearby **Phantom Ranch**. The route more or less follows a path that Native Americans and 19th-century prospectors took into the canyon.

Although more primitive, the **South Kaibab Trail** is a slightly shorter path and offers better day-hike options. The total distance from trailhead to the river is 6.7 miles (10.78 km). But several stops along the way offer spectacular views for those who don't want to trek the entire way to the canyon floor, including **Ooh-Aah Point** (1.8-mile/2.9 km round-trip), **Cedar Ridge** (3-mile/4.8 km return) and **Skeleton Point** (6-mile/9.6 km return).

A sunset glow tints the textured canyon walls carved by the Colorado River.

The only path into the canyon from the opposite rim is the **North Kaibab Trail**, a 14-mile (22.5 km) hoof down to Phantom Ranch and the river. Several trails wind through the canyon, including the rugged, multiday **Tonto Trail** which wanders 70 miles (112.65 km) from east to west below the South Rim.

Mule trips into the canyon are offered from both rims. The South Rim features day trips and multiday pack trips with stops at Phantom Ranch; the North Rim offers only day trips.

Sixteen companies own concessions from the Park Service to run **float trips** down the Colorado River between **Lee's Ferry** and **Diamond Creek**. Four types of craft are used: paddled rafts, oared rafts, motorized rafts, and wooden dories that recall Powell's landmark 1869 journey down the river. Trips range from three to 18 days and include riverside camping throughout. A full list of river rafts is posted at nps.gov/grca/planyourvisit/river-concessioners.htm. ∎

LAY YOUR HEAD

Hotels

South Rim

Reservations: 888-297-2757 or grandcanyonlodges.com

• **El Tovar:** Historic national park lodge opened in 1905 by the Fred Harvey Company; air-conditioning, restaurant, bar; from $217.

• **Bright Angel Lodge:** Modern rooms and rustic cabins on the edge of the canyon, designed by Mary Colter in 1935; restaurant, saloon, soda fountain; from $97.

• **Phantom Ranch:** Very basic cabins and dorm rooms, and shared baths. It is the only indoor lodging at the bottom of the canyon; air-conditioning, restaurant; reserve up to 13 months ahead; from $51.

North Rim

Reservations: 877-386-4383 or grandcanyonforever.com

• **Grand Canyon Lodge**: Cozy cabins and motel-style rooms on the North Rim; restaurants, bar; open mid-May to mid-October; from $132.

Camping

Campground reservations: 877-444-6777 or recreation.gov

• **Three campgrounds:** Mather at Grand Canyon Village (all year), North Rim (May 15 to October 15), and Desert View (mid-April to mid-October); $12-18 per night.

• **Trailer Village:** RV campground with full hookups; from $51 per night. *visitgrandcanyon.com/trailer-village-rv-park*

Zion & Bryce Canyon National Parks
Utah

Less than 40 miles (64.37 km) apart as the crow flies, Zion and Bryce Canyon showcase the incredible geology of southern Utah, a red-rock wonderland created by wind, water, and snow. Among the nation's most beloved (and photographed) parks, they are also active outdoor areas that offer varied hiking opportunities, challenging rock climbing faces, and winter cross-country skiing trails.

ZION

Arriving in the 1860s, Mormon pioneers were so overwhelmed by the "natural temples" near the headwaters of the Virgin River they decided to call it Zion after the heavenly city of the Old Testament. Although Brigham Young considered it blasphemy—and actually forbade its use—the name endured as a symbol of the nature that blesses so much of southern Utah.

The park revolves around Zion Canyon—15 miles (24.14 km) long and almost 3,000 feet (914.4 m) deep in places. It also includes much of the surrounding terrain, landscapes that range from red-rock

THE BIG PICTURE

Established: Zion (1919); Bryce Canyon (1928)

Size: Zion (146,597 acres/593.26 sq km); Bryce Canyon (35,835 acres/145 sq km)

Annual Visitors: Zion (4.5 million); Bryce Canyon (2.5 million)

Visitor Centers: Zion Canyon, Bryce Canyon

Entrance Fees: $30 per vehicle, $15 per person

nps.gov/zion; nps.gov/brca

desert to the high-altitude forests sprawling across the plateaus above the canyon. The park's various ecosystems support more floral diversity (around 800 native plant species) than anywhere else in Utah, and more than 80 percent of the park (124,000 acres/501.8 sq km) is designated wilderness area.

After making the transition from till to tourism over the past century, the old riverside town of **Springdale** is the park's main gateway. The main drag (Highway 9) is flanked by heaps of hotels, restaurants, art galleries, and shops, as well as outfitters who arrange adventure activities in and around the park. Choose between rock climbing and rappelling, helicopter and 4x4 tours, guided hikes along the Narrows, and tubing on the Virgin River downstream from the park. The **Zion National Park Forever Project**, the park's official nonprofit partner, organizes a number of outdoor learning adventures, service projects, classes, lectures, and special events through its field institute, in addition to operating three stores inside the park.

Pedestrian and vehicle bridges connect Springdale with the national park **Visitor Center** on the other side

More than 18 hiking trails are on offer at Zion National Park.

The hike along Sunset Park in Bryce Canyon leads to views of multihued sandstone cliffs.

of the Virgin. In addition to exhibits and information, the visitor center is the southern terminus of the **Zion National Park Shuttle**, which is the only way to reach the heart of the canyon between spring and fall when visitation peaks. Private vehicles are not allowed beyond Canyon Junction, turnoff to the **Zion-Mount Carmel Highway**. Even if you're not headed for south-central Utah, the highway makes an interesting detour through what was once the world's longest auto tunnel to a geological oddity called **Checkerboard Mesa**, a sandstone facade scarred by hundreds of vertical and horizontal fissures.

The first stop on the shuttle route is the **Zion Human History Museum**, which details the heritage of Native Americans and Mormon pioneers in the region. Entering the

canyon, the shuttle makes seven stops, including viewpoints of celebrated stone formations like **Court of the Patriarchs** (Abraham, Isaac, and Jacob) and **Weeping Rock**, as well as historic **Zion Lodge**, a classic national park lodging designed by Gilbert Stanley Underwood and opened in 1927. The park's most celebrated landmark—the **Great White Throne**, a 1,500-foot (457.2 m) rock face—can be seen from numerous places along the canyon road.

The road (and shuttle route) ends with a dramatic flourish inside the **Temple of Sinawava**, a colossal natural amphitheater. A riverside path continues to the **Narrows**, where the thousand-foot-high (304.8 m) canyon walls are sometimes just 20 to 30 feet (6.1-9.1 m) apart. Anyone is free to hike the Narrows as far as

MEET THE NEIGHBORS

• **Cedar Breaks National Monument:** This miniature version of Bryce Canyon is focused on a half-mile-deep (0.8 km) natural amphitheater.

• **Pipe Springs National Monument:** Historic frontier fort in a desert oasis setting near the Utah-Arizona border.

• **Capitol Reef National Park:** A giant geological "wrinkle" called the Waterpocket Fold extends nearly 100 miles (160.9 km) through this central Utah park.

• **Snow Canyon State Park:** Cliffs and canyons, sand dunes, and lava formations are the allure of this reserve near St. George Utah.

Snow dusts the mountains of Zion, Utah's first national park.

upstream Big Springs (beyond that you need a backcountry permit). But be prepared to get wet: much of the trail is through waist-high water.

Zion Canyon is laced with other popular trails, from easy hikes like **Emerald Pools** (2.2 miles/3.5 km) to strenuous uphill slogs that lead to **Angel's Landing, Hidden Canyon,** and **Observation Point.** Backpackers can trek the **West Rim Trail** (14.2 miles/22.85 km) across the wilderness **Horse Pasture Plateau** to **Lava Point,** where another trail connects to **Kolob Canyons** in the far north.

Drivers can explore the high country via two motor routes that start outside the park. **Kolob Terrace Road** runs 22 miles (35.4 km) from Virgin, Utah, to Lava Point and its scenic overlook. Exit 40 on Interstate 15 drops down to **Kolob Canyons Visitor Center** and the start of a road that leads 5.4 miles (8.7 km) to a vista of the impressive red-rock gorges. High country hikes are possible from both of the Kolob roads.

BRYCE CANYON

Unlike the early Mormons who viewed Zion Canyon as a heavenly gift, rancher Ebenezer Bryce viewed the badlands that ran through his 1870s ranch as a bane. "It's a hell of a place to lose a cow," he once famously quipped.

The area's indigenous people were far more amazed. According to Paiute Indian legend, the canyon's hoodoo rock formations were created by that old trickster Coyote, who turned the gluttonous To-when-an-ung-wa ("legend people") into stone.

Truth be told, Bryce isn't a canyon. It's a natural amphitheater carved into the eastern flank of the Paunsaugunt

Thor's Hammer in Bryce Canyon, seen from the Navajo Trail

Plateau by millions of years of wind and water erosion (and perhaps a little help from the Coyote god). While the fantastical hoodoos are certainly what draws most visitors to Bryce, the park's extreme altitude (the rim hovers between 8,000 and 9,000 feet/2,438.4 to 2,743.2 m) means that visitors can also explore alpine meadows and coniferous forests that provide habitats for a wide variety of flora and fauna.

To help alleviate heavy summertime traffic, visitors are encouraged to park outside the park and hop the free **Bryce Canyon Shuttle** from a station off Highway 63 in Bryce Canyon City. The shuttle runs to the **Visitor Center,** lodge, campground, and several overlooks. However, you will need your vehicle to reach viewpoints at the southern end of the main park road.

By far the park's most popular activity is walking all, or part, of the 11-mile (17.7 km) **Rim Trail** between **Fairyland Point** and **Bryce Point.** Offering panoramic views of the kaleidoscopic topography, the trail can be accessed from several places along the rim, including **Sunrise Point** and **Sunset Point,** as well as the old and esteemed **Bryce Canyon Lodge** (opened in 1925).

The easiest way to dip down into

the canyon is the **Queen's Garden Trail,** a 1.8-mile (2.89 km) route that starts from Sunrise Point. At the opposite extreme are routes like the **Under-the-Rim Trail** (23 miles/ 37 km) and **Rigg Springs Loop** (8.8 miles/14.16 km) that meander through stone formations and forested areas below the plateau; backcountry campsites along both of these trails enable multiday treks through the best of Bryce.

The **classic auto tour** of Bryce runs 18 miles (28.97 km) south from the visitor center to **Rainbow Point,** where the view encompasses all five colorful layers (pink, gray, white, vermilion, and chocolate) of the **Grand Staircase** formation. From nearby **Yovimpa Point,** the view extends all the way to the North Rim of the Grand Canyon on a clear day.

Bryce Canyon is also an extraordinary winter park. Seeing the hoodoos covered in a shroud of fresh snow is surreal. The **Bryce Canyon Snowshoe Program** includes free ranger-led hikes along the rim and among the hoodoos. **Cross-country skiing** is encouraged on park trails above the rim and in adjacent Dixie National Forest. Permits for backcountry hiking during the winter months are issued only to experienced and well-equipped campers. ∎

Valles Caldera National Preserve

New Mexico

THE BIG PICTURE

Established: 2000

Size: 89,216 acres (361 sq km)

Annual Visitors: 120,000

Visitor Center: Valle Grande

Entrance Fee: $20 per vehicle, $10 per person

nps.gov/vall

The eruption of a primordial supervolcano created a massive 13-mile (20.9 km)-wide caldera in the Jemez Mountains of what is now northern New Mexico. Fast-forward more than a million years, and it's now the focus of New Mexico's exquisite national preserve, a diverse green space where modern tourism and outdoor recreation blend easily with ancient ways and means.

Evergreen forest, alpine meadows, and perennial streams are not your typical image of New Mexico. But Valles Caldera is a park like no other. In bygone times, these highlands were a place of seasonal hunting or grazing for a variety of Native American peoples and early Spanish settlers. Obsidian quarried in the caldera was traded throughout the Southwest and southern Great Plains to be made into arrowheads and tools.

Between 1876 and 2000, when the federal government purchased the property, Valles Caldera was part of a huge private ranch where grazing, logging, and hunting were the primary activities. Rather than a national park in the strictest sense, its new national preserve status means that seasonal grazing and hunting are still allowed on a carefully managed basis, alongside recreational pursuits like hiking, mountain biking, horseback riding, and winter sports.

The only paved route into the park, the **Jemez Mountain Trail National Scenic Byway** (Route 4), threads along the southern boundary of the aptly **Valle Grande**. It's the largest of the five valleys that comprise the caldera and the best place in the park for spotting some of the 3,000-plus elk that roam the area. A short side road leads to the log cabin–style **Valle Grande Visitor Center,** where visitors can pick up backcountry and fishing permits, as well as schedule ranger-led hikes, snowshoe tours, and van tours.

The easy **Movie Set Cabin Route** (0.9 mile/1.45 km) leads to replica wooden shacks used in Western films and television shows, including *The Missing* (2003) and *The Lone Ranger* (2013). The **History Grove Loop** is a triangular path to the old ranch house that now serves as the **interpretive museum**. A spur trail climbs to the

Daisies bloom in a field of flowers at Valles Caldera National Preserve.

"History Grove" is home to 300- to 400-year-old trees, overlooking foggy Valle Grande.

summit of **South Mountain** with its sky-high views of the caldera. In winter, the valley trails transition from hiking to cross-country skiing and snowshoeing. Meandering across the valley is the **East Fork of the Jemez River**, where visitors can cool their feet or angle for brown and rainbow trout.

Hikers, horses, and 4x4s share the **Backcountry Vehicle Route,** which leads from the staging area to narrow **Valle Jaramillo** in the heart of the caldera, and then on to **Valle Toledo** and **Valle San Antonio** in the far north. Running 12 miles (19.3 km) through the preserve, **San Antonio Creek** and its waterfront meadows are a great place to spot elk, bear, coyotes, and other animals that call the preserve home.

All vehicles and horses require permits for venturing behind Valle Grande. And no matter how they explore the backcountry, visitors are basically on their own in terms of transportation, food, lodging, and other necessary supplies. There is no overnight lodging or camping (backcountry or otherwise) inside the preserve. Camping is available at adjacent **Bandelier National Monument** and **Santa Fe National Forest**.

Among the annual events at Valles Caldera National Preserve are the **Jemez Mountains Elk Festival** (viewing, not hunting) in the fall and **fly-fishing clinics** for children and adults conducted by volunteers from New Mexico Trout during the summer months. ■

MEET THE NEIGHBORS

• **Bandelier National Monument:** Cliff dwellings and petroglyphs detail 11,000 years of human occupation in the wooded highlands west of the Rio Grande.

• **Santa Fe National Forest:** Much of the highlands around Valles Caldera is protected within the confines of this federal forest reserve, renowned for its hot springs, hiking trails, scenic rivers, and numerous wilderness areas.

• **Kasha-Katuwe Tent Rocks National Monument:** Formed by the same volcanic events that formed Valles Caldera, this park managed by the Bureau of Land Management, harbors unusual cone-shaped rock formations.

• **El Mapais National Monument:** Lava tube caves and cinder cones are among the geological wonders of this rugged volcanic badlands, southwest of Valles Caldera.

Glen Canyon NRA & Canyonlands National Park
Utah & Arizona

Nearly 300 miles (482.8 km) of the Colorado River in southern Utah are protected within the confines of parks with vastly different personalities. Glen Canyon National Recreation Area revolves around Lake Powell, the nation's second largest reservoir. Upstream the river runs wild and free through the red-rock chasms of Canyonlands National Park.

THE BIG PICTURE

Established: Glen Canyon (1972); Canyonlands (1964)

Size: Glen Canyon (1.2 million acres/ 4,856.2 sq km); Canyonlands (337,598 acres/1,366.21 sq km)

Annual Visitors: Glen Canyon (4.5 million); Canyonlands (742,000)

Visitor Centers: Glen Canyon Dam, Bullfrog, Island in the Sky, the Needles

Entrance Fees: Glen Canyon ($25 per vehicle, $12 per person); Canyonlands ($25 per vehicle, $10 per person)

nps.gov/glca; nps.gov/cany

GLEN CANYON

Finished in 1966, **Glen Canyon Dam** remains one of the most controversial infrastructure projects in American history. Environmentalists fought long and hard to keep the Colorado River free flowing but ultimately lost. The nation's second-highest concrete-arch dam (726 feet/ 221.26 m) created **Lake Powell**, a massive desert reservoir that provides recreation for millions each year.

Carl B. Hayden Visitor Center near Page, Arizona, offers museum exhibits, ranger programs, and a bookstore, as well as guided tours of the dam and power plant. Just up the lakeshore, **Lake Powell Marina** in Wahweap, Arizona, is ground zero for watercraft rentals, a flotilla that includes power boats, jet skis, pontoons, and houseboats. The marina also offers sunset dinner cruises on the lake as well as guided boat tours to **Rainbow Bridge National Monument** and flooded **Antelope Canyon** with its towering Navajo Sandstone walls. The best place along the south shore for a dip is **Lone Rock Beach**.

Only three other points on the lakeshore are accessible by paved road. Lying on opposite sides of the same bay, **Bullfrog** and **Halls Crossing** offer marinas, boat ramps, and campgrounds, as well as the *Charles Hall*, a vehicle/passenger ferry that travels back and forth across Bullfrog Bay. The only bridge that spans the Colorado River between Moab and Glen Canyon Dam leaps across a gorge at **Hite**, where the lake gives way to the

On Walnut Knob, centuries-old petroglyphs cover rock formations.

The Escalante River curves its way through portions of Glen Canyon National Recreation Area.

mighty **Cataract Canyon** with its 14 miles (22.5 km) of rapids.

CANYONLANDS

Set at the confluence of the Colorado and Green Rivers, Canyonlands is a giant jigsaw puzzle of mesas, buttes, arches, pinnacles, and deep canyons, all of the assorted pieces chiseled from stone.

A river trip is the classic way to discover the park—through **Labyrinth Canyon** and **Stillwater Canyon** on the Green River or **Meander Canyon** and Cataract Canyon on the Colorado. Other parts of Canyonlands are best explored by foot, mountain bike, or four-wheel drive. And others still are nearly impossible to reach, with some of the most remote points in the lower 48 states.

More than a dozen commercial outfitters are authorized by the Park Service to run river trips through the park. The adventure ranges from single-day float trips to multiday journeys offered by, for example, **Sheri Griffith Expeditions** in Moab.

Rafting is the most popular means, but guided kayak and canoe trips are also available.

Landlubbers can explore the park on mountain bike tours with **Magpie Cycling** or 4x4 camping tours organized by **NAVTEC Expeditions** and other adventure outfits in Moab.

Those exploring the park on their own should always start at one of the two visitor centers—**Island in the Sky** in the north (32 miles/51.5 km from Moab) or the **Needles** in the east (74 miles/119.1 km from Moab)—to check on road, weather, and water conditions.

The road across **Island in the Sky mesa** leads to overlooks along the **White Rim** that hover as much as 1,500 feet (457.2 m) above the rivers. From **Grand View Point**, you can gaze across Stillwater Canyon to an untamed rock wilderness, the **Maze**, or the red-and-white striped pinnacles of the **Needles** region on the far side of Meander Canyon. ◼

MEET THE NEIGHBORS

• **Arches National Park:** More than 2,000 stone arches are clustered just upstream from Moab in this unique national park.

• **McInnis Canyons National Conservation Area:** Sprawling on both sides of the river, this Bureau of Land Management reserve safeguards 75,000 acres (303.5 sq km) of western Colorado wilderness.

• **Colorado National Monument:** Desert canyons and wooded plateaus are the focus of this park near Grand Junction, Colorado.

• **Grand Staircase-Escalante National Monument:** The nation's largest national monument (1.9 million acres/7,689.5 sq km) protects scenic watersheds that drain into Lake Powell and Canyonlands.

Known as false kiva, Anasazi ruins are preserved in Canyonlands National Park.

❶ Mount Washington, New Hampshire

Whether you ride the cog railway to the summit, drive the historic toll road, or hike the Six Presidents, the view from the highest mountain in the Northeast United States is always commanding—and normally breezy: A weather station at the top of Mount Washington recorded a world-record 231 miles an hour (371.76 km/h) wind gust in 1934.

❷ Statue of Liberty, New York

It's far from being the highest outlook in the Big Apple, but it just might be the best. Look through Lady Liberty's crown to view the Manhattan skyline and a harbor that has welcomed millions of immigrants to America since the statue was dedicated in 1886.

❸ Washington Monument, Washington, D.C.

Recently refurbished elevators speed visitors to the summit of the monolith that honors America's founding father and first president. Perched 555 feet (169.17 m) above the grassy Mall, the viewing deck looks down on the Capitol Building, White House, Lincoln Memorial, and other national landmarks. The 897 stairs to the top have been closed to the public since 1976.

❹ Clingman's Dome, North Carolina and Tennessee

The highest point along the entire Appalachian Trail, the 6,643-foot (2,024.78 m) peak in Smoky Mountains National Park can be reached by foot, car, or cross-country skis when the road is closed in winter. On clear days, the view easily extends 100 miles (160.9 km).

❺ Gateway Arch, Missouri

After years of renovation, the 630-foot-high (192 m) stainless steel arc above downtown St. Louis is once again open to visitors. To get an appreciation for what it took to build the iconic structure, be sure to catch the film "Monument to the Dream" at the National Park Visitor Center.

THE TOP

10

PANORAMIC PARK VIEWS

Nature's peaks and man-made perches offer plenty of awesome panoramas.

❻ Navajo Bridge, Arizona

The Grand Canyon boasts dozens of world-class views. As for which one is best, that's largely up to personal taste. But it would be very hard to top the vertigo-inducing view from the historic Navajo Bridge, opened in 1929 and still the only span across the Colorado River between Lake Powell and the Hoover Dam.

The Statue of Liberty watches over the Manhattan skyline with torch raised.

❼ Half Dome, California

Sliding your chin over the granite edge at the top of Half Dome and staring down at Yosemite Valley 8,844 feet (2,695.6 m) below is one of America's essential national park experiences. But it doesn't come easy: The adrenaline rush entails a 16-mile (25.75 km) round-trip hike from the valley. The last leg up is a vertiginous cable ladder on the mountain's slick granite backside.

❽ Marin Headlands, California

The verdant hills on the north shore of Golden Gate National Recreation Area provide a literal bird's-eye view of the park's namesake span and San Francisco Bay. On a foggy summer day, the bridge's burnished towers are often the only parts protruding above the thick mist.

❾ Haleakala, Hawaii

Watching sunrise from the summit of the highest peak on Maui has been a tradition for decades, so much so that early risers must make reservations with the Park Service to visit the mountaintop at dawn. The experience is spectacular: the golden orb rising over the Pacific with Hawaii's other volcanic peaks floating to your left and right.

❿ Glacier Skywalk, Alberta

If you think it's cool to walk across the massive Athabasca Glacier at the southern end of Jasper National Park, try looking down on the frozen behemoth from this translucent pedestrian platform that floats more than 900 feet (274.32 m) above the visitor center and Sunwapta Valley. It's also the perfect place to see how the glacier flows down from the massive Columbia Icefield in the Canadian Rockies.

Four Corners Parks

Arizona, Utah, Colorado & New Mexico

Four Corners is the only place in the United States where four states—Arizona, Utah, Colorado, and New Mexico—come together at one spot. And beyond the region's dramatic desert landscapes is something much deeper: more than 10,000 years of human history expressed in numerous cliff dwellings, kivas, and pueblos clinging to mesas or tucked into remote canyons protected within the confines of several parks.

MONUMENT VALLEY

Sprawling across the Arizona-Utah border in the northeast corner of the Navajo reservation, Monument Valley is one of the places that summons instant déjà vu. You feel you've been here before because the valley's iconic Southwest scenery has appeared in so many movies, especially the classic Westerns of John Ford and John Wayne.

Tse'Bii'Ndzisgaii ("Valley of the Rocks") is the Navajo name for a landscape that comprises sandstone

THE BIG PICTURE

Established: Monument Valley (1958); Mesa Verde (1906); Canyons of the Ancients (2000)

Size: Monument Valley (91,696 acres/371.08 sq km); Mesa Verde (52,485 acres/212.4 sq km); Canyons of the Ancients (176,000 acres/712.25 sq km)

Annual Visitors: Monument Valley (350,000); Mesa Verde (613,000); Canyons of the Ancients (30,000)

Visitor Centers: Monument Valley, Anasazi Heritage Center, Hovenweep, Mesa Verde

Entrance Fees: Monument Valley ($20 per vehicle, $10 per person); Mesa Verde ($15-$20 per vehicle, $7-10 per person); Canyons of the Ancients ($3)

navajonationparks.org; nps.gov/meve; blm.gov/visit

pinnacles, buttes, and mesas towering as much as a thousand feet (305 m) above the valley floor. Visitors can explore the park on their own via a 17-mile (27.36 km) **unpaved scenic loop** or join a **Jeep tour** hosted by Navajo guides that ventures into areas off-limits to self-drive visitors.

Set on a high bluff beneath a sheer red-rock escarpment, the **Navajo Tribal Park Visitor Center** offers an information desk, souvenir shop, and restaurants specializing in Navajo foods. But some people never make it past the parking lot with its stunning panoramic views of **Merrick Butte** and the twin **Mitten Buttes** (named for the resemblance to a pair of woolen mittens).

Starting off from the visitor center, **Valley Drive** dips into a gap between the buttes and hulking **Merrick Mesa**, rambling across a sand-and-sagebrush landscape that's featured in

Cliff Palace, built by Ancestral Puebloans, is the largest cliff dwelling in the U.S.

A rainbow pierces through dark skies between the Mittens in Monument Valley, Arizona.

classic films like *Stagecoach* (1939) and *The Searchers* (1956). Around 5 miles (8 km) out, a junction with a spur road leads west to **John Ford's Point** near the base of the **Three Sisters**—a trio of tall, red-rock pinnacles. The main road loops around **Rain God Mesa** to an outlook for the lanky **Totem Pole**, a dreamy view across the valley from **Artist's Point** and the **North Window**.

Navajo Spirit and **Sacred Mountain Jeep Tours** are two of the outfitters that offer guided 4x4 explorations of Monument Valley.

MESA VERDE

One of the nation's 10 oldest national parks, Mesa Verde received federal protection in 1906 in order to safeguard its 600 cliff dwellings and thousands of other archaeological sites from treasure hunters and souvenir seekers who

were carting away so much of the region's treasured ancient heritage around that time.

Drawn to the woodlands, water, and wildlife of the massive outcrop, humans have lived on or around Mesa Verde since the 10th century B.C. But it wasn't until the arrival of the Ancestral Puebloans around A.D. 650 that the mountain's iconic stone villages and cliff dwellings began to take shape.

The new energy-efficient **Mesa Verde Visitor and Research Center** lies at the base of the 8,500-foot (2,590.8 m) mountain, just off U.S. Highway 160 about 10 miles (16.1 km) east of Cortez, Colorado. In addition to exhibits highlighting the three-million-strong artifact collection, the visitor center offers a bookshop, modern artwork interpretations of Mesa Verde, and reservations and tickets for Cliff

Palace, Balcony House, and Long House—three notable cliff dwellings that can only be visited on ranger-led tours.

Although there's a temptation to rush straight to the celebrated cliff dwellings, Mesa Verde is also about celebrating nature. Several hikes along the **North Rim** bring the park's mosaic of trees and shrubs into sharper focus. Morefield Campground marks the start of the 2.2-mile (3.5 km) **Point Lookout Trail** to a lofty viewpoint over the Mancos Valley and a 7.8-mile (12.5 km) loop called the **Prater Ridge Trail** that's especially rewarding around dawn when the resident wildlife is out and about.

Reaching the **Far View** area with its lodge and restaurant, the park road splits into two branches. The right fork zigzags down to **Wetherill Mesa**, named for the pioneer rancher who rediscovered many of the cliff dwellings in the 1880s and 1890s. The road dead-ends at a parking lot and the start of walking and hiking trails to the area's most notable ruins.

Built into a large cave-like gap beneath the mesa rim, **Long House** is a large 13th-century structure with three levels, a central plaza, and around 150 rooms. The strenuous ranger-led hike descends 130 feet (39.6 m) down the cliff face via two ladders. The remainder of Wetherill Mesa is self-guided, including the ruins of the **Badger House Community**, the looping trail down to an overlook for **Kodak House**, and an off-the-beaten-path hike to **Nordenskiold Site No. 16.**

Hanging a left at Far View takes you along the main park road to **Chapin Mesa** and the most renowned ruins. The largest cliff dwelling in North America, **Cliff House** is a masterpiece of Ancestral Puebloan architecture. Built around A.D. 1190, it features numerous rooms, kivas, and towers. Many of the interior walls are still decorated with ancient murals. **Balcony House** is tucked so far into the mesa it's almost like a cave residence rather than a cliff dwelling.

Both Cliff House and Balcony House can only be visited on tick-

eted ranger tours, but the rest of Chapin Mesa is free to explore. **Mesa Top Loop** is a 6-mile (9.65 km), one-way motor route to a dozen viewpoints or archaeological sites including **Sun Temple** and **Square Tower House**. In addition to artifacts, **Chapin Mesa Archeological Museum** is the jumping-off point for the self-guided trail down to **Spruce Tree House** and the **Petroglyph Point Trail** (2.4-mile/3.86 km round-trip) to a rock-art panel along the rim.

CANYONS OF THE ANCIENTS

With more than 6,300 structures already recorded and an estimated 30,000 archaeological sites in total, this national monument managed by the Bureau of Land Management has the highest density of ancient ruins and remains in North America. Some areas of the park boast an astounding 100 sites per square mile. Many of the sites were occupied as long as 10,000 years ago by the Ancestral Puebloan peoples, the first humans who settled the Four Corners.

The **Anasazi Heritage Center** in Dolores, Colorado, doubles as the park headquarters and interpretive museum. In addition to artifacts, exhibits, bookshop, nature trails, and two 12th-century archaeological sites, the center provides guided tours of the main gallery, behind-the-scene curator tours, and astronomy programs.

Most of the actual park is remote and difficult to access. **Lowry Pueblo**, one of the most significant sites, is the easiest to reach—a half-hour drive from the visitor center via U.S. Highway 491 and County Road CC. Founded in the 11th century and occupied for more than

Totem Pole and Yei Bi Chei are just two of many popular rock formations in Monument Valley.

A 7-mile (11.3 km) round-trip hike leads to Painted Hand Pueblo, one of the Anasazi dwelling ruins in the Canyons of the Ancients.

100 years, the ruins encompass eight kivas and 40 total rooms rendered in the Chaco architectural style popular at the time.

Two other noteworthy sites inside the park are harder to reach. **Painted Hand Pueblo**, with its distinctive stone tower and namesake pictograph, is about a half hour south of Lowry. The zigzag trail down to the ruins is less than a half mile (0.8 km) long, with views across much of park's rugged canyonlands. **Sand Canyon Pueblo** is a large 13th-century village built in a U shape around a spring. The trailhead is on Road N about 20 miles (32.2 km) west of the visitor center.

Adjacent **Hovenweep National Monument** preserves the impressive ruins of six Ancient Puebloan villages on **Cajon Mesa** and nearby canyons. Among the scores of structures found along this popular mesa are the three-story **Square Tower** and the mammoth **Hovenweep Castle**. ■

LAY YOUR HEAD

Monument Valley

• **The View Hotel:** The only accommodation inside the tribal park, with views to die for; restaurant, guided tours on offer; from $69. *monumentvalleyview.com*

• **Far View Lodge:** In Mesa Verde, modern mesa-top accommodations with Southwest styling and awesome views of the Four Corners region; restaurant, bar, private balconies; from $136. *visitmesaverde.com*

• **Canyon of the Ancients Guest Ranch:** Rustic log cabins and adobe houses on a working ranch in McElmo Canyon on the south side of the park; from $190. *canyonoftheancients.com*

Camping

• RV/tent camping available at the View in Monument Valley, Square Tower in Hovenweep, and Moorefield in Mesa Verde.

Carlsbad Caverns & Guadalupe Mountains
New Mexico & Texas

One dives deep underground, and the other rises high into the sky, polar opposites located along the same ridgeline. Among the world's great show caves, Carlsbad Cavern attracts thousands of visitors each year to its subterranean wonders. Nearby Guadalupe National Park, less than 20 miles (32.2 km) away, offers desert and mountain wilderness to the few hardy souls who bravely trek its vast backcountry.

Claret cup cactus flowers bloom toward the sun.

THE BIG PICTURE

Established: Carlsbad Caverns (1930); Guadalupe Mountains (1972)

Size: Carlsbad Caverns (46,766 acres/189.26 sq km); Guadalupe Mountains (86,367 acres/349.5 sq km)

Annual Visitors: Carlsbad Caverns (520,000); Guadalupe Mountains (225,000)

Visitor Centers: Carlsbad Caverns, Pine Springs

Entrance Fees: Carlsbad Caverns ($10), Guadalupe Mountains ($5)

nps.gov/cave; nps.gov/gumo

CARLSBAD CAVERNS

"A whale of a big cave," is how teenage ranch hand Jim White described the massive cavern he discovered in 1898. Using a homemade kerosene lantern and wire ladder, he explored what's now known as the Carlsbad Caverns and named many of the underground chambers that people visit today.

The caverns trace their roots to the Permian period (250 million years ago) when the area was a reef on the edge of a shallow inland sea, later uplifted and subjected to eons of erosion and other forces. Although the park boasts rugged desert mountains and canyons, most visitors make straight for the caves. **Carlsbad Caverns Visitor Center** doubles as a cave entrance for those exploring on their own or on ranger-guided tours.

Starting with an elevator ride from the surface, the **Big Room Self-Guided Trail** is a 1.25-mile (2 km) route to the largest underground chamber in North America, a space so big Will Rogers called it "the Grand Canyon with a roof." About the same

In the shadows of rocky walls, hikers wind down the graveled path to the natural entrance of the Carlsbad Caverns.

length, the **Natural Entrance Self-Guided Trail** offers a steep descent to the **Devil's Den, Whale's Mouth**, and other limestone landmarks discovered by Jim White and other early explorers and spelunkers.

Ticketed ranger-guided "wild cave" tours explore six subterranean areas beyond the self-guided trails, including the **King's Palace** (1.5 hours) into the deepest part of the caverns open to the public, and **House of the White Giant** (4 hours) via an underground obstacle course of ladders, tight spaces, and slippery surfaces. Amateur spelunkers will enjoy heading away from the main cavern, where ranger tours are also conducted through **Slaughter Canyon Cave** (5.5 hours) with its towering columns and claustrophobia-inducing **Spider Cave** (4 hours), where crawling through supernarrow apertures on your belly is part of the adventure.

Between May and October, hundreds of **Brazilian free-tailed bats** exit the natural entrance around sunset in search of food, a spiraling cloud of screeching, flying mammals that either freaks out or fascinates visitors. The park also offers evening **Star Parties**, **Full Moon Hikes**, and other night sky activities.

GUADALUPE MOUNTAINS

It's only a 45-minute drive along the **National Parks Highway** (U.S. 62) from Carlsbad Caverns to the **Pine Springs Visitor Center** in Guadalupe Mountains National Park, but the experience is so different the two attractions might as well be a million miles apart.

LAY YOUR HEAD

Hotel

• **Trinity Hotel:** Erected in 1892 as the First National Bank, this stout brick building in Carlsbad is now a cute boutique hotel; restaurant, bar; from $189. *thetrinityhotel.com*

• **Fiddler's Inn:** Cozy five-room B&B tucked inside a 1912 Victorian-style manse in downtown Carlsbad, with breakfast two doors down at the Blue House Bakery & Cafe; outdoor hot tub, barbecue area, garden; from $189. *fiddlersinnbb.com*

Camping

• Two campsites available at Guadalupe Mountains National Park: Pine Springs and Dog Canyon; $8 per night.

• Primitive camping is allowed in Carlsbad Caverns National Park with a permit from the visitor center.

Above: El Capitan's peak sits at 8,085 feet (2,464.3 m). Opposite: Stalactites line the Carlsbad Caverns.

The Pine Springs area is by far the park's most user friendly—in both past and present times. Freshwater springs nurture a lush riparian area where pioneers once established a cattle ranch and station coach stop. The whitewashed **Frijole Ranch House** (1876) now houses the park's history collection. Those who bring their own horses for exploring the park's many multiuse trails can keep their mounts stabled at the ranch corral overnight.

The stone ruins of the **Pinery Butterfield Stage Station** (1858) are a short walk from the visitor center. But there are plenty of more challenging hikes that start at Pine Springs, including the **Devil's Hall Trail** (3.8-mile/6.1 km round-trip) to a supernarrow rock gorge and the steep climb to the summit of **Guadalupe Peak** (8.5-mile/13.7 km round-trip), the highest point in Texas at 8,749 feet (2,666.7 m).

Two other areas of the park are accessible by motor vehicle. **McKittrick Canyon** is renowned for its fall foliage, an explosion of color among the native big-toothed maple trees. Hikes in the area include the **Permian Reef Geology Trail** (3.5 miles/5.6 km) and a longer walk through the middle of the canyon to the historic **Pratt Cabin** and a damp, shady overhang called the **Grotto**.

Around the north side of the park, out-of-the-way **Dog Canyon** can be reached from Carlsbad, New Mexico. There's a short **Indian Meadows Nature Trail** (0.6 mile/.97 km), but otherwise Dog Canyon is used as a staging ground for hikes and horseback trips into the park's rugged and remote backcountry. ■

DID YOU KNOW

• A legendary 19th-century longhorn cattle route called the Goodnight Loving Trail ran along the Pecos River just east of Carlsbad Caverns and the Guadalupe Mountains.

• Notorious outlaw Billy the Kid—who terrorized the New Mexico Territory in the late 1870s and early 1880s—was known to frequent the area.

• The two parks boast a surprisingly wide array of plant life, more than 900 species and subspecies, including 26 kinds of cacti, 135 different kinds of grass, and 153 members of the sunflower family.

• Discovered in 1986, Lechuguilla Cave is the longest in the park—more than 140 miles (225 km) in length.

Access to the underground behemoth is currently limited to scientific researchers and survey and exploration teams.

• African-American buffalo soldiers clashed with Mescalero Apaches in the Guadalupe Mountains shortly after the Civil War.

Big Bend National Park
Texas

THE BIG PICTURE

Established: State park (1933); national park (1944)

Size: 801,163 acres (3,242.19 sq km)

Annual Visitors: 440,000

Visitor Centers: Panther Junction, Chisos Basin, Rio Grande Village, Castolon, Persimmon Gap

Entrance Fee: $25 per vehicle, $12 per person

nps.gov/bibe

"Texas seemed to be half Mexico . . . and half Will Rogers," quipped the British writer Graham Greene after a 1939 visit to the Lone Star State. While the rest of Texas may have settled down, Big Bend retains its raw edge. Set along the north bank of the Rio Grande, the massive national park offers an adventurous blend of mountains, desert, water, and Wild West.

On its way from the Rocky Mountains to the Gulf of Mexico, the **Rio Grande** suddenly makes a huge left turn, a geographical oddity that 19th-century explorers and settlers simply called the Big Bend. It wasn't just no country for old men—it was no country for anyone during pioneer days.

Unrelenting desert, impenetrable canyons, and a wild river kept the region largely uninhabited and unvisited until the parks came along in 1933.

One of the nation's largest national parks is also one of the least visited, a vast expanse of desert and mountain—and 118 miles (189.9 km) of the Rio Grande—where few people have ever lived. But that's what makes Big Bend so intriguing: a glimpse of what much of the American West was like once upon a time.

Despite its arid facade, Big Bend boasts incredible biodiversity, an array of habitats including forests, grasslands, and oases that foster a variety of flora and fauna. More than 450 bird species call the park home, together with 75 types of mammals and 67 varieties of reptiles and amphibians. Even more astounding is the fact that such a harsh environment nurtures more than a thousand plant species.

Panther Junction Visitor Center is the place to top-up on fuel, food, and information before heading out to more remote corners. Route 12 reaches the river at **Rio Grande Village**, the put-in/take-out spot for many of the float trips organized by **Big Bend River Tours** and other outfitters. It's also a great place for riverside hikes. The vertiginous **Boquillas Canyon Trail** (1.4-mile/2.25 km round-trip) affords a glimpse of the park's most imposing chasm, while the **Hot Springs Historic Trail** (1-mile/1.6 km round-trip) meanders

Casa Grande towers over agave plants and grassland in Big Bend National Park.

After rainfall, the desert comes alive as sagebrush and ocotillo bloom in vivid color before the Chisos Mountains.

down to an old homestead and riverside rock pool with 105°F (40.6°C) water to soak in. A tiny border station facilitates visits to the Mexican village of **Boquillas** across the river, so bring your passport.

Rising to 7,825 feet (2,385.1 m), the **Chisos Mountains** form the park's rugged core and hiking center. The crater-like **Chisos Basin** shelters another visitor center and the rustic **Chisos Mountains Lodge** for sleep and eats. Seven trails head up into the highlands, ranging from relatively easy jaunts like the **Chisos Basin Loop** (1.8 miles/2.9 km) to the much more strenuous **Window Trail** (5.6-mile/9 km round-trip) through **Oak Creek Canyon** to an incredible desert overlook and the day-long climb to the crest of **Emory Peak**.

Another way to reach the river is via the 22-mile (35.4 km) **Ross**

Maxwell Scenic Drive through the park's western sector. After tumbling through the bottom of **Tuff Canyon**, the road flows into **Castolon**, a riverside ghost town where the old **La Harmonia Store** (1921) is now a seasonal visitor center with historic exhibits. The road continues along

the Rio Grande to an overlook for spectacular **Santa Elena Canyon**. Visitors can trace their path back along the scenic road or take **Old Maverick Road** through the national park's back door to **Terlingua Ghost Town** and **Big Bend State Park**. ■

Palo Duro Canyon State Park

Texas

THE BIG PICTURE

Established: 1934

Size: 29,182 acres (118.1 sq km)

Annual visitors: 279,000

Visitor Center: El Coronado Lodge

Entrance Fee: $5

palodurocanyon.com

The nation's second largest canyon, Palo Duro, is a 120-mile-long (193.12 km) gouge in the Earth's crust on the outskirts of Amarillo. Featuring numerous caves, rock formations, and cliffs towering up to a thousand feet (304.8 m), the canyon offers a dramatic contrast to the flatness of the surrounding Llano Estacado ("staked plain"), as well as the best place in the Texas Panhandle for hiking, biking, and horseback riding.

Georgia O'Keeffe rendered its multicolored walls on canvas, and American composer Samuel Jones was moved to create an entire symphony about this geographical landmark. But most Americans have probably never even heard of Palo Duro Canyon. That might have something to do with its extremely remote location in the Texas Panhandle and that most of the chasm was privately owned until well into the 20th century.

Palo Duro means "hard wood" in Spanish, a name that refers to the Rocky Mountain junipers that thrive in the canyon and around the rim. But for the most part, it's an arid landscape that blends short grass prairie and deeply eroded palisades carved by the Prairie Dog Town Fork of the Red River, which flows through the canyon.

The state park visitor center is located in the historic **El Coronado Lodge**, built in the 1930s by the Civilian Conservation Corps (CCC) and now home to interpretive exhibits and an information desk where visitors can get the scoop on hiking, camping, and other Palo Duro activities. The **scenic overlook** beside the lodge gives visitors their first glimpse of the canyon.

Drive the Park Road or hike the old **CCC Trail** (1.4 miles/2.25 km) from the rim of the **Caprock Escarpment** to the **Pioneer Amphitheater** on the canyon floor, a descent of 500 feet (152.4 m) through four layers of the canyon's geological history. A patriotic musical drama, *Texas*, takes the stage at the outdoor theater on evenings

Riders make their way through Lighthouse Trail in Palo Duro.

Three miles (4.8 km) from the road, the famous Lighthouse rock formation towers 300 feet (91.4 m) above sightseers.

between June and August. The adjacent **Palo Duro Trading Post** vends meals, souvenirs, and camping supplies, while **Old West Stables** is one of several outfitters that offer guided trail rides in the canyon. A bit farther down the road is the **Charles Goodnight Dugout**, a replica of the rustic dwelling where the legendary Texas rancher lived in the 1870s and 1880s when he ran cattle in Palo Duro.

Thirty miles of multiuse trail (hike, bike, and horse) lead through the main part of Palo Duro and many spectacular side canyons. Most popular of these is the **Lighthouse Trail** (5.5-mile/8.85 km round-trip) to a large hoodoo rock column that's long been the park's geological mascot. Among the easy hikes on the canyon floor are the mile-long (1.6 km) **Paseo del Rio** along the Prairie Dog Town Fork and the half-mile (0.8 km) **Pioneer Nature Trail**. At the opposite end of the sweat spectrum, the **Rock Garden Trail** (2.4 miles/ 3.86 km) follows a side canyon up to the northeast rim, where it intersects

with the **Rylander Fortress Cliff Trail** (3.7 miles/5.95 km) to several striking viewpoints.

Just outside the state park, **Palo Duro Canyon Adventure Park** offers a quarter-mile (0.4 km) zip line that hangs nearly 500 feet (152.4 m) above the canyon floor, as well as a half-day cliff rappelling and bouldering experience. Over

on the other side of the canyon, **Cowgirls and Cowboys in the West** at Los Cedros Ranch offers open-range horseback riding along trails on the rim, as well as the six-hour **Step Into the Real Texas** experience, which includes a canyon tour, cowboy demonstration, hiking or horseback riding, and a steak lunch. ■

LAY YOUR HEAD

Cabins

• **CCC Rim Cabins:** Three vintage stone cottages with canyon views outfitted with modern conveniences including heating and air-conditioning, and an outdoor charcoal grill; $110-$125 per night. *tpwd.texas .gov/state-parks/palo-duro-canyon/ fees-facilities/cabins*

• **Cow Camp Cabins:** Four smaller stone dwellings on the canyon floor offering bunk beds, a mini-fridge, microwave, and outdoor charcoal grill; $60 per night.

Camping

• Drive-up campsites with electrical hookups at Hackberry, Mesquite, and Sagebrush; $24 per night.

• Mesquite equestrian campsite and primitive campsites; $12 per night.

Outside the park

• **Hudspeth House:** An elegant B&B in a 1909 mansion, located in Canyon, Texas, about 15 minutes from the park entrance; from $115. *hudspethhouse.com*

California
& Nevada

The Mesquite Flat Dunes in Death Valley, California

Yosemite National Park

California

"Everybody needs beauty as well as bread, places to play in and pray in, where Nature may heal and cheer and give strength to body and soul alike," wrote John Muir in his beloved 1912 book *The Yosemite*. More than a century later, the giant California park still reaches those lofty goals via its dramatic landscapes, diverse outdoor pursuits, and the possibility of soul-searching reflection.

THE BIG PICTURE

Established: Federal protection (1864); National Park (1890)

Size: 748,436 acres (3,028.8 sq km)

Annual Visitors: 4.3 million

Visitor Centers: Yosemite Valley (year-round), Wawona and Big Oak Flats (May–October), Tuolumne Meadows (June or July–late September)

Entrance Fee: $30 per vehicle, $15 per person

nps.gov/yose

YOSEMITE VALLEY

Stretching nearly 8 miles (12.8 km) from east to west and with granite walls more than twice the height of the Empire State Building, Yosemite Valley is one of the wonders of the natural world. Carved by glacial dynamics and weathering and erosion spanning 30 million years, few other places reflect in such remarkable fashion the geological forces that have shaped our planet.

There is nothing quite as striking as viewing the valley for the first time while exiting the **Wawona Tunnel**, a view that stretches all the way to **Half Dome** and that impressed even the great Ansel Adams. For an even better view (and far fewer people to share it with), hike the 1.2-mile (1.9 km) trail to **Inspiration Point** from the tunnel's upper parking lot.

A circular one-way road system cruises past all of the valley's major landmarks. The first of the many astonishing sights is the aptly named **Bridalveil Fall**, 620 feet (188.9 m) of delicate white water tumbling down a granite face beneath **Cathedral Rocks**. **Southside Drive** soon runs along the **Merced River**, a slow-flowing scene for swimming, tubing, rafting, and fishing during the valley's hot summer months. **Cathedral Beach** is a great place to get your feet wet or stare up at 3,593-foot (1,095.15 m) **El Capitan** looming high above the valley. One of the holy grails of extreme adventure, the imposing cliff is on the bucket list of every serious rock climber. Bring binoculars to watch their slow but steady progression up El Cap.

The road eventually leads into **Yosemite Village**, the valley's human hub and home to the park's main **Visitor Center.** In addition to a grocery store, gas station, post office, medical clinic, and other facilities, the village

The Majestic Yosemite Hotel, formerly the Awahnee Hotel, sits in Yosemite Valley.

Seen from a distance, Bridalveil Fall, the most prominent waterfall in the park, plunges 620 feet (188.9 m) into Yosemite Valley.

offers the **Yosemite Museum** of Native American culture, the **Ansel Adams Gallery** of photographic art, and the **Yosemite Wilderness Center**, where backpackers can obtain wilderness permits, bear canisters, and other backcountry essentials.

Many of the landmarks scattered around the valley's eastern end are best reached on foot or shuttle from Yosemite Village. Tumbling down an enormous rock face just west of the village, **Yosemite Falls** is impressive not so much in water volume but the sheer height from which it falls. Split into three sections, the cascade plunges 2,425 feet (739.1 m); it is the highest waterfall in North America and fifth on the planet. A supereasy trail leads to the falls' rock-strewn base. Those with more time (and a lot more energy) can hike a 7.2-mile (11.59 km) trail to the summit of **Upper Yosemite**

Fall and its spectacular views across the valley.

Other trails lead from the village to **Ahwahnee Meadow**, the best place on the valley floor to look at or photograph Half Dome no matter what the season. Soaring 4,788 feet (1,459.4 m) above the

valley, the distinctive granite dome has been literally sheared in half by weathering, erosion, and earthquakes. Secreted in a stand of trees beyond the meadow is the old **Ahwahnee Hotel** (now the Majestic), opened in 1927 and now a national historic monument.

CHOW DOWN

- **Majestic Hotel dining room**: Breakfast, lunch, dinner and Sunday brunch beneath 34-foot-high (10.36 m) pine ceilings and granite pillars; Bracebridge "Old English" dinners during the Christmas season. *bracebridgedinners.com*

- **Yosemite Lodge at the Falls:** Mountain Room Restaurant and Lounge, food court.

- **White Wolf Lodge Dining Room:** Serving breakfast and dinner.

- **Half Dome Village:** Meadow Grill, Pavilion Restaurant, Pizza Deck, coffee and ice cream bar.

- **Big Trees Lodge Dining Room:** Breakfast, lunch, dinner, and Saturday barbecues.

- **Glacier Point Snack Stand:** Sandwiches, light bites; open 9 a.m.-7 p.m.

- **Tuolumne Meadows Lodge Dining Tent:** Serving breakfast and dinner.

Sunset lights the Tuolumne River and Meadows, with Lembert Dome in the distance.

Continuing eastward, the trails curve up **Tenaya Canyon** to legendary **Mirror Lake**, which reflects Half Dome and other monoliths.

Perched along the south side of the Merced River are the **Yosemite Conservation Heritage Center** (interpretive programs, natural history exhibits, library) and **Half Dome Village** (formerly Curry Village) with its myriad food, beverage, and accommodation options. During the winter, the village **ice rink** hosts skating under the stars. The **Nature Center at Happy Isles** offers family-oriented, interactive nature displays and exhibits.

Happy Isles is also a jumping-off spot for a branch of the **John Muir Trail** that leads up to **Vernal Fall** and **Nevada Fall** before leveling in **Little Yosemite Valley** and the high

country beyond. A spur trail leads up the back side of Half Dome via a vertiginous cable walkway. Placing your chin on the outer lop of the dome and peering down almost a mile (1.6 km) to the valley floor is an iconic Yosemite experience.

TIOGA ROAD AND THE HIGH COUNTRY

The bulk of Yosemite National Park lies above the valley, a vast expanse of high country meadows, mountains, and forest that includes the headwaters of several mighty rivers and more than 1,100 square miles (2,848.9 sq km) of designated wilderness. Most of this region is accessible only by foot or horse. But two long, winding roads open up much of the Yosemite backcountry to motorists and casual hikers too.

Tioga Road, one of the nation's most scenic highways, literally splits the park in half between Crane Flat near the park's western border to Tioga Pass at the crest of the High Sierra. Often closed until early or even midsummer due to snowpack, the road is the only drivable route between Yosemite Valley and the eastern side of the Sierra. Flanking **Crane Flat** (gas station, store) are two of the park's lesser-known wonders—the **Tuolumne Grove** and **Merced Grove** of giant sequoias, the only spots in Yosemite where you can occasionally have the redwoods to yourself, especially during the snowy winter months. Another "secret" spot is the forest and flower-filled alpine wonderland around little **Lukens Lake**, 20 miles (32.19 km) up the road from Crane Flat. Other

LAY YOUR HEAD

Hotels

Lodging reservations: 888-413-8869 or travelyosemite.com

• **Majestic Yosemite** (formerly the Ahwahnee Hotel): Historic park lodge in Yosemite Valley; pool, restaurant, bar; from $399.

• **Half Dome Village** (formerly Curry Village): Cabins, tent cabins, and Stoneman House rooms; pool, restaurant; from $39.

• **Big Trees Lodge** (formerly the Wawona Hotel): Vintage 1876 wilderness retreat; pool, golf, restaurant; from $99.

• **Yosemite Lodge at the Falls:** Motel-style accommodation in the village; pool, restaurant; from $99.

• **High Sierra Camps:** Six remote tent-cabin camps along the John Muir Trail in eastern Yosemite accessible only by hiking; $151 per person, including three daily meals.

Camping

Campground reservations: 877-444-6777 or recreation.gov

• Thirteen campgrounds spread across the park, including Yosemite Valley, Tuolumne Meadows, and Wawona; $12-$26 per night.

Outside the Park

• **Evergreen Lodge:** Historic 1920s family-friendly resort near Hetch Hetchy and Big Oak Flats; from $148. *evergreenlodge.com*

• **Tenaya Lodge:** Modern luxury retreat 7 miles (11. 3 km) south of Wawona; from $159. *tenayalodge.com*

---

turnoffs along Tioga Road provide parking for a few hiking trails leading to the north side of Yosemite Valley and vertigo-inducing viewpoints like **North Dome, Eagle Peak, Indian Arch**, and **El Capitan** that perch 3,000 to 4,000 feet (914.4-1,219.2 m) above the valley floor.

Olmsted Point tenders one of the high country's best views, a sweeping vista of Tenaya Lake and the flank of Half Dome in the hazy distance. Look out for marmots frolicking on the rocky slope beside the parking lot. Largest of the park's water bodies, **Tenaya Lake** is a great place to picnic or paddle—and perhaps even swim if you can stand the chilly water temperatures, even at the height of summer. A 2.5-mile (4 km) trail leads around the lake.

With its visitor center, campground, tented lodge, and other services, **Tuolumne Meadows** is the "Times Square" of the high country. Trails meander across the giant meadow to **Sunset Lakes, Soda Springs, Lembert Dome**, and other natural landmarks. Both the **Pacific Crest Trail** and **John Muir Trail**

transit the meadow. The Wild and Scenic **Tuolumne River** runs slow and gentle so close to its source in the High Sierra. Sunset is especially moody here, the soft pinks, purples, and golds of alpenglow coloring **Mount Dana** (13,057 feet/3,979.7 m) and other Sierra crest peaks. A free hiker's shuttle connects Tuolumne Meadows and Yosemite Valley. Beyond the meadows, the road cuts through 9,945-foot (3,031.24 m) **Tioga Pass**

and down the eastern slope of the Sierra to **Mono Lake** and the town of **Lee Vining**.

The river eventually tumbles through the remote **Grand Canyon of the Tuolumne** (accessible only by hiking) down into deep **Hetch Hetchy Canyon**—an almost identical twin of Yosemite Valley until it was dammed and transformed into a lake in 1923 to provide water for San Francisco. Visitors can walk

El Capitan pokes through the clouds that hover over the massive peak.

across the 430-foot-high (131.1 m) **O'Shaughnessy Dam** and gaze up the flooded canyon via **Evergreen Road**, which starts just outside the **Big Oak Flat Entrance Station**. Below the dam (and outside the park), the increasingly rugged river provides a venue for adventurous multi-day rafting trips through companies like **OARS**.

GLACIER POINT AND WAWONA

Above the tunnel, **Wawona Road** climbs the valley wall into the park's low-key southwest corner. Roughly 7.6 miles (12.23 km) beyond the tunnel is the turnoff to **Glacier Point Road**, which follows the southern edge of Yosemite Valley to "Wow!" inspiring **Glacier Point.** From the point parking lot, the

8.7-mile (14 km) **Pohono Trail** leads across the top of the valley's lofty wall to **Sentinel Dome**, **Taft Point**, and **Dewey Point** above Bridalveil Fall. Directly opposite El Capitan, Taft Point is a great place to watch climbers scaling the famed vertical face.

About halfway along Glacier Point Road is the **Badger Pass** winter sports area, originally developed for Yosemite's failed bid to host the 1932 Winter Olympics. In addition to family-oriented skiing and snowboarding, Badger Pass also facilitates ranger-led snowshoe tours and cross-country skiing along the road (closed to vehicles in winter) to the **Glacier Point Ski Hut** (open December to March).

Yosemite's frontier side is on display in **Wawona Village**, where the

Climbers ascend Half Dome, the iconic rock formation that rises nearly 5,000 feet (1,524 m) from the Yosemite Valley.

Pioneer Yosemite History Center offers horse-drawn carriage rides, a working blacksmith shop, covered wooden bridge, and other relics of the era before National Park status. **Big Trees Lodge** (the old Wawona Hotel) opened in 1876 to host early visitors to Yosemite. The lodge's nine-hole **golf course** (created in 1918) is one of the few found in the National Park System. The 3.5-mile (5.6 km) **Wawona Meadow Trail** loops through the mosaic of meadows and woods around the golf course.

Among other Wawona activities are horseback trips through the surrounding woods and wandering the **Mariposa Grove**, the park's largest stand of giant sequoias (more than 500 trees). The grove's most celebrated tree is the **Grizzly Giant**, standing at 209 feet (63.7 m) tall and more than 1,800 years old (plus or minus a few centuries). A free shuttle runs between the grove and **Wawona Visitor Center** in the village. From the village, a 5-mile (8 km) trail leads to **Chilnualna Falls**, a beautiful series of five cascades that tumble 690 feet (210.3 m) down a granite slope. The trail continues deep into the park's southern backcountry and hard-core (read: expert-only) hiking to secluded spots like **Chain of Lakes**, the fin-shaped **Clark Range,** and the Fernandez Pass route into the **Ansel Adams Wilderness**. ∎

The John Muir Trail leads to the top of 317-foot-tall (96.6 m) Vernal Fall.

DID YOU KNOW

• Yosemite has sister national parks in China (Huangshan and Jiuzhaigou), Chile (Torres del Paine), Germany (Berchtesgaden), and Mongolia (Lake Hovsgol and Tengis-Shishged).

• Violence broke out in Yosemite on July 4, 1970, when rangers tried to evict hundreds of hippies who were camped illegally in Stoneman Meadow. The National Guard was called in to quell the disturbance; 138 people were arrested.

• African-American cavalry troops protected Yosemite in its early days as a national park, and the "Montana Peak" cap of the famed Buffalo Soldiers was later adopted for the Park Service ranger uniform.

• Sheep were once the biggest threat to the environment prior to national park status. As many as 100,000 sheep grazed Yosemite's high country each summer.

Daredevils stand atop Eichorn's Pinnacle (10,680 feet/3,255.3 m).

Sequoia & Kings Canyon National Parks
California

Rambling across a massive expanse of the Sierra Nevada, these twin parks have a lot in common: snowcapped peaks, voluminous canyons, raging rivers, and the world's largest living things. But their differences make them even more intriguing—Kings Canyon's "lost world" feel and the sense of history exuded by Sequoia, one of the first places to inspire the global environmental movement.

THE BIG PICTURE

Established: Sequoia (1890); Kings Canyon (1940)

Size: Sequoia (404,063 acres/ 1,635.18 sq km); Kings Canyon (461,901 acres/ 1,869.25 sq km)

Annual Visitors: Sequoia (1.3 million); Kings Canyon (692,000)

Visitor Centers: Grant Grove, Cedar Grove, Lodgepole, Foothills, Mineral King

Entrance Fees: Both parks $30 per vehicle, $15 per person

nps.gov/seki

SEQUOIA

From cave exploration and horseback trips to scaling the highest peak in the lower 48, Sequoia offers a greater range of activities than its big sister to the north. Most of the park's major sights and visitor facilities are found along **Generals Highway**, including the **Foothill Visitor Center** and its exhibits on oak and chaparral ecosystems that dominate Sequoia's lower elevations. Farther up the road is **Potwisha Campground** and a trail that leads 3.6 miles (5.79 km) to **Marble Falls**, tucked into a narrow boulder-filled canyon shaded by oaks.

Switchbacks carry the highway up to **Giant Forest** and its celebrated sequoia grove. Located in the old market building (1928), the **Giant Forest Museum** provides a great introduction to the park's history.

Tucked up at the north end of Giant Forest is the park's main event: the massive **General Sherman Tree**. Towering 275 feet (83.82 m) above the forest floor, it measures 36 feet (10.97 m) in diameter at the base and weighs an estimated 2.4 million pounds (1.08 million kg). In other words, the tree is nearly as tall as London's Big Ben clock tower and more than seven times heavier than the Statue of Liberty. Follow the popular **Congress Trail** (2.1-mile/3.4 km loop) to other wooden behemoths. Perched on the southern edge of Giant Forest is **Moro Rock**, which offers an unusual bird's-eye view looking *down* on giant sequoias.

A sinuous side road leads to **Crystal Cave**, an underground wonderland of stalagmites and stalactites fashioned by subterranean streams. Guided tours are offered May to November by Sequoia Parks Conservancy.

The park's southern region centers around **Mineral King**, an old mining

A supermoon hovers above the Eastern Sierra.

A woman is dwarfed by the massive Cedar Grove trees during a winter snowshoe expedition.

camp that Walt Disney nearly turned into a huge ski resort until a fierce environmental campaign thwarted the scheme. Now it's a launchpad for Sequoia's vast backcountry, trails leading to **Kern Canyon** and 14,494-foot (4,417.8 m) **Mount Whitney**, the highest point in the United States outside of Alaska.

KINGS CANYON

Thirty miles from Giant Forest in Sequoia, **Grant Grove** was its own small national park from 1890 until 1940 when it was folded into the newly created Kings Canyon. It's still the park's most popular area, home to both the **Kings Canyon Visitor Center** and the world's second largest living thing—the 267-foot-high (81.38 m) **General Grant Tree**. The Grant Tree was declared the "Nation's Christmas Tree" by President Coolidge in 1926. The looping trail through the grove leads to other landmarks like the **Cen-**

tennial Stump (all that remains of a redwood cut for the 1876 Philadelphia world's fair), a massive tumbled-over tree called the **Fallen Monarch**, and the pioneer-era **Gamlin Cabin**.

Kings Canyon Scenic Byway (Highway 180) meanders through 29 miles (46.67 km) of Sequoia National Forest from Grant Grove Village to Cedar Grove. Much of the route hugs the **South Fork Kings River**, which, along with glacial action, helped form the mile-deep chasm. **Cedar Grove**

Visitor Center offers displays on the canyon's inhabitants, as well as advice on day hikes and backcountry exploration. Easy trails lead along the valley bottom to **Zumwalt Meadow** and **Roaring River Falls**. Armed with a wilderness permit for overnight camping, you can trek the **Woods Creek Trail** (6.5 miles/10.46 km) to Paradise Valley, the challenging **Cooper Creek Trail** (9 miles/14.48 km) to Granite Pass, or the popular **Rae Lakes Loop** (42 miles/67.59 km). ■

DID YOU KNOW

• The parks boast three of the world's 10 longest-living tree species: the giant sequoia (3,266 years old), western juniper (2,675 years old), and foxtail pine (2,123 years old).

• In 1903, Capt. Charles Young became the first African-American superintendent of a national park as head of the Buffalo Soldiers protecting Sequoia and Grant Grove.

• Around half of the world's sequoia groves are found in the recently created Giant Sequoia National Monument on the south side of Sequoia National Park.

Redwood National & State Parks

California

An inspiring example of cooperation between federal and state agencies, the Redwood parks shelter the world's tallest trees in cathedral-like groves beside the Pacific. Spread along 37 miles (59.5 km) of the Northern California coast, the four reserves also offer copious wildlife, scenic rivers, rolling grasslands, and tranquil lagoons, as well as insights into the native peoples and pioneers who lived among these gargantuan trees.

REDWOOD NATIONAL PARK

Running north from the Golden Gate Bridge, the **Redwood Highway** (U.S. 101) weaves through several big tree groves before reaching the national park. At **Kuchel Visitor Center**, exhibits and a film illuminate the park's natural history, and the information desk has updates on ranger-led walks and talks.

Nearby **Orick** has transformed itself from a logging town into an adventure sports hub. Local outfitters offer guided kayak trips on **Stone**

The redwoods of Del Norte State Park can reach heights of 379 feet (115.5 m).

THE BIG PICTURE

Established: State parks (1925); national park (1969)

Size: 139,000 acres (562.5 sq km)

Annual Visitors: 445,000

Visitor Centers: Kuchel, Prairie Creek, Crescent City, Hiouchi

Entrance Fees: Most of the park is free, but $8 day-use fees are charged at Gold Beach, Del Norte Coast Redwoods, and Jedediah Smith Redwoods state parks.

nps.gov/redw

Lagoon and horseback rides and mountain biking along Redwood Creek. The town also hosts the **Orick Rodeo** each summer.

One mile north of Orick, a right turn onto **Bald Hills Road** leads into the old-growth forest and restored areas along **Redwood Creek**. In the 1960s and 1970s, this valley was the front line of the struggle between the timber industry and conservationists over the future of the redwoods. Much of the landscape was devastated by clear-cutting. But you would hardly know it driving up Bald Hills Road today to the **Lady Bird Johnson Grove** and the **Tall Trees Trail**, where National Geographic senior scientist Paul Zahl famously discovered the world's tallest tree in 1963—a *Sequoia sempervirens* towering 367.8 feet (112.1 m) high. Since then, the record has been surpassed by the **Hyperion Tree** (380.1 feet/115.85 m), which stands at a secret location in the Redwood Creek watershed.

REDWOOD STATE PARKS

Prairie Creek is the first of three state parks that stretch along the coast between Orick and Crescent

High Bluff Overlook in Redwood National Park offers an ideal spot for picnicking and whale-watching.

City. Established in the 1920s when conservationists started protecting the redwoods, it has much more of a traditional national park feel than the much newer federal reserve. **Newton B. Drury Scenic Parkway** leads to the "prairie"—a large meadow often grazed by elk. From the small state park **visitor center**, trails lead down to **Gold Bluffs Beach** and through primeval **Fern Canyon**, where Steven Spielberg filmed scenes for *The Lost World: Jurassic Park*.

The **Klamath River** is another hub for park activities, including the **Coastal Drive Loop** down to the World War II radar station on **Klamath Beach**, several cliff-top overlooks, and river fishing or boating on the **Yurok Reservation**, home to California's largest Native American tribe.

Much of **Del Norte Coast Redwoods** is inland and inaccessible to all but the hardiest hikers. Nevertheless, several spots along Highway 101 are

easy to access, including **Enderts Beach** with its sandy stretches and tide pools and **Damnation Creek Trail**, which ambles through old-growth forest to a secluded beach.

Named for the legendary trapper and explorer who "discovered" these redwood groves in 1828, **Jedediah Smith Redwoods** is the northernmost of the four parks. Tall trees flank the **Smith River** as it flows through

the heart of the park, past campgrounds and the **Hiouchi Visitor Center**. Among great hikes in this area is the **Boy Scout Tree Trail** (2.8 miles/4.5 km one way to Fern Falls) and the solemn **Stout Memorial Grove**. Adventurous souls can drive unpaved **Howland Hill Road**, an old stagecoach route that leads to the **National Tribute Grove** of old-growth redwoods. ■

MEET THE NEIGHBORS

• **Redwood Creek Buckarettes** specializes in guided horseback rides into the big trees on the heavily forested ridgeline just east of town.

• **Kayak Zak's** rents kayaks and paddleboards, organizes guided float trips on Stone Lagoon and Big Lagoon, and can facilitate kayak camping.

• **Redwood Adventures:** Based at Elk Meadow Cabins, this eclectic outfitter offers guided mountain biking, birding, and hiking tours of the redwood groves and coastline.

• **Orick Rodeo:** Started in 1961, the July event includes bull riding, steer wrestling, calf roping, mounted archery, and deep-pit barbecue.

Lake Tahoe Basin Management Unit

California & Nevada

THE BIG PICTURE

Established: 1973

Size: 150,000 acres (607.03 sq km)

Annual Visitors: 3 million

Visitor Center: Taylor Creek

Entrance Fees: LTBMU is free of charge, but parking is $5-$8 at some trailheads/beaches; California state parks, $10; Nevada state parks, $7-$12

fs.usda.gov/main/ltbmu/home

Whether you see it covered in a blanket of fresh winter snow or shaded deep blue under a summer sun, Lake Tahoe is an absolute stunner. North America's largest alpine lake sits high in the Sierra Nevada mountains, an emphatic divide between California and Nevada that also counts among the world's deepest lakes (1,645 feet/ 501.4 m). Year-round recreation makes the Tahoe Basin one of the West's leading outdoor playgrounds.

Mark Twain called it a "beautiful relic of fairy-land forgotten," that giant lake that sits astride the boundary between California and Nevada. For many years, Lake Tahoe and its surrounding mountains were protected by various parklands. But in 1973, in order to better manage the lake's environment quality and recreational activities, the U.S. Forest Service created the Lake Tahoe Basin Management Unit (LTBMU). This coalition of three national forests works closely with state parks and nonprofits in both California and Nevada to preserve this incredible asset.

The Nevada side is the wilder in both nature and nightlife with the longest stretch of roadless shoreline, as well as casinos and showrooms. Far more populated, the California side flaunts more human history and offers a much bigger selection of places to sleep, eat, and play.

Visitors can circumnavigate the lake via three means. The motor route meanders 71.6 miles (115.23 km) through lakeshore towns and various parks included in the LTBMU. This includes the **Lake Tahoe Eastshore Drive National Scenic Byway**, a long stretch on the Nevada side. Alternatively, you can walk around the lake via the 165-mile (265.6 km) **Tahoe Rim Trail**. The trail can be accessed at two points on the lakeshore: Tahoe City on the California side and Stateline on the Nevada side. There's also an official **Lake Tahoe Water Trail**, a 72-mile (115.9 km) canoe/kayak route along the lakeshore.

The blue waters of Lake Tahoe are refreshing on a hot summer day.

Knife-edge ridges are open to ski tours and hikers and offer some of the best views of Lake Tahoe's immensity.

CALIFORNIA SHORE

Home to nearly half the people who live year-round in the basin—and possibly half of the area's hotels, restaurants, and other tourist services—**South Lake Tahoe** (pop. 21,000) sprawls along the south shore. Winter activities include snow sports like skiing, tubing, and snowboarding at **Heavenly Mountain Resort** and the **SnowGlobe** electronic music festival held every December. But the town really comes into its own when the snow starts to melt. That's when a wide range of summer activities, including powerboating, parasailing, paddleboarding, kayaking, jet skis, and pontoon boats, take over the lake.

Tahoe South Visitor Center gives the lowdown on everything lake related. Next door, the **Lake Tahoe Museum** offers artifacts, photos, movies, and books on local history inside Osgood Toll House, the town's oldest commercial building. Get your

feet wet—and discover how cold Lake Tahoe is even at the height of summer—at **Regan Beach**, **Lakeview Commons**, or **Conolley Beach** with its waterfront restaurant and lengthy pier. Meanwhile, Heavenly Resort morphs into a summer hotbed for hiking, biking, and other adventure sports, as well as the

Scenic Gondola Ride to mountaintop vistas of the lake.

Emerald Bay Road leads into the national forest along the lake's western shore. **Taylor Creek Visitor Center** is the official information hub for the basin management unit, as well as the place to shop for books, maps, and souvenirs. Walk or

MEET THE NEIGHBORS

Lake Tahoe offers numerous opportunities to get out on the water in motorized and muscle-powered craft:

• **Tahoe Sailing Charters:** Daily sightseeing and sunset cruises in summer on a 50-foot (15.24 m) sailboat, plus motor yacht and sailboat charter.

• **Action Watersports:** Speedboat, Jet Ski, kayak, and paddleboard rentals; parasailing; thunder boat excursions; water taxi service.

• **Tahoe Gal:** Brunch, lunch, sunset, happy hour, and dinner cruises on a 120-passenger paddle wheeler with indoor and outdoor decks.

• **Tahoe Tastings:** Sip classic California wines while cruising the lake on a vintage Venetian water taxi; discounts for designated drivers.

• **Tahoe Adventure Company:** Guided kayak tours as well as kayak and paddleboard rentals are available for those who want to explore on their own.

EVENT HORIZON

• **WinterWonderGrass Tahoe:** Squaw Valley bids adieu to winter with this early April festival that meshes bluegrass and other acoustic music with California wines and craft beers, comfort food, and one last chance to hit the slopes. *winterwondergrasstahoe.com*

• **Great Gatsby Festival:** The Roaring Twenties return to the lakeside mansions of Tallac Historic Site during an August weekend that includes vintage cars and clothing. *tahoeheritage.org/gatsby*

• **Lake Tahoe Shakespeare Festival:** Bard beside the lake since 1972. The summer program, currently staged at Sand Harbor on the Nevada side, also includes ballet, philharmonic, jazz, and other performing arts. *laketahoeshakespeare.com*

• **Lights on the Lake:** Gawkers gather around the shoreline and in hundreds of boats to watch a Fourth of July fireworks show rated as one of the nation's best.

• **SnowGlobe Music Festival:** Electronic music aficionados flock to South Lake Tahoe for this annual outdoor bash spread across the last three days of December. *snowglobemusicfestival.com*

drive to nearby **Tallac Historic Site**, where three lavish lakeside estates (Baldwin, Pope, and Valhalla) host museum exhibits, interactive tours, afternoon teas, and living history presentations. The Taylor Creek area also offers **three beaches** (Pope, Baldwin, and Camp Richardson) and a trail to the summit of **Mount Tallac** (9,735 feet/2,967.23 m).

Emerald Bay State Park surrounds a thumb-shaped inlet that's probably the most photographed landmark in all of Tahoe. Floating in the bay is **Fannette Island** with its stone teahouse. The lake's only island is said to be haunted with the ghost of a hermit who once lived there. Overlooking the bay is **Vikingsholm**, a rustic 28-room mansion built in 1929 by Swedish architect Lennart Palme and considered one of the nation's outstanding examples of traditional Scandinavian architecture; tours are offered in summer. **Emerald Bay Underwater Preserve** draws scuba divers with its wooden wrecks, prehistoric sites, and incredibly translucent waters. Across the road, trails lead through the woods to **Lower Eagle Falls** and the 63,960-acre (258.84 sq km) **Desolation Wilderness**.

Adjacent to Emerald Bay, **D. L. Bliss State Park** offers a wonderful

From Eagle Falls, Fannette Island and Emerald Bay are seen through the trees.

stretch of sand called **Lester Beach** (a great place to slip a canoe, kayak, or paddleboard into the water) and a short .75-mile (1.2 km) trail to the old wooden **Rubicon Point Lighthouse** (1919). Farther up the coast is **Ed Z'berg-Sugar Pine Point State Park** with thick lakeside woods, historic structures, and 20 miles (32.2 km) of groomed winter trails for snowshoeing and cross-country skiing. Set between the lake and north shore ski resorts, **Tahoe City** is another hub for sleeps and eats, plus the **Tahoe Maritime Museum** featuring a fleet of 30 vintage watercraft, outboard engines, and other boating paraphernalia.

The mountains behind the shore shelter resorts like **Northstar** and **Alpine Meadows** that revolve around snow sports in winter and outdoor adventure during the warmer months. The most renowned is **Squaw Valley**, founded in 1931 and host of the 1960 Winter Olympics. Pedestrian-friendly Squaw Valley village boasts numerous places to eat, drink, shop, and rent snow sports equipment. No matter the season, the valley's **aerial tram** climbs to 8,200 feet (2,499.36 m) above the lake and a multitude of skiing and snowboarding runs, as well as hiking trails around **High Camp**. Memorabilia from the 1960 Winter Games are on display at the summit's **Olympic Museum**.

NEVADA SHORE

Just across the border from South Lake Tahoe is **Stateline**, an alter ego urban area where casinos and show biz momentarily grab the limelight from the lake. The town's public **Edgewood Tahoe Golf Course** offers 18 holes, including three greens that are right on the lakeshore.

Kayakers paddle through clear waters on the east shore of Lake Tahoe.

Lincoln Highway (U.S. 50) runs north from town into the Nevada portion of the LTBMU. Superquiet **Nevada Beach** is set aside for swimming and nonmotorized boating like kayaking and paddleboarding. Just up the coast is lively **Zephyr Cove Resort and Marina**, where horseback riding and hiking complement water-based activities like powerboating, parasailing, waterskiing, and fishing. There's also a long golden-sand strand and scenic lake cruises on the paddle wheeler **MS Dixie II.** The highway continues along the shore to **Cave Rock Lake Tahoe Nevada State Park**, named for a massive rock outcrop that rises from the lake waters. It offers a small beach and a boat ramp, but the main event is hiking an 0.8-mile (1.29 km) trail to the crest of Cave Rock.

The coast gets even more rugged a few miles farther north as the highway veers around **Deadman Point**. The only way to explore this off-road area is by foot or boat.

Trails lead down to secluded strands at **Skunk Harbor, Whale Beach,** and clothing-optional **Secret Harbor.** Road finally meets lake again at **Sand Harbor State Park**, where the boulder-strewn coves are equally fine for swimming and photography. The park also stages the **Lake Tahoe Shakespeare Festival** over two summer months on an outdoor stage with the lake as a backdrop.

The north end of the Nevada shore is anchored by laid-back **Incline Village**, another town that rotates between summer activities along the lakeshore and winter snow sports at **Diamond Peak Ski Area**. Tucked among the village pines, the **UC Davis Tahoe Science Center** offers docent tours and interactive exhibits on the lake's ecosystem. High above the lakeshore, a walk along the picturesque **Tahoe Meadows Whole Access Interpretive Trail** combines well with an easy cruise down the **Mount Rose Scenic Byway** through the Nevada mountains. ∎

Sunset at Bonsai Rock in Lake Tahoe, Nevada

Anza-Borrego Desert State Park

California

THE BIG PICTURE

Established: 1933

Size: 600,000 acres
(2,428.11 sq km)

Annual Visitors: 2 million

Visitor Center: Borrego Springs

Entrance Fee: None unless
camping

www.parks.ca.gov/?page_id=638

Larger than many other national parks, Anza-Borrego sprawls across 937 square miles (2,428.11 sq km) of rocky outcrops, sandy flats, and oasis canyons in the Colorado Desert of eastern San Diego County. The second largest state park in the lower 48 takes its name from its location centered around the Borrego Valley and the fact that 18th-century Spanish explorer Juan Bautista de Anza passed this way.

The state park **Visitor Center** in the desert town of Borrego Springs is the best place to begin your exploration—browsing the natural history exhibits; watching a short documentary film, *A Year in the Desert;* and gathering maps and other information. Come spring, this is also your best source for the latest scoop on wildflower blooms and the best places to spot indigenous wildlife like the desert bighorn sheep. The adjacent **Desert Garden** provides a preview of the plants you can expect to see across the park, as well as a small pond full of desert pupfish.

The western edge of the Borrego Valley is peppered with oasis canyons where natural springs nourish the California fan palm—the state's only native palm tree. The oases are ripe for bird-watching or escaping the scorching desert sun. Just up the road is **Borrego Palm Canyon**, with a campground and nature trail.

At the valley's north end, off-roaders, hikers, and equestrians can follow unpaved desert tracks into **Coyote Canyon** and historical markers along the **Anza Trail**, the route the Spanish explorer trekked in 1774. Near the upper end of Coyote Canyon, the **Pacific Crest Trail** briefly dips into the park. The **Borrego Badlands** on the valley's eastern edge is a nearly plantless moonscape of deeply eroded hills and dales. Jeep trails lead to desert overlooks like **Font's Point** and **Vista del Malpais,** as well as the trailhead into the **Slot,** a narrow twisting slot canyon.

County Road S3 connects the Borrego Valley with southern portions of the park via **Yaqui Pass,** where the short **Kenyon Overlook Trail** leads uphill through ocotillo, creosote, and

During a superbloom, wildflowers cover the desert floor of Anza-Borrego.

Across 600,000 acres (2,428.1 sq km), there are more than 110 miles (177 km) of hikes available to Anza-Borrego visitors.

cacti to a great vantage point of a rocky plain, called the **Mescal Bajada**. From Scissors Crossing junction, County Road S2 follows the route of the **Southern Overland Trail** to the park's southernmost extreme. This is one of the routes that 19th-century pioneers traveled to California, their story told in historical markers and the ruins of old Butterfield stage-coach stations along the way.

Blair Valley is the jumping-off point for several interesting desert hikes, including a trail to ancient Indian **pictographs** rendered over several thousand years. The segment of the route through **Box Canyon** was famously hacked out by the Mormon Battalion during the 1847 Mexican War that brought California into the Union. Farther along, **Vallecito Stage Station** (1857) has been faithfully reconstructed with adobe and wood.

As the name suggests, **Agua Caliente** offers indoor and outdoor naturally heated swimming pools surrounded by a desert campsite.

Tucked at the base of the Tierra Blanca range, **Mountain Palm Springs** feeds a cluster of six palm groves connected by short trails. Veteran hikers can undertake a 6-mile (10 km) return to **Goat Canyon**

Trestle, the world's longest all-wooden railway bridge. **Carrizo Badlands Overlook** offers one last chance to gaze across the desert before the county road intersects with Interstate 8. ■

MEET THE NEIGHBORS

Surrounded by the state park, the town of Borrego Springs (pop. 3,429) is the center for art and adventure activities in the Anza-Borrego region.

• The nonprofit **Anza-Borrego Desert Nature Center** organizes hikes, lectures, motor tours, and other desert-related activities.

• Professional astronomer **Dennis Mammana** offers evening tours that look at the heavens from vantage points around California's only International Dark Sky Community.

• Metal artist **Ricardo Breceda** has sprinkled the valley with more

than 100 rust-colored sculptures of animals, dinosaurs, and mythological creatures.

• **Bike Borrego** rents mountain bikes, road bikes, and fat bikes for cycle-related excursions around the valley or state park.

• **California Overland Tours** offers guided off-road adventures and overnight camping trips in modern air-conditioned Jeeps or vintage military vehicles.

• The eclectic **Borrego Art Institute** offers a painting and sculpture gallery, pottery studio, café, kids' programs, and ArtFarm Garden.

Red Rock Canyon & Valley of Fire
Nevada

Perched on either side of Las Vegas, Red Rock Canyon National Conservation Area and Valley of Fire State Park offer a striking, stony contrast to the neon-studded Strip. The backdrop of many TV shows and movies, Red Rock flaunts chromatic cliffs, historic ranches, and oasis canyons. On the east, Valley of Fire preserves more twisted geology, prehistoric rock art, and a petrified forest.

RED ROCK CANYON CONSERVATION AREA

Flanking the western edge of the Las Vegas Valley, Red Rock Canyon National Conservation Area was created by the Bureau of Land Management to protect the area's fragile desert ecosystem and facilitate all sorts of recreation. Hiking, biking, horseback riding, and rock climbing are the main activities, but the park also caters to stargazers, photographers, and people who just want to soak in a secluded oasis pool.

Red Rock Canyon Road (Highway 159) arches through the heart of the park to various points of interest, including **Red Rock Canyon Visitor Center**. The center offers maps, information, outdoor nature exhibits, a desert tortoise habitat, and an eco-oriented gift shop. It's also the starting point for a 13-mile (20.9 km) **Scenic Drive** that leads to various overlooks and trailheads. Among the dozen or so hikes in this area are **Ice Box Canyon** (2.6 miles/4.18 km) with its seasonal waterfalls, the challenging 5-mile (8 km) trek to the summit of **Turtlehead Peak**, and the easy **Children's Discovery Trail** (.75 mile/ 1.2 km) along **Lost Creek**.

Veteran climbers flock to the park's stupendous Aztec sandstone walls, formed 180 to 190 million years ago. Guides from **Red Rock Climbing Center** can help you find your vertical limit. Several local stables offer desert horseback adventures including **Cowboy Trail Rides**, or discover the park's rugged off-road routes on a **Pink Jeep Tour**.

Roughly 5 miles (8 km) south of the visitor center, **Spring Mountain Ranch** was founded in 1876 and has seen many wealthy owners, including recluse billionaire Howard Hughes and German actress Vera

THE BIG PICTURE

Established: Red Rock Canyon (1990); Valley of Fire (1935)

Size: Red Rock Canyon (195,819 acres/792.45 sq km); Valley of Fire (45,938 acres/185.9 sq km)

Annual Visitors: Red Rock Canyon (2.5 million); Valley of Fire (698,000)

Visitor Centers: Red Rock Canyon, Valley of Fire

Entrance Fees: Red Rock Canyon ($7 vehicle; $3 individual); Valley of Fire ($10 vehicle)

redrockcanyonlv.org
parks.nv.gov/parks/valley-of-fire

Ancient petroglyphs cover rocks in the Valley of Fire.

Colorful striations formed wavelike striped patterns into Fire Wave rock in the Valley of Fire, accessed by an easy 1.25-mile (2 km) hike.

Krupp. It pays homage to pioneer-era Nevada by preserving some of the state's oldest buildings and organizing living history events. The ranch also offers a popular **outdoor summer theater series**.

VALLEY OF FIRE STATE PARK

Whether it's named for its brightly colored rock formations or the fact that summer temperatures often hit triple digits, Valley of Fire has been a red-hot destination for desert aficionados since it was declared Nevada's first state park in 1935. Like Red Rock it's also been a Hollywood star,

appearing in pictures like *Viva Las Vegas* (1964), *Total Recall* (1990), and *Star Trek Generations* (1994).

Located 52 miles (83.7 km) northeast of downtown Las Vegas, the **Valley of Fire Visitor Center** offers exhibits on the park's geology, ecology, and human history, as well as maps and information on park roads, trails, and wildlife.

Mouse's Tank Road leads north from the visitor center to many of the park's geological landmarks, most of them carved from the same Aztec sandstone that colors Red Rock Canyon. Along the way are the **Rainbow Vista** overlook, a swirling stone formation called **Fire**

Wave, and **Mouse's Tank**—a seasonal rock pool named for a renegade Paiute Indian ("Little Mouse") who used the valley as a hideout in the 1890s. At the road's end is a trailhead for the easy, 1-mile (1.6 km) **White Domes Loop** and the demanding **Prospect Trail** (4.6 miles/7.4 km) through the arid, rocky wilderness.

The Atlatl area harbors several other natural monuments—the swirling **Beehives** sandstone formation, **Arch Rock**, and the **Petrified Logs**—as well as the 2,000-year-old petroglyphs of **Atlatl Rock** that depict animals, humans, trees, and geometric designs. ■

LAY YOUR HEAD

Hotels

• **Bonnie Springs Ranch:** Motel rooms with a Wild West theme; pool, restaurant, saloon; from $85. *bonniesprings.com*

• **Red Rock Casino, Resort and Spa:** Guided hikes, horseback riding,

bike tours, and rock climbing in the national conservation area; from $80. *redrock.sclv.com*

• **North Shore Inn:** 15 miles (24 km) from Valley of Fire in Overton, Nevada; pool, pets, laundry from $89. *northshoreinnatlakemead.com*

Camping

• Red Rock Canyon Bureau of Land Management campground; $15.

• Valley of Fire: Arch Rock and Atlatl Rock; $20.

The sun rises over Red Rock Canyon, Nevada.

Golden Gate NRA & Point Reyes National Seashore

California

Mingled together like pieces of a jigsaw puzzle, Golden Gate National Recreation Area (NRA) and Point Reyes National Seashore protect a massive stretch of the northern California coast between San Francisco and Sonoma. In addition to beaches, bays, and windswept cliffs, the parks embrace history, culture, towering redwood trees, and lofty peaks, as well as one very famous bridge.

GOLDEN GATE

One of the nation's most diverse parks, Golden Gate National Recreation Area features a huge segment of San Francisco's historic, handsome waterfront and the rambling Marin Headlands on the north side of the bay. Recent additions have extended the park to the shores of Tomales Bay in the north and nearly as far as Half Moon Bay in the south. For hikers, bikers, and drivers, the most convenient way to travel between the park's northern and southern domains is the **Golden Gate Bridge**, opened in 1937 and still one of the planet's most recognizable landmarks.

Golden Gate harbors 19 different ecosystems, more than 200 plant and animal species, and a vast array of historical treasures representing every era of California history, from the Native American and Spanish colonial periods through the Civil War and 20th century. And living up to its name, it facilitates dozens of ways to enjoy the great outdoors.

Just up the bay shore from Fisherman's Wharf, the park's **Fort Mason** sector includes the celebrated ships (seven in total) of the **San Francisco Maritime National Historic Park**, as well as the eclectic galleries, museums, cafés, and performance spaces of the **Fort Mason Center for Arts and Culture**. Protected by a breakwater, **Aquatic Cove** is popular with local swim-

THE BIG PICTURE

Established: Golden Gate (1972); Point Reyes (1963)

Size: Golden Gate (82,000 acres/331.84 sq km); Point Reyes (71,000 acres/287.3 sq km)

Annual Visitors: Golden Gate (15 million); Point Reyes (2.4 million)

Visitor Centers: Fort Mason, the Presidio, Marin Headlands, Muir Woods, Bear Valley, Point Reyes Lighthouse, Drakes Beach

Entrance Fees: None

nps.gov/goga; nps.gov/pore

Cypress trees form a tunnel over a road in Point Reyes.

The Golden Gate Bridge stretches across the Golden Gate Strait, which connects the Pacific Ocean with San Francisco Bay.

mers. Floating offshore is **Alcatraz**, the notorious federal prison that operated from 1934 to 1963. Ferries (adults $38, children $23.25) shuttle visitors from Pier 33 to the island for ranger-guided tours of the old cell blocks.

A former army base, the **Presidio**, contains the largest slice of the park south of the Golden Gate. Arrayed around the Main Parade Ground are **Mott Visitor Center**, **Presidio Dance Theatre**, and **Walt Disney Family Museum**, as well as a bowling alley, yoga studio, and various eateries. A former military airstrip called **Crissy Field** provides a breezy bayside location for windsurfing or flying a kite, as well as hiking and biking along the **Golden Gate Promenade**. At the far end of the walkway is **Fort Point National Historic Site**, a stout Civil War–era bastion that literally squats in the shadow of the bridge. Surfers and seals often share the waves breaking beside the fort.

LAY YOUR HEAD

Hotels

• **Inn at the Presidio:** 22-room boutique hotel in Pershing Hall, the former bachelor officers' quarters on the Main Parade Ground; from $295. *innatthepresidio.com*

• **Cavallo Point Lodge:** Victorian-era military housing at Fort Baker morphed into an upscale hotel with sweeping views of the bay, bridge, and city; restaurant, bar, spa, guided hikes; from $327. *cavallopoint.com*

• **Marin Headlands Hostel:** Dorms and private single or double rooms in Hostelling International-affiliated lodging in the Rodeo Valley; from $28. *norcalhostels.org/marin*

• **Point Reyes Hostel:** Dorms and family-style rooms in the wooded Inverness Hills near Limantour Beach; from $29. *norcalhostels.org/reyes*

Camping

• Point Reyes National Seashore offers primitive, hike-in campsites at Wildcat Beach, Santa Maria Beach, Mount Wittenberg, and Glen, and boat-in camping on Tomales Bay. Golden Gate NRA has no public campgrounds.

On the ocean side of the Presidio, **Baker Beach** and **China Beach** provide secluded sands and dramatic bridge views. The NRA wraps around rugged **Land's End** and runs all the way down **Ocean Beach** to hilly **Fort Funston** with hiking trails and favorable hang-gliding conditions. Even farther south is **Rancho Corral de Tierra**, 3,848 acres (15.57 sq km) of pristine coastal hills and vales added to the park in 2005.

MARIN HEADLANDS

On the north shore of the Golden Gate, the Marin Headlands sector provides dramatic vantage points for looking down on the bridge and across the bay to San Francisco. The views are especially good along cliff-hugging **Conzelman Road**, which meanders out to precipitous **Point Bonita Lighthouse** and the **Marin Headlands Visitor Center** in Rodeo Valley. The valley is also home to an old **Nike missile launch site** (and Cold War museum) and the **Marine Mammal Rescue Center**.

Tennessee Valley tenders some of the park's best hiking opportunities,

while sea, sand, and sun (on days when it's *not* foggy) are the lures at 3-mile-long (4.8 km) **Stinson Beach**.

On the bayside of the headlands, **Fort Baker** is a sailing hub and home to the interactive, hands-on **Bay Area Discovery Museum**. The mountains behind the coast shelter **Muir Woods National Monument**, a lush grove of coastal redwoods that namesake John Muir dubbed "the best tree-lovers monument that could possibly be found."

Newer segments of the NRA north of Muir Woods revolve around the **Olema Valley**, a giant trench created by the **San Andreas Fault** as it carves a quake-riddle path between Bolinas and Tomales Bays. Trails along the crest of **Olema Ridge** render incredible views of the Marin coast. The funky little town of **Point Reyes Station** is the main gateway to the adjacent national seashore.

POINT REYES

Wild beaches and imposing cliffs, copious wildlife, and pastoral landscapes are enough to make Point Reyes one of the most

alluring stops on the West Coast. But it's the area's quirky history that makes it even more compelling.

Miwok Indians inhabited the peninsula when Sir Francis Drake and the crew of the *Golden Hind* sojourned there in the summer of 1579 during their circumnavigation of the globe. Drake christened the landfall "New Albion" and claimed it for his queen, Elizabeth I. The English never returned to back up their claim, however. In Drake's wake came Spanish Sebastián Vizcaíno, whose party landed on January 6, 1603, on the Epiphany. Being the Feast of the Three Kings, he dubbed it Punta de los Reyes ("Point of the Kings").

During the latter half of the 19th century, American settlers transformed the foggy, faraway peninsula

Just north of San Francisco, the hilly Marin Headlands emerge in fog.

into cattle ranches and dairy farms. As their rural lifestyle and livelihood became threatened by coastal development, ranchers formed an unusual alliance with the Sierra Club and the National Park Service to create the national seashore in the early 1960s—the reason you can still find a few working ranches inside the preserve.

Located near the town of Point Reyes Station, **Bear Valley Visitor Center** provides maps, information, and exhibits on the national seashore, as well as ranger-led walks along the San Andreas Fault. The visitor center is also the jumping-off spot for hikes up 1,407-foot (428.85 m) **Mount Wittenberg** (the park's highest peak) and the 9-mile (14.5 km) drive to secluded **Limantour Beach**, inhabited by harbor seals, shorebirds, and migratory gray whales. Farther west along the shore is **Alamere Falls**, which tumbles 39 feet (11.9 m) onto **Wildcat Beach**.

Sir Francis Drake Boulevard wanders 21 miles (33.79 km) along the shore of **Tomales Bay** and former ranchlands to the very end of the peninsula. Along the way are side roads leading down to 11-mile-long (17.7 km) **Great Beach**, one of the longest stretches of pristine sand in California, and **Drakes Beach** on the bayside. **Patrick Visitor Center** at Drakes Beach offers exhibits on maritime exploration and hosts a sandcastle-building competition over Labor Day weekend. East along the beach is **Drakes Estero**, which historians say is likely the place where the dashing English sea captain landed in 1579.

At the tip of the peninsula (and down 308 steps) sits the historic **Point Reyes Lighthouse** (built in 1870) and a small visitor center with exhibits on coastal lighthouse-keeping and marine mammals. The

The Point Reyes Lighthouse has sat over the Gulf of the Farallones since 1870.

land's end area also offers an **observation deck** for watching migrating whales, overlooks for California sea lion and elephant seal colonies, and the old **Point Reyes Lifeboat Station**, built in 1927 and the only remaining rail-launch lifesaving facility on the West Coast.

The northern section of the national seashore ends in skinny **Tomales Point**, where a herd of around 350 very large deer find shelter in the **Tule Elk Reserve**. Once thought to be extinct, the elk are best observed from a distance along trails or roads. Explore historic **Pierce Point Ranch** on a self-guided trail or plunge down paths to secluded strands like **Kehoe Beach** with its wetlands and sand dunes. ∎

MEET THE NEIGHBORS

• **Golden Gate Park:** Not to be confused with the national recreation area, this dynamic green space is San Francisco's oldest and largest city park.

• **Mount Tamalpais State Park:** The birthplace of modern mountain biking is also perfect for a hike to the 2,571-foot (783.6 m) summit and its views of the Bay Area.

• **Samuel P. Taylor State Park:** Camp amid the giant coastal redwoods of this popular state reserve along Lagunitas Creek.

• **Sonoma Coast State Park:** Spectacular seascapes at the mouth of the Russian River and its renowned wine country.

Channel Islands National Park

California

A bucolic blast from the past, the five-island archipelago offers a glimpse of what much of Southern California was like before freeways, theme parks, and movie studios. Once the home of Native Americans and pioneer ranchers, the secluded landfalls are now the realm of kayakers, hikers, and scuba divers, as well as a diverse array of marine, aerial, and terrestrial creatures.

Seventy miles (112.7 km) from downtown Los Angeles, **Ventura Harbor** is the park's main gateway. Perched at the end of Spinnaker Drive, **Lagomarsino Visitor Center** provides information on ferries, camping, hiking trails, and ranger-led activities available within the park.

Island Packers runs ferries for day-trippers and campers to Santa Cruz, Anacapa, Santa Rosa, and San Miguel, as well as whale-watching cruises. In the same building, **Channel Islands Adventure Company** offers guided kayak trips around Santa Cruz, Anacapa, and Santa Barbara.

THE BIG PICTURE

Established: 1980

Size: 249,561 acres (1,009.9 sq km)

Annual Visitors: 383,000

Visitor Center: Open daily 8:30 a.m. to 5 p.m. (closed Thanksgiving and Christmas)

Entrance Fee: None for the park; various for ferries and other services

nps.gov/chis

SANTA CRUZ ISLAND

An hour by sea from Ventura Harbor, Santa Cruz is renowned for its sea caves, surf breaks, and secluded beaches. Jointly administered by the National Park Service (76 percent) and the Nature Conservancy (24 percent), the largest of the islands also offers the park's longest hiking trails—along the coast, through two parallel mountain ranges, and into a deep central valley.

Scorpion Anchorage on the island's east coast is the main ferry stop and staging area for hiking and kayaking. Tucked into the valley behind the beach are a ranger station and two campgrounds. From the ferry pier, trails lead over the mountains to **Smugglers Cove** (7.5 miles/12 km) with its old ranch house and olive grove, the bluffs above **Potato Harbor** (5 miles/8 km), and the remote cobblestone beach at **Chinese Harbor** (15.5 miles/24.9 km).

The island's north shore is framed by spectacular cliffs riddled with some of the world's largest sea caves. A mosaic of colorful rocks, moss, and algae, **Painted Cave** is the largest—a water-filled grotto that measures 160 feet (48.7 m) tall and more than

Off Anacapa Island, a kelp forest thrives underwater.

Resplendent at sunset, the Channel Islands coast is lined with small, rocky cliffs.

a quarter-mile (0.4 km) long. The Island Packers ferry hovers near the cave's mouth during the return trip from Santa Rosa.

OUTER ISLANDS

Santa Rosa Island combines human and natural history with some of the park's most scenic trails. **Vail and Vickers Ranch** near the ferry pier offers a glimpse of 19th-century pioneer life in the Channel Islands. Among the historic buildings are a bunkhouse, barn, one-room schoolhouse, and handsome ranch house. A popular trail runs along the shore of Bechers Bay to a grove of **Torrey pines** (America's rarest native pine), the **Black Rock** lava flow, and snowy plover nesting area amid the rolling dunes of **Skunk Point.**

Home to 265 plant species and colonies of California sea lions and harbor seals, **Anacapa Island** is rich in flora and fauna. Yet its most

recognizable landmark is not part of the natural landscape—historic **Anacapa Lighthouse** (1932), an easy half-mile (0.8 km) hike from the landing cove. Other trails lead across the lofty summit of East Anacapa to **Inspiration Point** and **Cathedral Cove**.

A four-hour ferry from Ventura Harbor, **San Miguel Island** is only for those who crave extreme solitude

or close encounters of the pinniped kind. The island is home to four different species of seal and sea lion, as many as 30,000 animals at any one time who come to breed, give birth, and raise their young. A monument at **Cuyler Harbor** honors the memory of Spanish explorer Juan Rodríguez Cabrillo, leader of the first European expedition to chart the California coast (1542). ■

Lassen Volcanic National Park
California

Three million years of geological history are laid bare at this low-key national park in the Cascade Range of Northern California. One of only two volcanoes to erupt in the lower 48 states during the 20th century, 10,457-foot (3,187.3 m) Lassen Peak towers over a warped wonderland of black cinder cones, lava fields, mud flows, hot springs, and geysers.

Those who lived nearby were caught off guard when Lassen Peak, which nearly everyone assumed to be dormant, suddenly roared to life in 1914. By then, the mountain was already part of the National Park System. But the three-year volcanic episode that followed made Lassen even more alluring to scientists and visitors with an affinity for geological drama.

In addition to being one of the few places on the planet where all four volcano types (plug dome, cinder cone, shield, and composite) occur within a short distance of one

THE BIG PICTURE

Established: 1916

Size: 79,062 acres (319.95 sq km)

Annual Visitors: 507,000

Visitor Centers: Kohm Yah-mah-nee and Loomis Museum

Entrance Fee: $20 per vehicle, $10 per person

nps.gov/lavo

another, the park is also blessed with rich conifer forest, alpine meadows, and copious wildlife.

Many of the geothermal wonders are found along **Lassen Volcanic National Park Highway**, a 30-mile (48.3 km) scenic drive that meanders through the middle of the park between **Kohm Yah-mah-nee Visitor Center** in the south and Manzanita Lake in the north. Along the way are panoramic turnoffs, picnic areas, and trailheads into the wilderness and volcanic wastelands.

From the visitor center, the highway climbs quickly up to **Sulphur Works**, a smoldering slope of mudpots and fumaroles (steam vents) ejecting clouds of odoriferous gas. On either side of placid **Lake Helen** are trailheads for two classic hikes. A 1.5-mile (2.4 km) trail leads down to **Bumpass Hell**, the park's largest geothermal area with 16 acres (.06 sq km) of bubbling pools, belching mudpots, and hissing steam vents explored on elevated boardwalks. Farther up the road is the start of the arduous 2.5-mile (4 km) **Lassen Peak Trail** to the summit of the often snow-capped volcano.

Summit Lake offers a woodsy respite before the highway crosses a pyroclastic flow called the **Devastated Area** and an avalanche area dubbed the **Chaos Jumbles** before

A boardwalk winds through Bumpass Hell, the largest geothermal area in the park.

Reflection Lake mirrors the peaks of Chaos Crags, six dacite domes formed approximately 1,000 years ago.

gliding past **Manzanita Lake**, where the bulk of the park's visitor services are located. Visitors can rent kayaks and cabins at lakeside or marvel at dramatic black-and-white photos of Lassen's last eruption in the little **Loomis Museum**.

Away from the highway, the park is dominated by roadless wilderness that can be explored only on foot. The **Pacific Crest Trail** and other paths lead to remote landmarks like the **Cluster Lakes**, a large meadow called the **Grassy Swale**, and the **Red Cinder Cone**—places that see few visitors even during the height of summer because they are so far off the beaten path.

Here and there, roads penetrate the wilderness, giving drivers and day hikers a chance to explore Lassen's far-flung corners. From the town of Chester on the park's south flank, a lonely road shoots into the Warner Valley and the historic **Drakesbad Guest Ranch**, a base for hikes and

horseback rides through the woods to an active geothermal field called the **Devil's Kitchen** and **Terminal Geyser**. Another road from Chester ends at **Juniper Lake** with its campground and boat ramp.

The **Volcanic Legacy Scenic Highway** (Route 44) runs all the way across the park's north side between the towns of Old Station and Susanville. Along the way is a turnoff to an unpaved forest road that leads to **Butte Lake** and its

volcanic attractions. Hikers can follow a section of the 19th-century **Nobles Emigrant Trail** (3.5 miles/ 5.6 km) along the edge of the **Fantastic Lava Beds**, a jagged, jet-black basalt flow between Butte Lake and secluded **Snag Lake**. Looming over the twisted landscape is the 690-foot (210.3 m) **Cinder Cone**. A spur trail ascends to the summit with its dusky crater and view across the lava beds to the **Painted Dunes** and distant Mount Lassen. ∎

LAY YOUR HEAD

Hotels

• **Drakesbad Guest Ranch:** Historic Warner Valley dude ranch; restaurant, thermal-heated swimming pool, horseback riding; from $166. *drakesbad.com*

• **Manzanita Lake Camping Cabins:** Self-service cabins on the lakeshore; store, gas station, Laun-

dromat, ATM; from $70. *lassen recreation.com/where_to_stay*

Camping

• Developed campgrounds available at Butte Lake, Crags, Juniper Lake, Manzanita Lake, Summit Lake North, Summit Lake South, Southwest, and Warner Valley; $10-$26 per night.

1 Mont-Tremblant, Quebec

Tremblant offers two distinct winter adventures. Inside the Quebec provincial park, it's all about going slow, exploring the snowy wilderness via cross-country, snowshoe, fat bike, or Ski-Vel for the mobility impaired. Mont Tremblant Ski Resort on the park's southwest side revolves around expert downhill and snowboarding.

2 Adirondacks, New York

Lake Placid is the only North American snow resort that can boast hosting two Winter Olympics (1932 and 1980). Eight Adirondack resorts offer downhill skiing and snowboarding. Cross-country skiers can groove to the tunes on musical trails at Cascade and Sarnac. The region also offers one of the nation's few biathlon courses.

3 Voyageurs, Minnesota

The waterways that make the Minnesota park a summer paddling paradise freeze over during the colder months, creating a vast network of winter sports routes. In addition to snowmobile, snowshoe, and cross-country ski trails, the park offers ice roads on which motorists can drive to areas normally reached only by boat.

4 Black Hills, South Dakota

In addition to seeing Mount Rushmore with a snowy mantle, the South Dakota highlands offer a wide range of winter sports. Black Hills National Forest maintains more than 400 miles (643.7 km) of groomed snowmobile trails, as well as winter routes for cross-country skiers and snowshoe trekkers. Ice fishing is allowed on all lakes found in the national forest.

5 Yellowstone, Wyoming

The annual "snowover" may close most of the park's roads to vehicular traffic, but snowmobile and snow-coach tours take visitors to Old Faithful geyser, the Grand Canyon of the Yellowstone, and other landmarks. The park also offers cross-country ski trails, ranger-led snowshoe jaunts, winter wildlife viewing, and winter backcountry camping.

THE TOP

10

SPOTS FOR WINTER SPORTS

Olympic gold medals and black diamond ski runs highlight winter adventures in the parks.

6 Sawtooth, Idaho

One of the cradles of winter sports in North America, Sawtooth National Forest in central Idaho offers a broad range of cold weather activities, from the legendary downhill ski runs on Bald Mountain and cat skiing on Soldier Mountain to cross-country skiing and snowshoeing at Rock Creek and the snowboard half-pipe at Pomerelle.

Lake Tahoe appears as a snowboarder takes to the air at Heavenly Ski Resort.

7 Banff, Alberta

It doesn't get any better than Banff in winter—ice-skating on frozen-over Lake Louise, the black diamond runs on offer at Norquay and Back Bowls, curling and ice hockey at the Fenlands outdoor rink, more than 100 miles (160.9 km) of cross-country and snowshoe trails, backcountry skiing through virgin powder, and all those après-ski activities in the village.

8 Yosemite, California

The High Sierra park may have lost out to Lake Placid for the right to host the 1932 Winter Olympics, but the bid created Badger Pass ski area and the ice-skating rink in Yosemite Valley. Among other cold weather activities are the legendary cross-country ski route to Glacier Point and snowshoeing through giant sequoias.

9 Lake Tahoe, California

"Big Blue" is ringed by a dozen winter sports resorts that offer downhill skiing, cross-country, snowboarding, and tobogganing. Heavenly is the largest (97 runs, 30 lifts), Kirkwood gets the most snow (472 inches/11.9 m per year), but Squaw Valley is the chicest and most renowned (it hosted the 1960 Winter Olympics).

10 Denali, Alaska

Given its lack of motor roads, the big Alaska park is actually easier to explore in winter using snowshoes, cross-country skis, fat bikes, or dog-sleds. For those with more time (and energy), cross-country camping trips venture even farther into the snowy wilderness that surrounds North America's highest peak.

Golden Gate Park

California

From the gold rush and quake to the Summer of Love and football's 49ers, Golden Gate Park has played an indelible role in San Francisco history. The rambling green space is many things: a place to bike or hike, view art or sip Japanese tea, roam with buffalo or commune with redwood trees. It's a true people's park in every sense of the term.

THE BIG PICTURE

Established: 1870

Size: 1,017 acres (4.1 sq km)

Annual Visitors: 13 million

Entrance Fee: None

*goldengatepark.com; sfrecpark
.org/parks-open-spaces/golden
-gate-park-guide*

Not to be confused with the nearby national recreation area, Golden Gate is San Francisco's old and venerable urban park, a patch of woodland, lawns, lakes, and museums that stretches nearly halfway across the city. Laid out in the 1870s and clearly inspired by Manhattan's Central Park, the park sheltered survivors of the devastating 1906 earthquake and flower children during the psychedelic sixties.

Flanked by many of the park's top attractions, the sunny **Music Concourse** is the closest thing to a central focus. Rebuilt with a stunning copper shell after the 1989 Loma Prieta earthquake, the **de Young Museum** showcases American, Asian, African, and Pacific art and artifacts. Across the concourse, the **California Academy of Sciences** features natural history exhibits, a four-story artificial indoor rain

forest, an aquarium and planetarium, as well as a "living roof" covered in 1.7 million native plants.

Founded in 1894, the beloved **Japanese Tea Garden** offers tea, snacks, and bonsai demonstrations. The adjacent **San Francisco Botanical Garden** cultivates the diverse flora of California, the Mediterranean, Asia-Pacific, and Mesoamerica on 55 acres (.22 sq km) explored on footpaths. The area's third botanical landmark, the **Conservatory of Flowers**, is a marvelous glass-and-wood greenhouse filled with rare and exotic plants from around the world. Erected in 1879, it's the park's oldest building.

The southeast corner is anchored by **Kezar Stadium**, an architectural dinosaur where the San Francisco 49ers played from 1946 to 1970. Across the street, the elaborate **Herschell-Spillman Carousel** (1914) stills goes around and around, as do the wheels that visitors can rent at **Parkwide Bike Rentals and Tours**. The scene of many peace and political demonstrations, the **Panhandle** is a thin, eight-block extension of the park into the renowned **Haight-Ashbury** neighborhood.

Stow Lake floats near the center of Golden Gate Park. The **Boathouse** rents pedal boats, rowboats, and electric boats for circuits around an island featuring **Strawberry Hill**

Golden Gate Park seen from the observation tower at the de Young Museum

Originally built as part of a 1894 world's fair, the Japanese Tea Garden is now a permanent and popular fixture in Golden Gate Park.

and the artificial Huntington Waterfall. The meadows and woods west of the lake are the park's favorite spots for picnics, walking, jogging, and impromptu sports.

The large **Polo Field** is mostly used for soccer these days, but nearby **Spreckels Lake** still draws model yachting. One of the more astonishing sights in the park is a small herd of buffalo that graze the **Bison Paddock** under the care of keepers from the San Francisco Zoo. The animals wouldn't look out of place on the grassy fairways of the public **Golden Gate Park Golf Course**, a nine-hole links formed around the indigenous coastal dunes.

Way out west, the graceful **Dutch Windmill** (1902) and massive **Murphy Windmill** (1908) once pumped water to irrigate the park. **Queen Wilhelmina Tulip Garden** is named after the Dutch monarch who donated the older windmill to San Francisco. The historic **Beach Chalet** flaunts iconic art deco murals and a craft brewery/ restaurant with panoramic sea views. On the other side of the Great Highway is windswept **Ocean Beach**, now part of Golden Gate National Recreation Area. ■

EVENT HORIZON

• **Pacific Orchid and Garden Exposition:** The nation's largest orchid show brings flowers to the park's San Francisco County Fair Building in February. *orchidsanfrancisco.org*

• **4/20 at Hippie Hill:** Relive the Summer of Love during this unofficial, unsanctioned event on April 20, even more retro with the legalization of weed in California. *420hippiehill.com*

• **Bay to Breakers 12K:** 30,000 runners clad in outlandish costumes (and sometimes nothing)

participate in an annual May race that stretches from downtown San Francisco to Golden Gate Park. *baytobreakers.com*

• **Outside Lands:** Big-name bands and thousands of fans pour into the park for this annual August music fest at the Polo Field. *sfoutsidelands.com*

• **Hardly Strictly Bluegrass:** More than 90 acts take the stage over the first weekend in October during a free festival that embraces bluegrass, folk, and indie rock. *hardlystrictlybluegrass.com*

Balboa Park
California

One of the nation's oldest urban reserves, Balboa Park was born shortly after the Civil War when San Diego's forward-thinking city fathers designated a large tract of canyon and mesa country as a public park. The sprawling green space overlooking downtown now harbors 17 museums, the San Diego Zoo, several outstanding performing arts venues, and numerous outdoor recreation areas.

THE BIG PICTURE

Established: 1868

Size: 1,200 acres (4.86 sq km)

Annual Visitors: 12-15 million

Visitor Center: House of Hospitality

Entrance Fee: None for the park; varies for museums and other attractions

balboapark.org

Balboa Park took on much of its present flavor during the Panama-California Exposition of 1915-16, which commemorated the opening of the Panama Canal and Spanish explorer Vasco Núñez de Balboa's 1513 discovery of the Pacific Ocean. The fair's architectural theme was Spanish colonial revival and many of the structures arrayed along a central avenue called the **Prado** were meant to be temporary. But they were so skillfully rendered that most were spared the wrecking ball and eventually were transformed into museums and other public spaces.

The 120-foot-high (36.6 m) **Cabrillo Bridge** leaps a heavily wooded canyon to the western end of the Prado and the park's most iconic structure: the cathedral-like **Museum of Man** with its distinctive dome and bell tower. The extensive collection revolves around the history and culture of the Americas before the European discovery, but there are also Egyptian mummies and other oddities on display. The adjacent **Old Globe,** with its Tudor theme, is one of the nation's premier theaters for Shakespeare and other plays.

Arrayed around the central **Plaza de Panama** are the **San Diego Museum of Art and Sculpture Garden**, the **Timkin Museum** with its Old Master paintings, the quirky folk-art-focused **Mingei International Museum**, and the **House of Hospitality** with its cool central courtyard and **Prado Restaurant** (a great place for lunch during your park exploration).

East of the plaza, the Prado morphs into a vehicle-free walking street flanked by even more collections, including the **Museum of Photographic Arts**, the fun **San Diego Model Railroad Museum**, the **San Diego History Center**, the superb **Natural History Museum**, and the cutting-edge **Reuben H. Fleet Science Center** with its IMAX theater, planetarium shows, and interactive exhibits.

The Prado area also tenders the **Spreckels Organ Pavilion** and its weekly outdoor concerts and the

The stunning architecture of Balboa Park comes to life at dusk.

A fountain marks the center of Plaza de Panama at Balboa Park, overlooking the tower at the Museum of Man.

adjacent **Japanese Friendship Garden**, which traces its roots to a tea pavilion created for the Panama-California Exposition.

The **San Diego Zoo** spreads across canyons and mesas north of the Prado. The zoo has evolved from a small menagerie created for the 1915-16 exhibition into one of the world's foremost wildlife collections, home to more than 3,500 animals from 650 species, as well as 700,000 exotic plants. Along with its Safari Park satellite in San Diego's backcountry, the zoo is also a world leader in captive breeding of rare and endangered species like the Arabian oryx, white rhino, and California condor. Just south of the zoo entrance are an **arts and crafts village, miniature railroad,** and vintage 1910 **carousel.**

Balboa Park's south side is dominated by structures dating to its second world's fair—the California Pacific International Exposition of 1935-36, including the art deco–style Ford Building (now home of the excellent **San Diego Air and Space Museum**). Among other attractions on the south mesa are the beloved **Marie Hitchcock Puppet Theater**, the **Starlight Bowl** (outdoor musical theater), the **San Diego Automotive Museum**, and a mock **Spanish village** with cottages that house goodwill and cultural clubs from 36 countries.

In addition to the 18-hole public **Balboa Park Golf Course**, the park also features a swimming pool, tennis courts, baseball diamonds, archery ranges, a cycling velodrome, and an extensive **trail network**. ■

Griffith Park
California

Rambling through canyons and mountains between Hollywood and downtown Los Angeles, Griffith Park is one of Southern California's most underrated treasures. Much of the park is wild and untamed, home to mountain lions and other creatures. But Griffith also has a more refined side, including world-class museums, entertainment venues, and the last resting place of many Hollywood show-business favorites.

THE BIG PICTURE

Established: 1896

Size: 4,310 acres (17.4 sq km)

Annual Visitors: 10 million

Visitor Center: Crystal Springs Drive

Entrance Fee: None

laparks.org/griffithpark

Since Griffith Park was founded in 1896, the City of the Angels has been completely engulfed with huge green space, preserving a surprisingly pristine piece of wilderness in the middle of the nation's second largest urban area.

Many of LA's leading cultural institutions are located in and around the park. But there's also plenty of space for recreational activities: picnics and ball games on manicured lawns; hiking, biking, and horseback riding on secluded trails; swimming, tennis, and golfing on four courses.

Rising to an elevation of 1,820 feet (554.7 m) at **Cahuenga Peak**, the park embraces several ecosystems, including oak woodland, coastal sage scrub, and riparian vegetation. With its picnic tables, shady trails, and parking areas, **Fern Dell** in the Los Feliz neighborhood is the starting point for many park outings.

If you didn't pack your own picnic, **Trails Cafe** offers a nice selection of drinks, baked goods, and other snacks.

Western Canyon Road twists uphill 2 miles (3.2 km) from the dell to the famous **Griffith Park Observatory** with its iconic views of Los Angeles. Opened in 1935, the observatory illuminates the heavens through exhibits, telescopes, and planetarium shows. The main road continues downhill to the **Griffith Park Bird Sanctuary** (with its summer storytelling series and upwards of 200 bird species) and the **Greek Theater**, popular for outdoor concerts since the 1920s. Trails lead uphill to **Dante's View** (with its even more spectacular outlook over the LA Basin), **Captain's Roost** on Mount Hollywood, and a network of footpaths over and along the park's mountainous spine.

Wedged between the mountains and Interstate 5, the eastern sector looks and acts more like a traditional city park than any other part of Griffith. The diverse flora and fauna of the **Los Angeles Zoo and Botanical Gardens** are the main attraction. But the flatlands also host picnic areas, a marvelous 1926 musical **merry-go-round** (and its playlist of 1,500 marches and waltzes), and the excellent **Autry Museum of the American**

Seemingly far from the city, a coyote pair snuggle in Griffith Park.

The Griffith Park Observatory offers a planetarium, public telescopes, and the best views of the Los Angeles Basin.

West, where more than a half million artifacts and artworks elucidate the region's Native American, Spanish, and American heritage. The **Visitor Center** on Crystal Springs Drive offers information on all park activities and attractions.

Big things that move dominate the park's north side. **Travel Town** preserves historic trains, buggies, and motor vehicles, while the **Los Angeles Live Steamers Railroad Museum** offers rides on two miniature railroads. On the other side of the Ventura Freeway, the **Los Angeles Equestrian Center** offers riding lessons and trail rides and hosts horse shows. The park wraps arms around nearly all of **Forest Lawn cemetery**, where Michael Jackson, Clark Gable, Bette Davis, Walt Disney, Humphrey Bogart, Liz Taylor, and many other luminaries are buried.

The park's secluded western extension is the hardest to reach—unless you're willing to hike along the area's hot and dusty trails. Pedestrian-only **Mount Lee Drive** climbs via a series of switchbacks to the celebrated **Hollywood Sign**, erected in 1923 to advertise a new subdivision called Hollywoodland. The **Aileen Getty**

Ridge Trail leads farther west to Mount Cahuenga and **Mount Burbank** with its bird's-eye view of Universal Studios. **Brush Canyon Trail** leads to the **Bronson Caves**, which have appeared in more than 100 movies, including *Invasion of the Body Snatchers* (1956), *Star Trek VI* (1991), and *The Scorpion King* (2002). ■

DID YOU KNOW

• Griffith Park started as an ostrich farm founded by Griffith J. Griffith, who later donated the property to the City of Los Angeles.

• From *Birth of a Nation* (1915) and *Rebel Without a Cause* (1955) to *The Terminator* (1984) and the *Batman* TV series, Griffith Park has appeared in many classic films and TV shows.

• During World War II, the park served as an internment camp for Japanese Americans suspected of spying, as well as a processing center for Japanese, German, and Italian POWs.

• America's most famous mountain lion (tagged "P22") was photographed in Griffith Park with the Hollywood sign as a backdrop in 2013.

Mojave Desert Parks

California & Nevada

Sprawling across much of California, Nevada, and Arizona, the Mojave Desert is one of North America's most formidable landscapes. While some may view it as barren wasteland, others find beauty in the undulating dunes, mirage-inducing salt flats, and noble Joshua trees. Two immense national parks, Death Valley and Joshua Tree, unveil the secrets and surprises of North America's most arid region.

DEATH VALLEY

The largest U.S. national park outside Alaska, Death Valley sprawls across an area larger than Connecticut. And that's not its only superlative. In 1913, local thermometers soared to 134°F (56.6°C)—the highest reliably recorded temperature in human history. The ultra-arid basin also boasts the lowest elevation in all of North America (282 feet/ 85.9 m below sea level). Despite these extremes, the valley offers pockets where flora and fauna thrive.

With its steady freshwater, **Furnace Creek** oasis attracted Timbisha Shoshone Indians, pioneer-era ranchers, borax miners, and Death Valley's first tourist services. The Timbisha never left; their modern

THE BIG PICTURE

Established: Death Valley (1933); Joshua Tree (1936)

Size: Death Valley (3.37 million acres/14,973.37 sq km); Joshua Tree (790,636 acres/3,199.6 sq km)

Annual Visitors: Death Valley (1.3 million); Joshua Tree (2.8 million)

Visitor Centers: Death Valley (Furnace Creek); Joshua Tree (Joshua Tree, Oasis, Cottonwood)

Entrance Fees: $25 vehicles, $12 per person

nps.gov/deva; nps.gov/jotr

village on the southern edge of Furnace Creek includes a **Tribal Gift Shop** open to the public. In addition to refreshing air-conditioning, **Furnace Creek Visitor Center** offers exhibits and ranger activities. Established in 1883, **Furnace Creek Ranch** has morphed from vaqueros to vacationers with a restaurant, golf course, stables, and swimming pool, as well as a **Borax Museum** that spins tales of the legendary 20-mule teams. The oasis comes into full bloom in the lush gardens of the **Furnace Creek Inn**, opened in 1927 and still the park's poshest accommodation.

True to its name, **Badwater** (11 miles/17.7 km south of Furnace Creek) is far too salty to be potable. But surprisingly, there is life in the shallow: Aquatic insects, plants, and even an endemic snail have adapted to the extreme salinity. Two of the park's iconic viewpoints overlook this part of the valley. **Zabriskie Point** is celebrated for its deeply eroded, multicolored rock formations, **Dante's View** for its sheer drop to the valley floor.

North of Furnace Creek, the main road leads to the old **Harmony**

Mud weaves its way through the white salt flats of Death Valley.

The Racetrack at Death Valley is known for its mysterious "moving rocks"—heavy stones that seem to slide across the desert.

Borax Works, the **Mesquite Flat Sand Dunes** (where scenes from the original *Star Wars* were filmed), and smaller clusters of visitor services at **Stovepipe Wells Village** and **Panamint Springs**. Lesser visited sites along the park's western edge are accessed via **Emigrant Canyon Road**, which meanders up into the Panamint Mountains to the remains of the **Skidoo** and **Eureka** mines, the panoramic views of **Aguereberry Point** (6,433 feet/1,960.8 m) and the beehive-shaped **Wildrose Charcoal Kilns** (built in the 1870s).

Some of the park's most eccentric landmarks are found in the far north. Colorful con man Walter Scott is the legend behind **Scotty's Castle**, a rambling Spanish revival mansion in Grapevine Canyon funded in the 1920s by a Chicago tycoon who thought he was investing in a Death Valley gold mine. **Ubehebe Crater**, a 600-foot-deep (182.88 m) gouge in the Earth's crust, reveals the area's volcanic origins. A two-hour drive down a remote desert road leads to the **Racetrack**, a dry lake bed renowned for its mysterious "moving rocks."

A few old towns around the park also beg a visit. **Rhyolite** is one of the region's best preserved ghost towns. Tucked up in the Bullfrog Hills, it prospered from 1905 to

DID YOU KNOW

- Joshua trees were allegedly named by Mormon pioneers who thought they resembled the biblical figure Joshua as he lifted his arms toward heaven.

- Death Valley nurtures around 1,000 different plant species— more than 50 of them found nowhere else on Earth.

- Cap Rock in Joshua Tree is an unofficial shrine to rock star Gram Parsons (of Byrds fame), who died nearby in 1973.

- In addition to being home to the endangered pupfish, the water in Devil's Hole in Death Valley has

been known to react to earth-quakes occurring on the other side of the world.

- Joshua Tree boasts more than 8,000 rock climbing routes.

- The highest ground temperature ever recorded in Death Valley (and possibly on our planet) was a sizzling 201°F (93.9°C) near Furnace Creek in 1972.

- The cover of the Eagles' self-titled debut album was shot in Joshua Tree, but, oddly, the cover of U2's epic *Joshua Tree* album was not.

1911 when the gold ran out. The old train station and the famous **Bottle House** are among the structures still standing. **Goldwell Open Air Museum** in Rhyolite preserves oversized works by Belgian artists who came to create in the Nevada desert. Although it counts less than 20 year-round residents, **Death Valley Junction** (founded 1914) is still a lively little town—at least on weekends between October and May, when the historic **Amargosa Opera House** stages its dance, comedy, music, and movie shows.

JOSHUA TREE

An enduring symbol of the Mojave, *Yucca brevifolia* might be the namesake of this national park in the desert east of Los Angeles, but it's certainly far from the only thing to see at Joshua Tree. Dozens of trails are open to hiking, biking, and horseback riding, and the stony terrain makes it one of America's rock-climbing meccas. Spring brings a carpet of wildflowers. And the superclear desert night

sky makes the park an oasis for stargazing.

The park actually embraces parts of two distinct deserts—the Mojave and Sonoran—as it tumbles down from the heights into the Coachella Valley near Palm Springs. There are only three ways visitors can enter the park: from Yucca Valley in the west, Twenty-Nine Palms in the north, and Cottonwood Springs in the south.

The main **Visitor Center** is actually outside the park, in the nearby town of Joshua Tree. Although the name seems like an oxymoron, Park Boulevard runs from the visitor center to **Lost Horse Valley** in the heart of the park, where three short interpretive trails (Hidden Valley, Barker Dam, and Cap Rock) are a great introduction to Joshua Tree's natural and human history.

Several of the parks have longer, more challenging trails that can also be accessed from the Hidden Valley area, including the 8-mile (12.9 km) **Boy Scout Trail** into the boulder-strewn **Wonderland of Rocks** and

the 35-mile (56.3 km) **California Riding and Hiking Trail** (normally done as a two- or three-day backpack trip). Another trail ascends to the summit of 5,456-foot (1,662.9 m) **Ryan Mountain**. Or cruise the paved road to **Keys View** at the crest of the Little San Bernardino Mountains for a mile-high (1.6 km) vista of the Coachella Valley, Salton Sea, and San Andreas Fault—a view that's especially enchanting after dark when Palm Springs sparkles with millions of lights.

In Joshua Tree National Park, sunsets create an ethereal landscape

From Lost Horse Loop, a 6.5-mile (10.5 km) trail, hikers can take in the arresting scenery of Joshua Tree National Park.

Park Boulevard continues over Sheep Pass into **Queen Valley** and another Joshua tree forest. The 18-mile (28.97 km) **Motor Geology Road** runs south through the valley, with 16 stops along the way that explain how the park's dramatic landscape was formed. Anchoring the valley's eastern edge is eerie **Skull Rock**, a natural formation that looks exactly like a skeleton's head. Exiting the valley, Park Boulevard makes a sharp turn to the north and a rendezvous with a lush palm grove, the **Oasis of Mara,** located beside the **Oasis Visitor Center**.

Alternatively, you can drive **Pinto Basin Road** into the park's lesser-known eastern expanse where other iconic desert plants—cholla cactus, ocotillo, cottonwood trees, and California fan palms—overshadow the Joshuas. **Cottonwood Visitor Center** anchors the park's southeast corner and a hiking area that includes trails to **Mastodon Peak** (3 miles/4.8 km) and the remote **Lost Palms Oasis** (7.5 miles/12 km). Just outside the park, the **General Patton Memorial Museum** at Chiriaco Summit includes a large collection of battle tanks and mementos of the general's military exploits. ∎

MEET THE NEIGHBORS

• **Mojave National Preserve:** This desert park between Joshua Tree and Death Valley shelters landmarks like the Kelso Dunes, Mitchell Caverns, and Hole-in-the-Wall.

• **Lake Havasu National Wildlife Refuge:** A ribbon of blue through the unrelenting desert, this Colorado River park fosters bird-watching, fishing, kayaking, and powerboating.

• **Inyo National Forest:** The mountains north of Death Valley shelter a forest of ancient bristlecone pines (*Pinus longaeva*), including one tree that sprouted around 3000 B.C.

• **Manzanar National Historic Site:** A museum, memorials, and historic structures mark the spot where more than 100,000 Japanese Americans were detained in this Mojave Desert relocation camp during World War II.

• **Sand to Snow National Monument:** Jointly managed by the Forest Service and Bureau of Land Management, this new park—established in 2016—includes the bird-rich Big Morongo Canyon Preserve.

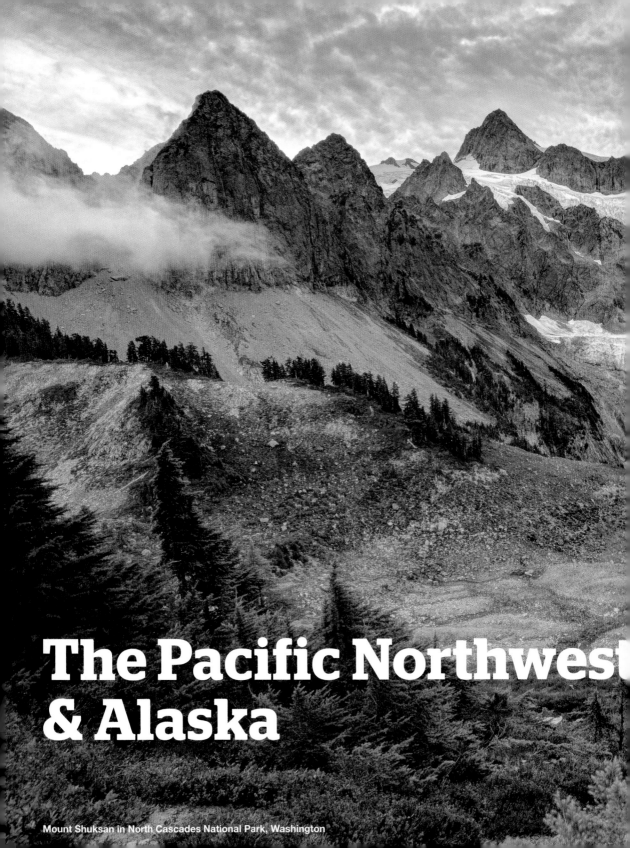

The Pacific Northwest & Alaska

Mount Shuksan in North Cascades National Park, Washington

Olympic National Park
Washington

One of the most primeval parts of the lower 48 states, Olympic covers nearly 1 million acres (4,046.9 sq km) of the eponymous peninsula in Washington State—95 percent of that designated wilderness. While the typical image of the park is a dark, damp, and overwhelmingly beautiful temperate rain forest, the park also shelters alpine highlands, tranquil lakeshores, and a wild Pacific coastline that seems totally untouched by humans.

THE BIG PICTURE

Established: 1938

Size: 922,650 acres (3,733.8 sq km)

Annual Visitors: 3.4 million (2017)

Visitor Centers: Port Angeles, Hurricane Ridge, Hoh Rain Forest, Lake Quinault

Entrance Fee: $25 vehicles, $10 per person

nps.gov/olym

Olympic is one of the places that Teddy Roosevelt recognized as an endangered national treasure, protecting the area's snowcapped peaks and lush forest with national monument status in 1909. That set the stage for a struggle between the timber industry and conservationists that segued into the ecological wave that later swept the Pacific Northwest.

While it's possible to enter the park from more than two dozen spots off the **Olympic Highway** (U.S. 101), the most popular is via **Port Angeles** on the peninsula's north shore. The city's **Olympic National Park Visitor Center** offers the usual range of information, books, and maps, as well as hands-on exhibits on the park's human and natural history

and a 25-minute film, "**Mosaic of Diversity.**" Two short nature walks, the **Living Forest Loop** (0.4 mile/ .64 km) and **Peabody Creek Trail** (0.5 mile/0.8 km), are a good introduction to the nature that lies ahead.

Mount Angeles Road meanders 17 miles (27.36 km) south into the heart of the park and a popular spot called **Hurricane Ridge**, where another visitor center offers exhibits and ranger-guided activities during the summer. Hikers have plenty of choices, from the short, flat **Big Meadow Loop** (a quarter mile/ 0.4 km) to challenging treks like the 8-mile (12.9 km) **Wolf Creek Trail** to Whiskey Bend. During winter, **snowshoeing** and **cross-country skiing** take over the Hurricane (equipment rentals are available at the gift shop).

Heading west from Port Angeles, Highway 101 makes a beeline for blue-green **Lake Crescent**, renowned for both its beauty and indigenous trout species. Get out on the water with a rental boat from **Fairholme Store**, hike or bike the north shore via the 10.5-mile (16.9 km) **Spruce Railroad Trail**, or take a refreshing dip at **East Beach**.

Just beyond the lake's western end, a side road leads to **Sol Duc Hot Springs** with its outdoor mineral pools

Camping is available on Shi Shi Beach at Point of the Arches.

The Deer Ridge Trail leads to an overlook of forests, mountains, and Sequim Bay in the distance.

(the hottest averages 104°F/40°C) and massage treatments. The valley is also renowned for its **ancient forest**, with many of the towering trees more than 200 years old. **Salmon Cascades** is a great spot to watch fish spawn in the fall, while trails lead off to **Mink Lake**, **Sol Duc Falls**, and the secluded **Seven Lakes Basin**.

Over on the park's supersaturated west side, the **Hoh Valley** is home to the park's most enchanting forest, a mosaic of moss, ferns, and giant trees that really does look like something from a medieval fairy tale (or Sasquatch movie). This is also the gateway to 7,980-foot (2,432.3 m) **Mount Olympus**, the park's highest point. Glacier-climbing skills are necessary to reach the peak, but day hikers can reach the base of **Blue Glacier** via the 18-mile (28.97 km) **Hoh River Trail**.

Separated from the rest of the park by private and tribal lands, **Kalaloch** area protects 65 miles (104.6 km) of an extremely wild Pacific coast carved by waves and tidal action. Riptides and floating logs inhibit swimming or surfing in these waters. The shoreline is more suited to long walks, exploring **tide pools**, and scouting for harbor seals, porpoises, sea otters, and other local denizens. ■

LAY YOUR HEAD

Hotels

• **Lake Crescent Lodge:** Founded in 1915, the south shore inn offers biking, fishing, and paddle sports; restaurant, gift shop; from $97. *olympicnationalparks.com/lodging*

• **Log Cabin Resort:** Perched on the north shore of Lake Crescent, the resort offers a wide range of choices from rustic camper cabins to A-frame chalets; restaurants, boat rental, general store; from $80. *olympicnationalparks.com/lodging*

• **Sol Duc Hot Springs Resort:** The mineral pools are just steps away from this historic retreat founded in 1912 in the Sol Duc Valley; restaurant, grocery store, gift shop, spa treatments; from $142. *olympic nationalparks.com/lodging*

• **Kalaloch Lodge:** Cabins and motel-style rooms overlooking the Pacific; restaurant, gift shop; from $129. *thekalalochlodge.com*

Camping

• Olympic National Park offers 14 developed campgrounds and scores of backcountry possibilities; $15-$24 per night.

Mt. Rainier & Mt. St. Helens National Volcanic Monument

Washington

Rising high above western Washington, stately Mount Rainier and menacing Mount St. Helens offer dramatic interpretations of how mountains can change the landscape as well as the flora, fauna, and people who inhabit the surrounding region. Both parks are easily explored by road and foot, including trails that ascend to both of the lofty volcanic summits.

Alpine flowers, including magenta paintbrush, cover meadows on Mount Rainier.

THE BIG PICTURE

Established: Mount Rainier (1899); Mount St. Helens (1982)

Size: Mount Rainier (236,381 acres/956.6 sq. km); Mount St. Helens (110,000 acres/ 445.15 sq km)

Annual Visitors: Mount Rainier (1.4 million); Mount St. Helens (295,000)

Visitor Centers: Sunrise, Paradise Jackson, Ohanapecosh, Johnson Ridge

Entrance Fees: Mount Rainier: ($25 per vehicle, $10 per person); Mount St. Helens: ($5-$8 per vehicle)

nps.gov/mora; fs.usda.gov/ giffordpinchot

A snowcapped backdrop to Seattle and the Puget Sound, Mount Rainier is a slumbering giant that last erupted in the 1890s. Just 40 miles (64.4 km) to the south, Mount St. Helens was the flashpoint for one of the most violent disasters in modern American history, a 1980 explosion that shook the world.

MOUNT RAINIER NATIONAL PARK

One of world's oldest national parks, Mount Rainier became part of the federal system in 1899, shortly after its last eruption. Park status was the culmination of a long campaign by John Muir and other conservationists to preserve a unique forest, field, and glacial landscape under threat from the timber and mining extraction that had already ravaged much of the American West.

That wasn't the last battle over the mountain. There was also a bitter feud over the name. British explorer George Vancouver originally christened the peak in 1792, naming it

Fifty miles (80 km) north of Portland, Oregon, Mount St. Helens, an active volcano, sits at 8,366 feet (2,549.9 m).

after his friend Rear Admiral Peter Rainier of the Royal Navy. With memories of the redcoats still fresh in their minds, Americans who settled the region in the early 19th century preferred the name Mount Tacoma. The lexical dispute continued into the 1920s, and returned again with the official designation of Denali as the name of Alaska's highest peak in 2015.

Despite its mountainous topography, the national park is easy to access from five different roads from the surrounding lowlands. One of the most popular areas is **Sunrise** in the northeast, easy to reach from the Seattle-Tacoma metropolitan area (around two hours) and also the highest point (6,400 feet/1,950.72 m) in the park that visitors can venture with their cars.

Renowned for its panoramic views of Mount Rainier and Emmons Glacier, **Sunrise Visitor Center** is well stocked with maps, books, and information on the park. Ranger-led

programs are a staple during the summer season. Snacks, drinks, and souvenirs are available at the nearby **Sunrise Day Lodge**.

Set amid a large alpine meadow, Sunrise is also the jumping-off point for numerous trails, both short and long, around the fringe of Mount Rainier. One of the easier hikes is

the **Silver Forest Trail** (2 miles/ 3.2 km) to the **Emmons Vista Overlook** and an old burn area where the grayish tree trunks glisten silver in a certain light. Far more difficult—and far more rewarding in scenery—is **Boroughs Mountain Trail**, which climbs steadily upward through wildflower-filled tundra to

Hikers follow a guide rope as they ascend snowy Mount Rainier, the highest mountain of the Cascade Range.

Frozen Lake and the edge of **Winthrop Glacier**. Another great route is the 7-mile (11.3 km) hike to the **Palisades Lakes** area, which starts at the parking lot for **Sunrise Point** (also the best place in the park to catch daybreak over the hazy plains of central Washington).

The park's most visited area is **Paradise** on the mountain's south side, which owes its name to Martha Longmire, a young settler who is said to have exclaimed "What a paradise!" when her family homesteaded the area in the 1880s.

Paradise Jackson Visitor Center tenders exhibits, ranger programs, and the park film. Even if you're not sleeping at the historic **Paradise Inn** (opened in 1917), grab a meal or check out the iconic "parkitecture." Permits for climbing Rainier and hiking the backcountry are available at the **Paradise Climbing Information Center** in Guide House. With

the entrance road plowed throughout the winter, Paradise is also the park's favorite spot for cross-country skiing, snowshoeing, and tubing.

Right down the road from Paradise is the **Longmire Historic District**, where James Longmire (the father of Mount Rainier tourism) and his family settled in the 1880s. The two old park headquarters buildings are now home to the **Longmire Museum** of local history and the **Longmire Wilderness Information Center** (another place that issues climbing and backcountry permits).

Tucked in Rainier's southeast corner is the **Ohanapecosh Visitor Center**, nestled in a thick old-growth forest that offers a dramatic contrast to the park's higher altitudes. The **Grove of the Old Patriarchs** shelters trees as tall as 300 feet (91.44 m) and 1,000 years old, while the **Silver Falls Loop** (2.8 miles/4.5 km) leads to the eponymous cascade.

Separated from the rest of the park by Rainier's bulk, the **Carbon River** area in the northwest has few facilities and few visitors but offers excellent hikes through the temperate rain forest. **Carbon Glacier**—the lowest elevation glacier in the lower 48 states—is a 17-mile (27.36 km) round-trip walk from the ranger station. **Mowich Lake**, the park's largest water body, is the best place to canoe or kayak at Rainier.

MOUNT SAINT HELENS NATIONAL VOLCANIC MONUMENT

Mount St. Helens was a largely unheralded mountain—not nearly as fabled as Rainier, Adams, Hood, Shasta, or other Cascade Range peaks—until 1980 when it suddenly roared to life after nearly 200 years of scant volcanic activity.

With a mighty rumble that would be felt hundreds of miles away,

St. Helens erupted May 18 in an explosion that collapsed the entire north face, reduced the height of the mountain by 1,300 feet (396.24 m), and generated the largest debris avalanche in recorded history. The massive pyroclastic flow that followed devastated 230 square miles (595.7 sq km) of Washington State wilderness, killed millions of animals, and took the lives of 57 people.

Two years later, President Reagan created the national monument to preserve the bizarre, posteruption landscape and encourage both recreation and research within its bounds. Given that Mount St. Helens was part of Gifford Pinchot National Forest before the 1980 explosion, the park is managed by the U.S. Forest Service with help from Washington State Parks. Volcanic activity continued through 2008, and the mountain is still considered an active volcano.

The drive up **Highway 504** on the park's northwest side affords incredible scenic views of the crater and blast zone. Not long after entering the park, the **Forest Learning Center** at Clearwater Lake features a virtual helicopter tour of the mountain, an Eruption Chamber with sights and recorded sounds from the eruption, and a walk-through exhibit that shows how the forest has bounced back from the disaster. Outside is a viewing deck for watching the elk herds that often gather in the meadow below.

At the top of the road, deep in the blast zone, is **Johnson Ridge Observatory.** The official Forest Service visitor center offers ranger talks and exhibits on St. Helens flora, fauna, geology, and history. Outside, the half-mile (0.8 km) **Eruption Trail** leads to viewpoints of the crater, pumice plain, lava dome, and landslide area.

On the eastern flank of St. Helens, **Highway 99** climbs via a series of switchbacks to **Windy Ridge**—the closest point that vehicles can get to the crater. Along the way are views of **Spirit Lake,** the crushed **Miner's Car**, and the ghostly **blown-down forest**, as well as interpretive sites where motorists can gain more knowledge about the mountain.

Backpackers can circumnavigate Mount St. Helens on the 28-mile (45 km) **Loowit Trail**, a trek that takes two to three days. Serious hikers can also reach the crater rim, although anyone venturing above 4,800 feet (1,463.04 m) needs a Forest Service climbing permit. The most popular route to the summit is the **Monitor Ridge Trail** (10-mile/ 16.1 km round-trip), which starts from Climbers' Bivouac trailhead on the mountain's south side. **Mount St. Helens Institute** offers guided summit treks and into-the-crater hikes, as well as field seminars and group winter activities in the park. ■

Beargrass grows on a lava flow at Mount St. Helens National Volcanic Monument.

Wildflowers cover the grass on the way to snowcapped Mount Rainier.

Crater Lake National Park

Oregon

One of the nation's most impressive geographical features, Crater Lake occupies the caldera of an ancient volcano that exploded around 7,000 years ago and eventually filled with rainwater and snowmelt. Although the southern Oregon lake is a photographer's paradise, the park offers plenty of other ways to discover the great outdoors, from starry nights and savory sunsets to a spectacular segment of the Pacific Crest Trail.

One of the legends of the Klamath people is a story about how the god of the underworld (Llao) and the god of the sky (Skell) waged a great battle that destroyed Llao's mountaintop home, a tale that reflects the eruption of Mount Mazama in the sixth century B.C. That event—an explosion estimated to have been *42 times larger* than the eruption of Mount St. Helens in 1980—created Crater Lake.

THE BIG PICTURE

Established: 1902

Size: 183,224 acres (741.48 sq km)

Annual Visitors: 711,000

Visitor Centers: Steel, Rim Village

Entrance Fee: $10-$15 vehicles, $10 per person

nps.gov/crla

Rim Drive, one of the most breathtaking roads in the world, runs 33 miles (53.1 km) around the outside of the crater with 30 viewpoints along the way where visitors can gaze down into the deep blue belly of the lake and **Wizard Island**, a volcanic cinder cone that rises 755 feet (230 m) above the surface.

Perched on the crater's southern edge, **Rim Village** revolves around the **Sinnott Memorial Overlook**, with its panoramic views and ranger programs, and the historic **Crater Lake Lodge** (opened in 1915). During the summer, the village also offers guided **Rim Drive Trolley Tours**, as well as ranger-guided hikes to the summit of **Mount Garfield** and the overlook at **Sun Notch** with its bird's-eye view of the **Phantom Ship**, a jagged volcanic rock formation that forms a small island.

Heading clockwise around the rim, **Discovery Point** and the **Watchman** are two of the best spots to catch sunrise over the lake. The latter also overlooks **Wizard Island**, a volcanic cinder cone that rises more than 700 feet (213.36 m) above the lake's surface.

Cleetwood Cove on the north rim is the only place where visitors can access the lakeshore—via an extremely steep 1.1-mile (1.8 km) trail that drops 700 feet (213.36 m). During the summer, two-hour ranger-led **Crater Lake Boat Tours** depart from

Towering pinnacles, fossil fumaroles, were formed under sheets of volcanic pumice.

A snow-covered rocky expanse surrounds the Crater Lake Volcano, with Wizard Island in its center.

the Cleetwood Cove dock. In addition, the cove offers **fishing** and **swimming** in the chilly water (temperatures range from 55°-60°F/12.8°-15.6°C in summer).

Around the east side are **Cloudcap Overlook** (great for sunsets), **Phantom Ship Overlook**, and the trailhead for the 2.2-mile (3.5 km) hike to the summit of 8,929-foot (2,721.6 m) **Mount Scott**, the park's highest point. A side roads leads downhill to a cluster of volcanic spires called the **Pinnacles**, an easy 1-mile (1.6 km) trail leading to **Plaikni Falls** (which tumbles over a volcanic precipice), and gravel **Grayback Drive**, which is open to hikers, bikers, and horseback riders but not motor vehicles. Before completing the circle, Rim Drive runs past **Steel Visitor Center**, which screens a 22-minute film on Crater Lake.

Around a thousand feet (304.8 m) below the rim—at the junction where the roads from Klamath Falls

and Medford merge at the park entrance—lies **Mazama Village.** The park's other beehive of activity offers a restaurant, gas station, grocery store, and campground. It's also a convenient waypoint on the **Pacific Crest Trail** (PCT), which meanders 33 miles (53.1 km) through the park.

Those who want to escape the crowds that cluster around the crater rim should cruise the North Entrance Road, a 9-mile (14.5 km) section of the **Volcanic Legacy Scenic Byway** that includes a lava wasteland called the **Pumice Desert** and a parking lot for short day hikes along the PCT. ■

DID YOU KNOW

- At 1,949 feet (594 m), Crater Lake is the deepest lake in the United States and ninth deepest on Earth.

- An almost total absence of pollutants means Crater Lake boasts some of the world's cleanest water, a factor that also creates its intense blue color.

- Crater Lake has no native fish. The rainbow trout and kokanee salmon found in the water are descendants of fish introduced between 1888 and 1941.

- The park averages around 40 feet (12.2 m) of snow each winter, fresh powder that facilities snowshoeing, cross-country skiing, and other cold weather sports.

- The last time Crater Lake completely froze over was in 1949.

- Although Crater Lake is not currently considered an active volcano, hydrothermal activity on its floor suggests the possibility of future volcanic events.

North Cascades National Park Complex

Washington

They may not be as massive or explosive as Washington State's other great mountains, but in several ways, the North Cascades are even more formidable—a soaring wall of stone and ice just three hours outside Seattle or Vancouver. Numerous peaks over 8,000 feet (2,438.4 m), more than 300 glaciers, and nearly 500 lakes spangle a landscape that seems little changed from the days when Native Americans were the region's only inhabitants.

Given its majestic persona, it's surprising that North Cascades wasn't included among the nation's earliest national parks. But opposition from timber and mining interests—as well as a long-running scuffle between the Forest Service and National Park Service over stewardship of the land—delayed designation until the late 1960s.

Moss covers tree branches in the North Cascades forests.

THE BIG PICTURE

Established: 1968

Size: 504,781 acres (2,042.8 sq km)

Annual Visitors: 30,000

Visitor Centers: Newhalem, Stehekin

Entrance Fees: None

nps.gov/noca

Even today, North Cascades is one of the least visited American national parks, a boon rather than a bane for those who cherish lesser-trampled trails, solitary lakeshores, and uncrowded campgrounds.

The park's most easily accessible area is **Ross Lake National Recreation Area**, which wraps around the **Skagit Gorge** and three artificial lakes. **Ross Lake Resort** rents small motorboats, kayaks, canoes, and fishing equipment during the summer, while Skagit Tours offers guided visits of the historic **Gorge Powerhouse**—the oldest power plant on the Skagit River—and scenic cruises across Diablo Lake aboard the *Seattle City Light.*

Trails lead up the eastern shore of Ross Lake to **Desolation Peak** and **Hozomeen** on the U.S.-Canada border, an unstaffed post that hikers with passports can cross into **Skagit Valley Provincial Park** in British Columbia.

North Cascade's **North Unit** is 100 percent wilderness and can be accessed only on foot. For those with the time and fitness, the region is virtually untouched by humans. Among its most impressive features are massive **Challenger Glacier, Redoubt Glacier**, and the twin **Beaver Valleys**. The required backcountry permits are available at the **North Cascades National Park Service Wilderness Information Center** in Marblemount.

Aptly named Picture Lake reflects Mount Shuksan, rising behind the forest in the distance.

The **South Unit** below the Skagit Valley is nearly roadless, another vast expanse of wilderness that can be explored only on foot via paths like the 8-mile (12.9 km) **Thunder Creek Trail** (which starts at Diablo Lake), the **Bridge Creek** section of the Pacific Crest Trail (12.8 miles/20.6 km), or the extraordinary **Rainbow-McAlester Loop** (31.5 miles/50.7 km) to alpine lakes and lofty passes.

North Cascade's fourth and final segment—and many would say its most scenic—is **Lake Chelan National Recreation Area** in the far south. With a landscape that could easily be mistaken for the Swiss Alps, the area centers around **Lake Chelan** and the tiny waterfront town of **Stehekin**, which can be reached only by foot, boat, horseback, or airplane. The *Lady of the Lake* boat service makes the 50-mile (80.5 km) journey from the lake's south end at Chelan year-round, docking 60 to 90 minutes in Stehekin before the return leg.

Founded in the 1880s, the town features historic **Buckner Homestead**, the one-room **Stehekin School**, and the **Golden West Visitor Center** in a rustic 1920s structure that was originally a wilderness lodge. Visitors can explore the **Stehekin Valley** via hikes and bikes on 22 miles (35.4 km) of paved roads and numerous unpaved trails. Hikes range from the easy jaunt to **Rainbow Falls** (7-mile/11.3 km round-trip) to the strenuous **Purple Creek Trail** (15-mile/24.14 km return) and its 57 switchbacks to an aerie with stunning views across the lake and the entire North Cascades.

Red Bus Tours whisk day-trippers on a quick tour of the valley. **Stehekin Discovery Bikes** rents cycles by the day or hour, and **Stehekin Outfitters** offers guided horseback rides and overnight pack trips into the surrounding wilderness. ◼

LAY YOUR HEAD

Hotels

• **North Cascades Lodge at Stehekin:** Lakeview cabins and motel-style rooms in the heart of the village; restaurant, general store; from $210. *lodgeatstehekin.com*

• **Ross Lake Resort:** Floating cabins and bunkhouses; fully furnished including kitchens; from $205. *rosslakeresort.com*

• **Stehekin Valley Ranch:** Tent cabins and ranch cabins—plus three meals a day at the cookhouse—in this secluded spot in the Stehekin Valley; horseback riding, kayaking, bikes, massage; from $105 per person. *stehekinvalleyranch.com*

Camping

• Developed campsites at Goodell Creek, Newhalem Creek, George Lake, Colonial Creek, Hozomeen, Stehekin, Diablo Lake, Ross Lake, Lake Chelan; from free to $16 per night.

San Juan Islands
Washington

A stark contrast to the hustle and bustle of nearby Seattle, the San Juan Islands offer a bucolic lifestyle and an amazing array of nature both on land and in the water. Tucked into the extreme northwestern corner of the lower 48 states, the archipelago comprises more than a hundred islands and myriad parks managed by federal, state, and local authorities.

Once a backwater on the outer edge of American civilization, the San Juan Islands have evolved into one of the adventure playgrounds of the Pacific Northwest. Ferries serve the islands from Anacortes, Seattle, and Port Townsend, as well as Sidney, British Columbia.

SAN JUAN ISLAND

San Juan Island National Historical Park tells the story of the celebrated Pig War of 1859, a dispute between the United States and Britain over ownership of the islands that reached fever pitch after an American settler killed a pig owned by a local employee of the Hudson's Bay Company. The Americans sent troops; the British dispatched warships. But thankfully the boundary dispute was resolved with only a single shot being fired and no casualties.

THE BIG PICTURE

Established: San Juan Island NHP (1966); Moran SP (1921)

Size: San Juan Island NHP (2,072 acres/8.39 sq km); Moran SP (5,579 acres/22.6 sq km)

Annual Visitors: San Juan Island NHP (267,000); Moran SP (1 million)

Visitor Centers: English Camp, American Camp

Entrance Fees: San Juan Island NHP (none); Moran SP ($10 per vehicle)

nps.gov/sajh
parks.state.wa.us/547/moran
visitsanjuans.com

The park is split between **American Camp** and **English Camp,** where the two sides staged their forces in 1859. The latter offers a **visitor center** in the old barracks where the Royal Marines lived during a dozen years of joint occupation. In addition to ranger activities, English Camp also features a self-guided history walk, an **English formal garden**, and the 1-mile (1.6 km) **Bell Point Trail** along the shore. American Camp is more renowned for sandy shores like **Fourth of July Beach** and long **South Beach**.

About halfway down the island's west coast, **Lime Kiln Point State Park** is considered the best place on the planet to view marine mammals from the shore—including orcas, gray whales, minke whales, humpbacks, porpoises, and sea lions. A vintage **1919 lighthouse** and sea cliffs provide the best vantage points.

ORCAS ISLAND

The largest of the San Juans harbors the best woodland parks, areas that have bounced back from an

A family of orcas travels through Haro Strait.

The San Juan Islands consist of 172 named islands and reefs in the Salish Sea, split between the United States and Canada.

era when the islands were heavily lumbered. **Moran State Park** (the fourth largest in Washington State) protects more than 5,000 acres (20.23 sq km) of forest and wetlands that can be explored via 38 miles (61.15 km) of hiking trails and boating on five lakes. There are also trails for horseback riding and mountain biking, as well as five campsites. Trails and a motor road snake to the summit of 2,409-foot (734.3 m) **Mount Constitution** and its stone viewing tower.

Turtleback Mountain Preserve offers an even more pristine slice of nature, a densely forested area that can be entered only on foot, bike, or horse. In addition to hiking the 1.2-mile (1.9 km) trail to the crest of the 1,000-foot (304.8 m) **Turtle-head**, with its views across the water to Canada, visitors can traverse the entire park on a series of trails between the two parking lots (4.4 miles/7.08 km).

Those with their own boat can venture to more remote parts of the San Juans. **Patos Island**, jointly managed by the state and federal governments, features a **historic lighthouse**, primitive **campsite**, and 1.5-mile (2.4 km) loop trail. **San Juan Islands National Wildlife Refuge**, which includes **Matia Island State Park**, is a prime spot for bird-watching. Keep your eye out for the archipelago's resident bald eagles. ∎

CHOW DOWN

• **The Mansion:** Lodged inside the former home of tycoon Robert Moran, who bequeathed the rest of his Orcas Island property to the state park system, this elegant eatery offers gourmet dining beside Cascade Bay. *rosarioresort.com*

• **Westcott Bay Shellfish Company:** Right beside English Camp, this family-run aquaculture farm offers visitors fresh oysters, clams, and mussels during the summer. *westcottbayshellfish.com*

• **West Sound Cafe:** Round off a hike up Turtleback Mountain with Pacific Northwest wine and seafood at this cozy waterfront eatery near the park's south end. *kingfishinn.com/cafe*

• **San Juan Island Cheese:** Everything from artisan cheeseboards and quiche to homemade cheesecakes and cheesy pasta is on the menu at this mom-and-pop café in Friday Harbor. *sjicheese.com*

A waterfall spills into a remote area of Oregon's Columbia Gorge.

Oregon Dunes NRA

Oregon

THE BIG PICTURE

Established: 1972

Size: 31,566 acres (127.7 sq km)

Annual Visitors: 382,000

Visitor Center: Reedsport

Entrance Fee: $5 per vehicle per day

fs.usda.gov/recarea/siuslaw/recreation/recarea/?recid=42465

Like no other place along the Pacific Northwest coast, Oregon's otherworldly dunescape stretches more than 40 miles (64.4 km) along the shore and reaches a height of about 500 feet (152.4 m) in places, a sea of rolling golden sand between the blue-gray Pacific and the evergreen forest. Renowned for its off-roading, the national recreation area also has quiet corners for hiking, paddling, or solitary contemplation.

Formed by eons of storms, tides, and erosion along the tempestuous Oregon Coast, the Oregon Dunes National Recreation Area dominates the shoreline between Florence and Coos Bay. Siuslaw National Forest looks after most of the land, while the beaches are managed by Oregon State Parks.

Oregon Coast Highway (Route 101) provides multiple points to access the dunes and beaches, and the **Oregon Dunes NRA Visitor Center** in Reedsport tenders exhibits, books, brochures, and maps on the granular wilderness.

All-terrain vehicles and dune buggies can roar across the dunes at **off highway vehicle (OHV)** areas near Florence, Winchester, and Coos Bay. Off-road camping in the dunes is allowed at marked sites in all three areas. Those who don't have their own buggies can experience the dunes on guided dune buggy trips offered by outfits like **Sandland Adventures**. Motorized vehicles are forbidden on most of the beaches.

While some might love the smell of gasoline in the morning, others are more inclined to relish the sea spray, mulchy wetlands, or the tranquil "tree islands" scattered among the dunes.

Honeyman State Park near Florence offers dune access, nature trails, campsite and yurt rentals, and swimming and boating on freshwater **Cleawox Lake** and **Woahink Lake** on the inland side of the dunes. The park is only a 10-minute drive from long and often empty **South Jetty Beach**, which stretches nearly three miles (4.8 km) along an isthmus on the Siuslaw River.

The mouth of the **Sitcoos River** near Dune City is another fine place for beachcombing and camping. A little farther south, the **Oregon Dunes Day Use Area** provides viewing platforms, a 3-mile (4.8 km) loop trail through the shifting sands, and the leafy **Tahkenitch Creek**

Gorse flowers bloom along Route 101 overlooking the Oregon Dunes.

Wind and snow shape and decorate the Umpqua Dunes, a 1.7-mile (2.7 km) trail near Lakeside, Oregon.

Trail (1.4 miles/2.25 km) through the coastal woods. Sparrow Park Road leads to another long, underused beach area at the mouth of **Threemile Creek**.

After passing through **Reedsport** and the Oregon Dunes NRA visitor center, the coastal highway swings back to the coast at **Winchester Bay**, a hub for **sports fishing** on the Pacific Ocean and the Umpqua and Smith Rivers. The stretch of coast south of Winchester Bay includes the 1894 **Umpqua Lighthouse**, family-friendly **Ziolkouski Beach** (with its jetty-protected ocean swimming area), and the towering **Umpqua Dunes,** which reach their highest point at 500-foot (152.4 m) **Banshee Hill** in the OHV area.

The **Lakeside** area trailheads start some of the best Oregon Dunes hikes, including the roller-coaster **John Dellenback Trail** to the beach (10.5-mile/16.9 km round-trip) and a figure-eight trail that loops through the dunes and forest around **Hall and Schuttpelz Lakes**. **Spinreel Rentals** in Lakeside offers Jeep tours of the dunes, as well as ATV and dune buggy rentals.

Horsfall Beach anchors the southern end of Oregon Dunes.

The north shore is open to off-road vehicles year-round; the south shore is open only to hikers and horses. **Wild Mare Campground** is an equestrian-only site at the start of a scenic horse trail leading to the beach. ■

EVENT HORIZON

• **Florence Fest:** Oregon wine, art, and jazz are the triple crown of this annual April event on the north bank of the Siuslaw River. *florencefestoregon.com*

• **Oregon Dunes Triathlon:** Swim a freshwater lake, bike wilderness roads, and finish with a run up the sand dunes at this May event hosted by Dune City. *oregondunestriathlon.com*

• **Oregon Chainsaw Carving Championship:** One of the top semiprofessional events on the national chainsaw carving circuit

unfolds along the Reedsport waterfront over Father's Day weekend. *oregonccc.com*

• **Dune Fest:** This five-day jamboree draws thousands of off-roaders to Winchester Bay in late July for dune bashing, drag racing, and tricked-out show buggies. *dunefest.com*

• **Fiddle on the Beach:** Campgrounds, docks, and indoor venues around Winchester Bay host this annual jam of live fiddle, guitar, banjo, and mandolin music. *fiddleonthebeach.info*

① Long Range Traverse, Newfoundland

Trek across the top of Newfoundland on this 21-mile (33.8 km) trail through the highlands of Gros Morne National Park. While the route can certainly be hiked in a single day, five primitive campsites are spread along the traverse for those who want to linger in the tundra-laden landscape.

② Presidential Traverse, New Hampshire

The 10 presidential peaks of New Hampshire's White Mountains National Forest are normally conquered in a single day. Stretching 23 miles (37 km) between Mount Madison and Mount Jackson, the hike typically includes a break at Mount Washington with its summit visitor center, café, and museums.

③ Appalachian Trail, Maine to Georgia

Stretching around 2,200 miles (3,540.6 km) from Maine to Georgia, America's most celebrated hiking route provides a woodsy, rocky pathway through some of the great American parks, from White Mountain National Forest and Harpers Ferry to Shenandoah and Great Smoky. On average, the hike takes around six months to complete.

④ Ouachita NR Trail, Arkansas and Oklahoma

One of the longest routes in the South that's *not* in the Appalachians, the trail meanders across Ouachita National Forest between Perryville in central Arkansas and Talimena State Park in eastern Oklahoma. Much of the 192-mile (308.9 km) route is open to both hikers and bikers as it makes its way over remote ridges and through wilderness valleys.

⑤ Tonto Trail, Arizona

Avoid the crowds on the Kaibab and Bright Angel trails and hike the unfettered wilderness along this horizontal route that runs east-west through the Grand Canyon about halfway between the South Rim and the Colorado River. For experienced hikers only, the 70-mile (112.6 km) route requires multiple overnights at primitive campsites.

THE TOP

10

HIKING TRAILS

From challenging day hikes to six-month journeys, parks offer a wide range of routes.

⑥ John Muir Trail, California

Named for the legendary Scottish-American naturalist, the 211-mile (339.6 km) path leads across the High Sierra between Yosemite, Kings Canyon, and Sequoia National Parks. Anchoring the southern end of the Muir is the climb up 14,505-foot (4,421.12 m) Mount Whitney, the highest point in the lower 48 states. The trail draws the most hikers between late May and October.

A mother and daughter hike the Appalachian Trail.

⑦ Tahoe Rim Trail, California and Nevada

Circle the big blue lake that straddles the California-Nevada border on this 165-mile (265.5 km), single-track route through the mountains that ring Tahoe. The trail wanders through three national forests, three wilderness areas, and one state park at elevations of 6,300 to 10,300 feet (1,920.2-3,139.4 m). Around a third of the route overlaps with the Pacific Crest Trail.

⑧ Pacific Crest Trail, Mexico to Canada

Although this 2,650-mile (4,264.76 km) long trail runs all the way from Mexico to Canada and through three states, one of its most spectacular sections is the stretch in western Washington State that links the Columbia River Gorge with Mount Rainier and North Cascades National Parks.

⑨ West Coast Trail, Vancouver Island

This path along the western edge of Vancouver Island traces a route blazed centuries ago by the First Nations people who lived along this shore. Most hikers undertake the 46-mile (74 km) trail in six to eight days, including a short interlude at Ditidaht tented camp at Tsuquadra Point.

⑩ Mauna Loa Summit Trail, Hawaii

Trek the world's second largest volcano—and the planet's second highest mountain when measured from base to peak—on this path in Hawaii Volcanoes National Park. Normally done over two or three days, the 30-mile (48.3 km) return hike rises from the upper rain forest to the moonscape summit of 13,679-foot (4,169.4 m) Mauna Loa, a massive active shield volcano that last erupted in 1984.

Columbia River Gorge National Scenic Area

Washington & Oregon

THE BIG PICTURE

Established: 1986

Size: 292,000 acres
(1,181.7 sq km)

Annual Visitors: 4 to 5 million

Visitor Center: Columbia Gorge
Interpretive Center

Entrance Fees: None to the
national scenic area; various
fees for state parks

gorgefriends.org
gorgecommission.org
columbiarivergorge.info

Stretching 85 miles (136.8 km) along both sides of the Columbia River Gorge between Oregon and Washington, the national scenic area safeguards the natural and human heritage of one of the great landmarks of the American West. Managed jointly by the U.S. Forest Service and the Columbia Gorge Commission with input from four Native American tribes, the park blends recreation and conservation with the gorge's role as a vital transportation corridor.

A winter fog covers the peaks and falls of the gorge.

Created in 1984 to prevent urban sprawl and wanton tourism development from trashing the gorge, the national scenic area extends more than 80 miles (128.7 km) between Portland and the Deschutes River. The **Historic Columbia River Highway** (Route 30) runs the Oregon shore and the **Lewis and Clark Highway** (Route 14) the Washington bank, with only a handful of bridges to cross the mighty waterway.

Leaving Portland behind, the initial stretch of Route 30 could easily be called Waterfall Row, such is the wealth of liquid that tumbles down from Oregon's aptly named Cascade Range. Of the dozen major waterfalls, **Multnomah Falls** is the most renowned for its height (627 feet/191.1 m) and sublime nature—a double cascade with a bridge that leaps across the misty gap.

Another 10 miles (16 km) up the gorge is the **Bonneville Lock and Dam**, structures that expedite river traffic and hydroelectric generation. On the Oregon shore are **Bradford Island Visitor Center**, an observation deck to watch ships pass through **Navigation Lock**, and the

In full color, wildflowers decorate the meadow floors of the Columbia River Gorge.

Bonneville Fish Hatchery, where salmon are raised for release into the river. Over on the north bank are the **Washington Shore Visitor Complex** (with its fish-viewing windows) and **Fort Cascades National Historic Site**, one of the waypoints along the Oregon Trail.

Visitors can't cross the Columbia (or switch states) at Bonneville Dam. But a little farther upstream is **Bridge of the Gods**, a majestic cantilever span that stretches more than 1,800 feet (548.64 m) across the river. In addition to motor traffic, the bridge carries the **Pacific Crest Trail** across the Columbia. Literally in the shadow of the bridge, the town of **Cascade Locks** is home port for the *Columbia Gorge* sternwheeler, which offers scenic river cruises between May and October. On the other side of the bridge, the

Columbia Gorge Interpretive Center details the region's 40-million-year history.

Hood River has morphed from a timber town into an outdoor recreation hub that includes whitewater rafting on a branch of the Columbia called the **White Salmon River**, as well as visitor-oriented orchards and vineyards along the **Fruit Loop**

MEET THE NEIGHBORS

- **Mount Hood National Forest:** One of the nation's most visited national forests protects more than a million acres (4,050 sq km) south of the Columbia Gorge including 11,249-foot (3,429 m) Mount Hood—the highest point in Oregon.

- **Fort Vancouver National Historic Site:** This dual site includes the Hudson's Bay Company post on the north bank of the Columbia (established in 1824) and the historic McLoughlin and Barclay houses in Oregon City, Oregon.

- **John Day Fossil Beds National Monument:** Forty million years of Oregon's remarkable history is exposed in this remote park, which includes the Thomas Condon Paleontology Center.

- **Lewis & Clark National Historical Park:** The spot where the Corps of Discovery wintered in 1805-1806 is marked by a Fort Clatsop replica, historic canoe landing, and trails down to the river.

Above: An evening view of the gorge from Vista House Opposite: Multnomah Falls in autumn

trail. **Panorama Point Park** offers outstanding views of perpetually snowcapped **Mount Hood**.

Located on the site of a longtime Native American trading center and pioneer trading post, the **Dalles** anchors the eastern end of the national scenic area. The largest city along the gorge offers several worthwhile sights, including historic **Fort Dalles** (1850), **Old St. Peter's Church** (1897), and the excellent **Columbia Gorge Discovery Center and Museum**.

Over on the Washington side, **Columbia Hills Historical State Park** revolves around a treasure trove of ancient Native American rock art, the rustic trails of the old **Dalles Mountain Ranch**, rock climbing on riverside **Horsethief Butte**, and various water sports on the Columbia River (swimming, boating, windsurfing, and fishing). There's also culture—the **Maryhill Museum of Art** in a 1914 mansion overlooking the river. ■

EVENT HORIZON

• **Menucha Mountain Dulcimer Festival:** Four days of concerts, jam sessions, and workshops mark this April shindig at Menucha Retreat near Corbett, Oregon. *menucha.org/ programs/dulcimer-festival*

• **Hood River Hard-Pressed Cider Fest:** More than 50 locally made ciders are on tap at this April event that showcases Hood River's thriving craft cider scene. *hoodriver.org/cider-fest*

• **Northwest Cherry Festival:** The Dalles hails the arrival of spring with a downtown bash that features a parade, classic car show, 10K race, Cherry Idol singing contest, and lots of treats made with locally grown cherries. *thedalleschamber.com/ northwest-cherry-festival*

• **GorgeGrass Festival:** Top bluegrass acts from around the nation play beside the river in this annual July fest at Skamania County Fairgrounds in Stevenson, Washington. *new.columbia gorgebluegrass.net*

• **Roy Webster Cross Channel Swim:** This charity swim, 1.1 miles (1.8 km) across the Columbia River, has been a Hood River tradition since 1943 when the annual Labor Day weekend event was founded. *hoodriver.org/ roy-webster-cross-channel-swim*

Wrangell-St. Elias & Kluane

Alaska & the Yukon

Sprawling across an area nearly as large as Switzerland, Wrangell-St. Elias National Park in Alaska and adjacent Kluane National Park in the Yukon are the most significant parts of North America's single largest conservation area. This vast expanse of wilderness—almost completely without roads—offers a majestic blend of snowcapped peaks and deep valleys, massive glaciers and coastal fjords, untamed rivers and wild creatures.

Ironically, the very thing that kept settlers away or otherwise carving up the Wrangell-Kluane region is the same thing that makes it so alluring today: extreme nature. Mountains so high and rugged they couldn't be crossed. Glaciers larger than some American states. Rivers that couldn't be tamed, a coastline defended by icebergs, and animals that view humans as just another form of prey.

While the region certainly boasted its fair share of mineral wealth, copper and gold in particular, there wasn't enough to set off a local equivalent of the Klondike gold rush or North Slope oil boom.

THE BIG PICTURE

Established: Wrangell-St. Elias (1980); Kluane (1972)

Size: Wrangell-St. Elias (4.8 million acres/19,424.9 sq km); Kluane (5,439,530.8 acres/22,013 sq km)

Annual Visitors: Wrangell-St. Elias (68,000); Kluane (27,000)

Visitor Centers: Copper Center and Kennecott (Alaska); Haines Junction and Thachäl Dhäl (Yukon)

Entrance Fees: None

nps.gov/wrst; pc.gc.ca/en/pn-np/yt/kluane

So by the 1970s, when the U.S. and Canadian governments finally got around to creating the two national parks—and UNESCO declared the entire region a World Heritage site—there was still plenty left to preserve, including large numbers of animals such as brown bears, wolves, mountain goats, Dall sheep, moose, caribou, and bald eagles.

WRANGELL-ST. ELIAS NATIONAL PARK AND PRESERVE

It's difficult to describe America's largest national park without lapsing into facts and figures worthy of *Jeopardy*. With more than 150 glaciers and ice fields, Wrangell harbors the world's largest concentration of ice outside the polar regions. Nine of North America's 16 highest peaks are in the park, including the planet's most imposing coastal mountains.

Given the lack of roads—and the fact that bush planes, all-terrain vehicles, snowmobiles, and hiking are the main modes of getting around—it takes an entire year for Wrangell to get as many visitors as the Grand Canyon sees in just four days. It's

An aerial view of a glacier within Wrangell-St. Elias

At more than 13 million acres (52,609.1 sq km), Wrangell-St. Elias is larger than Switzerland—and the largest U.S. national park.

almost impossible *not* to be alone once you leave the McCarthy-Kennecott area.

For those driving in from Anchorage or Fairbanks, **Copper Center Visitor Center** near Glennallen is the first point of contact with Wrangell-St. Elias. In addition to ranger programs and nature exhibits, the visitor center shows a short film about the park. The neighboring **Ahtna Cultural Center** offers interpretive displays and artifacts on the region's indigenous people. Explore the surrounding woods on the half-mile (0.8 km) **Boreal Forest Loop** or the half-mile (0.8 km) **Copper River Bluff Trail**, which leads to a scenic overlook view across the bush toward 14,163-foot (4,316.9 m) **Mount Wrangell**, an active volcano that last erupted in 2002.

The main park entrance is located across the Copper River from **Chitina**, 57 miles (91.7 km) south of the visitor center. From there, the gravel McCarthy Road meanders through 60 more miles (96.6 km) of wilderness to the town of **McCarthy** at the foot of **Kennicott Glacier**. Although it originally served the interests of local copper miners,

A bush plane flies over crevices formed in the glaciers of Wrangell-St. Elias National Park.

McCarthy now serves as a base camp for guides, bush pilots, and adventure outfitters offering various ways to explore the park. **St. Elias Alpine Guides** organizes backpacking, mountaineering, river rafting, ski trips, and more.

Visitors can hike or catch a shuttle bus along the old wagon road (5 miles/8 km) to the **Kennecott Mines**, a national historic monument that preserves the remains of an early 20th-century copper mill camp. The **Kennecott Visitor Center** in the former schoolhouse offers ranger-guided tours of the grounds and buildings. Trails lead to old **copper mines** on the slopes above Kennecott, as well as nearby **Root Glacier**.

Ranging out from the McCarthy-Kennecott area, there are a number of ways to explore the park, including **whitewater rafting** the Copper River, **scenic bush plane flights,** climbing the perpetually snowcapped peaks of the St. Elias Range, and hiking the backcountry. Backpackers can reach several alluring areas—including the spectacular **Donoho Lakes** and **Eire Lake/Stairway Icefall**—by striking out on foot from McCarthy. Air taxis drop backpackers into other popular hiking spots such as the historic **Goat Trail** at Skolai Pass and **Iceberg Lake** in the Tara River Basin.

The park's only other auto route is the unpaved 42-mile (67.6 km) **Nabesna Road** between Slana and Nabesna around the park's north side. This little-visited region offers a blend of lakes, wetlands, and boreal forest that can be explored in several day hikes, including the **Skookum Volcanic Trail** (2.5 miles/4 km) and the **Reeve's Field Trail** (4.2 miles/ 6.8 km) down to the banks of the Nabesna River. The relatively flat terrain makes this an ideal place for cross-country skiing, snowmobiling, and snowshoeing in winter.

Unless you've got your own boat, the only realistic way to access the Wrangell-St. Elias coast is via bush plane from either McCarthy or **Yakutat** on the Gulf of Alaska. The region includes the massive **Malaspina Glacier** and **Icy Bay**, a wonderland of glaciers, waterfalls, icebergs, and thousand-foot (304.8 m) cliffs that emerged over the last century because of glacial retreat. **Expeditions Alaska** is one of the few outfitters that offers guided kayak trips on Icy Bay.

KLUANE NATIONAL PARK AND RESERVE

The colossal ice fields and high peaks of the St. Elias Range form both the international border between the United States and Canada and an imposing barrier between Wrangell-St. Elias and Kluane national parks. Unless you're a veteran mountaineer, it's nearly impossible to travel between the parks without flying over the mountains and driving around the north end via the **Alaska Highway**, a distance of 400 to 500 miles (653.7-804.7 km).

Located on the Alaska Highway between Destruction Bay and Whitehorse, **Haines Junction** is the main gateway to Kluane. The Parks Canada **visitor center** offers detailed advice on how to discover the giant park, as well as exhibits and videos, audio recordings by local First Nations elders, and interactive games. The adjacent **Da Kų Cultural Centre** stages exhibits and demonstrations on the culture of the local Champagne and Aishihik people.

Flight-seeing trips over the park—showcasing a bird's-eye view of 19,551-foot (5,959.15 m) **Mount Logan**, the highest point in Canada—are available through **Kluane Glacier Air Tours**. **Icefield Discovery** offers glacier camping and Mount Logan expedition air charters.

Although Kluane is largely a roadless wilderness, the eastern edge of the park is easily explored by motor vehicle at stops along the Alaska and Haines Highways. A 20-minute drive south of Haines Junction, **Kathleen Lake** is set against a stunning backdrop of snow-capped Kluane peaks. In addition to the park's only drive-in campground, the lake offers kayaking and canoeing, a short nature trail, and the tougher **King's Throne Trail** (6 miles/9.7 km) to an alpine cirque with incredible views across the park's landscape. It's also the trailhead for the adventurous **Cottonwood Trail** (53 miles/85.3 km), a

four- to six-day hike that requires numerous stream crossings.

One hour north of Haines Junction, the Alaska Highway reaches the southern shore of **Kluane Lake**. Here the park's **Thachäl Dhäl Visitor Centre** features a viewing deck where it's often possible to see Dall sheep on the nearby slopes. **Soldier's Summit Trail** (0.6 mile/0.9 km) leads to the spot where the Alaska Highway was officially opened in

1942. Hikes in the adjacent Slims River Valley range from moderate walks like the **Sheep Creek Trail** (6 miles/9.7 km) to major treks like the two-day **Ä'äy Chù Trails** (on either side of the Slims River) to the foot of **Kaskawulsh Glacier**. Farther up the lakeshore, the **Kluane Museum of Natural History** in Burwash Landing revolves around local nature and the area's Southern Tutchone people. ∎

A trio of Dall sheep look on curiously from Sheep Mountain in Kluane.

Denali National Park & Preserve

Alaska

One of the world's most impressive mountains is the focal point of this massive national park and preserve in central Alaska. But there is much more to Denali than just a towering peak. Legendary for its wildlife, the park rambles across an area the size of New Jersey, nearly all of it untamed wilderness without roads, trails, or any other human touch.

"Coppers and purples, and reds and golds, browns and blacks streaked across the earth violently, and sweeping up and over, a kaleidoscope of dirt and rock that challenges even the most jaded of hearts to not fall under her spell." That's how naturalist Danielle Rohr describes her one-year sojourn in the park in the autobiographical *Denali Skies*.

THE BIG PICTURE

Established: 1917

Size: 4.7 million acres (19,020.23 sq km)

Annual Visitors: 642,000

Visitor Centers: Denali, Eielson, Murie (September through May only)

Entrance Fee: $10

nps.gov/dena

Even though the park revolves around perpetually snowcapped **Denali**—the highest mountain in North America at 20,310 feet (6,190.5 m)—it's often the rest of the park that leaves a lasting impression on visitors: the boreal forest and tundra, the wild rivers and glaciers, and the creatures that wander this amazing Alaska landscape, in particular the formidable brown bears that call Denali home.

Located about halfway between Anchorage and Fairbanks, Denali National Park and Preserve can be reached via the **Parks Highway** (Alaska Route 3), air services into **McKinley National Park Airport**, or the **Denali Star Train**.

Both the airport and train station are within a very short walk of the **Denali Visitor Center**, open summer only. During the other three seasons, **Murie Science and Learning Center** (MSLC) across the street assumes the role of park visitor center. The third (and perhaps most important) of the buildings clustered near the park entrance is the **Wilderness Access Center** (WAC), where visitors can reserve campsites, obtain backcountry permits, hop a shuttle bus, or purchase tickets for the park's popular bus tours.

There's plenty to do near the park entrance, including day hikes to **Triple**

An Alaska bull moose displays his large rack in Denali National Park.

The aurora borealis dances above the Toklat River and its surrounding mountains and glaciers.

Lake (9.5 miles/15.3 km), the lofty **Mount Healy Overlook** (5.4-mile/8.7 km round-trip), and the relatively easy **Taiga Trail** to **Horseshoe Lake** (0.9 mile/1.45 km). Visitors can also pop into the **Denali Sled Dog Kennels** to watch a demonstration of how the dogs help patrol the park in winter. The paved road (and private vehicle access) ends at **Savage River**, where there's a campground and a 1.7-mile (2.7 km) loop trail that crosses the river on a wooden footbridge.

Denali Park Road meanders 92 miles (148.06 km) through the heart of the park to scenic spots like the **Toklat River** crossing, **Wonder Lake** with its remarkable views of the Alaska Range and Denali's north flank, the old gold mining town of **Kantishna**, and **Eielson Visitor Center** with its interactive exhibits and ranger-guided activities. But only the first 15 miles (24.14 km) of the road are open to private vehicles. The only ways to cruise the rest of the route are by foot, bicycle, or bus. **Traveling Park Road** is the best way to spot wildlife,

in particular bears, moose, caribou, Dall sheep, and a variety of birds.

Three narrated bus tours ply the route during the warmer months (May-September), including the **Denali History Tour** to the Teklanika River, the **Tundra Wilderness Tour** to Stony Overlook, and the **Kantishna Experience** to the very end of the road. Along the way, the buses stop at prime wildlife viewing spots. Back-

country hikers, campers, or those who merely want to explore on their own can hop on a nonnarrated shuttle bus from the WAC to four different stops along the road.

While anyone with a backcountry permit is free to hike the wilderness and camp overnight, several outfitters offer guided treks into the Denali wilderness. **Alaska Alpine Adventures** has guided backpack camping trips

DID YOU KNOW

• William McKinley was only a candidate for president in 1896 when an Alaska gold miner named the massive peak in honor of the Ohio politician.

• Although the national park changed its name from McKinley to Denali in 1980, the peak itself retained the presidential name until officially changed by the Department of the Interior in 2015.

• While Denali is indisputably the highest peak in North America,

it wouldn't even rank in the top 100 of highest mountains in the Himalaya range.

• Only two other continents (Asia and South America) boast peaks higher than Denali.

• Although many Alaska mountains are volcanic, Denali is actually an enormous granite pluton that originally solidified beneath the Earth's surface before it was thrust up by plate tectonics.

of one week or more at distances ranging from 20 to 50 miles (32.19 to 80.47 km) through the park. Six companies are authorized by the Park Service to guide ascents of Denali peak and other mountains in the park, including **Alpine Ascents International**, which offers three-week expeditions between May and July.

Another way to explore more of the backcountry is overnighting at **campgrounds** along Denali Park Road (in particular, Wonder Lake or Igloo Creek) and striking out on hikes from there. The **three private lodges** in Kantishna are also perfect for day hikes, with or without a guide.

McKinley Airport is home base for many of the park's scenic flight operations. A variety of aerial choices are available during the summer. **Fly Denali** is one of several aviation companies that offer flightseeing around the big peak, glacier landing trips, and climbing support for mountaineers. **Talkeetna Air** does helicopter sightseeing over the glaciers and valleys leading up to Denali's south side.

Winter activities also revolve around the park entrance. The roads and trails around the visitor center are ideal for cross-country skiing, snow-

Hikers make their way up snow-covered mountains.

shoeing, and fat-tire biking, as are Denali Park Road and the temporary trails created by the park's dogsledding teams. **Riley Creek Campground** remains open through the winter, and visitors are free to overnight as long as they have a backcountry permit.

Or you can opt for organized winter activities. **Earth Song Lodge** arranges dogsledding trips, as well as overnight cross-country skiing trips to Wonder Lake and Igloo Creek. **Denali Wilderness Winter Guides** specializes in single-day activities like guided snowshoeing, a winter photography workshop, and a motorized "selfie tour" with park landmarks as your backdrops.

Outside the park, the Nenana River/Parks Highway corridor is also rife with outdoor activities, as well as most of the hotels and restaurants in the Denali region. Visitor services cluster in the little backcountry towns of **McKinley Park**, **Cantwell**, and **Healy** along the park's eastern edge, as well as **Talkeetna** in the southeast.

Brave the whitewater of the Nenana Gorge and Talkeetna River—rapids that range up to Class IV—with **Raft Denali**, which also offers a multiday, heli-rafting experience along 33 miles (53.1 km) of river. Home to arctic grayling and rainbow trout, both rivers are also great for angling, either on

your own or with services like **Denali Fly Fishing Guides**.

Another way to get your Alaska adrenaline fix is motorized exploration via the all-terrain vehicles of **Denali ATV Adventures** or the military-style off-road vehicles of **Denali Backcountry Safari**. The latter has tours in both summer and winter, including a 4x4 excursion along the **Stampede Trail**, where Christopher McCandless spent his last days in Bus 142, a tragedy that inspired the book and film *Into the Wild*.

Motorists can drive the old **Denali Highway** on their own, although they should be well aware that the 135-mile (217.26 km) route between Cantwell and Paxson is primarily gravel, often washboard, and very lightly traveled. Four-wheel drive is highly recommended. The payoff is a spectacular drive along the south side of the Alaska Range east of the park, with much of the road above the tree line and spectacular vistas of tundra, glaciers, and snowy peaks.

The Denali region is also active after dark. As the name implies, **Aurora Quest** in Healy offers evening "aurora chasing" tours to view and photograph the northern lights. And for something completely different, **Alaska Cabin Nite Dinner Theatre** offers gold rush–era music, comedy, and storytelling. ∎

CHOW DOWN

• **Morino Grill:** The only sit-down restaurant inside the park serves a standard selection of sandwiches, soups, and more during the summer high season. *reservedenali.com*

• **229 Parks:** A short drive from the park entrance, the Denali area's best restaurant features an ever changing menu of Alaskan game, seafood, and vegetarian dishes. *229parks.com*

• **Denali Park Salmon Bake:** This local favorite runs a culinary gamut from traditional burgers and salmon platters to offbeat dishes like the hydroponic salad, yak burrito, and elk sliders. Pack lunches are available for taking on hikes into the park. *denaliparksalmonbake.com*

• **49th State Brewing Company:** Local craft beers, live music, and the

bus from the movie *Into the Wild* are the attraction at this energetic little joint in Healey. *49statebrewing.com/denali/*

• **The Black Bear:** Coffee, tea, shakes, and smoothies, plus brunch and dinner menus, near the main gate. *blackbeardenali.com*

Fall colors overwhelm the Alaska Range, Denali National Park.

Katmai & Lake Clark National Parks
Alaska

Although both Katmai and Lake Clark were born of volcanic fury—and are only 50 miles (80.47 km) apart as the eagle flies—they present entirely different takes on the Alaska wilderness experience. With its crater lake and sprawling lava fields, Katmai's geothermal landscape continues to evolve. More set in its ways, Lake Clark unfolds as a glacier-shaped wonderland of lakes, fjords, and broad forest-filled valleys.

Set along the western edge of the Cook Inlet, Katmai and Lake Clark are largely wilderness and accessed only by boat or plane from Anchorage or Homer. Around five million of the parks' 8 million acres (32,274.95 sq km) is designated federal wilderness.

KATMAI

Nature doesn't get any more extreme than Katmai, renowned for its salmon-snatching bears and the largest volcanic eruption of the 20th century. The park also boasts some fine fishing and incredible backcountry trails where hikers can go days (sometimes even weeks) without seeing another human being.

Brooks Camp in the heart of the park is the entry point for most visitors, as well as the starting point for nearly all adventures in Katmai. Perched at the shore of **Naknek Lake**, the wilderness outpost is home to the **Katmai Visitor Center** and **Brooks Lodge**. Wooden boardwalks lead to elevated viewpoints of **Brooks Falls**, world-renowned as a place to see salmon-fishing grizzlies.

During the summer, the park offers guided tours from Brooks Camp to the famed **Valley of Ten Thousand Smokes**. The day trip includes an optional ranger-led hike to the lava-encrusted valley floor. The twisted landscape was formed in 1912 when **Novarupta volcano** blew its top with an explosion estimated at 30 times greater than the 1980 Mount St. Helens eruption. The collapsed **Mount Katmai** created the crater lake that now crowns the peak and caused a massive pyroclastic ash flow that gushed down the valley.

Exploring the rest of the park requires a carefully planned hiking

THE BIG PICTURE

Established: Katmai (1980); Lake Clark (1980)

Size: Katmai (4.09 million acres/16,551.64 sq km); Lake Clark (4.03 million acres/16,308.83 sq km)

Annual Visitors: Katmai (37,000); Lake Clark (22,000)

Visitor Centers: Brooks Camp, King Salmon, Port Alsworth

Entrance Fees: None

nps.gov/katm; nps.gov/lacl

Brown bear cubs explore the summer tundra at Katmai National Park.

Volcanic Mount Katmai, 6.3 miles (10.1 km) in diameter, has a lake-filled caldera, formed during an eruption in 1912.

trip into the vast backcountry or arrangements with one of the wilderness lodges along Katmai coast or remote lakes.

LAKE CLARK

Farther north along Cook Inlet, Lake Clark revolves around **Port Alsworth** village and a National Park Service **visitor center** that offers exhibits and a film on naturalist Dick Proenneke, who spent 30 years living alone in the park's backcountry.

There's plenty of action around Port Alsworth: kayaking out to **Tommy Island** in Lake Clark, fly-fishing near **Tanalian Falls**, or ascending 3,900-foot (1,188.72 m) **Mount Tanalian** on the park's only maintained trail (8.6-mile/ 13.84 km round-trip). Across the lake is **Kijik National Historic Landmark**, an area of great cultural significance to the local Dena'ina Athabascan people that spans

prehistoric archaeological sites to a 19th-century ghost town.

Despite its tranquil facade, Lake Clark has several volcanoes including 10,016-foot (3,052.87 m) **Mount Iliamna** and 10,197-foot (3,108.05 m) **Mount Redoubt**; the latter last erupted in 2009 to the dismay of Alaska aviation.

Whitewater rafting is possible on the **Tlikakila, Mulchatna,** and **Chilikadrotna**.

There are plenty of bears too, especially at **Chinitna Bay** and **Silver Salmon Creek** on the coast. Backpackers can hike 25 miles (40.23 km) along Cook Inlet between the two grizzly clusters. ◼

DID YOU KNOW

• Katmai's gray wolves are also known to "fish" salmon from the park's streams and rivers, as well as harbor seals and sea otters along the coast.

• "Grizzly Man" Timothy Treadwell spent 13 summers living with brown bears in the Katmai backcountry until he was killed and eaten by one in 2003.

• With more than 900 prehistoric sites, Brooks Camp in Katmai boasts one of North America's

most densely concentrated archaeological areas.

• The Alaska National Interest Lands Conservation Act of 1980 created a number of national parks, including Katmai (which was already a national monument) and Lake Clark.

• Port Alsworth is named for Alaska bush pilot Leon "Babe" Alsworth and his wife, Mary, who homesteaded the secluded site with their floatplane in 1944.

Kenai Fjords National Park

Alaska

Kenai Fjords is a look into our planet's past, a vision of what most of North America was like 12,000 years ago during the last ice age—massive glaciers covering most of the land, icebergs floating across fjords along the coast. Remote and largely roadless, Alaska's most photogenic park is best explored by foot or paddle along routes blazed thousands of years ago by wildlife and early humans.

THE BIG PICTURE

Established: 1980

Size: 669,984 acres (2,711.33 sq km)

Annual Visitors: 303,000

Visitor Center: Seward

Entrance Fee: None

nps.gov/kefj

The staging point for most journeys into the fjords, **Seward** lies at the end of the railroad line, highway, and Iditarod dogsledding trail from Anchorage, 120 miles (193.12 km) to the north. The national park **visitor center** on the waterfront features an Alaska-focused bookstore and short film about the Kenai Peninsula. The **Alaska SeaLife Center** in Seward previews some of the animals that visitors see in the park.

Many of the outfitters that take visitors into Kenai are located down Fourth Avenue from the visitor center, including **Major Marine**, which offers half-day and full-day narrated boat trips in spring and summer, as well as special orca and gray whale cruises. Paddling is an option for those with more time and an adventurous spirit. **Liquid Adventures**—guided kayak trips range from an easy half-day near Seward to week-long expedition trips in the park's nether regions.

Resurrection Bay, which reaches south from Seward into the Gulf of Alaska, was named by early 19th-century Russian governor Alexander Baranov, whose ship took refuge in the bay on Easter Sunday. Ice free throughout the winter, Resurrection is the year-round gateway to the wonders of Kenai and a wildlife haven in its own right, a place where it's not unusual to see sea otters and sea lions, humpbacks and orcas, or even puffins perched on the sea cliffs.

The national park starts in spectacular fashion along the bay's western shore with **Bear Glacier**, a 13-mile (20.92 km) tongue of ice that flows down from the **Harding Icefield**. Local outfitters can arrange kayaking and paddleboarding (with boat or helicopter transfer) on the iceberg-filled lagoon at the bottom of Bear.

Boats from Seward take day trips and kayak campers deeper into the

Horned puffins are native to the Lake Clark area.

The largely unexplored Neacola Mountains range includes peaks as high as 9,426 feet (2,873 m).

fjords. With its many arms and coves, elongated **Aialik Bay** offers more landing beaches with overnight campsites than anywhere else in the park, as well as the **Kenai Fjords Glacier Lodge**, the park's only hotel. Looming over the bay are **Aialik Glacier** and **Pedersen Glacier** with its mirror-like lagoon and rocky frontal moraine.

Paddlers who really want to get away from it all make a beeline for **Harris Bay** and the **Northwestern Fjords**, a supersecluded area visited by only a handful of die-hard kayakers each summer. Seven glaciers line a waterway marked by sea stalks and natural arches that's also considered the best place in the park to paddle alongside the resident orcas.

Exit Glacier, the only part of the park that is accessible by road, lies a half hour's drive from Seward. From the **Nature Center**, trails lead uphill to the very edge of the glacier and along the boulder-strewn outwash plain at the bottom. This is also the start of the **Harding Icefield Trail**, a tough 8.2-mile (13.2 km) trek into the frozen heights that span the park's 40 glaciers. The road to Exit Glacier is closed in winter, but visitors are free to explore the area by snowshoe, dogsled, snowmobile, and other means of winter movement. ∎

MEET THE NEIGHBORS

The Kenai Peninsula harbors a number of other parks that showcase the region's flora, fauna, and scenery.

• **Kenai National Wildlife Refuge:** Three times larger than the adjoining national park, the sprawling refuge is home to wolves, bears, moose, lynx, bald eagles, and other iconic Alaska species.

• **Kachemak State Park:** Located along the western edge of the national park, Alaska's oldest state park continues the theme of glaciers, mountains, forests, and fjords.

• **Chugash National Forest:** Hiking, camping, kayaking, and fishing the salmon-filled Russian River are a few of the outdoor pursuits on tap in the East Kenai section of this massive forest reserve.

• **Caines Head State Recreation Area:** Reachable by boat or foot from Seward, this coastal park boasts numerous hiking trails and the ruins of World War II military gun emplacements.

The American Tropics

Kauai's Na Pali Coast, awash in emerald colors

Haleakalā National Park
Hawaii

Haleakalā means "house of the sun" in the Hawaiian language, an apt description for a place that witnesses sunrise before anywhere else in Maui. While the national park revolves around its namesake volcano, there's much more to contemplate—rare plants and animals, Hawaiian history and culture, outdoor adventure sports, untamed wilderness, and even a small strip of wave-splashed coast.

THE BIG PICTURE

Established: 1961

Size: 33,265 acres
(134.62 sq km)

Annual Visitors: 1.1 million

Visitor Centers: Park
Headquarters, Summit, and
Kīpahulu

Entrance Fee: $25 per vehicle,
$12 per person

nps.gov/hale

Thousands of people make the twisting drive to the top of Haleakalā volcano each day to watch the sun rise over the Hawaiian Islands. The ritual has become so popular—and the summit so crowded—that authorities have implemented a reservation system. When sunrise ends, most of the sun seekers retreat to the coast and miss out on the other wonders offered by this diverse national park.

The drive along **State Highway 378** to the summit is spectacular, a zigzag route that climbs from around 3,500 feet (1,066.8 m) to more than 10,000 feet (3,048 m) in just 21 miles (33.79 km). Drink plenty of water to avoid altitude dizziness and sickness. This is the also the road that **Haleakalā Bike Company** uses for its adrenaline-pumping downhill rides through Maui forest, farmland, and upcountry villages.

Tucked just inside the entrance, the **Park Headquarters Visitor Center** offers exhibits, ranger-guided activities, and the **Hana No'eau** series of native Hawaiian storytelling and cultural workshops.

The road continues up to the **Summit Area**, where views are literally breathtaking because of the lofty elevation. Haleakalā's ever changing interplay of clouds, sky, and volcanic desert makes for an otherworldly landscape that really does look like something from another planet. The **stone hut** (built in 1936) near the summit houses another small visitor center with a rear walkway that offers crater views. From there you can either walk or drive the short distance to **Pu'u 'Ula'ula** (Red Hill), at 10,023 feet (3,055 m), the highest point on the mountain. At night, the **Summit Area** is a great place to set up a telescope for a view of the night sky almost completely devoid of air pollution and urban lights.

Visitors can venture into the crater via several routes from the summit. Both the **Keonehe'ehe'e "Sliding Sands" Trail** (9.2 miles/14.8 km)

A massive banyan tree shades the Pipiwai Trail in Haleakalā

A Maui must-do: taking in sunrise from the top of Haleakalā crater, elevation 10,023 feet (3,055 m)

and **Halemau'u Trail** (10.3 miles/ 16.58 km) lead all the way across the crater floor to **Palikū** cabin and campsite on the eastern side of the great depression. But you don't have to make the entire trek; even a short walk into the crater is enough to sample the remarkable volcanic landscape and glimpse the strange *'āhinahina* ("silversword") plants that survive in the harsh highland habitat.

From **Palikū,** experienced hikers can head down the rugged 8.6-mile (29.9 km) **Kaupo Trail** to the Piilani Highway and the coast; however, more than half of this route is via private land outside the national park.

Much of it still unpaved, the vertiginous **Piilani Highway** is the "secret" back way into the national park's **Kīpahulu District**. The more common means of reaching the coastal area is via the 64-mile (102.9 km) **Hana Highway**, a winding route that takes hours and should

not be driven after dark. A totally different experience from the summit, Kīpahulu boasts rain forest, rock pools, and remnants of ancient human settlement.

Kīpahulu Visitor Center offers Hawaiian cultural demonstrations and guided ranger hikes along the **Pīpīwai Trail** through the coastal

rain forest to several waterfalls. The short and easy **Kuloa Point Trail** leads to an ocean overlook and the edge of **'Ohe'o Gulch** with its **Seven Sacred Pools**. There is no safe place to enter the sea at Kīpahulu, and the pools are often closed to swimming because of safety concerns, so check the visitor center before entering. ∎

LAY YOUR HEAD

Although Haleakalā National Park doesn't offer lodges or hotels, there are other ways for visitors to spend the night in the shadow of a great volcano:

• **Wilderness Cabins:** Located on the crater floor, the Hōlua, Kapalaoa, and Palikū cabins offer rustic accommodation. Pit toilets, nonpotable water, and wood-burning stove. Permit required; $75 per night per cabin.

• **Hike-In Campsites:** Hōlua and Palikū on the crater floor; pit toilets, nonpotable water.

• **Drive-In Campsites:** Hosmer Grove in the Summit Area and Kīpahulu on the coast; picnic tables, BBQ grills, drinking water, pit toilets.

Reservations can be made up to 180 days in advance via recreation.gov or 877-444-6777.

Hawaii Volcanoes National Park
Hawaii

Two celebrated volcanoes—one of them very tall, the other very active—frame this large national park. From glowing lava flows and earth-shaking tremors to wind, rain, and waves, the geological and meteorological forces that shaped our planet are fully on display on the Big Island. While volcanism rules the day, pockets of rain forest and grassland shelter rare Hawaiian flora and fauna.

THE BIG PICTURE

Established: 1916

Size: 323,431 acres (1,308.88 sq km)

Annual Visitors: 2 million

Visitor Center: Daily 9 a.m. to 5 p.m.

Entrance Fee: $25 per vehicle, $12 per person

nps.gov/havo

"Double, double toil and trouble; fire burn and caldron bubble." Shakespeare could just as easily have been describing Hawaiian volcanoes rather than a witch's brew in *Macbeth*. No other national park produces so much drama on a regular basis.

Erupting since 1983, **Kīlauea** volcano is one of our planet's most active hot spots; red-hot lava continually rushes across the land and into the Pacific Ocean—and most recently erupting to devastating effect in spring 2018. The park also harbors **Mauna Loa**, a massive 13,679-foot (4,169.36 m) mountain and the world's largest volcano, active for around 700,000 years.

Two outstanding auto routes provide easy access to the park's main attractions. **Crater Rim Drive** hugs the edge of **Kīlauea Caldera** and leads to viewpoints where visitors can gaze into the belly of the beast and inhale its pungent sulfur scent. Near the start of the route, the park **Visitor Center** offers exhibits and important safety information, as well as an excellent film, *Born of Fire, Born of the Sea*.

Across the road, **Volcano House** (1846) is one of the oldest lodges in the entire National Park System; the back terrace is a great place to get your first glimpse of the crater. Located in another historic structure, **Volcano Art Center** offers classes and workshops, a gallery dedicated to local artists, hula performances, and free guided hikes into the **Niaulani rain forest**.

Learn all about lava at the **Jaggar Museum** of volcanology and then watch magma exploding from **Halema'uma'u Crater** in the caldera from the terrace behind the museum. The pyrotechnic display is even more awesome after dark. Crater Rim Drive also leads to **Kīlauea Iki Crater** and **Nāhuku Thurston Lava Tube**, reached via a short hike through a forest of prehistoric fern trees.

Chain of Craters Road meanders 20 miles (32.19 km) through tortuous volcanic landforms between

Lava flows into the ocean from Hawaii Volcanoes National Park.

At night, molten lava creates bright red smoke and embers as it meets the sea.

Kīlauea Caldera and **Hōlei Sea Arch**. Numerous places en route beg a stop, including lofty **Kealakomo Overlook**, the Martian-like landscape of **Mau Loa o Mauna Ulu lava field**, and the boardwalk trail that leads to the **Puʻu Loa Petroglyphs**, where more than 23,000 images were rendered by native Hawaiians between A.D. 1200 and 1450.

Farther east along the coast is **Kamokuna**, where molten lava from **Puʻu ʻŌʻō Crater** sometimes reaches the ocean. The hot zone is best approached from Pāhoa village (outside the park) with experienced guides from **Active Lava Hawaiian Tours** or similar outfitters. The hike normally takes around four hours (7 to 10 miles/11.26-16.1 km) over rough volcanic terrain. At times when the lava is flowing into the sea, **Lava Ocean Tours** runs boat excursions to the steamy entry point.

Reaching the summit of **Mauna Loa** is a herculean effort. A narrow, paved road ascends to a lookout point at 6,662 feet (2,030.58 m). The rest of the route is on foot, a 16-mile (25.75 km) trail that quickly morphs from native woodland into lava rock wilderness. Most people undertake the trek over four days, with overnights in national park mountain huts.

The park's other iconic backcountry hike is the **Kaʻū Desert Trail**, a rugged 18-mile (28.97 km) trek that leads from the trailhead off of Highway 11 across undulating lava fields to **Hilina Pali** cliffs and overnight campsites along the Pacific coast like **Halape** with its sandy beaches and coconut grove. ■

MEET THE NEIGHBORS

• **Mauna Kea National Natural Landmark:** At 13,803 feet (4,207.15 m), this volcano is the nation's highest insular mountain, as well as the highest point in Hawaii. Onizuka Center for International Astronomy facilitates public stargazing on the peak.

• **Ala Kahakai National Historic Trail:** This 175-mile (281.6 km) coastal route around the Big Island features eight sites significant to native Hawaiian culture and history, including Puʻuhonua o Hōnaunau and Kaloko-Honokōhau national historical parks.

• **Puʻu O Umi Natural Area Reserve:** Perched on the Big Island's north shore, this remote reserve harbors 13 native ecosystems including rare montane bog and ʻohiʻa forest.

• **Hawaii Tropical Botanical Garden:** Just north of Hilo, this 17-acre (.07 sq km) preserve showcases more than 2,000 plant species including palms, bromeliads, and heliconias.

Kīlauea volcano erupts across from a lava field in Hawaii.

Nāpali Coast State Parks

Hawaii

THE BIG PICTURE

Established: Nāpali Coast (1983)

Size: Nāpali Coast (6,175 acres/ 24.9 sq km); Waimea Canyon (1,866 acres/7.63 sq km); Kōkeʻe (4,345 acres/17.58 sq km)

Visitor Center: Kōkeʻe Natural History Museum

Entrance Fees: None

dlnr.hawaii.gov/dsp/parks/kauai kokee.org

It's no wonder that Steven Spielberg chose the Nā Pali Coast as a backdrop for *Jurassic Park*—the north side of Kauai has always had a primeval feel. Secluded beaches framed by 400-foot-high (121.92 m) cliffs, waterfalls tumbling into jungle pools, canyons so thick with rain forest that anything could be hiding back there. And nothing made by humans—other than ancient taro terraces—exists in the parks that protect Hawaii's wildest shoreline.

The **Nāpali Coast** and its hinterland are protected by a patchwork of conservation units including state parks, natural areas, and forest reserves. Foot and boat are the only means to reach its remote beaches, but a scenic highway provides easy access to the dramatic canyonlands behind the coast.

NĀPALI COAST

The most popular way to explore the shore is the **Kalalau Trail**, a rugged 11-mile (17.7 km) path that crosses five valleys on a roller-coaster route between **Haʻena State Park** and Kalalau Beach in **Nāpali Coast State Wilderness Park**. All are free to hike the trail's first 2 miles (3.2 km)

to idyllic **Hanakapiʻai Beach**, where you can soak up some sun or head inland on a strenuous 3.3-mile (5.3 km) spur trail through a jungle canyon to slender 300-foot (91.44 m) **Hanakapiʻai Falls.**

Anyone trekking beyond Hanakapiʻai needs an overnight camping permit from the Hawaii Division of State Parks—and a strong constitution—because the Kalalau Trail quickly climbs from sea level to 800 feet (243.84 m) as it enters **Hono O Nā Pali Natural Area Reserve**. Dead ahead is the **Hanakoa Valley**, where hikers can overnight at a primitive campsite on stone taro terraces beside a stream. The home stretch to **Kalalau Beach** is not for the faint of heart, a vertigo-inducing path chiseled into the cliffs with sheer dropoffs into the deep blue sea.

Towering palisades render the western end of the Nāpali Coast inaccessible to anything other than boats. Zodiac tours make day trips to **Nuʻalolo Kai Beach** for snorkeling, swimming, and sunbathing. But the best way to discover this wild, remote shore is kayak camping. Veteran paddlers can make the trip on their own; less experienced

An aerial view of the rainbow-colored Nā Pali Coast

Kayakers explore sea caves and cliffside waterfalls along Nā Pali's coastline.

voyageurs can sign on with outfitters like **Kayak Kauai** for multiday guided tours that overnight at Kalalau and **Miloli'i Beach**.

For those short on time, several aviation outfits offer **helicopter tours** of the Nā Pali Coast. Chopper is the only way to visit **Manawaiopuna Falls**, a towering cascade located on private land behind the Nāpali Coast that appears near the opening of *Jurassic Park*. And **Island Helicopters** is the only company allowed to land there.

WAIMEA & KŌKE'E

The lush hinterland behind the coast is every bit as spectacular—and much easier to reach for those who don't want to hike or paddle. State Highway 550 provides a scenic 14-mile (22.5 km) route into

the heart of **Waimea Canyon State Park**. Often called the "Grand Canyon of the Pacific," the multicolored gorge stretches 10 miles (16.1 km) and drops 3,000 feet (914.4 m) from its jungle-draped rim.

The first landmark along Highway 550 is a trailhead for the short **Iliau Nature Loop** (0.3 mile/ 0.48 km) with its panoramic views of the canyon. The adjacent **Kukui Trail** dips 2,000 feet (609.6 m) into

DID YOU KNOW

• Thousands of native Hawaiians once lived along the Nā Pali Coast, tending to the taro plants in lava rock terraces.

• The 1893 "leper war" in Kalalau Valley broke out when authorities tried to relocate local residents afflicted with leprosy to Molokai. Jack London immortalized the bloody encounter in the short story "Koolau the Leper."

• Waimea Canyon was carved over thousands of years by runoff from Mount Wai'ale'ale. Often cited as the wettest place on Earth, the volcano feeds the Waimea River in the canyon bottom.

• Other than camping, the only public accommodation inside the Nāpali Coast parks is the rustic Cabins at Kōke'e Park (*westkauai lodging.com*).

Above: Take in Kauai's coastal mountain landscape via helicopter or by foot (opposite) along the Nāpali hiking trails.

the gorge, a 2.5-mile (4.02 km) trek to the river for those who want to sample the majesty of Waimea without camping overnight. Experienced hikers can continue downstream along the **Waimea Canyon Trail** (11.5 miles/18.5 km) to Waimea Town on Kauai's south shore or upstream along the **Koaie Canyon Trail** (6 miles/9.65 km) to supersecluded **Lonomea Camp** with its jungle swimming holes.

Highway 550 continues into **Kōkeʻe State Park** and several lofty viewpoints where you can gaze down at the stunning Nā Pali Coast. With its natural history exhibits, bookshop, and information counter, **Kōkeʻe Natural History Museum** functions as a visitor center.

The park features nearly two dozen trails, often with spectacular coastal views along the way. Among these vertiginous routes are **Poomau Canyon Lookout Trail** (0.3 mile/ .48 km) and **Nuʻalolo Cliffs Trail** (2.1 miles/3.4 km). Elsewhere in the park, the **Kawaikoi Stream Trail** (1.8 miles/2.9 km) meanders through lush rain forest, and the **Alakai Swamp Trail** (3.5 miles/5.6 km) uses boardwalks to leap across shallow bogs rich in native plant life. ∎

MEET THE NEIGHBORS

• **Kīlauea Point National Wildlife Refuge:** One of the best places in Hawaii to view native wildlife, the refuge harbors nēnē geese, Laysan albatross, Newell's shearwater, monk seals, spinner dolphins, and a historic lighthouse.

• **Princeville Botanical Gardens:** Three-hour walking and chocolate-tasting tours are offered four days a week at a tropical garden with more than 600 flora species, including many that are species native to Hawaii.

• **Polihale State Park:** Perched on the island's northwest coast, the park is renowned for its sand dunes, sunsets, and shore fishing along a pristine beach with views of the Nā Pali Coast.

• **Wailua River State Park:** Kayaking is the best way to explore Hawaii's only navigable river, a watery trail that leads to waterfalls, a fern-covered grotto, coconut groves, and the Wailua Complex of Heiau —a cluster of archaeological sites hidden deep in the park's rain forest.

One of many waterfalls on offer in Nāpali Coast State Wilderness Park, Hawaii

San Juan & El Yunque

Puerto Rico

One of history's largest and most complex fortifications is the focus of San Juan National Historic Site, a rambling, shoreline park that wraps around Old San Juan. Looming in the misty mountains behind Puerto Rico's capital city is El Yunque, the only tropical rain forest in the U.S. national forest system and one of the largest stands of native woodland remaining in the Caribbean.

SAN JUAN NATIONAL HISTORIC SITE

Two massive stone forts— San Cristóbal and El Morro— anchor this historic waterfront park. The castles are connected by walls, bastions, and embrasures along the entire Atlantic coast of Old San Juan and much of the town's harborside. Built by the Spanish during their long colonial occupation of Puerto Rico, the forts helped repel invasions by the British, Dutch, and pirates. However, the bastions were no match for modern naval weapons and fell to invading U.S. forces during the Spanish-American War in 1898. The U.S. military occupied the forts until the 1960s, when the compound was bequeathed to the National Park Service.

THE BIG PICTURE

Established: San Juan (1949); El Yunque (1903)

Size: San Juan (75 acres/0.3 sq km); El Yunque (29,000 acres/117.36 sq km)

Annual Visitors: San Juan (1.18 million); El Yunque (1.25 million)

Visitor Centers: San Cristóbal in San Juan; El Portal in El Yunque

Entrance Fees: San Juan NHS ($5); El Yunque NF (none)

nps.gov/saju; fs.usda.gov/elyunque

Many visitors head straight for **El Morro,** the hulking castle that overlooks the entrance to San Juan Bay. But the best starting point for those interested in exploring all of the historic park is the larger but lesser-known **Castillo San Cristóbal.** Constructed during the late 18th century, San Cristóbal is the largest fortification built by the Spanish during their 400 years in the New World and a textbook example of 18th-century military engineering.

Behind the thick stone walls lies a warren of tunnels, gunpowder magazines, artillery batteries, and living quarters, as well as five giant cisterns for storing drinking water in case the fort was besieged. The casemates around the castle's **Plaza de Armas** are now filled with historical displays, a bookstore, and reconstructed barracks. There's also a dungeon where prisoners of war, criminals, and political dissenters were jailed in colonial times. A tunnel leads upward to the **Main Firing Battery** with its World War II observation posts and views of a legendary sentry post, the **Garita del Diablo.** Another tunnel leads to the **Visitor Center,** set inside a bunker

A wall path leads to a gun turret of the Castillo San Felipe del Morro.

El Yunque National Forest protects 28,434 acres (11.5 sq km) of lush greenery, waterfalls, and mountains.

constructed in 1942 when the Americans were beefing up defense against possible enemy attack.

Visitors can catch a free tram or walk **Calle Norzagaray** along the top of its walls. The colorful barrio along the shore is **La Perla**, founded in the early 1800s when the slaughterhouses and cemetery were moved outside the walls for health reasons. A large grassy area called the **Esplanade** acts as a front yard for El Morro. Several pitched battles were fought on the open space during colonial times. The U.S. military transformed the Esplanade into a sports ground with a golf course, baseball diamond, tennis courts, and swimming pool. It's now Puerto Rico's favorite kite-flying spot. If you didn't remember to pack your own kite, buy one at **El Angel** street stall on Norzagaray.

Crowning a rocky headland at the entrance to San Juan Bay,

Castillo San Felipe del Morro (to use its full name) is the most renowned of the city's Spanish colonial bastions. Construction started in 1539 and continued through the late 18th century as the fortification grew in both size and complexity.

A bridge leads across the dry moat into the heart of the castle, a six-story beehive of barracks and

gun batteries. One of the casemates in the central plaza houses a chapel, and another doubles as a theater showing a short film on El Morro. The **Main Battery** on Level 4 affords the best views of the harbor entrance and its busy ship traffic. Hidden below is the fort's oldest section, the 16th-century **Round Tower**, its ceiling pierced by the

DID YOU KNOW

• The walls of San Juan NHS and Barrio La Perla provide a backdrop for the 2017 hit music video "Despacito," the most streamed song of all time, as of 2018.

• America's opening shots of World War I were fired from El Morro on March 21, 1915, by U.S. soldiers trying to prevent a German navy supply ship from exiting San Juan Bay.

• The cobblestones of Old San Juan are blue because they're made from iron slag used as ballast in Spanish galleons returning to Puerto Rico.

• Although none of them are navigable, the Río Mameyes, Río de la Mina, and Río Icacos in El Yunque National Forest are designated as part of the National Wild and Scenic Rivers System.

Puerto Rico's 20 state forests (bosques estatal) preserve other swatches of native flora and fauna:

• **Guajateca:** Karst hills and limestone caverns underpin this rain forest area on the island's west side. It features 46 hiking trails, a visitor information center, campground, and observation tower.

• **Toro Negro:** The "Black Bull" cloud forest embraces Puerto Rico's three highest peaks, nine rivers, and numerous waterfalls.

• **Guánica:** Arrayed along the south coast, this biosphere reserve protects the Caribbean's largest remaining tract of tropical dry forest.

rusting remains of a shell from the Spanish-American War. In addition to a Moorish revival–style lighthouse, **Level 6** offers spectacular views across the Esplanade to Old San Juan.

That colossal building on the other side of the lawn is the **Ballajá Barracks**. Although not part of the national park, the 19th-century structure was once an integral part of the fort's Spanish military infrastructure. Now, the meticulously restored barracks house dance and music academies (where visitors can take classes), the hip **Cine Bar 1950** movie lounge, and the eclectic **Museum of the Americas** with art and artifacts from all around the Western Hemisphere.

Behind the barracks is lively **Calle San Sebastián**, the old town's celebrated bar-hopping street where a raucous street festival takes place

each year after **Three Kings Day** (January 6). Spanish explorer Ponce de León once lived on the same street in a lovely villa called **Casa Blanca.** The oldest European house in the Americas is now a museum with period artwork, antique furniture, and splendid views across the bay.

Over on the bay side of the Esplanade, a leafy lane, **Caleta de las Monjas**, leads downhill to the **Plazuela de la Rogativa** (with its wild parakeets) and the hulking **San Juan Gate**, the only survivor among the old town's six colonial-era portals. Rising beside the gate is **La Fortaleza**, built in 1533 and now the oldest surviving section of San Juan's fortifications. The whitewashed villa crowning the bastion is the official home of Puerto Rico's governor (and unfortunately not open to the public). Those venturing outside the gate find themselves on the brink of the **Paseo del Morro**, a 1-mile (1.6 km) national recreation trail along the bay shore.

EL YUNQUE NATIONAL FOREST

Among the different types of woodlands in the National Forest system, the only tropical rain forest is found at El Yunque in the cordillera of eastern Puerto Rico. Located about an hour from Old San Juan, the island's only national forest provides a refreshing escape from city life, an oasis of indigenous flora and fauna that can be explored by car or on foot along various hiking trails leading to misty mountaintops and wilderness campsites.

In addition to the critically endangered Puerto Rican parrot and more than a dozen types of coqui frogs, the park provides a refuge for 23 plants found nowhere else on Earth. All told, El Yunque harbors 240 native tree species, more than 150 kinds of

Bromeliads draw nutrients and moisture from the forest air.

Built in the 16th century, Castillo San Felipe del Morro lies on the northeasternmost point of Old San Juan overlooking the ocean.

ferns, and around 50 different orchids. El Yunque was severely damaged by the hurricanes of 2017, but in the year that followed, the forest bounced back with amazing speed.

El Portal Visitor Center on the park's northern edge is equipped with an information desk, rain forest displays, and a short nature trail through the surrounding forest. **Highway 191** rises from the visitor center into the **Sierra de Luquillo** mountains. The first stretch includes pull-offs for **La Coca Falls** and the 75-foot-tall (22.86 m) **Yokahú Tower** with its far-reaching views across the forest to the coast. Just beyond is **Juan Diego Falls** and the start of the **Big Tree Trail** down to **La Mina Falls** and its refreshing swimming hole.

The **Palo Colorado** area in the middle of the rain forest park features an information center, picnic areas, and Baño Grande pool. It's also the jumping-off spot for a half dozen other trails, including a steep climb through the rain forest to 3,543-foot (1,079.9 m) **El Yunque Peak.** Just beyond Palo Colorado, Highway 191 is closed to vehicular traffic. The rugged and remote **El Toro Wilderness** safeguards around half of the national forest and can be accessed only on foot. ■

LAY YOUR HEAD

Hotels

• **Olive Boutique Hotel:** Cozy lagoon-side digs near Old San Juan; restaurant, pool, roof bar, El Yunque hikes and private tour; from $154. *oliveboutiquehotel.com*

• **Decanter Hotel:** Wine-themed boutique lodging opposite the cathedral in Old San Juan, just steps away from El Morro; from $149. *decanterhotel.com*

• **Wyndham Grand Rio Mar:** This sprawling beach resort is just 15 minutes from El Yunque's main entrance; restaurants, bars, beach, pools, golf, spa, casino, water sports; from $207. *wyndhamriomar.com*

• **Royal Isabela:** Upscale resort set in a 200-acre coastal reserve; restaurant, bar, pools, golf, tennis, beach, kayaking, paddleboarding, guided hikes in Guajataca Forest; from $331. *royalisabela.com*

Camping

• **El Yunque National Forest:** Primitive camping at seven sites, including three hike-in camps. Permits must be requested two weeks in advance and retrieved at El Portal Visitor Center. *fs.usda.gov/elyunque*

Virgin Islands National Park

U.S. Virgin Islands

THE BIG PICTURE

Established: 1956

Size: 14,737 acres (59.64 sq km)

Annual Visitors: 304,000

Visitor Center: Cruz Bay

Entrance Fee: None, other than at Trunk Bay ($5 per person)

nps.gov/viis

"Virgin" aptly describes the pristine coastline and countryside that composes this dazzling tropical reserve on St. John. For 200 years, the island was dominated by sugar plantations worked by African slaves and their descendants. It wasn't until the early 20th century—after the United States purchased the Virgin Islands from Denmark—that the island began its devolution back into Caribbean wilderness.

Carib Indians inhabited St. John when Christopher Columbus sailed to the islands in 1493. He named them after the 11,000 virgins martyred with St. Ursula, then sailed on to larger, richer landfalls. Denmark claimed the Virgin Islands in 1718. The colony endured until 1917, when the United States paid $25 million for the Danish Virgins. By the 1950s, American tycoon Laurence Rockefeller owned much of the island and bequeathed his land to the National Park Service.

A 45-minute ferry ride from Charlotte Amalie, the territorial capital, **Cruz Bay** is the gateway for St. John and a hub for boat charters and guided water sports excursions in the park's offshore waters. Here, scuba diving, snorkeling, sailing, and kayaking prevail. **Cruz Bay Visitor Center** offers a great orientation to the national park, including information on ranger-led hikes and snorkeling. Those who want to dive right into the park can follow the easy **Lind Point Trail** 1 mile (1.6 km) from the visitor center to nearby **Salomon Beach** and **Honeymoon Beach** for swimming, snorkeling, and sunbathing.

North Shore Road meanders along the coast to many of the park's best bays and beaches, a mosaic of private and public lands that reaches all the way across the top of St. John. **Hawksnest Bay** offers boat-free swimming and snorkeling, as well as short trails to the **Peace Hill Windmill** and ruins of the **Dennis Bay Great House**. In addition to a long white-sand strand, **Trunk Bay** is renowned for its **Underwater Snorkeling Trail**, a 225-yard (205.74 m) route with waterproof plaques that identify the different fish and corals.

With its cottages, campground, and store, busy **Cinnamon Bay** is the park's epicenter, a place to eat, sleep, and shop, as well as swim,

A wild iguana basks in the sun within the park's open spaces.

Aquamarine Maho Bay sits within white-sand beaches shaded by towering coconut palms, perfect for sunbathers and sailors alike.

paddle, and snorkel in the aquamarine bay. **Cinnamon Bay Water Sports** offers kayak, paddleboard, and sailboat rentals, as well as sailing and windsurfing lessons and a daily sunset cruise. On dry land, the short **Cinnamon Bay Nature Loop and Boardwalk** is a self-guided nature trail to the ruins of an old sugar plantation. Alternatively, the 1-mile (1.6 km) **Cinnamon Bay Trail** leads uphill through a forest spangled with mango, kapok, and other large tropical trees. **Cinnamon Bay Heritage Center and Archaeology Lab** offers exhibits on island history and a chance to watch archaeologists at work.

Continuing along North Shore Road, **Maho Bay** attracts sea turtles with its grassy underwater meadows. Just past the bay is a turnoff to the ruins of the **Annaberg Sugar Mill** (once the island's largest producer) where the national park hosts cultural demonstrations Tuesday through Friday. The nearby **Francis Bay Trail** loops 1 mile (1.6 km) around a salt pond to sandy **Francis Bay Beach**.

The backcountry is accessed via **Centerline Road,** a route that runs from Cruz Bay across the island's mountainous spine to **Coral Bay** and **East End** peninsula. Along the way are the ruins of the 18th-century **Catherineberg Plantation** and trailheads for many of the park's longer, more interesting hikes, including the popular **Reef Bay Trail** (3 miles/ 4.8 km) down to an old sugar mill of the same name on the south shore. Visit the 18th-century **Emmaus Moravian Church** and **Manse** in Coral Bay, and then head south to **Saltpond Bay** and **Lameshur** for

swimming, snorkeling, or trekking the area's dry tropical forest on a half dozen trails. ■

1 Outer Beach, Massachusetts

The Atlantic side of Cape Cod is actually one long, singular strand—40 miles (64.37 km) of sand between Provincetown and Chatham, the only interruption being the narrow passage into Nauset Harbor. From swimming and shore fishing to Marconi's radio station and the artsy dune shacks, the Outer Beach offers incredible variety.

2 Cape Point, North Carolina

Flanked by sandy strands, Cape Point offers just about everything that visitors love about Cape Hatteras National Seashore: beach driving and people-only stretches, a maritime museum and historic lighthouse, oceanfront camping, coastal villages with tasty seafood eateries, and even a now-you-see it, now-you-don't disappearing island.

3 Cumberland Island, Georgia

Sixteen miles (25.7 km) of uninterrupted and undeveloped sand define the east coast of Georgia's largest barrier island. Visitors share the shore with wild horses, sea turtles, and horseshoe crabs. Tucked into the dunes and woods behind the beach are campgrounds, hiking trails, and turn-of-the-century tycoon mansions.

4 Cinnamon Bay, U.S. Virgin Islands

Although Virgin Islands National Park offers more than a dozen beaches, none of them boast the range of activities available along the crescent curve of Cinnamon Bay on the north shore of St. John. Visitors can dive, swim, snorkel, sail, and paddleboard; follow self-guided nature trails; or nose around the shoreline history center and archaeology lab.

5 Padre Island, Texas

The world's longest stretch of undeveloped barrier island is protected within the confines of a national seashore with 70 miles (112.65 km) of sand along the Gulf of Mexico. The north end near Corpus Christi offers plenty of family-friendly beach activities. The rest of the shore is wild and free—and open to motorists with four-wheel drive.

THE TOP

10

BEACH DESTINATIONS

Along the open ocean and tranquil lakeshores, many parks offer close encounters of the sandy kind.

6 Twelve Mile Beach, Michigan

Wedged between the park's namesake cliffs and the 300-foot (91.44 m) Grand Sable Dunes, this photogenic strand at Pictured Rocks National Lakeshore offers waterfront camping, solitary beachcombing, gorgeous sunsets, and a chance to take a dip in always chilly Lake Superior. Beaver Basin Wilderness shelters bears, wolves, and bald eagles.

A couple snorkels in the clear waters of Cinnamon Bay.

7 Ruby Beach, Washington

Breathtakingly beautiful in both sunshine and storm, Ruby Beach anchors the northern end of the Kalaloch coast in Olympic National Park. Scattered with seamounts, tide pools, and driftwood, the beach is easy on the eye and even better through a camera lens. But the turbulent offshore waters are best left to the resident sea otters and other ocean dwellers.

8 Umpqua Beach, Oregon

The middle section of Oregon Dunes National Recreation Area revolves around multitalented Umpqua Beach, which provides both a safe jetty-shelter swimming area for children and one of the nation's most radical off-road playgrounds, crowned by a 500-foot (152.4 m) dune called Banshee Hill.

9 Hanakapi'ai Beach, Hawaii

The only beach along the rugged Nāpali Coast that is easily reached by foot, Hanakapi'ai slumbers beneath towering cliffs on Kauai's north shore. Without a boat, the only way to get there is hiking the first 2 miles (3.2 km) of the precipitous Kalalau Trail. But it's well worth the sweat to visit a tiny slice of paradise that channels bygone Hawaii.

10 Ofu Beach, American Samoa

The quintessential paradise beach, this palm-shaded strand in the National Park of American Samoa looks as if it were conjured by an artist's mind rather than sculpted by the hand of nature. Jagged volcanic peaks rise high above the talcum-powder-fine sand and aquamarine water flush with coral and colorful tropical fish.

National Park of American Samoa

American Samoa

The National Park of American Samoa, 4,700 miles (7,563.9 km) off the U.S. mainland—roughly halfway between Hawaii and New Zealand—is the most distant unit of the National Park Service. Scattered across three islands, the park preserves a primal slice of the South Pacific, an untouched paradise of beaches, coral reefs, rain forest, volcanic landforms, and ancient Samoan culture.

A quirky footnote in American history, the seven islands and atolls that compose American Samoa came under Washington's control in 1899 following a decade-long colonial dispute that was finally resolved by a treaty that split the archipelago between the United States and Germany. Beyond Pago Pago, the territorial capital, the islands remain largely off the grid, including three large tracts that form the nucleus of the national park.

An orange-fin anemonefish and damselfish swim near a protective sea anemone.

THE BIG PICTURE

Established: 1988

Size: 13,500 acres (54.63 sq km)

Annual Visitors: 69,000

Visitor Center: Pago Pago; open weekdays 8 a.m. to 4:30 p.m.

Entrance Fee: None

nps.gov/npsa

TUTUILA

The largest and most populous of the islands, Tutuila has long been a crossroads of the South Pacific. The **Visitor Center** on the Pago Pago waterfront offers interactive exhibits on Samoa's culture and natural history, as well as useful information on how to reach the park's three scattered units. Above the town, the **World War II Heritage Trail** leads to hilltop gun emplacements that once protected the island from Japanese invasion.

The Tutuila section is reached via Route 6, which breaches Afona Pass on its way to splendid beaches at **Amalau Bay** and **Vatia Bay** on the north shore. The island's offshore waters are rich with marine life—more than 950 fish species and 250 types of coral—that can be explored via snorkeling or walk-in shore diving. The **Lower Sauma Ridge Overlook** is a great perch to snap coastal photos; a 0.2-mile (.32 km) trail leads to an archaeological site and swimming holes at the bottom of a rocky peninsula.

The road peters out on the far side of Vatia Bay, where the easy **Pola Island Trail** (0.1-mile/.16 km round-trip) leads to a viewpoint of the **Vaiava Strait National Natural Landmark**, where giant waves crash into steep volcanic cliffs. Vatia Bay is

At the center of the National Park of American Samoa sits Tafeu Cove, a national marine sanctuary.

also the jumping-off point for the **Mount 'Alava Adventure Trail**—a 5.6-mile (9 km) jungle loop that takes you to the peak's 1,610-foot (490.73 m) summit via a series of earthen steps and rope ladders.

OFU AND TA'U

It could be the most beautiful beach in the South Pacific—the long white strand along the south shore of **Ofu Island** that falls within the national park. Shaded by coconut palm trees and jungle cliffs, the beach provides a paradise setting for swimming, snorkeling, or just lazing on the sand. Looming in the background are shark-toothed **Sunu'itao** and hulking **Piumafua**, surreal peaks that look as if they were painted on the sky.

The island's only good hike is outside the park. The **Tumu Mountain Trail** runs 52.7 miles (84.8 km) from Ofu Harbor through a thick stand of rain forest to the 1,621-foot

(494.08 m) summit of the island's highest peak. Ofu boasts a small airfield, but the most common way to reach the island (60 miles/96.56 km east of Tutuila) is by flying to nearby Ta'u and paying a fisherman to take you across the channel.

Ta'u Island offers up the wildest and most remote part of the park,

a knot of jungle peaks, volcanic geology, and beaches that can be reached only by sea. **Si'u Point Trail** (5.7-mile/9.1 km round-trip) passes the **Saua archaeological site** as it makes its way around the coast to the south shore, where an even more primitive path leads through the rain forest to the stunning **Laufuti Falls**. ◾

MEET THE NEIGHBORS

Some of the world's largest and most diverse maritime environments are protected within the confines of U.S. wildlife refuges and marine sanctuaries in the South Pacific.

• **National Marine Sanctuary of American Samoa:** From Fagatele Bay on Tutuila to far-off Swain Island, this largest of America's marine sanctuaries protects both inshore reef and open ocean.

• **War in the Pacific National Historical Park:** Six sites on Guam preserve battlefields, gun emplacements, trenches, and other relics of the 1944 siege to retake the island from the Japanese.

• **Pacific Remote Islands Marine National Monument:** Seven national wildlife refuges compose this supersecluded sanctuary in the Central Pacific that safeguards endemic land and sea and air creatures on numerous atolls and reefs.

Ofu Island's coral reefs, within the National Park of American Samoa

Vieques National Wild-life Refuge

Puerto Rico

Consistently named one of the nation's best wildlife refuges, Vieques lies in the Spanish Virgin Islands east of Puerto Rico. It covers around half of Vieques Island and includes a diverse range of habitats from beaches, bays, and lagoons to mangrove swamps and tropical forest. The refuge shelters 190 types of birds, 22 kinds of reptiles and amphibians, and hundreds of marine species.

O ne of the oddest little islands in the Caribbean, Vieques was largely ignored by its Spanish colonial masters until the sugar boom of the 19th century. The U.S. government purchased many of the sugar

plantations during World War II and transformed Vieques into a Navy base with a weapons test ground and live firing range.

Under growing pressure from residents and environmentalists, the

THE BIG PICTURE

Established: 2001

Size: 17,771 acres (71.92 sq km)

Annual Visitors: 300,000

Visitor Center: Puerto Ferro

Entrance Fee: None

fws.gov/refuge/vieques

Navy relinquished control of the base to the U.S. Fish and Wildlife Service in the early 21st century. In many respects, 60 years of military occupation was detrimental. But it also sheltered much of the island from modern tourism and residential development. Some parts of the refuge are still off-limits to visitors due to the presence of live ammunition; cleanup is an ongoing process. And Hurricane Irma ravaged parts of the refuge in 2017. But the areas that are currently open to the public offer a rare glimpse of the wild Caribbean.

The refuge is split into eastern and western sectors at either end of the island. The main entrance to the much larger eastern tract is on Highway 997, about a 15-minute drive from the **Vieques Ferry Terminal**. The **FWS Visitor Center** offers maps, information, and displays on some of the animals that inhabit the refuge. Among the wide variety of creatures are manatees; dolphins; four sea turtle species; pythons; boa constrictors; nine bat species; various types of sharks; whales; an amazing variety of fish, coral, and other reef dwellers; and even a few caimans.

Most of the eastern sector's natural attractions are strung along a gravel road that meanders along the south shore. The main park road leads to a string of pristine beaches: **Playa Caracas** (Red Beach) on kayak-friendly

The crystal-clear waters of Playa Caracas welcome swimmers.

Within Vieques National Wildlife Refuge, Playa Caracas offers white-sand beaches and picturesque views.

Bahia Corcho, superlong **Playa la Chiva** (Blue Beach), and **Playa La Plata**. The **Vereda Cerro Playuela** peninsula offers three short hiking trails down to the shore. Other than this gorgeous beach-and-bay strip, the rest of the eastern sector is closed to the public.

Another gravel road runs due south from the visitor center to the old **Puerto Ferro Lighthouse**. Constructed in 1896 during the waning years of Spanish rule, the lighthouse continued to operate through the early years of the American occupation, guiding sugarcane boats and other vessels along the south coast until 1926.

Although much smaller, the refuge's **western sector** offers plenty of variety. Among its half dozen pristine beaches are big **Playa Grande** on the south shore and **Playa Punta Arenas** at the island's northwest tip. Almost lost amid the jungle behind the beach are the historic ruins of the 19th-century **Playa Grande Sugar Mill**.

Nature activities mostly revolve around **Laguna Kiani**, where a wooden boardwalk leads through mangroves to places where you can spot and photograph many of the shorebirds that frequent the refuge. An information kiosk at the start of the trail details the flora and fauna found around the lagoon. And a 1-mile (1.6 km) hiking and biking trail leads through thick vegetation to the summit of 987-foot (300.8 m) **Monte Pirata** ("pirate mountain"), the island's highest peak. ■

MEET THE NEIGHBORS

• **Bahía Bioluminiscente Nature Reserve:** This bay on Vieques island lights up each night with one of the world's most intense bioluminescent displays. Watch the show on a guided kayak trip.

• **Isla de Mona Nature Reserve:** Often called the "Galápagos of the Caribbean" because of its land iguanas and rich birdlife, Monkey Island sits 41 miles (65.98 km) off Puerto Rico's west coast. However, there are no monkeys.

• **Navassa National Wildlife Refuge:** Located halfway between Haiti and Jamaica, this remote, uninhabited piece of U.S. territory harbors large seabird colonies.

• **La Cordillera Nature Reserve:** This string of a dozen tiny islands and reefs off Puerto Rico's northeast coast features coral gardens, crested iguanas, virgin beaches, and a dozen great dive spots.

Canada

Sea ice on the Gulf of St. Lawrence in Prince Edward Island National Park

Banff & Jasper National Parks

Alberta

Much like its neighbor to the south, Canada's national park movement first took root in the Rockies, the majestic valleys and mountains around the frontier towns of Banff and Jasper—a mingling of rock, wood, water, and ice that continues to awe. Add an array of outdoor pursuits, abundant wildlife, and absorbing human history, and you've got all of the makings of two parks that are among the globe's most iconic wild places.

As Canada pursued its westward push, the Rockies were only a temporary impediment to reaching the Pacific coast. Some men lingered in the mountains, convinced their own manifest destiny could be found among the secluded valleys and snowcapped peaks. And in some cases, it was. Banff started life as a railway whistle-stop and Jasper as a fur-trading outpost. Yet by the end of the 19th century, the unbridled wilderness that had earlier seemed like something to master was being viewed as a legacy to be preserved for everyone.

BANFF NATIONAL PARK

Banff was originally called Siding 29, a remote stop on the

THE BIG PICTURE

Established: Banff (1885); Jasper (1907)

Size: Banff (6,641 sq km/1.64 million acres); Jasper (10,878 sq km/2.68 million acres)

Annual Visitors: Banff (4 million); Jasper (2.3 million)

Visitor Centers: Banff village, Lake Louise, Jasper village

Entrance Fees: C$19.60 per family/group or C$9.80 per person (per day)

pc.gc.ca/en/pn-np/ab/banff
pc.gc.ca/en/pn-np/ab/jasper

Canadian Pacific Railway created in the 1880s as the transcontinental tracks were driven through the Rockies of western Alberta. Three railway workers chanced on hot springs near the siding. Rather than continuing with the grueling construction work, they decided to jump ship and start a health resort centered around the Cave and Basin Hot Springs.

When development (and competing claims) threatened to spoil the site, the Canadian government took control of the springs, designating Canada's first and the world's third national park. As a means to ensure the profitability of the new railway, the government and Canadian Pacific began promoting the park as a tourist destination. Railway big shot Lord Strathcona was awarded the privilege of renaming the park after his Scottish hometown—Banff.

Even in their wildest dreams, none of the original founders could have foreseen that Banff would grow into Canada's most visited national park and one of the world's most cherished scenic wonders.

Cave and Basin Hot Springs is now a national historic site that offers

Peaks of the Canadian Rockies are surrounded by low-lying clouds in Banff.

A hiker looks out over glacier-fed Peyto Lake in Banff. The lake is easily accessed via the Icefields Parkway.

a high-definition movie, living history activities, a ranger-led **Biodiversity Experience** in the surrounding marshlands, and evening **Lantern Tour**. It's no longer possible to take a dip in the soothing waters, but just 10 minutes away is **Banff Upper Hot Springs**, a modern spa with outdoor pools, changing rooms, and a café.

Banff village has evolved from a whistle-stop into a thriving year-round resort town with hotels, restaurants, art galleries, and outdoor adventure outfitters. Lodged inside a mock-Tudor building, **Banff National Park Visitor Centre** has everything you need to know about places, activities, road conditions, and weather in the park.

Two blocks down the main street is the **Banff Park Museum**

National Historic Site, which doubles as a rustic architectural wonder and storehouse of Victorian-era zoological, botanical, and geological specimens. The nearby **Whyte Museum of the Canadian Rockies** specializes in regional art and architecture, including paintings, sculptures, photography, and heritage homes on display in the gardens.

Outdoor recreation of one sort or another surrounds the village. Laid

EVENT HORIZON

• **Lake Louise Ice Magic Festival:** Ice sculptures, sleigh rides, and skating on the lake highlight this January bash. *banfflakelouise.com*

• **Mountain Madness:** Relay teams in wacky costumes compete in a Banff race that combines ski, skate, and snowshoe in January. *banff.ca*

• **Banff Mountain Film and Book Festival:** Nine days of adventure-related readings, movies, and exhibitions at the Banff Centre for Arts and Creativity. *banffcentre.ca*

• **Jasper Dark Sky Festival:** "Power down, loop up" is the motto of this October event that combines stargazing and celebrity astronauts. *jasperdarksky.travel*

• **Christmas in November:** Holiday music and tacky sweaters complement the food and drink of this 10-day event at Jasper Park Lodge. *christmasinnovember.com*

out in 1911, the public nine-hole **Banff Springs Golf Club** takes full advantage of its location in the Rockies with epic mountain views and fairways along Bow River. Along the river's north bank, the **Banff Legacy Trail** (26.8 kilometers/16.65 mi) between Canmore town and Banff village is just one of the park's many scenic cycling and mountain biking routes. **Bow River** between Lake Louise and Canmore offers plenty of scope for fly-fishing, self-guided kayaking, and guided float trips of the type offered by **Rocky Mountain Raft Tours**.

Towering high above the village, **Mount Norquay** provides skiing, snowboarding, and tubing in winter; hiking and biking trails; a **via ferrata** rock climbing route; and chairlift flightseeing in summer. Just 20 minutes outside town is **Lake Minnewanka**, a long fjord-like body of water with plenty of options to get wet, including swimming, kayaking, fishing, motor boating, or even scuba diving the ruins of a sunken village. One-hour scenic boat tours cruise the lake to **Devil's Gap**.

An hour farther up the Bow River Valley via the **Trans-Canada Highway** is drop-dead-gorgeous **Lake Louise**. Named after Queen Victoria's fourth daughter, the stunning alpine lake is a bit cold for swimming but ideal for paddle sports in summer or lake fishing and ice-skating come the winter freeze-over.

Looming above the east shore is the historic **Château Lake Louise**, opened in 1911 and still Canada's premier national park lodge. **Afternoon tea** in the lounge—with huge picture windows overlooking the lake—is a long tradition. Of the area's many hikes, **Plain of the Six Glaciers Trail** is the most popular, a 13-kilometer (8.1 mi) round loop along the lakeshore and up a glacial valley, with a chance to sip at the log cabin **Lake Agnes Tea House** located on the mountainside.

Brewster Stables organizes summer trail rides to the teahouse, as well as a full-day expedition ride up Paradise Valley and winter horse-drawn sleigh rides around the shore. Another way to discover the lake area is by the private guided hikes offered by **Great Divide Nature Interpretation**. Themed treks revolve around glaciers, grizzlies, birding, autumn leaves, or dozens of other topics.

Down in the village, **Lake Louise Visitor Centre** offers another chance

Snowcapped mountains are reflected in the waters of a Banff park lake.

to fetch information, brochures, maps, and books about the park. Clinging to the eastern side of the valley is **Lake Louise Ski Resort**, which sets itself apart from other winter sports resorts in the region with activities like **Torchlight Dinner and Ski** evenings, a spring music festival, guided snowshoe tours, and backcountry ski tours.

Just north of Lake Louise, the Trans-Canada Highway veers off to the west and into British Columbia. But another famous roadway continues north along Bow River: the celebrated **Icefields Parkway** (Highway 93), which meanders 268 kilometers (166.5 mi) through the heart of the Canadian Rockies to Jasper. Flanked by rivers, waterfalls, snowy peaks, and more than 100 glaciers, the route offers plenty of reasons to pull over, snap a photo, take a short walk, or simply take in views of nature's splendid canvas.

Bow Lake is a great place to pause, for a peek at historic **Num-Ti-Jah Lodge** or a hike along the **Bow Glacier Falls Trail** (9.3-kilometer/ 5.78 mi round-trip) to the namesake cascade fed by meltwater from Wapta Glacier. The parkway reaches its highest point at **Peyto Lake**, with its jaw-dropping views back down the valley. Another waterfall tumbles through the slot canyon at **Mistaya** before the parkway leaps across the **Saskatchewan River** at a place called the **Crossing**, which marks the halfway point between Banff and Jasper villages. Fifty kilometers (30.1 mi) farther up the parkway is Columbia Icefield (see below) and the start of Jasper National Park.

JASPER NATIONAL PARK

Jasper's more northerly location spared it the large-scale tourism development that marked the Bow

Bighorn sheep graze along the Canadian Rockies.

River Valley. As a result, Jasper National Park is much less crowded than its southern brother but just as impressive. Set around the awesome **Athabasca River Valley**, the sprawling wilderness preserve blends land and water, rock and ice into a smorgasbord of summer and winter outdoor adventure.

Jasper House, the early 19th-century fur-trading post that served as the nucleus for the area's first community, is long gone. Other than a national historic marker beside the **Yellowhead Highway** (Route 16), nothing remains of the original settlement. Nearby **Miette Hot Springs** are the hottest hot

---

LAY YOUR HEAD

Hotels

• **Château Lake Louise:** Iconic national park lodging at a classic location; restaurants, bars, spa, kids' camp, summer and winter activities; from C$319. *fairmont.com/lake-louise*

• **Baker Creek Mountain Resort:** Log cabins along the Bow River south of Lake Louise; restaurant, bikes, fishing rods; from C$195. *bakercreek.com*

• **Banff Springs Hotel:** Historic national park property founded in 1888; restaurants, bars, spa, golf, swimming pool, winter and summer activities; from C$59. *fairmont.com/banff-springs*

• **Pyramid Lake Resort:** Modest but comfy digs on the edge of Jasper village; restaurant, bar, summer boat and bike rentals, and winter snowshoe, ice-skate, and fat bike rentals; from C$178. *mpljasper.com*

• **Jasper Park Lodge:** Queen Elizabeth II and Marilyn Monroe are just two of the many celebrities who have slept here; restaurants, bars, spa, golf, extensive summer and winter activities; from C$279. *fairmont.com/jasper*

springs in the Canadian Rockies (40°C/104°F) and the outdoor pools offer awesome mountain views.

Another 50-odd kilometers (30.1 mi) up the Athabasca River, modern **Jasper** is a thriving wilderness town where the bulk of the park's visitor services are situated. With the **Two Brothers Totem Pole** out front, the log-and-stone **Jasper Park Information Centre** offers information on activities and events in both the village and park. Over on the west side of town, the **Jasper-Yellowhead Museum and Archives** mounts exhibits on early exploration, the fur trade, and railway, as well as art inspired by local history and nature.

Arrayed around the town are multi-use trails (hiking, biking, horses) and alpine lakes ripe for canoeing, fishing, and traction kiting. **Jasper Discovery Trail** (8.3 kilometers/ 5.16 mi), the longest path, loops around the entire village. **Jasper Riding Stables** is one of several equestrian facilities offering summer trail rides and winter carriage rides in the park. On the outskirts of town, **Maligne Canyon's** medley of waterfalls, rock walls, and forest trails is like a miniature version of the whole park.

Icefields Parkway heads south from Jasper village on its long and scenic run down to Banff. One of the must-see stops along the route is

Above: Athabasca Falls in Jasper Opposite: Three glaciers surround Jasper's Maligne Lake.

powerful **Athabasca Falls**, which plunges 23 meters (75.46 ft) down a rock face into a slot canyon. Below the falls, outfitters like **Maligne Rafting Adventures** start whitewater float trips back to the village.

The main attraction along the entire parkway is the massive **Columbia Icefield**—325 square kilometers (125.48 sq mi) of snow and ice that feed meltwater into both the Pacific and Arctic Oceans. The **Icefield Interpretive Centre** offers exhibits and guided snowcoach tours to **Athabasca Glacier**, one of the six large "arms" flowing down from the Columbia. Some of the tours include a guided walk across the glacier. Perched 300 meters (984.24 ft) above the visitor center, the glass-floored **Glacier Skywalk** provides a bird's-eye view of the frozen landmark.

Beyond the Athabasca Valley and Icefields Parkway, more than 90 percent of Jasper National Park is wilderness that can be explored via more than 1,000 kilometers (621.37 mi) of hiking, biking, skiing, and horseback routes. ■

CHOW DOWN

Between them, Banff and Jasper boast some of the finest food among all national parks.

• **Eden:** One of the best eateries between Vancouver and Toronto cooks up ambrosial French cuisine and stunning mountain views on a hillside above Banff village. *banffeden.com*

• **Park Distillery Restaurant & Bar:** The Banff favorite blends vodka made with glacial meltwater and Alberta grains with wood-fired rotisserie fish and meat dishes. *parkdistillery.com*

• **Tekarra:** New Canadian cuisine (fresh from field, forest, and sea) is the specialty at this Jasper dining hot spot—although breakfast is more like old-style Canadian cooking. *tekarrarestaurant.ca*

• **Oka Sushi:** An oasis of Japanese cuisine in one of the most unlikely places, this tiny (12-seat) sushi bar hides inside the Jasper Park Lodge. *fairmont.com/jasper/dining/okasushi*

Moraine Lake, in the Valley of Ten Peaks, Banff National Park

Dinosaur Provincial Park

Alberta

THE BIG PICTURE

Established: 1955

Size: 80 square kilometers (19,768.4 acres)

Annual Visitors: 120,000

Visitor Center: Dinosaur

Entrance Fees: C$6 per person

albertaparks.ca/parks/south/ dinosaur-pp

The deeply eroded badlands of central Alberta are where the real-life denizens of the Jurassic world roamed millions of years ago, a legacy preserved in the geological formations of Dinosaur Provincial Park, where paleontologists have discovered the remains of more than 50 dinosaur species from the Age of Reptiles.

Located along the banks of the Red Deer River in the badlands region east of Calgary, Dinosaur Provincial Park is one of the world's great treasures of prehistoric fossils, as well as a marvelous place to learn about the creatures that walked the earth 75 million years ago.

Since the first bones were uncovered in the 1880s, the area has yielded more than 500 separate dinosaurs, including 150 complete skeletons. Fossils from around 450 other prehistoric flora and fauna species have also been found, many of these now exhibited in various preeminent natural history museums around the world.

"The property is outstanding in the number and variety of high quality specimens representing every known group of Cretaceous dinosaurs," reads the UNESCO citation that declared the park a World Heritage site in 1979. "The diversity affords excellent opportunities for paleontology that is both comparative and chronological."

A 40-minute drive off the Trans-Canada Highway, **Dinosaur Visitor Centre** offers interactive exhibits, dinosaur-related films, and interpretive tours throughout the year. Other facilities in the park headquarters area include a general store and café that are open between early May and late October. The adjacent **John Ware Cabin** was built by a renowned African-American cowboy and former slave who settled the area in the 1880s.

Guided activities in the park range from a two-hour **Explorer Bus Tour** around the park and a family-friendly, very hands-on **Fossil Safari** to the 2.5-hour guided hike to the famous **Centrosaurus Quarry** and a paleontologist-for-a-day experience called the **Bonebed Guided Excavation**, during which participants pitch in at an authentic dinosaur fossil dig.

Boys climb the clay badlands looking for fossils.

Mud deposits from 75 million years ago created the valley walls, hills, and hoodoos of Dinosaur Provincial Park.

Visitors who sign up for the **Cast from the Past** program learn about the tools of the trade and make an authentic fossil cast (which they get to keep) inside the **Paleo Lab**. Reservations for all of these activities are strongly recommended. If you're feeling "fossiled out" by day's end, sign up for the two-hour **Sunset Tour** with stops at photogenic spots in the badlands like **Valley of the Gold, Valley of the Castles,** and **Valley of the Moon.**

Dinosaur offers many self-guided activities including biking, hiking, or driving a 3.5-kilometer (2.17 mi) **Scenic Loop Road** through the badlands to several **Fossil Houses** where dinosaur bones are displayed in situ. Five interpretive hikes range in length from the very easy **Prairie Trail** (300 meters/984.25 ft) to the **Cottonwood Flats Trail** (1.4 kilometer/.87 mi) through the lush vegetation along the **Red Deer**

River. For visitors who hauled along their own canoe or kayak, a **public boat launch** makes it easy to paddle the slow-flowing river.

Many of the bones uncovered in the park are sent to the **Royal Tyrrell Museum** for study and display. Located about two hours by road northwest of the park, the museum collection easily rivals other great "boneyards" like the American Museum of Natural History. Among its prehistoric treasures are a *Tyrannosaurus rex* called Black Beauty, the original *Albertosaurus* skeleton, and a giant *Camarasaurus.* ∎

Mont-Tremblant National Park

Quebec

Most renowned of the Laurentian region's many nature reserves, Mont-Tremblant is one of the oldest and largest national parks in eastern Canada. Less than two hours from downtown Montreal, the park is a popular getaway year-round with its myriad outdoor recreation activities and enticing blend of lakes and forest that lure urban dwellers to the wilder side of Quebec.

Like many of Quebec's other nature areas, Mont-Tremblant has evolved from blatant resource extraction in the 19th century to a mixed-use provincial park to full-blown (and completely protected) national park status in 1981. The park's time line parallels Quebec's evolution into one of the most conservation-conscious political entities in North America.

Although its long been renowned for winter sports, Mont-Tremblant shines in every season, a place where

THE BIG PICTURE

Established: State forest reserve (1895); national park (1981)

Size: 1,510 square kilometers (373,129.13 acres)

Annual Visitors: 410,000

Visitor Center: Lac Monroe

Entrance Fees: C$8.50 per person per day

sepaq.com/pq/mot

visitors can paddle on numerous lakes and rivers, camp along supersecluded backcountry trails, or photograph the wildlife that inhabits its mix of eastern and boreal forest.

In addition to more traditional outdoor pursuits, the park offers offbeat wilderness experiences like wheelchair-enabled Ski-Vel, via ferrata rock climbing, rabaska Algonquin birchbark canoes, and electric-assisted bikes—e-bikes—of both the mountain and road variety).

La Diable Sector is the park's equivalent of Yosemite Valley, both a hub of activity and a scenic wonder flanked by granite cliffs and dissected by the copper-colored waters of the **Rivière du Diable** as it flows through a chain of lakes.

Lac-Monroe Visitors Centre is the place to pick up information on what to do and where to stay in the park, as well as snacks and drinks at the center's general store. The center rents a variety of watercraft, including standup paddleboards, birch-bark and aluminum canoes, pedal boats, and rowboats, as well as bicycles, snowshoes, and cross-country skis. The nearby **Discovery Centre** hosts ranger talks, campfire chats, various adventure activities, and guided trips during the summer. Farther upriver is the **Plage de la Crémaillère**, a small sandy shore

A 9.3-km (5.8 mile) round-trip hike leads to Chute-aux-Rats.

An autumn forest is mirrored in a mountain lake within the park limits of Mont-Tremblant.

reserved for recreational swimming and family-friendly beach games.

Among the adventure activities are two days of unguided **river-canoe camping** along a 25-kilometer (15.5 mi) stretch of the Rivière du Diable and two days of unguided **lake-canoe camping** at four different spots in the park (with boat rental and ground transport included in the rates).

A number of **guided trips** are also on offer, from a slow paddle down the **"Devil's River"** with a ranger-naturalist and lake kayaking in search of loons, to a **mountain e-bike adventure** along 20 kilometers (12.43 mi) of trail, treks to the top of **Pic Johannsen** and **Mont-Tremblant** (the park's highest peaks), and a day-long **van tour** of park highlights. And then there's the **via ferrata**, a unique vertigo-inducing climb 182.88 meters (600 ft) up a rock wall above the Rivière du Diable via a series of cables, beams, and narrow ledges.

The Diable area is laced with hiking trails, including short jaunts to the **Chutes-Croches** and **Chute-du-Diable** waterfalls and more demand-ing treks to viewpoints over the valley like **La Roche** (5.4-kilometer/3.35 mi round-trip) and **La Corniche** (3.4-kilometer/2.1 m round-trip).

Once snow starts to fall, the Diable Sector transforms into a winter wonderland with 43 kilometers (26.7 mi) of **cross-country skiing** trails, 26 kilometers (16.15 mi) of dedicated **snowshoe** trails, **Ski-Vel** for the mobility impaired, as well as **winter hiking** and **fat bike** routes. There's also access to 77 kilometers (47.8 mi) of backcountry trails with ski huts for overnight stays. ■

DID YOU KNOW

• Mont-Tremblant National Park has two other (far more remote) regions: La Pimbina Sector in the middle of the park and L'Assomption Sector in the far east. A range of summer and winter activities is available in both.

• Tremblant Ski Resort, founded by American adventurer Joe Ryan in 1939, borders the park's southwestern corner. The resort features 96 trails available to downhill skiers and snowboarders.

• La Diable draws its demonic name from a French interpretation of the Algonquin term for the area—*Manitonga Soutana* ("mountain of the devil")—a reference to evil spirits that were thought to dwell there.

• The national park is home to 40 mammal species, including bears, wolves, and moose, and nearly 200 types of birds such as the bald eagle and great horned owl.

Cape Breton Highlands National Park

Nova Scotia

Canadian Maritimes nature comes into full bloom at this diverse park near the northern end of Nova Scotia. Wedged between the Gulf of St. Lawrence and the open Atlantic, Cape Breton offers plenty of coastal adventures, one of North America's best scenic drives, and a rugged wilderness plateau that gradually rises from thick boreal forest into windswept tundra.

THE BIG PICTURE

Established: 1936

Size: 949 square kilometers (234,503 acres)

Annual Visitors: 302,000

Visitor Centers: Chéticamp, Ingonish

Entrance Fee: C$7.80 per person per day

pc.gc.ca/en/pn-np/ns/cbreton

A captivating glimpse of long ago, the Cape Breton coast and highlands are what a lot of Atlantic Canada must have been like when Mi'kmaq migrated into the region, when the Norsemen came this way a thousand years ago, and when explorer John Cabot reached this coast in 1497 as the first "modern" European to set foot on the North American continent.

The park harbors three distinct landscapes. The coast wears a crown of high bluffs and soaring cliffs, occasionally broken by sandy beaches and tranquil bays. Acadian forest covers much of the interior, a blend of evergreens and deciduous trees that delivers a riot of colors come autumn. Tundra takes over at the highest elevations, an ethereal expanse of stunted trees, rocky outcrops, and boggy barrens.

Most park visitors never stray far from the **Cabot Trail**, the renowned road that frames three sides of the Cape Breton Highlands. Around a third of the route (110 kilometers/ 68.35 mi) passes through the park, but it's far and away the most spectacular part, a vertiginous drive or bike ride along bluff tops, through deep canyons, and along wave-splashed shores.

Among the many items on offer at **Le Nique** nature bookstore in the **Chéticamp Visitor Centre** on the gulf (west) coast is an audio driving guide that describes the landscapes and landmarks along the Cabot Trail. The store also sells hiking guides to the park's 26 trails, including two that start from the visitor center: the **Acadian Trail** (8.4-kilometer/ 5.2 mi loop) to a lofty viewpoint over the Gulf of St. Lawrence, and the **Salmon Pools Trail** (7.8-kilometer/ 4.85 mi round-trip) along the Chéticamp River.

Meandering up the gulf coast, Cabot Trail passes **La Bloc** beach

A native yellow-rumped warbler perches on a branch.

The Cabot Trail, a Canadian highway, winds its way parallel to the ocean and into small fishing villages.

(a great place to take a dip in the sea) and the scenic **French Lake** area, the jumping-off point for several worthwhile hikes. One of the park's most spectacular walks, **Skyline Trail** leads just over 3 kilometers (1.86 mi) to a bluff perched high above the water. Moose, bear, and other critters frequent the area, and it's often possible to see humpbacks, finbacks, pilots, and other whales swimming in the gulf.

Switchbacking down a steep grade, the highway cruises into **Pleasant Bay** and its **Whale Interpretation Centre**, where visitors can learn more about the 16 species of whale that frequent the waters around Cape Breton.

Leaving the gulf behind, the Cabot climbs into the wooded highlands on a 30-kilometer (18.64 mi) leg that crosses the island to **Aspy Bay** and the Atlantic Ocean. Two of the best landlocked stops are **MacIntosh Brook** with its old-growth forest and the **Aspy Trail** (9.6-kilometer/

5.97 mi return), which leads uphill to **Beulach Ban Falls** and an overlook in the highlands.

The park's rugged Atlantic coast offers swimming at **Black Brook Cove** and **Ingonish Beach**, awesome overlooks like **Lakies Head**, and a spectacular seaside **Highlands Links**, a golf course that ranks

among the top 100 in North America. In addition to the **Coastal Trail** (6 kilometers/3.7 mi) along the rocky shore, the area offers several great ways to hike into the highlands, in particular the **Branch Pond Trail** (8.4-kilometer/5.2 mi round-trip), a hiking and biking route into the high tundra barrens. ∎

Whitepoint, Cape Breton Island

Gros Morne National Park

Newfoundland

It's all about tall at Gros Morne, the national park that dominates the wild west coast of Newfoundland: towering fjords and soaring sea stacks, some of the highest mountains of Atlantic Canada, and waterfalls that seem to tumble from the clouds. But there's plenty down at ground level too, in a landscape formed by powerful earth forces over millions of years.

It's no wonder the Vikings felt at home when they came upon this coast a thousand years ago and decided to stay for a while. The gargantuan fjords, boreal forests, and barren tablelands of Gros Morne are virtually a carbon copy of Iceland, Norway, and other lands the Norsemen hailed from.

The park's over-the-top topography was created by primordial tectonics forces, the collision of massive plates that started around a half billion years ago and eventually raised

THE BIG PICTURE

Established: 1973

Size: 1,805 square kilometers (446,025.2 acres)

Annual Visitors: 244,000

Visitor Centers: Rocky Harbour, Woody Point

Entrance Fee: C$9.80 per person per day

pc.gc.ca/en/pn-np/nl/grosmorne

remnants of the earth's mantle and the ancient ocean floor high above sea level. That ancient rock lies at the core of modern Gros Morne, a national park with a distinctively different feel than anywhere else in eastern Canada.

Founded in the early 1800s, the old fishing village of **Rocky Harbour** is the main staging point for visits to the park and adjacent Gulf of St. Lawrence. **Visitor Centre Rocky Harbour** renders advice on how to explore the park by road, trail, and sea (or skis, snowshoes, and snowmobiles if it happens to be winter). They can also give the lowdown on nearby Parks Canada sites worth exploring like Port au Choix and L'Anse aux Meadows in western Labrador and Red Bay in southern Labrador.

Boat tours are the park's top activity, especially for those who have only a short time to discover the wonders of Gros Morne. **Bon Tours** on the Rocky Harbour waterfront launches day tours of **Bonne Bay** fjord and landlocked **Western Brook Pond**—a thoroughly mild-mannered name for the park's most astounding geology feature. They also offer a **cod jigging cruise** that combines Newfoundland tradition and angling.

Woody Point Lighthouse overlooks Bonne Bay.

The sun sets over Trout River Pond, bordered by larch scrub and serpentine barrens.

Boone Bay Marine Station, a working research facility, offers tours. On the south side of Boone Bay, the **Discovery Centre at Wood Point** offers exhibits on Gros Morne nature, geology, and the region's ancient inhabitants, as well as park films, an art gallery, and guided activities like the **Mi'kmaq Medicine Walk**.

Gros Morne's trails are the stuff of hiking legend, not so much because of their difficulty but the unusual terrain through which many of them traipse. The **Tablelands Trail** (4-kilometer/2.48 mi round-trip) leads across a moonscape of rust-colored peridotite rock that was once part of the earth's mantle. A steep 16-kilometer (9.9 mi) loop reaches the summit of 806-meter (2,644.36 ft) **Gros Morne Mountain**, Newfoundland's second highest peak, while the **Long Range Traverse** rambles 35 kilometers (21.75 mi) through the backcountry between Western Brook Pond and Gros Morne Mountain, with five primitive campsites along the way.

The **Viking Trail** (Highway 430) runs north from Rocky Harbour to the beach at **Shallow Bay** and beyond. Not far out of town is **Lobster Cove Head Lighthouse**, another hub of park activity that hosts exhibits on the area's maritime history, outdoor fire circles in summer, and indoor storytelling and musical programs throughout the year. Across the highway, **Berry Hill Campground** offers trailheads for several short hikes. Farther up the shore, the **Broom Point Fishing Exhibit** revolves around the **Mudge Family Cabin**, where three fishermen and their families lived for 35 years while working this coast. ▪

MEET THE NEIGHBORS

• **L'Anse aux Meadows National Historic Site:** At the northern end of the Viking Highway, this combination archaeological dig and historic re-creation preserves the only verified Norse settlement located in North America.

• **Red Bay National Historic Site:** See the remains of a 16th-century Basque whaling station on the southern Labrador coast via preserved original whaling boats and other artifacts.

• **Battle Harbour National Historic District:** A throwback to bygone days, this seaside town was the unofficial capital of Labrador during the territory's British Empire days.

• **Akami-Uapishk^U-KakKasuak-Mealy Mountains National Park Reserve:** Farther up the Labrador coast, this vast expanse of wilderness is Canada's newest national park and the largest along the Atlantic seaboard.

Saguenay-St. Lawrence Marine Park

Quebec

Set at the confluence of two mighty rivers, this watery wonderland protects a unique environment where freshwater flowing down the fjord-like Saguenay blends with saltwater in the St. Lawrence estuary to create an environment where all sorts of marine life thrives. Whale-watching, kayaking, and sailing count among the park's varied aquatic activities.

Like Captain Ahab, visitors to Saguenay–St. Lawrence are obsessed with a white whale—albeit a much smaller one: the rare St. Lawrence beluga, which congregates in the river and upper estuary during the warm summer months. They are not alone: nine other species frequent the area, including humpbacks, minkes, finbacks, blue whales (the

THE BIG PICTURE

Established: 1998

Size: 1,246 square kilometers (307,893.3 acres)

Annual Visitors: 1.1 million

Visitor Centers: Pointe-Noire, Cap de Bon-Désir, Les Escoumins, Baie-Éternité, Baie-Ste-Marguerite

Entrance Fee: None

pc.gc.ca/en/amnc-nmca/qc/saguenay

largest animals on the planet), and even sperm whales like in the fictional *Moby Dick*.

The giant creatures are drawn by the rich food supply stirred up at the rendezvous of the two rivers, a unique blend of currents, tides, and underwater topography that traps the krill, plankton, and fish that form the bulk of the whale diet.

Whales aren't the only creatures that come for the maritime smorgasbord. Several types of dolphin and porpoises are also found in park waters, as well as Greenland sharks, three species of seal, and more than 1,600 species of birds that call this home—one of the most biodiverse marine environments found in North America.

Perched on the north side of the confluence, **Tadoussac** is the main focal point of park accommodations and activities. Down along the waterfront, the **Marine Mammals Interpretation Centre** offers an excellent introduction to the marine park and its resident cetaceans with interactive exhibits, videos, an extensive skeleton collection, and even whale song classes (for humans).

Mer et Monde Écotours specializes in kayak whale-watching in the

An underwater seascape of coral and urchins

Saguenay Fjord is the world's longest fjord at 146 miles (234.9 km) and surrounded by rugged, craggy mountains.

estuary and paddling the Saguenay Fjord. Several companies offer whale-watching day trips in larger boats from Tadoussac, including **Dufour** and **AML**.

A passenger and vehicle ferry links Tadoussac and **Baie-Sainte-Catherine** on the south bank, where the **Pointe-Noire Interpretation and Observation Centre** offers the opportunity to spot whales from land. Ste. Catherine is also home port for more whale-watching cruises.

Visitors can head north along Quebec's **Côte-Nord**, following Highway 138 along the left bank of the St. Lawrence estuary to other national park landmarks like the **Cap de Bon-Désir Interpretation and Observation Centre** (another chance to watch whales from shore).

The **Marine Environment Discovery Centre** near Les Escoumins renders one of the park's most unusual experiences, **St. Lawrence Live**, a theater that streams live video images from biologist-divers encountering various life-forms in the estuary. The Discovery Centre is

also the park's **dive base**, offering guided dives, customized packages, diving platforms, air tank fills, and equipment rentals.

Upstream from the confluence, **Saguenay Fjord** is split between water and dry land parks that work in tandem to preserve one of eastern Canada's geological landmarks: The sunken glacial valley stretches 100 kilometers (62.14 mi) inland from Tadoussac to Saguenay city, with walls towering as high as 450 meters (1,476.38 ft). More than 100 kilometers (62.1 mi) of hiking trails along the sunken gorge range from long, multiday treks like **Le Fjord Trail** (41 kilometers/25.5 mi) to easy jaunts like the **Méandres-à-Falaises Loop** (1.6 kilometers/ 1 mi) and the **Trail De l'Estuaire** (800 meters/2,624.6 ft).

Le Fjord du Saguenay Discovery and Visitors Centre at Baie-

Éternité highlights the fjord's geology and wildlife through exhibits and a simulated flight experience. Baie-Éternité is also the base for guided kayak trips, as well as Zodiac, sailing, and bateau-mouche (fly boat) tours along the fjord. Over on the north bank, the **Beluga Discovery and Visitors Centre** near Baie-Ste-Marguerite is the place to learn more about the adorable white whales. ∎

Above: A whale breaches the waters in Tadoussac. Opposite: An aerial view of Cap de la Tête au Chien Lighthouse

Wapusk National Park
Manitoba

THE BIG PICTURE

Established: 1996

Size: 11,475 square kilometers (2.83 million acres)

Annual Visitors: 10,000

Visitor Center: Churchill Heritage Railway Station

Entrance Fee: None

pc.gc.ca/en/pn-np/mb/wapusk

It's not all about polar bears at this wilderness park along the shore of Canada's Hudson Bay, but the big white bruins are the main reason people venture to this isolated outpost in northern Manitoba. Around 1,000 polar bears—one of the world's largest populations—mate, mother their cubs, and migrate through the park's beautiful mix of boreal forest and tundra.

*W*apusk means "white bear" in the language of the indigenous Cree people who inhabit this region. And it's those very bears that have put the national park and the nearby town of Churchill on the bucket list of avid nature lovers and wildlife photographers.

One of the great spectacles of North American nature unfolds in and around the park: the migration of polar bears onto land when the sea ice begins to melt in the early summer and their famished return to the frozen-over Hudson Bay when winter takes over again. Pregnant females remain ashore during the winter, giving birth and nurturing their youngsters in underground dens deep in the park.

Polar bears may be the main attraction, but the national park shelters many other subpolar animal species, from small creatures like lemmings, arctic foxes, and snowshoe hares, to larger kinds like moose, timber wolves, and caribou. More than 270 bird species have been recorded in and around the park, while the offshore waters are known to attract beluga whales and other marine mammals.

The park's gateway is **Churchill**, reachable via daily flights or a twice-weekly 40-hour train journey from Winnipeg. The **Parks Canada Visitor Centre** in the town's **Heritage Railway Station** is the place to get the lowdown on Wapusk and other area parks, and browse exhibits like the replica polar bear den. The town's small but excellent **Eskimo Museum** revolves around the art, lifestyles, and traditions of the area's human inhabitants.

Visitors who haven't prearranged a park visit can find out about local outfitters that offer land-based tundra buggy and aerial helicopter tours. Other than paddling on the Owl River, a licensed tour operator is required for all journeys inside the park so that visitors don't disturb the bears or their pristine habitat.

Cape Churchill, which crowns the park's northern end, is considered

A polar bear and her two cubs play in the snow.

The northern lights cast an alien glow over the snowy landscape of Wapusk National Park.

the single best place on the planet to observe and photograph polar bears in the wild. But it's not easy to reach.

Hudson Bay Helicopters, which helps wildlife authorities transport mischievous polar bears from town to remote areas, also offers aerial tours of the cape and park. **Frontiers North Adventures** organizes tundra buggy day tours during the summer and fall, as well as winter **aurora borealis** excursions. Visitors can spend the night at a mobile lodge in the prime migration zone by booking a multiday polar bear safari with **Natural Habitat**.

Wat'Chee Lodge, about 60 kilometers (37.28 mi) south of Churchill, specializes in a whole different type of Wapusk wildlife encounter: winter trips to watch polar bear mothers frolicking with their adorable newborn cubs.

The only section of the park that visitors can experience on their own (without a licensed guide) is paddling the **Owl River**, which runs all the way across Wapusk from **Herchemer** rail stop to the **Hudson Bay**. With a total length of 168 kilometers (104.39 mi), the trip normally takes four to seven days through an epic wilderness that evolves from boreal forest and tundra to the rocky, barren bay shore. Paddlers can arrange to have a helicopter or aircraft pick them up at the end of the worthwhile journey. ■

MEET THE NEIGHBORS

Churchill offers a number of other outdoor adventures and historical encounters.

• **Beluga whales:** Around 3,000 belugas gather at the mouth of the Churchill River in summer. Numerous local outfitters offer boat trips; Churchill Wild lets you swim and snorkel with the great white creatures. churchillwild.com

• **Dogsledding:** The finishing point of the annual Hudson Bay Quest sled-dog race, Churchill is a hub for kennels like Blue Sky that offer

backcountry mushing adventures. blueskymush.com

• **Prince of Wales Fort National Historic Site:** This massive stone bastion was built 250 years ago at the mouth of the Churchill River by British seeking to protect the lucrative Hudson Bay fur trade.

• **Itsanitaq Museum:** Galleries feature a world-class collection of fascinating Inuit art and artifacts rendered in whalebone, caribou antlers, and soapstone.

1 L'Anse aux Meadows, Newfoundland

Walk where ancient Vikings once trod at this archaeological dig at the top of Newfoundland's Great Northern Peninsula. The earliest evidence of European presence in the Western Hemisphere, the site preserves the remains of a small timber-and-sod encampment the Norsemen built more than a thousand years ago after voyaging from Greenland in their longboats.

2 Red Bay Basque Whaling Station, Labrador

Around the same time that Jacques Cartier was exploring the St. Lawrence River, Basque whalers were establishing a major whaling station on the Labrador shore. They stayed for around 70 years before abandoning the station. Many of the artifacts they left behind are on display at the national historic site museum.

3 Signal Hill, Newfoundland

Perched high above St. John's on the Newfoundland coast, this breezy hilltop witnessed the final battle of the Seven Years' War in 1762 and Marconi's first successful transatlantic wireless radio transmission in 1901. Not nearly as old as it looks, the hill's Cabot Tower was erected in 1897 to commemorate the 400th anniversary of explorer John Cabot's Canadian landfall.

4 Fortress of Louisbourg, Nova Scotia

Designed to protect New France from enemy attack, this massive stone bastion played a pivotal role in the 18th-century struggle between France and Britain over control of North America. Living history programs and rangers clad in period outfits provide a time-trip back into Canada's past.

5 Roosevelt Campobello International Peace Park, New Brunswick

FDR spent much of his childhood in his family's summer home on this island bordering New Brunswick and Maine. The Roosevelt Cottage exhibits mementos from those days, while the surrounding park offers forest and seaside trails, and tributes to the long friendship between Canada and the United States.

THE TOP

10

CANADIAN HISTORICAL PARKS

From the Maritimes to the Rockies, Canada's history comes alive at these parks.

6 Fortifications of Quebec City, Quebec

The only walled town in North America is surrounded by massive stone bastions erected by the French and British. A visit includes walking tours and living history programs, as well as a crypt with the remains of 17th-century Fort St. Louis beneath Dufferin Terrace.

Teepee camping is available at Head-Smashed-In Buffalo Jump.

7 HMCS *Haida,* Ontario

Permanently docked along the Hamilton waterfront, Canada's legendary "fightingest ship" served in World War II, the Korean War, and the Cold War. The Tribal class destroyer is now a floating museum that illuminates on the life aboard the *Haida* and Canadian naval history through walking tours, hands-on exhibits, and demonstrations.

8 Head-Smashed-In Buffalo Jump, Alberta

Once upon a time, the Blackfeet hunted bison by stampeding them off a high cliff that came to be called the Head-Smashed-In Buffalo Jump. Designated a UNESCO World Heritage site in 1981, the park features an underground visitor center and museum with exhibits on communal hunting techniques and the Blackfeet people.

9 Bar U Ranch, Alberta

During its heyday, the Bar U ran 30,000 head of cattle and attracted characters as diverse as England's Prince of Wales and notorious outlaw Sundance Kid. Now an ode to pioneering life on the Canadian prairies, the historic site offers wagon rides, rodeo demonstrations, and campfire talks about life in the Old West.

10 Dawson Historical Complex, Yukon

After the discovery of gold along the Klondike in 1896, the Great Stampede of miners flocked to Dawson to find their fortune. Eight blocks of that boom town are preserved as part of a national historic site that includes the Old Territorial Court House, Old Post Office, St. Paul's Anglican Church, Red Feather Saloon, and Harrington's Store.

Wood Buffalo National Park

Alberta & Northwest Territories

Canada's largest national park offers an unspoiled landscape of wild rivers, glacial lakes, wetlands, prairie, and forest that see few visitors, even at the height of summer. In addition to protecting wild bison, the mammoth park harbors many other North Country creatures, abundant outdoor recreation, and extraordinarily dark skies for excellent stargazing.

L arger than nine U.S. states, Wood Buffalo straddles the border between northern Alberta and the Northwest Territories, an incredible hulk of a park where nature reaches amazing extremes.

The park was created to protect the largest free-roaming herd of wood bison *(Bison bison athabascae),* a population that has grown from around 200 animals to more than 2,500 since the park was established in the 1920s. It also safeguards hundreds of other boreal creatures like the timber wolf, black bear, lynx, and moose. Wood Buffalo also boasts the world's

THE BIG PICTURE

Established: 1922

Size: 44,807 square kilometers (11 million acres)

Annual Visitors: 3,300

Visitor Center: Fort Smith

Entrance Fee: none

pc.gc.ca/en/pn-np/nt/ woodbuffalo

largest beaver dam—an 850-meter-long (2,788.71 ft) barrier accidentally discovered in 2010 by researchers studying satellite images of the park—and the last natural nesting place of the endangered whooping crane.

Reaching the park is easier than one might expect (even during the depths of winter) by driving the all-weather **Mackenzie Highway** roughly 590 kilometers (366.6 mi) between Grimshaw in northern Alberta to Hay River on the southern shore of Great Slave Lake. From there, Highway 5 meanders eastward into the park and the **Wood Buffalo Visitor Centre** in Fort Smith, a distance of around 270 kilometers (167.8 mi) along a mostly gravel road. In addition to information and exhibits, the visitor center is the place to sign up for the park's guided hikes, activities, and interpretive programs.

The drive along **Highway 5** offers a number of unique adventures, including the **Angus Sinkhole**, a viewpoint that looks out over the wetlands where the whooping cranes nest, and a chance to wander across the quirky **Salt Plains**, the remnant of an ancient sea that once covered the entire region.

From Fort Smith, take the gravel, all-weather **Pine Lake Road** due south into the heart of the park with

A wood bison grazes in Sedge Meadow.

The park's salt flats are the last remnants of an ancient inland sea that used to cover large swaths of North America.

several intriguing stops along the way. **Salt River Day Use Area** features more saline terrain and several good hikes, including the **North Loop Trail** (7.5 kilometers /4.7 mi) and **South Loop Trail** (9 kilometers/ 5.6 mi) around sinkholes and salt lakes. But the area's real claim to fame is the slithery spectacle that unfolds each May as thousands of red-sided garter snakes emerge from winter dens.

Pine Lake offers a woodsy campground and a chance to swim in a natural sinkhole, albeit a chilly one. Parks Canada provides canoes for paddling across the lake and evening campfire chats during the summer. Pine Lake Road continues another 62 kilometers (38.5 mi) to **Peace Point**, the jumping-off point for one of the park's main water routes—an epic week-long (224-kilometer/139.2 mi) paddle down the Peace and Slave Rivers to **Fort Fitzgerald** (near Fort Smith).

Intense aurora activity makes Wood Buffalo an excellent place to view the night sky, and in 2013 it

was designated the world's largest dark sky preserve. The park hosts a **Dark Sky Festival** in August, but the **northern lights** are most intense on the clear nights between December and February.

With temperatures dropping as low as -40°C (-40°F), many people assume that the park must close in winter. But quite the opposite: the colder months in Wood Buffalo attract **cross-country skiers** and **snowshoers**, as well as photographers intent on getting a classic shot of a snow-mantled buffalo.

Founded in 1788, **Fort Chipewyan** on the park's south side can be reached by air year-round or by ice road from Fort Smith or Fort McMurray during the winter. The town offers a national park visitor center, a replica **Hudson's Bay Company Store**, and prime boating on **Lake Athabasca**. ∎

LAY YOUR HEAD

Hotels

• **Whooping Crane Guest House:** Log cabin B&B near Aurora College in Fort Smith; open year-round; from C$115. *whoopingcraneguesthouse.com*

• **Ptarmigan Inn:** Modern accommodation in Hay River, 100 kilometers (62 mi) from the park entrance; restaurant, bar, fitness center; from C$161. *ptarmiganinn.com*

• **Lily's on Wylie:** Views of Lake Athabasca and the aurora borealis from this B&B in Fort Chipewyan near the park's south end; from C$157. *lilysonwylie.com*

Camping

• **Developed campground:** At Pine Lake; $C16 per night. Backcountry camping C$10 per person per night.

Pacific Rim National Park Reserve

British Columbia

Clinging to the outer edge of Vancouver Island, Pacific Rim feels like the legendary end of the world, a place so removed from modern civilization it sometimes feels like a different planet. Split almost 50/50 between marine and mainland sections, the park supports a wide variety of action, from wave surfing and scuba diving to long-distance hiking and encounters with First Nations people.

THE BIG PICTURE

Established: 1970

Size: 511 square kilometers (126,271 acres)

Annual Visitors: 1 million

Visitor Centers: Long Beach, Cox Bay

Entrance Fee: C$7.80 per person

pc.gc.ca/en/pn-np/bc/pacificrim

The rugged west coast of Vancouver Island offers both a cautionary tale in how humans can affect the natural environment and indigenous peoples, as well as an example of how a region can survive and thrive again with park status and other factors.

When Captain Cook sailed this way in 1778—stepping ashore just 96 kilometers (59.7 mi) north of Long Beach—the coast was home to a large population of indigenous people and some of the most prosperous tribes in North America. The very things that underpinned that prosperity, the resources of the sea and forest, also caused the decline that followed over the next century as the region's native population fell by an estimated 75 to 90 percent, millions of trees were cut, and marine resources strained.

Efforts to preserve the area began in the early 20th century, culminating in the establishment of Pacific Rim National Park in 1970. The park is split into three distinct units, each with its own personality: Long Beach in the north, the secluded Broken Group Islands in Barkley Sound, and the West Coast Trail section down south.

One of the most alluring strands along North America's west coast, **Long Beach** and its sandy cousins stretch a gorgeous 16 kilometers (10 mi) down the shoreline. The area is reached by small plane or by driving **BC Highway 4** through the Vancouver Island wilderness. **Kwisitis Visitor Centre** revolves around the region's marine and terrestrial wildlife, as well as the Nuu-chah-nulth people. But the main attraction is outside: **trekking** the beach, **surfing** the waves, or joining **ranger-guided interpretive walks**

A boardwalk cuts its way through Vancouver's lush rain forest.

Waves surge over the rocks of Halfmoon Bay, reached via a short hike through forest and cliff-hugging steps.

along the shore or through the nearby rain forest.

Green Point Theatre, located in the campground of the same name at Long Beach, offers an eclectic calendar during the summer and fall, from film nights and guest speakers to shows about local wildlife and **Hippies, Pioneers and Outcasts** who once populated this coast. Novice surfers can sign up for lessons at surf shops in **Tofino** and **Ucluelet**, the small coastal towns that bookend Long Beach.

Comprising more than 100 islands, exposed reefs, and rocky outcrops, the **Broken Group Islands** (BGI) harbor rocky shores, thriving rain forest, and many areas of First Nations significance.

The remote archipelago can be explored by boat only via day trips or kayak camping. **Keith Island** is the only one open to day visitors; however, kayak camping is allowed on seven of the islands. Paddlers can park

and launch kayaks from the Toquaht Nation's **Secret Beach Campground**, 30 kilometers (18.6 mi) from Kwisitis Visitor Centre. Tseshaht Beachkeepers, who patrol BGI in summer, provide information and cultural interpretation.

Bringing up the bottom of the park, the **West Coast Trail** (WCT) is an epic 75-kilometer (46.6 mi)

hike along ancient shoreline paths and paddle routes used by First Nations people for hundreds of years. The trek normally takes six to eight days across rugged terrain and often in wet weather. Other than the **Ditidaht First Nation's tented camp** at Tsuquadra Point, hikers are on their own when it comes to food and shelter along the WCT. ■

MEET THE NEIGHBORS

• **Gulf Islands National Park Reserve:** Across the watery divide from the San Juan Islands, this British Columbia park offers many of the same treasures, from forest walks and sandy shores to kayaking with killer whales.

• **Carmanah Walbran Provincial Park:** Sitka spruce and cedar old-growth forest are the highlights of this temperate rain forest park adjacent to the Pacific Rim.

• **Cape Scott Provincial Park:** Wrapped around the northern tip of Vancouver Island, the park embraces rocky headlands, salt marshes, and 30 kilometers (18.64 mi) of remote sandy strands.

• **Butchart Gardens:** Victoria's celebrated flower show, which started life in 1908 as a Japanese tea garden, offers an incredible range of blooms from around the world on the sunken site of an old quarry.

Schooner Cove, Pacific Rim National Park Reserve, British Columbia

Thousand Islands National Park

Ontario

One of Canada's smallest national parks presents a broad canvas of forest, field, and water in the St. Lawrence Valley downstream from Lake Ontario. Formed eons ago by glacial action, 20 island spots and three mainland areas fall within the confines of a park best explored by boat.

Technically there are 1,864 islands in this scenic archipelago that straddles the Canada-U.S. border. But "thousand" sounded much more alluring to those who flocked there in the late 19th century with the advent of the islands as a summer vacation retreat and Gilded Age playground.

Reaching farther back, the leafy isles were once home to First Nations people who called them *Manitouana* ("garden of the great spirit") because of their beauty and bounty. During the War of 1812, the St. Lawrence corridor saw furious fort building and pitched battles on both banks.

THE BIG PICTURE

Established: 1904

Size: 24.4 square kilometers (6,029.37 acres)

Annual Visitors: 90,000

Visitor Center: Mallorytown Landing

Entrance Fee: C$6.80 per vehicle per day

pc.gc.ca/en/pn-np/on/1000

Mallorytown on the Canadian side was founded by Loyalists fleeing the 13 colonies and protected during the 1812 conflict by a British garrison at **Chimney Island**, now a national historical site. **Mallorytown Landing Visitor Centre** offers park-related exhibits, interpretive programs, geocaching adventures, wildlife interactions, short hiking trails, and boat launching.

Just up the road from the visitor center, the **Jones Creek** unit doubled the size of the national park when it was added in 2005. Ranging from freshwater marshes to indigenous forest, the area features 12 kilometers (7.5 mi) of hiking trails and a **wetlands boardwalk**. The park's third mainland section is **Landon Bay Centre**, where the **Lookout Trail** leads to a lofty viewpoint over the St. Lawrence Valley.

The national park's 20 insular sections can be reached only by boat. Commercial **sightseeing cruises** are home-based at several Canadian river ports, including Rockport, Gananoque, and Kingston. However, these are primarily glide-by trips that don't make landfall on any of the park isles.

The alternative is voyaging out to the islands in your own craft or rentals from local outfitters like **1000**

Boldt Castle is located on the U.S. side of the Thousand Islands National Park.

Cottages sit along the St. Lawrence River, dotting the Thousand Island regions with boat docks and resting spots.

Islands Kayaking in Gananoque, which offers day watercraft rentals, guided trips, shuttle service to the park, and multiday kayak camping packages. No matter what your craft, all vessels must have a valid mooring or beaching permit, and all overnighters must purchase a camping permit.

The park islands offer plenty of choices when it comes to kayak camping—27 reservable and 34 nonreservable campsites along the shores of the tightly packed **Admiralty Islands**, big **Grenadier Island**, the **Navy Islands**, the **Lake Fleet Islands**, and others. Boaters can tackle them individually or as part of an epic voyage along the **Thousand Island Paddling Trail**, a nine-segment route along roughly 80 kilometers (49.7 mi) of the river between Kingston and Brockville.

Thousand Islands Parkway is a 40-kilometer (24.85 mi) scenic route along the Canadian side of the St. Lawrence between Butternut Bay and Gananoque, a convenient way to visit the park's three mainland sections and towns with riverboat and paddling services. Running alongside the parkway is a 50-kilometer (31.1 mi) portion of the **St. Lawrence Recreational Trail**, a dual path for bikers and hikers with great views of the river and islands.

Reaching Selton, drivers, bikers, and hikers can detour across a mighty green giant called the **Thousand Islands Bridge** to midstream **Hill Island**, the venue for the international border crossing and the 130-meter-high (426.5 ft) **1000 Islands Tower** with its lofty café and open-air viewing deck. ■

MEET THE NEIGHBORS

• **Wellesley Island State Park:** Sandy shores, a full-service marina, nature center, canoe program, and nine-hole golf course highlight this large New York state park.

• **Boldt Castle and Yacht House:** One of the largest private homes in the United States dominates little Heart Island; accessible by tour boat or private boat from Canada. *boldtcastle.com*

• **Singer Castle:** The sewing machine fortune built this mock medieval manse on Dark Island; accessible only by tour boat from Canada or the United States. *singercastle.com*

• **Rock Island Lighthouse State Park:** One of six lights commissioned in the 1840s along the St. Lawrence; accessible by Clayton's glass-bottom boat tour. *claytonislandtours.com*

Prince Edward Island National Park
Prince Edward Island

THE BIG PICTURE

Established: 1937

Size: 27 square kilometers (6,036 acres)

Annual Visitors: 530,000

Visitor Centers: Cavendish, Greenwich

Entrance Fee: C$8 per person

pc.gc.ca/en/pn-np/pe/pei-ipe

One of North America's smallest and most unusual national parks, Prince Edward Island offers an enticing blend of Maritimes nature, pastoral landscapes, and literary history inspired by one of Canada's most beloved books and the woman who penned the coming-of-age tale *Anne of Green Gables* by island-born Lucy Maud Montgomery.

Split into three sections along a 60-kilometer (37.28 mi) stretch of the island's north shore, the park harbors an amazing array of landscapes in a short distance: golden sands and russet sandstone cliffs, bays and barrier islands, wild dunes and manicured lawns where the rich and famous once frolicked beside the sea. Visitors can explore by road or 50 kilometers (31.1 mi) of biking and hiking trails.

Although the park was originally established to protect a pristine slice of the Maritimes coast, over time it became just as important for preserving the area's human history, a mission that echoes in the park's official theme: "The Sea, People, and the Changing Landscape."

The Mi'kmaq people, French Acadians, and Scottish settlers all left their mark on both the park area and Prince Edward Island as a whole. However, the two people who contributed the most to the future national park were far more recent—author Lucy Maud Montgomery and tycoon Alexander Macdonald, who lived just a few kilometers apart from each other along the north yet lived distinctly different lives.

Montgomery grew up around **Cavendish**, a bucolic lifestyle and landscape that inspired her to write a fictional story about an orphaned farm girl growing up in the same environment. Published in 1908, *Anne of Green Gables* has sold more than 50 million copies worldwide.

Green Gables Heritage Place in Cavendish revolves around all sorts of old-fashioned fun: sack races, carriage rides, ice-cream making, and nature trails through places like the **Haunted Wood** (0.9 kilometer/.55 mi) and **Balsam Hollow** (0.8 kilometer/ 0.5 mi) that feature in the author's prose, as well as interpretive programs by rangers dressed like characters from the books.

Down the road is **Green Gables House**, a lovingly restored national historic site where Montgomery's cousins lived. **Cavendish Destination Centre**, with information on other

Young red foxes pick a fight in the snow.

A boardwalk traverses the large and mobile Greenwich dunes, part of a fragile coastal wetland with numerous rare plant species.

park sights and activities, is right across the road. In another part of the national park, **Green Gables Golf Course** rambles through the middle of the village. Paths lead to **sandy beaches** along the Cavendish coast.

The park's central region lies between dune-backed **Brackley Beach** and a Queen Anne Revival manse, **Dalvay-by-the-Sea**. Alexander Macdonald's seaside escape is now a seasonal resort with a restaurant and outdoor activities. The beach and

manor are connected by the popular **Gulf Shore Parkway East** (10 kilometers/6.2 mi) for bikes and hikes, which passes landmarks like **Covehead Lighthouse** and **Stanhope Beach**.

A new mountain biking trail system makes its way around **Robinson Island** to the west of Brackley Beach. The bays behind the park's central shore—**Rustico, Brackley, Covehead**, and **Tracadie**—are among the best places in the park for paddle sports and windsurfing.

Added to the park in 1998, the **Greenwich Peninsula** shelters a parabolic sand dune system and archaeological sites stretching across the 10,000-year human history of Prince Edward Island. The **Greenwich Interpretation Centre** offers interactive exhibits on the unique island habitat and a saltwater wildlife touch tank, while the **Greenwich Dunes Trail** loops an easy 4.5 kilometers (2.8 mi) through the sandy wilderness. ◾

CHOW DOWN

Straight-off-the-boat seafood is one of the enduring delights of Prince Edward Island.

• **MacMillan Dining Room:** Make like a tycoon, if only for a single meal, in the elegant restaurant of the historic Dalvay-by-the-Sea hotel; afternoon tea is offered on weekends. *dalvaybythesea.com/dining*

• **Blue Mussel Café:** Lobster, oysters, scallops, chowder, fish, and of course mussels flavor the menu at this low-key eatery along the waterfront in the old Acadian village of North Rustico. *bluemusselcafe.com*

• **Dunes Studio Gallery and Café:** Canadian crafts and Asian flavors mix at this combination gallery and restaurant at Brackley Beach. *dunesgallery.com*

• **Richard's Fresh Seafood:** This popular seafood shack near Covehead Lighthouse has lobster rolls, steamed clams, fish and chips, and other maritime favorites. *richardsfreshseafood.com*

• **Inn at St. Peter's Village:** Panoramic ocean views complement the cuisine at this gourmet eatery near the Greenwich Peninsula. *innatstpeters.com/dining*

Algonquin Provincial Park

Ontario

The largest park of any kind in eastern Ontario, Algonquin offers unscathed wilderness and countless outdoor recreation options only a three-hour drive from Toronto and Ottawa. Canada's oldest provincial park embraces more than 2,400 lakes and ponds, dozens of hiking and biking trails, more than 2,100 kilometers (1,304.88 mi) of canoe and kayak routes, and myriad winter trails for those who like to escape on cross-country skis or snowshoes.

Ontario formed a royal commission in the early 1890s to study a proposal for a large reserve that would protect the headwaters of five major rivers and the rich timber resources within. But on their arrival they discovered much more than trees.

In their final report, the commissioners remarked that the creation of Algonquin Provincial Park would afford "the citizen, tired of close-packed houses and of crowded streets, the means of passing summers surrounded by every pleasure which varied scenery can afford, amid the perfect response of a district almost uninhabited by man."

More than 120 years later, the park retains its pristine state and continues to provide the residents of Ontario and people from around the world the same degree of outdoor pleasure. Spread over an area nearly as big as Yellowstone, the park sprawls across a massive hunk of wilderness between the Ottawa River and Georgian Bay.

Frank McDougall Parkway (Highway 60) between Madawaska and Huntsville is the major route into the park, 56 kilometers (34.8 mi) of scenic road that passes many of the park's trailheads and landmarks. In addition to exhibits on the park's natural and human heritage, **Algonquin Visitor Centre** includes a restaurant, book store, movie theater, and outdoor viewing deck. Across the road, **Spruce Bog Boardwalk Trail** (1.5-kilometer/0.9 mi loop) offers a great introduction to the park's forest and wetland habitats.

Located near the park's east entrance, the **Algonquin Logging Museum** provides insight into timber extraction that spans 200 years of local

THE BIG PICTURE

Established: 1893

Size: 7,653 square kilometers (1.89 million acres)

Annual Visitors: 1 million

Visitor Center: Algonquin (Highway 60)

Entrance Fee: C$17–$20 per vehicle per day

ontarioparks.com/park/algonquin

An American pine marten lives in the Algonquin woodlands.

Early morning fog hides much of the forestland that makes up Ontario's Algonquin Provincial Park.

history and continues in the park today. Arrayed along the museum's 1.5-kilometer (0.9 mi) **interpretive trail** are a replica *camboose* ("lumbermen's cabin") and a vintage "alligator" steam-powered amphibious tug.

Heading west along the Highway 60 Corridor, the **Algonquin Art Centre** specializes in wilderness and wildlife painting and sculpture, with regular shows by some of the Canadian masters of the genre.

Scattered along the corridor are trailheads for a dozen other interpretive walks that explore various aspects of the park, including a 2-kilometer (1.24 mi) loop to an observation tower overlooking **Brent Meteorite Crater**, a 10.8-kilometer (6.7 mi) trek to the wildlife-rich **Mizzy Lake** area, and the **Big Pine Trail** (2.9-kilometer/1.8 mi) through old-growth forest to the remains of an 1880s logging camp.

With so many water bodies, Algonquin is a paradise for paddlers. Many of the lakes along the corridor are ideal for casual kayaking and canoeing. The park also tenders a number of **backcountry paddle routes** for more advanced paddlers, with 29 access points along Highway 60 and around the outer edge of the park. For those who don't have their own boats, the **Portage Store** on aptly named **Canoe Lake** provides canoe rentals and campground delivery, guided paddle trips, and complete outfitting for paddle camping trips. **Algonquin Outfitters** on **Lake Opeongo** provides similar services for the eastern half of the park.

For those who would rather walk, Algonquin offers three backcountry hiking routes: the **Eastern Pines Trail** (15-kilometer/9.3 mi loop), the **Highland Trail** (35-kilometer/21.75 mi loop), and the more challenging **Western Uplands Trail** (88-kilometer/54.7 mi loop). **Algonquin Adventure Tours** offers guided biking and fishing in the park. ∎

LAY YOUR HEAD

Hotels

• **Killarney Lodge:** Log and pine cabins beside the Lake of Two Rivers in the heart of the park; restaurant, canoes, art gallery; from C$234. *killarneylodge.com*

• **Bartlett Lodge:** This historic (1917) wilderness resort is on the north shore of Cache Lake; log cabins, artists' studios, and "glamping" platform tents; restaurant; from C$115. *bartlettlodge.com*

• **Arowhon Pines:** Secluded, all-inclusive resort on Little Joe Lake; restaurant, canoes, sailboats, tennis court, bikes; from C$243 per person per night, including all meals. *arowhonpines.ca*

Camping

• Eleven vehicle-access campgrounds (C$39.83 to $51.13 per night), plus scores of backcountry sites, 14 backcountry cabins, and yurts at Mew Lake and Achray.

Algonquin Provincial Park, Ontario, Canada

Mount Royal Park

Quebec

Montreal's great escape is Mount Royal, a densely wooded ridgeline that rises above the city's tallest skyscrapers. No matter what the season, Montrealers flock to the park for outdoor recreation and entertainment, close encounters with an amazing array of urban flora and fauna, or wistful views of across the city and the St. Lawrence Valley.

THE BIG PICTURE

Established: 1876

Size: 2 square kilometers (494.2 acres)

Annual Visitors: 5 million

Visitor Center: Smith House

Entrance Fee: None

lemontroyal.qc.ca/en

Ville-Marie was the name the French gave to their first settlement in Canada, established on an island in the St. Lawrence River in 1642. As the settlement grew into a proper town and then a city, it eventually adopted the name of the island's highest point, Mount Royal, which explorer Jacques Cartier christened in honor of the French king.

Although the rest of the island morphed into one of North America's largest metropolitan areas, the wooded peak endured through four centuries of urban growth and today forms the nucleus of Montreal's iconic city park. Frederick Law Olmsted, who designed Manhattan's Central Park, was tasked with sculpting Mount Royal in the

1870s, but only a few of his ideas were ever realized.

Named after the Huron chief who signed a 1701 peace treaty with the French, **Belvédère Kondiaronk** is a semicircular terrace with stunning views over downtown Montreal, the perfect place to snap a selfie with the city's skyline as a backdrop. The **Chalet du Mont-Royal** behind the terrace harbors a café and gift shop.

Trails head north through the woods to an even taller point, the 233-meter-high (764.4 ft) **Mount Royal summit** and its illuminated **Mount Royal Cross**, erected in 1924 by a local group that has long advocated for Quebec autonomy. Just below the summit, the parking lot along **Voie Camillien-Houde** offers more lofty panoramic views, terraces with views over the city's northern quarters to the Olympic Stadium. This lookout is also the terminus of the No. 11 public bus that runs to and from downtown Montreal.

A popular walking and biking path, **Chemin Olmsted**, runs the entire length of the park from north to south, with side trails leading off to most of Mount Royal's landmarks and activities.

Mount Royal's northern flank is dominated by the towering **Georges-**

The steel Mount Royal Cross is 31.4 meters (103 ft) tall.

From the hills above, a view of Mount Royal Park and downtown Montreal at sunrise

Étienne Cartier Monument, topped by an art deco version of the Goddess of Liberty and dedicated to one of the fathers of Canadian independence. On Sundays, the plaza around the monument is taken over by **Tam Tams**, a legendary drum circle that attracts thousands of artists, dancers, street performers, food vendors, and tourists.

Farther down Avenue du Parc are **Mordecai Richler Gazebo**, named after the celebrated Jewish-Canadian author who grew up in the adjacent Mile End neighborhood, and the **McGill University** campus. Perched on the park's northeast corner, **Percival Molson Memorial Stadium** provides a venue for football, soccer, and Ultimate Frisbee matches, including home games of the Montreal Alouettes of the Canadian Football League (CFL).

Beaver Lake (Lac aux Castors)

EVENT HORIZON

• **City Lights Snowshoe Excursions:** Guided after-dark treks through the park, in English and French, in January, February, and early March. *lemontroyal.qc.ca/en*

• **Nuit Blanche:** The after-dark portion of the annual Montréal En Lumière winter fest includes an all-night choir concert at St. Joseph's Oratory, one of many musical events the church stages. *saint-joseph.org*

• **Mont Royal Clean-Up:** Anyone can volunteer for the park's annual spring cleaning, which unfolds over three days in April or May. Hosted by the nonprofit Les Amis de la Montagne ("friends of the mountain"). *lemontroyal.qc.ca/en*

• **Musical Sundays:** Mont Royal Chalet presents a series of concerts between May and October featuring some of the best young musicians from around Montreal. *lemontroyal.qc.ca/en*

• **Shakespeare in the Park:** The great lawn at Mont Royal Cemetery provides an especially atmospheric venue for outdoor summer productions by the Repercussion Theatre. *repercussiontheatre.com*

Above: Visitors enjoy an autumn stroll in Mount Royal Park. Opposite: Large flowered trillium

is the main attraction of the park's southern sector. There are no beavers, but the lake area is home to the **Salamandre Playground**, the **Café des Amis** bistro, and a former downhill ski slope now used for winter **tubing and tobogganing**.

Across Voie Camillien-Houde from the park, sprawling **Mount Royal Cemetery** offers guided historic, flora, and birding walking tours, as well as a tour booklet and map to the graves of celebrated people buried in the cemetery like author Mordecai Richler, governess Anna Leonowens of *The King and I* fame, and ice hockey legend Howie Morenz. Anchoring the mountain's southwest end is the Italian Renaissance–style **Saint Joseph's Oratory**, Canada's largest church. Able to seat more than 1,000 worshippers, the massive basilica was built over 43 years (1924-1967) and boasts one of

the world's largest domes. The church is renowned for its many **musical events**.

Flanking the cemeteries on the west is **Outremont Summit**, a 211-meter (692.3 ft) hill with outstanding views of the Outremont neighborhood and the University of Montreal. The name of the rise was officially changed to Tiohtià:ke Otsira'kéhne ("place of the big fire") in 2017 to honor the summit's legacy as a gathering place for the Mohawk and other First Nations people in ancient times.

Rising beyond Beaver Lake—on the other side of a busy boulevard called the Chemin de la Côte des Neiges—is the third of Mount Royal's peaks. **Westmount (Bois) Summit** reaches just over 200 meters (656.2 ft), a heavily wooded hill with a network of hiking trails. Once a botanical garden for McGill University, the hill is now an urban nature reserve and bird sanctuary. ■

MEET THE NEIGHBORS

Parc Jean-Drapeau, which sprawls across two islands in the St. Lawrence, is a multifaceted park on the site of the Expo 67 world's fair. Among its features are:

• The Biosphère museum of ecology (in the sphere-shaped U.S. Pavilion from Expo 67).

• Montreal Casino (in the former France pavilion).

• La Ronde amusement park with numerous roller coasters.

• Fort de l'Île Sainte-Hélène (built in 1820) and its Stewart Museum.

• Circuit Gilles Villeneuve grand prix motor-racing track.

• An aquatic center with three outdoor pools.

Stanley Park
British Columbia

Canada meets the Pacific Ocean at Stanley Park in Vancouver, a green space that channels both its vibrant city and the British Columbia wilderness. From summer hiking and biking to winter trails through evergreen forest, as well as sandy beaches and seaside swimming spots, the park is cherished for many reasons in all seasons.

Located on a peninsula jutting into the Strait of Georgia, Stanley Park is bounded by Vancouver Harbor, English Bay, and downtown Vancouver. Named after Lord Stanley—the same Canadian governor general who inspired ice hockey's championship Stanley Cup—the area was occupied by indigenous people of the Squamish Nation and European settlers who were evicted when the woodsy waterfront parcel was declared a park in the 1880s.

Stanley Park offers scores of ways to pass the day. The best known is the **Seawall**, a combined walking, biking, skating, and jogging path that defines 9 kilometers (5.6 mi) of the park's waterfront. Construction started after World War I and continued until the early 1970s. Along the way are towering sea cliffs and sandy patches like **Third Beach** and **Second Beach**, which is also home to a large heated outdoor **swimming pool**, the **Rhododendron Garden**, and a **pitch-and-putt golf course**.

In recent years, the path has been extended farther south along the coast; an elongated park called the **Seawall Greenway** is considered the world's longest continuous waterfront walkway at 26 kilometers (16.15 mi).

Twenty-seven kilometers (16.7 miles) of hiking and biking trails meander through the park's leafy interior, where an estimated a half million trees (some of them hundreds of years old) convey a sense of true wilderness. Paths lead to water-lily-filled **Beaver Lake,** the big trees along **Tallow Walk**, and **Prospect Point** with panoramic views of the harbor entrance and **Lion's Gate Bridge**. Opened in 1938, the 1,823-meter (5,980.9 ft) span features pedestrian and cycle lanes easily accessed from Prospect Point.

Stanley Park's eastern half is anchored by the **Vancouver Aquarium**, which showcases a variety of sea creatures from sea lions and sea otters to jellyfish and penguins. It's also home to marine animal research and rescue facilities.

Many of the park's other built attractions are found near the aquarium, including the beloved **Stanley Park Train**, which chugs a 2-kilometer (1.2 mi) circuit through the rain forest. Special editions of

THE BIG PICTURE

Established: 1888

Size: 4 square kilometers (988.4 acres)

Annual Visitors: 8 million

Visitor Center: Information booth at Coal Harbour parking lot

Entrance Fee: None

vancouver.ca/parks-recreation -culture/stanley-park.aspx stanleyparkvan.com

First Nations' totem poles decorate the park's landscape.

Viewed from above: Stanley Park, the Lost Lagoon, and the urban city of Vancouver

the train appear at Christmas, Easter, and Halloween. **Horse-drawn carriages** take passengers on a full circuit of the park from a station in the Coal Harbour parking lot, next to the **Stanley Park Information Booth**. Another way to get around is the **Stanley Park Shuttle**, a summer hop-on/hop-off motorized trolley with 15 stops around the park. Or rent a bike from **Spokes**, a cycle shop on West Georgia Street just outside the park.

Stanley Park's original inhabitants are remembered in the historic **totem poles** and modern First Nations sculptures at **Brockton Point**. X̱wáýx̱way, the area's largest Squamish village, was more or less located where the **Lumberman's Arch** snack bar and picnic area is today. The region's British Empire past is recalled with the **9 O'Clock Gun**, which has fired a daily salute

at 9 p.m. (21:00 hours) for more than a century.

Stanley Park Ecology Society offers two-hour walking tours, workshops with First Nations themes, and a **Native Planet**

Demonstration Garden on the south shore of **Lost Lagoon** beside the society's **Stanley Park Nature House**. Nearby **Harbour Cruises** offers lunch, dinner, and sightseeing voyages around Vancouver Harbour. ■

EVENT HORIZON

• **World Partnership Walk:** Thousands take to the trails of Stanley Park on a Sunday in June for an event that benefits development programs in Africa and Asia. *worldpartnershipwalk.com/en*

• **Theater Under the Stars:** Malkin Bowl is the evergreen-flanked venue for this annual summer musical theater production, staged in the park since 1940. *tuts.ca*

• **Ratha Yatra:** This August tribute to Asian Indian culture features a parade along Beach Avenue

followed by entertainment, free food, and craft stalls at Second Beach. *vanrathfest.com*

• **Skookum:** A new music, food, and arts festival brings headline acts to Brockton Field for three marvelous September days. *skookumfestival.com*

• **Bright Nights:** Three million lights illuminate the Stanley Park Train course as the miniature choo-choo transforms into a Christmas express over the holiday period. *brightnights.ca*

A seawall trail at sunset, Stanley Park, Vancouver

RESOURCES

New England & New York

Acadia National Park, Maine
nps.gov/acad/
Scenic Flights of Acadia:
scenicflightsofacadia.com

White Mountains, New Hampshire
fs.usda.gov/main/whitemountain/
New England Dogsledding:
newenglanddogsledding.com

Cape Cod National Seashore, Massachusetts
nps.gov/caco
The Goose Hummock:
goose.com
Art's Dune Tours: artsdunetours.org
Moment Sailing Adventures:
momentsailing.com
Provincetown Aquasports:
ptownaquasports.com

Boston Commons, Massachusetts
boston.gov/parks/boston-common

Blackstone River Valley National Heritage Corridor, Rhode Island & Massachusetts
nps.gov/blac/blackstoneheritage
corridor.org

Adirondack Park, New York
visitadirondacks.com
apa.ny.gov

Niagara Falls State Park, New York
niagarafallsstatepark.com
Maid of the Mist:
maidofthemist.com

Gateway National Recreation Area, New York & New Jersey
nps.gov/gate/
Wheel Fun Rentals:
wheelfunrentals.com/ny/
brooklyn/marine-park/

Central Park, New York
centralparknyc.org
nycgovparks.org/parks/
central-park/
Central Park Conservancy:
centralparknyc.org

The Mid-Atlantic

Shenandoah National Park, Virginia
nps.gov/shen/
goshenandoah.com

Assateague Island, Virginia & Maryland
nps.gov/asis
fws.gov/refuge/Chincoteague
dnr.maryland.gov
Assateague Tours:
assateaguetours.com

Gettysburg National Military Park, Pennsylvania
nps.gov/gett
Confederate Trails:
confederatetrails.com

Colonial National Historical Park, Virginia
nps.gov/colo

Chesapeake & Ohio Canal National Historical Park, Virginia, Maryland, District of Columbia & West Virginia
nps.gov/choh

National Mall, Washington, D.C.
nps.gov/choh/index.htm
nps.gov/nama/
Smithsonian Museums:
si.edu/museums

Pinelands National Reserve, New Jersey
nps.gov/pine
Pinelands Adventure:
pinelandsadventures.org
Palace Outfitters:
thepalaceoutfitters.com

Pennsylvania Wilds, Pennsylvania
pawilds.com
visitanf.com

Cape Hatteras National Seashore, North Carolina
nps.gov/caha
nps.gov/choh/index.htm

The South

Great Smoky Mountains National Park, North Carolina & Tennessee
nps.gov/grsm
Smokemont Riding Stables:
smokemontridingstable.com
Cades Cove Trading Company:
cadescovetrading.com
Fontana Marina:
fontanavillage.com

Ouachita National Forest, Arkansas & Oklahoma
fs.usda.gov/ouachita

Chattahoochee-Oconee National Forests, Georgia
fs.usda.gov/main/conf/
Nantahala Outdoor Center:
noc.com

Natchez Trace Parkway, Mississippi, Alabama & Tennessee
nps.gov/natr

Jean Lafitte National Historical Park & Preserve, Louisiana
nps.gov/jela
Creole Queen Paddlewheeler:
creolequeen.com

Everglades National Park, Florida
nps.gov/ever

Florida Keys, Florida
nps.gov/bisc
nps.gov/drto
Yankee Freedom III: drytortugas.com
Key West Seaplane Adventures:
keywestseaplanecharters.com

Key West Eco Tours:
keywestecotours.com
John Pennekamp Coral Reef State
Park: pennekamppark.com

**Mammoth Cave National Park,
Kentucky**
nps.gov/maca
Mammoth Cave Adventures:
mammothcave-adventures.com

Wild Texas Coast, Texas
nps.gov/pais
fws.gov/refuge/Aransas

**Cumberland Island National
Seashore, Georgia**
nps.gov/cuis
Cumberland Island Ferry:
cumberlandislandferry.com

**Wichita Mountains National
Wildlife Refuge, Oklahoma**
fws.gov/refuge/Wichita_Mountains

The Midwest

Isle Royale National Park, Michigan
nps.gov/isro
Isle Royale Seaplanes:
isleroyaleseaplanes.com

**Pictured Rocks National Lakeshore
and Hiawatha National Forest,
Michigan**
nps.gov/piro
fs.usda.gov/hiawatha
Pictured Rocks Kayaking:
paddlepicturedrocks.com
Grand Island Ferry Service:
grandislandup.com

**Mackinac Island State Park,
Michigan**
mackinacparks.com
mackinacisland.org
Great Turtle Kayak Trips:
mackinackayak.com
Cindy's Riding Stable:
cindysridingstable.com

Mackinac Wheels:
mackinacbikes.com

Ha Ha Tonka State Park, Missouri
mostateparks.com/park/
ha-ha-tonka-state-park
Cottage by the Castle B&B:
cottagebythecastle.com

**Boundary Waters Canoe Area
Wilderness and Voyageurs National
Park, Minnesota**
nps.gov/voya
fs.usda.gov/superior
Rainy Lake Houseboats:
rainylakehouseboats.com

**Mississippi and St. Croix National
Rivers, Minnesota & Wisconsin**
nps.gov/miss
nps.gov/sacn
Padelford Riverboats: riverrides.com
Hayward:
haywardflyfishingcompany.com
Fly Dog Fishing:
flydogflyfishing.com

**Missouri National Recreational
River, Nebraska & South Dakota**
nps.gov/mnrr

**Cuyahoga Valley National Park,
Ohio**
nps.gov/cuva

Forest Park, St. Louis, Missouri
forestparkforever.org

Chicago's Lakeside Parks, Illinois
chicagoparkdistrict.com
Divvy Bike: divvybikes.com
Chicago Sailboat Charters:
chicagosailboatcharters.com

The Rocky Mountains

**Yellowstone and Grand Teton
National Parks, Wyoming**
nps.gov/yell
nps.gov/grte
Barker-Ewing: barkerewing.com

Solitude: grand-teton-scenic-floats
.com
Snake River Angler:
snakeriverangler.com
Colter Bay Marina: gtlc.com
Yellowstone Forever: yellowstone
.org

**Glacier and Waterton Lakes
National Parks, Montana &
Alberta, Canada**
nps.gov/glac
pc.gc.ca/pn-np/ab/waterton
Glacier Adventure Guides:
glacieradventureguides.com

**Rocky Mountain National Park,
Colorado**
nps.gov/romo

Sawtooth National Forest, Idaho
fs.usda.gov/main/sawtooth
Sawtooth Adventure:
sawtoothadventure.com
White Otter: whiteotter.com

**Dinosaur National Monument,
Colorado & Utah**
nps.gov/dino
Adrift Adventures: adrift.com
Don Hatch River Expeditions:
donhatchrivertrips.com

Flathead Lake State Park, Montana
stateparks.mt.gov
Flathead Rafting Company:
flatheadraftco.com
Base Camp Bigfork:
basecampbigfork.com
Bagley Guide Service:
fishflatheadlake.com

**Black Hills National Forest, South
Dakota**
fs.usda.gov/blackhills

**Theodore Roosevelt National Park,
North Dakota**
nps.gov/thro

The Southwest

Grand Canyon National Park, Arizona
nps.gov/grca
Grand Canyon Railway:
thetrain.com

Zion & Bryce Canyon National Parks, Utah
nps.gov/zion
nps.gov/brca
Zion National Park Forever Project:
zionpark.org

Valles Caldera National Preserve, New Mexico
nps.gov/vall

Glen Canyon NRA & Canyonlands National Park, Utah & Arizona
nps.gov/glca
nps.gov/cany
Lake Powell Marina: lakepowell.com
Sherri Griffith Expeditions:
griffithexp.com
Magpie Cycling:
magpieadventures.com
NAVTEC Expeditions: navtec.com

Four Corners Parks, Arizona, Utah, Colorado & New Mexico
navajonationparks.org
nps.gov/meve
blm.gov/visit
Navajo Spirit: navajospirittours.com
Sacred Mountain Jeep Tours:
monumentvalley.net

Carlsbad Caverns & Guadalupe Mountain, New Mexico & Texas
nps.gov/cave
nps.gov/gumo

Big Bend National Park, Texas
nps.gov/bibe
Big Bend River Tours:
bigbendrivertours.com

Palo Duro Canyon State Park, Texas
palodurocanyon.com
Texas Show: texas-show.com
Old West Stables:
oldweststables.com

Palo Duro Canyon Adventure Park:
palodurozip.com
Cowgirls and Cowboys in the West:
cowgirlsandcowboysinthewest.com

California & Nevada

Yosemite National Park, California
nps.gov/yose
OARS: oars.com

Sequoia & Kings Canyon National Parks, California
nps.gov/seki
Crystal Cave: explorecrystalcave.
com

Redwoods National and State Parks, California
nps.gov/redw
Redcreek Buckarettes:
redwoodcreekbuckarettes.com
Kayak Zak's: kayakzak.com
Redwood Adventures:
elkmeadowcabins.com
Orick Rodeo: orick.net

Lake Tahoe Basin Management Unit, California & Nevada
fs.usda.gov/main/ltbmu/home
Tahoe Sailing Charters:
tahoesail.com
Action Watersports:
action-watersports.com
Tahoe Gal: tahoegal.com
Tahoe Tastings: tahoetastings.com
Tahoe Adventure Company:
tahoeadventurecompany.com

Anza-Borrego Desert State Park, California
parks.ca.gov/?page_id=638
Anza-Borrego Desert Nature Center:
abdnha.org
Dennis Mammana:
borregonightskytours.com
Ricardo Breceda: desertusa.com/
borrego/bs-art.html
Bike Borrego: bikeborrego.com
California Overland Tours:
californiaoverland.com
Borrego Art Institute:
borregoartinstitute.org

Red Rock Canyon National Conservation Area and Valley of Fire State Park, Nevada
redrockcanyonlv.org
parks.nv.gov/parks/valley-of-fire
Red Rock Climbing Center:
redrockclimbingcenter.com
Cowboy Trail Rides:
cowboytrailrides.com
Pink Jeep Tours:
pinkjeeptourslasvegas.com
Red Rock Summer Theatre Series:
supersummertheatre.org

Golden Gate National Recreation Area and Point Reyes National Seashore, California
nps.gov/goga
nps.gov/pore
Fort Mason Center for Arts and
Culture: fortmason.org
Presidio Dance Theatre:
presidiodance.org
Walt Disney Family Museum:
waltdisney.org
Marine Mammal Rescue Center:
marinemammalcenter.org
Bay Area Discovery Museum:
bayareadiscoverymuseum.org

Channel Islands National Park, California
nps.gov/chis
Island Packers: islandpackers.com
Channel Islands Adventure
Company: islandkayaking.com

Lassen Volcanic National Park, California
nps.gov/lavo

Golden Gate Park, California
goldengatepark.com
sfrecpark.org/parks-open-spaces/
golden-gate-park-guide
Parkwide Bike Rentals & Tours:
parkwide.com

Balboa Park, California
balboapark.org

Griffith Park, California
laparks.org/griffithpark

Mojave Desert Parks, California &
Nevada
nps.gov/deva
nps.gov/jotr

The Pacific Northwest & Alaska

**Olympic National Park,
Washington**
nps.gov/olym

**Mount Rainier National Park and
Mount St. Helens National Volcanic
Monument, Washington**
nps.gov/mora
fs.usda.gov/giffordpinchot
Mount Saint Helens Institute:
mshinstitute.org

Crater Lake National Park, Oregon
nps.gov/crla

**North Cascades National Park
Complex, Washington**
nps.gov/noca
Lady of the Lake: ladyofthelake.com
Stehekin Discovery Bikes:
stehekindiscoverybikes.com
Stehekin Outfitters:
stehekinoutfitters.com

San Juan Islands, Washington
nps.gov/sajh
parks.state.wa.us/547/moran
visitsanjuans.com

**Oregon Dunes National Recreation
Area, Oregon**
fs.usda.gov/recarea/siuslaw/
recreation/recarea/?recid=42465
Sandland Adventures:
sandland.com
Winchester Bay Fishing:
winchesterbayfishing.net
Spinreel Rentals:
ridetheoregondunes.com

**Columbia River Gorge National
Scenic Area, Washington & Oregon**
gorgefriends.org
gorgecommission.org
columbiarivergorge.info
Columbia Gorge Sternwheeler: port
landspirit.com/sternwheeler.php

**Wrangell-St. Elias and Kluane,
Alaska & the Yukon**
nps.gov/wrst
pc.gc.ca/en/pn-np/yt/kluane
St. Elias Alpine Guides:
steliasguides.com
Expeditions Alaska:
expeditionsalaska.com
Kluane Glacier Air Tours:
kluaneglacierairtours.com
Icefield Discovery:
icefielddiscovery.com

**Denali National Park and Preserve,
Alaska**
nps.gov/dena
Denali Star Train:
alaskarailroad.com
Alaska Alpine Adventures:
alaskaalpineadventures.com
Alpine Ascents International:
alpineascents.com
Fly Denali: flydenali.com
Talkeetna Air: talkeetnaair.com
Earth Song Lodge:
earthsonglodge.com
Denali Wilderness Winter Guides:
denaliwinter.com
Raft Denali: raftdenali.com
Denali Fly Fishing Guides:
denaliflyfishing.com
Denali ATV Adventures:
denaliatv.com
Denali Backcountry Safari:
denalisafari.com
AuroraQuest: akauroraquest.com
Alaska Cabin Nite Dinner:
denaliparkvillage.com

**Katmai and Lake Clark National
Parks, Alaska**
nps.gov/katm; nps.gov/lacl

Kenai Fjords National Park, Alaska
nps.gov/kefj
Major Marine: majormarine.com
Liquid Adventures:
liquid-adventures.com

The American Tropics

Haleakalā National Park, Hawaii
nps.gov/hale
Haleakalā Bike Company:
bikemaui.com

**Hawaii Volcanoes National Park,
Hawaii**
nps.gov/havo
Volcano Art Center:
volcanoartcenter.org
Active Lava Hawaiian Tours:
activelavahawaiiantours.com
Lava Ocean Tours: seelava.com

Nāpali Coast Parks, Hawaii
dlnr.hawaii.gov/dsp/parks/Kauai
kokee.org
Kayak Kauai: kayakkauai.com
Island Helicopters:
islandhelicopters.com

**San Juan and El Yunque, Puerto
Rico**
nps.gov/saju
fs.usda.gov/elyunque

**Virgin Islands National Park,
U.S. Virgin Islands**
nps.gov/viis

**National Park of American Samoa,
American Samoa**
nps.gov/npsa

**Vieques National Wildlife Refuge,
Puerto Rico**
fws.gov/refuge/vieques

Canada

**Banff and Jasper National Parks,
Alberta**
pc.gc.ca/en/pn-np/ab/Banff
pc.gc.ca/en/pn-np/ab/jasper
Rocky Mountain Raft Tours:
banffrafttours.com
Brewster Stables:
brewsteradventures.com
Great Divide Nature Interpretation: greatdivide.ca
Jasper Riding Stables:
jasperstables.com

Maligne Rafting Adventures:
raftjasper.com

Dinosaur Provincial Park, Alberta
albertaparks.ca/parks/south/
dinosaur-pp

**Mont-Tremblant National Park,
Quebec**
sepaq.com/pq/mot

**Cape Breton Highlands National
Park, Nova Scotia**
pc.gc.ca/en/pn-np/ns/cbreton

**Gros Morne National Park,
Newfoundland**
pc.gc.ca/en/pn-np/nl/grosmorne
Bon Tours: bontours.ca

**Saguenay-St. Lawrence Marine
Park, Quebec**
pc.gc.ca/en/amnc-nmca/qc/
saguenay
Mer et Monde Écotours:
meretmonde.ca/en
Dufour: dufour.ca
AML: croisieresaml.com/en

Wapusk National Park, Manitoba
pc.gc.ca/en/pn-np/mb/wapusk
Hudson Bay Helicopters:
prairiehelicopters.com
Natural Habitat: nathab.com

**Wood Buffalo National Park,
Alberta & Northwest Territories**
pc.gc.ca/en/pn-np/nt/woodbuffalo

**Pacific Rim National Park Reserve,
British Columbia**
pc.gc.ca/en/pn-np/bc/pacificrim

**Thousand Islands National Park,
Ontario**
pc.gc.ca/en/pn-np/on/1000
1000 Islands Kayaking:
1000islandskayaking.com

**Prince Edward Island National
Park, Prince Edward Island**
pc.gc.ca/en/pn-np/pe/pei-ipe

Algonquin Provincial Park, Ontario
ontarioparks.com/park/algonquin

Portage Store: portagestore.com
Algonquin Outfitters:
algonquinoutfitters.com
Algonquin Adventure Tours:
algonquinparkcanoetrips.com

Mount Royal Park, Quebec
lemontroyal.qc.ca/en

Stanley Park, British Columbia
vancouver.ca/parks-recreation
-culture/stanley-park.aspx
stanleyparkvan.com
Harbour Cruises: boatcruises.com

ILLUSTRATION CREDITS

Front cover: (Main image), Bill Vorasate/Getty Images, (UP LE), Stan Strange/EyeEm/Getty Images; (UP RT), fotog/Getty Images; (LO LE), Jordan Siemens/Getty Images; (LO CTR), Bill45/Shutterstock; (LO RT), cchoc/Getty Images; Back cover, Antonio Busiello/Robert Harding; Spine, Tom Salyer/Stock Connection/Aurora Photos; 2-3, roman_slavik/Getty Images; 4, LHN/Getty Images; 6, Patrick Endres/Visuals Unlimited, Inc./Getty Images.

New England & New York

12-3, Jon Bilous/Shutterstock; 14, Hal Horwitz/Science Source/Getty Images; 15, Raul Touzon/National Geographic Creative; 16, Austin Trigg/TandemStock.com; 17, Mauricio Handler/National Geographic Creative; 18, Richard Cavalleri/Shutterstock; 19, Greg Dale/National Geographic Creative; 20, Peter Unger/Getty Images; 20, lightphoto/Getty Images; 21, Mike Theiss/National Geographic Creative; 22, Dennis W. Donohue/Shutterstock; 23, Rolf_52/Shutterstock.com; 24, Tono Balaguer/Shutterstock; 25, Phil Schermeister/National Geographic Creative; 26-7, Michael Melford/National Geographic Creative; 28, Mitchell Funk/Getty Images; 30, Babak Tafreshi/National Geographic Creative; 31, Denis Tangney, Jr./Getty Images; 33, Norman Eggert/Alamy Stock Photo; 34, Jeffrey M. Frank/Shutterstock; 34, Mikhail Kolesnikov/Shutterstock; 36, Michael Melford/National Geographic Creative; 37, Michael Melford/National Geographic Creative; 38-9, Kevin A. Scherer/Getty Images; 40, Peter Unger/Getty Images; 42, Vicki Jauron, Babylon and Beyond Photography/Getty Images; 43, Tom Till/Alamy Stock

Photo; 44, Kajo Merkert/Getty Images; 45, Michael Yamashita/National Geographic Creative; 46, Joe Daniel Price/Getty Images.

The Mid-Atlantic

48-9, Cvandyke/Shutterstock.com; 50, Paul E Tessier/Getty Images; 51, Chris Murray/Aurora/Getty Images; 52, Wicker Imaging/Shutterstock; 53, Rob & Ann Simpson/Visuals Unlimited, Inc./Getty Images; 54-5, beklaus/Getty Images; 56, arlohemphill/Getty Images; 57, Danita Delimont/Getty Images; 58, Michael Melford/National Geographic Creative; 59, Tetra Images/Getty Images; 60, Richard Cummins/Getty Images; 61, drnadig/Getty Images; 62, Tono Balaguer/Shutterstock; 63, Kenneth Garrett/National Geographic Creative; 64-5, Jeffrey D. Walters/Getty Images; 66, Arthur Tilley/Getty Images; 68, Jon Bilous/Shutterstock; 69, Michael Rosebrock/Shutterstock.com; 70, Ritu Manoj Jethani/Shutterstock.com; 71, John S. Quinn/Shutterstock.com; 72-3, f11photo/Shutterstock; 74, stanley45/Getty Images; 75, Michele Paccione/Shutterstock; 76, Paul Staniszewski/Shutterstock; 77, K Steve Cope/Shutterstock; 78, Keith Ladzinski/National Geographic Creative; 79, Mark Van Dyke Photography/Shutterstock; 80, Andre Nantel/Shutterstock; 81, Stephen St. John/National Geographic Creative.

The South

82-3, BeachcottagePhotography/Getty Images; 84, Danita Delimont/Getty Images; 85, kurdistan/Shutterstock; 86, Dan Reynolds Photography/Getty Images; 87, Jim Vallee/Getty Images; 88-9, Malcolm Mac-

Gregor/Getty Images; 90, Buddy Mays/Getty Images; 91, Rex Lisman/Getty Images; 92, Lifer's Dream/Shutterstock; 93, James Randklev/Getty Images; 94, Marc Muench/TandemStock.com; 95, Marc Muench/TandemStock.com; 96, Karine Aigner/TandemStock.com; 97, Danae Abreu/Shutterstock; 98, Don Mammoser/Shutterstock; 99, Robin Hill/Getty Images; 100-101, Mac Stone; 102, Masa Ushioda/Alamy Stock Photo; 103, National Park Service/Shaun Wolfe; 104, Stephen Saks Photography/Alamy Stock Photo; 105, Varina C/Shutterstock; 106, Nagel Photography/Shutterstock; 108, Phil Schermeister/National Geographic Creative; 109, Stephen Alvarez/National Geographic Creative; 110, San Antonio Express-News/ZUMA Press/Alamy Stock Photo; 111, Paasch Photography/Getty Images; 112, George H.H. Huey/Alamy Stock Photo; 113, Klaus Nigge; 114, Jessa Jackson/Shutterstock; 115, Michael Shi/Getty Images; 116-7, Michael Shi/Getty Images; 118, Zack Frank/Shutterstock; 119, John Elk/Getty Images.

The Midwest

120-121, Prisma by Dukas Presseagentur GmbH/Alamy Stock Photo; 122, Layne Kennedy/Getty Images; 123, Posnov/Getty Images; 124, George Ostertag/Alamy Stock Photo; 125, genesisgraphics/Getty Images; 126-7, Rudy Balasko/Shutterstock; 128, Walter Bibikow/Getty Images; 129, James L. Amos/Science Source/Getty Images; 130, Michigannut/Getty Images; 131, Panoramic Images/Getty Images; 132, Danita Delimont/Getty Images; 133, tomofbluesprings/Getty Images; 134, Don Breneman/Alamy

Stock Photo; 135, Per Breiehagen/ Getty Images; 136, Geir Olav Lyngfjell/Shutterstock; 138, RRuntsch/Shutterstock; 139, Gary A Nelson/Dembinsky Photo Associates/Alamy Stock Photo; 140-141, Jorge Rimblas/Getty Images; 142, Collins93/Shutterstock; 143, Patrick Ziegler/Shutterstock; 144, Douglas Sacha/Getty Images; 145, Matthew Kuhns/TandemStock.com; 146, Pat & Chuck Blackley/Alamy Stock Photo; 147, James Schwabel/Alamy Stock Photo; 148, STLJB/Shutterstock; 149, JByard/Getty Images; 150, Thomas Barrat/Shutterstock; 151, Qoqazian/Getty Images; 152-3, Jens Siewert/EyeEm/Getty Images; 154, Hank Erdmann/Shutterstock; 155, Thomas Barrat/Shutterstock.

The Rocky Mountains

156-7, Brad McGinley Photography/ Getty Images; 158, Mike Cavaroc/ TandemStock.com; 159, Keith Ladzinski/National Geographic Creative; 160, Susanne Pommer/Shutterstock; 161, Barrett Hedges/National Geographic Creative; 162, Zack Frank/Shutterstock; 163, Andrew S/ Shutterstock; 164, Bob Gurr/Getty Images; 165, Bill45/Shutterstock; 166, Michael Bollino/TandemStock .com; 167, Miles Ertman/roberthard-ing/Getty Images; 168-9, Ian Shive/ TandemStock.com; 170, Art Wolfe/ Getty Images; 171, Ethan Welty/ Aurora/Getty Images; 172, Tim Fitzharris/Minden Pictures; 173, Carol Barrington/Aurora Photos; 174, Anna Gorin/Getty Images; 175, Nick Lake/TandemStock.com; 176-7, Anna Gorin/Getty Images; 178, Justin Bailie/TandemStock.com; 179, Tim Fitzharris/Minden Pictures; 180, William Mullins/Alamy Stock Photo; 181, Ami Vitale/National Geographic Creative; 182, Gavin Hellier/ Getty Images; 184, critterbiz/Shutterstock; 185, DC_Colombia/Getty Images; 186, Bill Kennedy/Shutterstock; 187, Eric Foltz/Getty Images.

The Southwest

188-9, Justin Reznick/Getty Images; 190, Whit Richardson/Aurora Photos; 191, IlexImage/Getty Images; 193, Matt Anderson Photography/Getty Images; 194, Fotos593/Shutterstock; 195, Jill Schneider/National Geographic Creative; 196-7, Cavan Images/Offset; 198, Rachid Dahnoun/TandemStock.com; 200, Ralph Lee Hopkins/Alamy Stock Photo; 201, Efrain Padro/Alamy Stock Photo; 202, David Hiser/ National Geographic Creative; 203, Adam Barker/TandemStock.com; 204-205, Rudy Balasko/Shutterstock; 206, Tetra Images/Getty Images; 208, Bryan Brazil/Shutterstock; 209, Bryan Jolley/TandemStock.com; 210, Derek von Briesen/ National Geographic Creative; 211, Witold Skrypczak/Alamy Stock Photo; 212, Michael Melford/National Geographic Creative; 213, Ben Herndon/TandemStock.com; 214, Lilly Husbands/Getty Images; 215, Efrain Padro/Alamy Stock Photo; 216, Tim Fitzharris/Minden Pictures; 217, jamespharaon/Getty Images; 218, Dianne Leeth/Alamy Stock Photo; 219, Jim Parkin/Alamy Stock Photo.

California & Nevada

220-21, Steve Spiliotopoulos; 222, Ian Shive/TandemStock.com; 223, Nick Fox/Shutterstock; 224, Ian Shive/TandemStock.com; 225, Shaun Jeffers/Shutterstock; 226, Kerrick James/Getty Images; 227, Ron Koeberer/TandemStock.com; 228-9, Nicholas Giblin/TandemStock .com; 230, Johnny Adolphson/Shutterstock; 231, Brent Durand/Tandem Stock.com; 232, Clint Losee/Tandem Stock.com; 233, Bennett Barthelemy/TandemStock.com; 234, Joshua Meador/TandemStock.com; 235, Rachid Dahnoun/Tandem Stock.com; 236, Rachid Dahnoun/ TandemStock.com; 237, pierdest/ Shutterstock; 238-9, Cory Marshall/TandemStock.com; 240,

Scott Kranz/TandemStock.com; 241, Brett Holman/TandemStock.com; 242, slowfish/Shutterstock; 243, Filip Fuxa/Shutterstock; 244-5, William Ducklow/Shutterstock; 246, Rachid Dahnoun/TandemStock.com; 247, ventdusud/Shutterstock; 248, Chaikom/Shutterstock; 249, yhelfman/ Getty Images; 250, Ian Shive/ TandemStock.com; 251, Matthew Connolly/Shutterstock; 252, Rachid Dahnoun/TandemStock.com; 253, Rachid Dahnoun/TandemStock.com; 254, John P. Kelly/Getty Images; 256, Lee Foster/Alamy Stock Photo; 257, Irina Kosareva/Shutterstock; 258, f11photo/Shutterstock; 259, f11photo/Shutterstock; 260, Sean Crane/Minden Pictures; 261, trekandshoot/Shutterstock; 262, Jim Patterson/TandemStock.com; 263, Bryan Brazil/Shutterstock; 264, CREATISTA/Shutterstock; 265, Andrew Peacock/TandemStock.com.

The Pacific Northwest & Alaska

266-7, Sierralara/Getty Images; 268, Rainer Grosskopf/Getty Images; 269, Michael Wheatley/Getty Images; 270, Bob Gibbons/Alamy Stock Photo; 271, Diane Cook and Len Jenshel/ National Geographic Creative; 272, Shane Miller/Shutterstock; 273, Diane Cook and Len Jenshel/ National Geographic Creative; 274-5, Roman Khomlyak/Shutterstock; 276, Dennis Frates/Alamy Stock Photo; 277, Matthew Connolly/Shutterstock; 278, Phil Schermeister/National Geographic Creative; 279, Meleah Reardon Photography/Getty Images; 280, Monika Wieland Shields/Shutterstock; 281, Bill Ross/Getty Images; 282-3, Chris Moore—Exploring Light Photography/Getty Images; 284, Christopher Kimmel/Getty Images; 285, Robert L. Potts/Design Pics/ Getty Images; 286, Kennan Harvey/ Getty Images; 288, Bennett Barthelemy/TandemStock.com; 289, Jesse Estes/TandemStock.com; 290, Freebilly/Shutterstock; 291,

ESB Professional/Shutterstock; 292, Peter Mather/Minden Pictures; 293, Mint Images—Frans Lanting/Getty Images; 294, Mint Images—Frans Lanting/Getty Images; 295, Paul Nicklen/National Geographic Creative; 296, Chase Dekker Wild-Life Images/Getty Images; 297, Daniel A. Leifheit/Getty Images; 298, Kiefer Thomas/EyeEm/Getty Images; 300-301, Yves Marcoux/Getty Images; 302, Design Pics Inc/Getty Images; 303, Danita Delimont/Getty Images; 304, Mint Images/Art Wolfe/Getty Images; 305, Carl R. Battreall/Design Pics/Getty Images.

The American Tropics

306-307, Maridav/Shutterstock; 308, Ralf Broskvar/Shutterstock; 309, M.M. Sweet/Getty Images; 310, Greg Vaughn/Getty Images; 311, Sami Sarkis/Getty Images; 312-13, Art Wolfe/Getty Images; 314, Mint Images—Frans Lanting/Getty Images; 315, Makena Stock Media/Getty Images; 316, Tyler Stableford/Aurora Outdoor Collection/Getty Images; 317, Maridav/Shutterstock; 318-9, Haizhan Zheng/Getty Images; 320, guvendemir/Getty Images; 321, dennisvdw/Getty Images; 322, Tom Bean/Getty Images; 323, CathyRL/Shutterstock.com; 324, George Burba/Shutterstock; 325, Laurie Chamberlain/Getty Images; 326, Macduff Everton/Corbis/VCG/Getty Images; 328, Seaphotoart/Alamy Stock Photo; 329, Danita Delimont/Getty Images; 330-31, Jon Cornforth; 332, John and Tina Reid/Getty Images; 333, John and Tina Reid/Getty Images.

Canada

334-5, John Sylvester/Getty Images; 336, Shah Selbe/National Geographic Creative; 337, Jordan Siemens/Getty Images; 338, Jeff R

Clow/Getty Images; 339, Juancat/Shutterstock; 340, Ryszard Stelmachowicz/Shutterstock.com; 341, Brandon van Son/TandemStock.com; 342-3, puttsk/Shutterstock; 344, Kelly Boreson/Shutterstock; 345, Wayne Lynch/Getty Images; 346, Nicolas Kipourax Paquet/Getty Images; 347, Barisev Roman/Shutterstock; 348, Scott Leslie/Minden Pictures; 349, Thomas Kitchin & Victoria Hurst/Getty Images; 350-51, Rachel McGrath/Getty Images; 352, Mike Grandmaison/Getty Images; 353, David Purchase Imagery/Shutterstock; 354, Robert La Salle/AquaPhoto/Alamy Stock Photo; 355, Christian Guy/ImageBROKER/Alamy Stock Photo; 356, Yves Marcoux/Getty Images; 357, NorthHatley/Getty Images; 358, AndreAnita/Shutterstock; 359, AndreAnita/Shutterstock; 360, Emily Riddell/Getty Images; 362, Raymond Gehman/Getty Images; 363, Mike Grandmaison/Getty Images; 364, Sara Winter/Alamy Stock Photo; 365, Robert Postma/Getty Images; 366-7, Carrie Cole/Alamy Stock Photo; 368, NelzTabcharani316/Shutterstock; 369, Panoramic Images/Getty Images; 370, John Sylvester/Getty Images; 371, marevos imaging/Shutterstock; 372, mlorenzphotography/Getty Images; 373, Curtis Watson/Shutterstock; 374-5, Ron Erwin/Getty Images; 376, Alina Reynbakh/Shutterstock; 377, Yves Marcoux/Getty Images; 378, Yves Marcoux/Getty Images; 379, Marc Bruxelle/Alamy Stock Photo; 380, Regien Paassen/Shutterstock; 381, David Nunuk/All Canada Photos/Alamy Stock Photo; 382-3, Michael Wheatley/Alamy Stock Photo.

INDEX

ACKNOWLEDGMENTS

Special thanks to Julia Clerk (my wife of almost three decades and a talented writer in her own right) for her research on so many of the parks that appear in the book, as well as her companionship and insights in the many parks we visited together—from the Everglades and Glacier to Anza-Borrego and Mont-Tremblant.

I also thank my daughters, Chelsea and Shannon, for the privilege of letting me introduce them to their first parks in the same way that my parents blazed that trail for me. Among our many adventures were razoring through Central Park in New York, that boat trip out to Baker Island in Acadia, hiking to the summit of Sentinel Dome in Yosemite, exploring the El Yunque rain forest, and the "civil war" that raged in our van at Gettysburg (Dad wanted to stay *much* longer than the rest of the family).

Kudos to the many National Park Service and Parks Canada personnel who provided information and insights for this book, as well as those at the various state and provincial parks, national forest, city parks, and national wildlife refuges whom I quizzed in person, over the phone, or by email. And let me not forget the people from city, state, and provincial tourist boards or convention and visitor bureaus who were also essential to making *100 Parks* a reality.

Last but far from least, I thank Hilary Black at National Geographic for believing in this book from the very start, and senior project editor Allyson Johnson for being so incredibly easy to work with and a valuable asset when it came to compiling the lists of parks and ideas. And to the rest of the Nat Geo team—designer Kay Hankins; art director Elisa Gibson; photo editors Matt Propert, Uliana Bazar, Jill Foley, and Moira Haney; and senior production editor Judith Klein—thank you for bringing the parks to life in these pages.

ABOUT THE AUTHOR

During three decades as an editor, writer, and photographer, Joe Yogerst has lived and worked on four continents: Asia, Africa, Europe, and North America. His writing has appeared in *National Geographic Traveler, Condé Nast Traveler,* CNN Travel, *Islands* magazine, the *International New York Times* (Paris), the *Washington Post,* the *Los Angeles Times,* and 35 National Geographic books, including the best-selling *50 States, 5,000 Ideas.* His first U.S. novel—a murder mystery called *Nemesis* set in 1880s California, was published in 2018. Yogerst is currently writing and hosting a National Geographic/Great Courses video series on America's state parks that debuts in fall 2019.

100 PARKS 5000 IDEAS

Since 1888, the National Geographic Society has funded more than 13,000 research, exploration, and preservation projects around the world. National Geographic Partners distributes a portion of the funds it receives from your purchase to National Geographic Society to support programs including the conservation of animals and their habitats.

National Geographic Partners
1145 17th Street NW
Washington, DC 20036-4688 USA

Get closer to National Geographic explorers and photographers, and connect with our global community. Join us today at nationalgeographic.com/join

For rights or permissions inquiries, please contact National Geographic Books Subsidiary Rights: bookrights@natgeo.com

The information in this book has been carefully checked and to the best of our knowledge is accurate. However, details are subject to change, and the publisher cannot be responsible for such changes, or for errors or omissions. Assessments of sites, hotels, and restaurants are based on the author's subjective opinions, which do not necessarily reflect the publisher's opinion.

ISBN: 978-1-4262-2010-4

Printed in the United States of America

21/WOR/7